PLATO
Republic

PLATO

Republic

Translated from the New Standard Greek Text, with Introduction, by

C. D. C. REEVE

Hackett Publishing Company, Inc.
Indianapolis/Cambridge

Printed in the United States of America

08 07 06 05 04   1 2 3 4 5 6 7 8

For further information, please address
    Hackett Publishing Company, Inc.
    P. O. Box 44937
    Indianapolis, Indiana 46244–0937

    www.hackettpublishing.com

Cover design by Abigail Coyle
Interior design by Jennifer Plumley
Composition by William Hartman
Printed at Sheridan Books, Inc.

Library of Congress Cataloging-in-Publication Data

Plato.
        [Republic. English]
        Republic / translated from the new standard Greek text, with introduction, by
C.D.C. Reeve.
        p. cm.
        Includes bibliographical references and indexes.
        ISBN 0-87220-737-4 (hardcover) -- ISBN 0-87220-736-6 (pbk.)
        1. Political science--Early works to 1800.   2. Utopias.   I. Reeve, C. D. C.,
1948–   II. Title.
JC71.P513 2004
321'.07--dc22

                                                                2004013418

The paper used in this publication meets the minimum requirements of American National Standard for Information Sciences—Permanence of Paper for Printed Library Materials, ANSI Z39.48–1984.

For Daddy on his 88th birthday,
with much love.

Contents

Preface

I have been a student of the *Republic* since I first encountered it as an undergraduate at Trinity College, Dublin. In 1988 I published a book about it (*Philosopher-Kings*). Four years later, I published a revision of G. M. A. Grube's excellent translation. Perhaps I should have rested content with that, but my desire to have a *Republic* translation of my own proved too strong. The fruit of five years' work, it is now in print. Naturally, I hope it improves on existing translations. If so, I have their producers largely to thank. Certainly, I have ransacked them for assistance. Tom Griffith has helped greatly, Robin Waterfield too, and also (in the case of Books 5 and 10) Stephen Halliwell. Over the years, my respect has grown for earlier translations—for that of George Grube, from which I learned a huge amount, but also for those of Allan Bloom and Paul Shorey.

Every translation, even the most self-consciously and flat-footedly slavish, is somewhat interpretative. There is no avoiding that. But I have tried to make this one as uninterpretative and close to the original as possible. One conscious deviation from strict accuracy, however, will be obvious at a glance. The *Republic* is largely in reported speech. Socrates is relating a conversation he had in the past. But I have cast his report as an explicit dialogue in direct speech, with identified speakers. In the *Theaetetus,* Plato has Eucleides adopt a similar stratagem. "This is the book," he says to Terpsion; "You see, I have written it out like this: I have not made Socrates relate the conversation as he related it to me, but I represent him as speaking directly to the persons with whom he said he had this conversation." Decades of teaching the *Republic* have persuaded me that the minimal loss in literalness involved in adopting Eucleides' stratagem is more than made up for in readability and intelligibility.

I renew my gratitude to John Cooper for his always judicious advice, and to Paul Woodruff for his. I am also grateful to the publisher's readers, Christopher Rowe and the team of Patrick Miller and Christopher Childers. The latter—in particular—saved me from numerous errors and omissions. My debt to their care and scholarship is unrepayable. I am grateful to Hackett Publishing Company itself for trusting me with what is, in many ways, its flagship text; to my editor, Deborah Wilkes, for her encouragement and support; to Jenevieve Maerker for her help with the Introduction and, with Abigail Coyle, for the cover design. Many warm thanks, finally, to Janet Zweig for suggesting the wonderfully appropriate cover photograph.

Chapel Hill, June 2004

Introduction

No one doubts that the *Republic* is one of the very greatest works of Western philosophy. Like nothing before it and very little since, it combines philosophical and literary resourcefulness of the highest order in an attempt to answer the most important question of all—how should we live if we want to live well and be happy? Justly or unjustly? Morally or immorally? Moreover, the answer it develops is based on an unusually rich account of our nature and the nature of reality. Ethics, politics, aesthetics, philosophy of religion, philosophy of mind, philosophy of science, epistemology, and metaphysics are all woven together in it, and their later developments have been decisively shaped by its contribution to them. Contemporary philosophers read the *Republic,* as their predecessors did, not out of piety, but because it continues to challenge, disquiet, and inspire. Western philosophy is not, to be sure, simply a series of footnotes to this amazing text, but many of its best stories begin here.

PLATO

Plato was born in Athens in 429 BCE and died there in 348/7. His father, Ariston, traced his descent to Codrus, who was supposedly king of Athens in the eleventh century BCE; his mother, Perictione, was related to Solon, architect of the Athenian constitution (594/3). While Plato was still a boy, his father died and his mother married Pyrilampes, a friend of the great Athenian statesman Pericles. Hence Plato was familiar with Athenian politics from childhood and was expected to enter it himself. Horrified by actual political events, however, including the execution of his mentor and teacher Socrates in 399 BCE, he turned instead to philosophy, thinking that only it could bring true justice to human beings and put an end to civil war and political upheaval (see *Seventh Letter* 324b–326b). In the *Republic,* written around 380 BCE, he lays out the grounds for this at once pessimistic and optimistic assessment.

Plato's works, which are predominantly dialogues, all seem to have survived. They are customarily divided into four chronological groups, though the precise ordering (especially within groups) is controversial:

Early: *Alcibiades, Apology, Charmides, Crito, Euthyphro, Hippias Minor, Hippias Major, Ion, Laches, Lysis, Menexenus, Theages*
Transitional: *Euthydemus, Gorgias, Meno, Protagoras*

Middle: *Cratylus, Phaedo, Symposium, Republic, Phaedrus, Parmenides, The-aetetus*

Late: *Timaeus, Critias, Sophist, Statesman, Philebus, Laws*

Besides writing his dialogues, Plato contributed to philosophy by founding the Academy, arguably the first university. This was a center of research and teaching, both in theoretical subjects and also in more practical ones. Eudoxus, who gave a geometrical explanation of the revolutions of the sun, moon, and planets, brought his own students with him to join Plato and studied and taught in the Academy; Theaetetus developed solid geometry there. But cities also invited members of the Academy to help them in the practical task of developing new political constitutions.

The Academy lasted for some centuries after Plato died, ending around 80 BCE. Its early leaders, including his own nephew, Speusippus, who succeeded him, all modified his teachings in various ways. Later, influenced by the early Socratic dialogues, which end in puzzlement (*aporia*), the Academy, under Arcesilaus, Carneades, and other philosophers, defended skepticism; later still, influenced by Plato's other writings, Platonists were more dogmatic, less unsure. Platonism of one sort or another—Middle or Neo- or something else—remained the dominant philosophy in the pagan world of late antiquity, influencing St. Augustine among others, until the emperor Justinian closed the pagan schools at Athens in 529 CE. Much of what passed for Plato's thought until the nineteenth century, when German scholars pioneered a return to Plato's writings themselves, was a mixture of these different "Platonisms."

Given the vast span and diversity of Plato's writings and the fact that they are dialogues, not treatises, it is little wonder that they were read in many different ways, even by Plato's ancient followers. In this respect nothing has changed: different schools of philosophy and textual interpretation continue to find profoundly different messages and methods in Plato. Doctrinal continuities, discontinuities, and outright contradictions of one sort or another are discovered, disputed, rediscovered, and redisputed. Neglected dialogues are taken up afresh, old favorites newly interpreted. New questions are raised, old ones resurrected and reformulated: is Plato's Socrates really the great ironist of philosophy or a largely non-ironic figure? Is Plato a systematic philosopher with answers to give or a questioner only? Is he primarily a theorist about universals, or a moralist, or a mystic with an otherworldly view about the nature of reality and the place of the human psyche in it? Is the *Republic* a totalitarian work, a hymn to freedom properly conceived, or a reductio ad absurdum of the very argument it seems to be advancing? Does the dramatic structure of the dialogues undermine their apparent philosophical arguments? Should Plato's negative remarks about the efficacy of written philosophy (*Phaedrus* 274b–278b) lead us to look behind his dialogues for what Plato's student Aristotle refers to as the "so-called unwritten doctrines" (*Physics* 209^{b}14–5)?

Besides this continued engagement with Plato's writings, there is, of course, the not entirely separate engagement with the problems Plato brought to philosophy, the methods he invented to solve them, and the solutions he suggested and explored. So many and various are these, however, that they constitute not just Plato's philosophy, but a large part of philosophy itself. Part of his heritage, they are also what we inevitably bring to our reading of his works.

SOCRATES

Socrates is the central figure in the *Republic,* as in most of Plato's works. In some dialogues he is thought to be—and probably is—based to some extent on the historical Socrates. These are often called "Socratic" dialogues for this reason. In the transitional, middle, and late dialogues, however, he is thought to be increasingly a mouthpiece for ideas that go well beyond Plato's Socratic heritage.

In the Socratic dialogues, philosophy consists almost exclusively in questioning people about the conventionally recognized moral virtues. What is piety (*Euthyphro*)? Or courage (*Laches*)? Or temperance (*Charmides*)? These are his characteristic questions. He seems to take for granted, moreover, that there are correct answers to them—that temperance, piety, courage, and the rest are each some definite characteristic or form (*eidos, idea*). He does not discuss the nature of these forms, however, nor develop any explicit theory of them or our knowledge of them. He does not, for that matter, explain his interest in definitions, nor justify his claim that if we do not know what, for example, justice is, we cannot know whether it is virtue, whether it makes its possessor happy, or anything else of any significance about it (*Republic* 354b–c).

Socrates' style of questioning is called (by us, not him) an *elenchus*—from the Greek verb *elengchein,* meaning to examine or refute. He asks what justice is. His interlocutor puts forward a definition he sincerely believes to be correct. Socrates refutes this definition by showing that it conflicts with other beliefs the interlocutor sincerely holds and is unwilling to abandon. In the ideal situation, which is never actually portrayed in the Socratic dialogues, this process continues until a satisfactory definition emerges, one that is not inconsistent with other sincerely held beliefs, and so can withstand elenctic scrutiny.

The definitions Socrates encounters in his examinations of others prove unsatisfactory. But through these examinations—which are always at the same time self-examinations (*Charmides* 166c–d, *Hippias Major* 298b–c, *Protagoras* 348c–d)—he comes to accept some positive theses that have resisted refutation. Among these are the following three famous Socratic "paradoxes":

> The conventionally distinguished virtues—justice, piety, courage, and the rest—are all identical to wisdom or knowledge, conceived of as a type of craft (*technē*)[1] or expertise (*Charmides* 174b–c, *Euthydemus* 281d–e, *Protagoras* 329b–334c, 349a–361d). This is often referred to as *the unity of the virtues* doctrine.
>
> Possession of this knowledge is necessary and sufficient for happiness (*Crito* 48b, *Gorgias* 470e).
>
> No one ever acts contrary to what he knows or believes to be best, so that weakness of will is impossible (*Protagoras* 352a–359a).

Together these three doctrines constitute a kind of *ethical intellectualism:* they imply that what we need in order to be virtuous and happy is expert craft knowledge.

The goal of an elenchus is not just to reach adequate definitions of the virtues or seemingly paradoxical doctrines about weakness of will and virtue, however. Its primary aim is *moral reform*. For Socrates believes that, by curing people of the hubris of thinking they know when they do not, leading the elenctically examined life makes them happier and more virtuous than anything else. Philosophizing is so important for human welfare, indeed, that Socrates is willing to accept execution rather than give it up (*Apology* 29b–d, 30a, 36c–e, 38a, 41b–c).

In the transitional dialogues, as well as in some earlier ones, Socrates, as the embodiment of true philosophy, is contrasted with the sophists.[2] *They* are, for the most part, unscrupulous, fee-taking moral relativists who think that moral values are based on convention; *he* is an honest, fee-eschewing moral realist, who thinks that the true virtues are the same for everyone everywhere. The problem latent in this contrast is that if people in different cultures have different beliefs about the virtues, it is not clear how the elenchus, which seems to rely wholly on such beliefs, can reach knowledge of objective or non-culture–relative moral truth.

THE *REPUBLIC*

The *Republic* is specifically about the virtue of justice and about whether it pays better dividends in terms of happiness than does injustice. It begins, therefore, with a characteristically Socratic search for justice's definition (331b–c). Polemarchus provides the first candidate: justice is giving to each what he is owed (331e). Socrates proceeds to examine this definition by

---

[1] See Glossary of Terms s.v. craft.

[2] See Glossary of Terms s.v. sophists.

testing its consistency with other beliefs Polemarchus holds and is unwilling to abandon. When it proves to be inconsistent with them, it is taken to have been refuted (335e). Socrates must be presupposing, therefore, that some of Polemarchus' sincerely held ethical beliefs are true, since inconsistency with false beliefs is no guarantee of falsehood. The problem is that there seems to be little reason to accept this presupposition.

Socrates' next interlocutor, Thrasymachus, explains why. He argues that those who are stronger in any society—the rulers—control education and socialization through legislation and enforcement. But he thinks that the rulers, like everyone else, are self-interested. Hence they make laws and adopt conventions—including linguistic conventions—that are in their own best interests, not those of their weaker subjects. It is these conventions that largely determine a subject's conception of justice and the other virtues. By being trained to follow or obey them, therefore, a subject is unwittingly adopting an ideology—a code of values and behavior—that serves his ruler's, rather than his own, interests. Consequently, Thrasymachus defines justice not as what socialized subjects like Socrates and Polemarchus think it is (something genuinely noble and valuable that promotes their own happiness), but as what it really is in all cities: *the interest of the stronger.*

As in the case of Polemarchus, Socrates again uses the elenchus to try to refute Thrasymachus. But his attempts are not found wholly adequate, either by Thrasymachus himself or by the other interlocutors (350d–e, 357a–b, 358b–c). And we can see why: by arguing that ethical beliefs are an ideologically contaminated social product, Thrasymachus has undercut the elenchus altogether. *He* may get tied up in knots by Socrates, but his *theory* is invulnerable to elenctic refutation (as Thrasymachus points out at 349a). For elenctic refutation appeals to ideologically contaminated ideas in order to counter his theory, but his theory maintains that these have no validity. That is why Plato has Socrates abandon the elenchus in subsequent books and attempt to answer Thrasymachus (whose views are taken over by Glaucon and Adeimantus) by developing a positive defense of justice of his own.

The Argument of the *Republic* in Outline

At the center of Socrates' defense of justice stand the philosopher-kings— who unite political power and authority with philosophical knowledge of the transcendent, unchanging form of the good (the good-itself)—and the ideal city they come to rule, Kallipolis ("beautiful city" or "noble city" in Greek). Because this knowledge is based, as Socrates argues, in mathematics and science, it is unmediated by conventionally controlled concepts of good and bad, just and unjust. Hence it is free from the distorting influence of power or ideology, and so immune to the challenge Thrasymachus poses to the elenchus.

What the philosopher-kings do is construct a political system—including primarily a system of socialization and education—that will distribute the benefits of their specialized knowledge of the good among the citizens at large. The system they construct relies on Plato's theory of the soul or mind (*psychê*), the seat of consciousness, emotion, desire, and decision-making. According to this theory, there are three fundamentally different kinds of desires: *appetitive* ones for food, drink, sex, and the money with which to acquire them; *spirited* ones for honor, victory, and good reputation; and *rational* ones for knowledge and truth (437b ff., 580d ff.). Each of these types of desire "rules" in the soul of a different type of person, determining his values. People most value what they most desire, and so those ruled by different desires have very different conceptions of what is valuable or good, or of what would make them happy. Just which type of desire rules an individual's soul depends on the relative strengths of his desires and on the kind of education and socialization he receives. The fundamental goal of ethical or political education isn't to provide knowledge, therefore, but to socialize desires, so as to turn people around (to the degree possible) from the pursuit of what they falsely believe to be happiness, to the pursuit of true happiness (518b–519d).

The famous allegory of the cave illustrates the effects of such education (514a). Uneducated people, tethered by their unsocialized appetites, see only images of models of the good (shadows cast by puppets on the walls of the cave). Such people are not virtuous to any degree, since they act simply on their whims. When their appetites are shaped through physical training and that mix of reading and writing, dance and song that the Greeks call *mousikê* (musical training), they are released from these bonds and are ruled by their socialized appetites. They have at least that level of virtue required to act prudently and postpone gratification. Plato refers to them as *money-lovers,* because they pursue money as the best means of reliably satisfying their appetitive desires in the long term (580d–581a). They see models of the good (the puppets that cast the shadows), for stable satisfaction of appetitive desires *is* a sort of good.

Further education, this time in mathematical science, leaves people who are eligible for it ruled by their spirited desires. They are *honor-lovers,* who seek success in difficult endeavors and the honor and approval it brings. They have the true beliefs about virtue required for such success, and hence that greater level of virtue Plato calls "political" virtue (430c).

Finally, yet further education in dialectic (a sort of philosophical training that is a descendant of the Socratic elenchus) and practical city management results in people who are bound only by their rational desires. They are free from illusion and see, not mere images of the good, but the good itself. They are *wisdom-lovers* or philosophers, who have knowledge rather than mere true belief about virtue, and so are fully virtuous.

Not everyone, however, is able to benefit from all these types of education: there are some at each stage whose desires are too strong for education to break. That is why there are producers, guardians, and philosopher-kings in the ideal city. That is why, too, these groups can cooperate with one another in a just system, where the money-loving producers trade their products for the protection provided by the honor-loving guardians and the knowledge provided by the wisdom-loving kings, rather than competing with them for the very same goods (462e–463b). Nonetheless, everyone in this ideal system is enabled to travel as far toward the sun (the good) as education can take him, given the innate strength of his desires. Thus everyone comes as close to being fully virtuous, and so to pursuing and achieving genuine happiness, as he can. It is this that makes Plato's city both an ethical and a prudential ideal, both maximally just and maximally happy. And because it is both, it constitutes a response to the Thrasymachean challenge raised anew by Glaucon and Adeimantus in *Republic* 2. For if maximal justice and maximal happiness go together, then it pays, in terms of happiness, to be just rather than unjust.[3]

THE THEORY OF FORMS

In a number of dialogues, Plato connects the relativist doctrines he attributes to the sophists with the metaphysical theory of Heraclitus, according to which the perceptible things or characteristics we see around us are in constant flux or change—always *becoming,* never *being.* In the *Theaetetus,* he argues that Protagoras' claim that "man is the measure of all things" presupposes that the world is in flux; in the *Cratylus,* he suggests that the theory of flux may itself be the result of projecting Protagorean relativism onto the world (411b–c). Nonetheless, Plato seems to accept some version of this theory himself (see Aristotle, *Metaphysics* 987^{a}32–4). In *Republic* 5, for example, he characterizes perceptible things and characteristics as lying "in between what purely is and what in every way is not" (478a–479d; see also *Timaeus* 52a).

The theory of flux clearly exacerbates the problem we noticed earlier with the Socratic elenchus. If perceptible things and characteristics are always in flux, how can justice and the other virtues be stable forms? How can there be stable definitions of them to serve as correct answers to Socrates' questions? And if there are no stable definitions, how can there be such a thing as ethical knowledge? More generally, if perceptible things and characteristics are always in flux, always *becoming,* how can anything *be* something definite or determinate? How can one know or say what anything *is?* Aristotle tells us that it was reflection on these fundamental questions that

---

[3] First-time readers may want to skim over the remainder of the Introduction, returning to it for more careful study after they have read the *Republic* itself.

led Plato to "separate" the forms from perceptible things and characteristics (Aristotle, *Metaphysics* 987^{a}29–^{b}1). The allegories of the sun and line (*Republic* 507a–511e), which divide reality into the intelligible part and the visible (perceptible) part, seem to embody this separation.

Conceived in this way, forms seemed to Plato to offer solutions to the metaphysical and epistemological problems to which the elenchus and flux give rise. As intelligible objects set apart from the perceptible world, they are above the sway of flux, and so available as stable objects of knowledge; stable meanings or referents for words. As real, mind-independent entities, they provide the basis for the definitions of the virtues that Socratic ethics needs.

Like many proposed solutions to philosophical problems, however, Plato's raises new problems of its own. If forms really are separate from the world of flux our senses reveal to us, how can we know them? How can our words connect with them? If items in the perceptible world really are separate from forms, how can they owe whatever determinate being they have to forms? In the *Meno, Phaedo,* and *Phaedrus,* Plato answers the first of these questions by appeal to the doctrine of recollection (*anamnêsis*). We have knowledge of forms through prenatal, direct contact with them; we forget this knowledge when our souls become embodied at birth; then we "recollect" it in this life when our memories are appropriately jogged. He answers the second question by saying that items in the world of flux "participate" in forms by resembling them. Thus perceptible objects possess the characteristic of beauty because they resemble the form of beauty, which is itself beautiful in a special and basic way (see *Phaedo* 100c, *Symposium* 210b–211e).

The doctrine of recollection presupposes the immortality of the soul—something Plato argues for in *Republic* 10 and elsewhere (*Phaedo* 69e ff., *Phaedrus* 245c ff.). It also presupposes some method of jogging our memories in a reliable way. This method is dialectic, which is a descendant of the Socratic elenchus. It is introduced in the *Republic* as having a special bearing on first principles—a feature it continues to possess in Aristotle (*Topics* 101^{a}37–^{b}4)—particularly on those of the mathematical sciences.

The importance of these sciences in Plato's thought is twofold. First, they provided a compelling example of a rich body of precise knowledge organized into a deductive system of axioms, definitions, and theorems—a model of what philosophy itself might be. Second, the brilliant mathematical treatment of harmony (musical beauty) developed by Pythagoras of Samos and his followers (Aristotle, *Metaphysics* 987^{a}29–8^{a}17) suggested a role for mathematics within philosophy itself. It opened up the possibility of giving precise definitions in wholly mathematical terms of all characteristics, including such apparently vague and evaluative ones as beauty and ugliness, justice and injustice, good and evil, and the other things of which Socrates sought definitions (*Republic* 530d–533e).

Despite the benefits these sciences promised, however, Plato found a problem with them: they treat their first principles as "absolute" starting points, to be accepted without argument (510c–d). Yet if these starting points are false, the entire system collapses. It is here that dialectic comes in. Dialectic defends these definitional starting points—it renders them "unhypothetical"—not by deriving them from something yet more primitive (which is impossible, since they are "starting" points), but by defending them against all objections, by solving all the *aporiai,* or problems, to which they give rise (534b–c, 437a). With the objections solved, our intellectual vision is cleared and we are able then to see the forms these definitions define in something like the way we did before our souls became embodied (540a–b).

In the process of their dialectical defense, the definitions themselves also undergo conceptual revamping, so that their consistency with one another—and hence their immunity to dialectical (elenctic) refutation—is revealed and assured. This enables the philosopher (to whom the craft of dialectic belongs) to knit them all together into a single unified theory of everything that exhibits "their kinship with one another and with the nature of what is" (537c). It is this unified, holistic theory that provides the philosopher—and him alone—with genuine knowledge (533d–534a).

The first principle of this entire theory, Plato claims, the greatest object of knowledge (505a), is the form of the good, which seems to be an ideal of rational order or unity expressed in mathematical terms. It is the model the philosopher uses to design his ideally just and happy Kallipolis (540a–b). On a larger scale, it also provides the maker of the cosmos—the Demiurge—with the knowledge he needs to perform his cosmic task (*Timaeus* 29e ff.). For even the gods are bound by the objective truths and values embodied in the forms (*Euthyphro* 10a ff.).

FORMS AND THE GOOD

In the discussion of music and poetry in *Republic* 2, Socrates says: "You and I are not poets at present, Adeimantus, but we *are* founding a city. And it is appropriate for the founders to know the patterns on which the poets must base their stories, and from which they must not deviate. But they should not themselves make up any poems" (378e–379a). Adeimantus responds by asking what these patterns for stories about the gods actually are. Socrates' lengthy answer may be summed up without much loss as follows: no bad images of "what the gods and heroes are like" (377e); only stories that will make the guardians "least likely to fear death" (386a); no "terrible and frightening names for the underworld" (387b–c); no "lamentations of famous men" who have suffered defeat and died (387e); no representation of "worthwhile people as overcome by laughter" (388e–389a); no representation of gods or heroes as failing "to rule over the pleasures of drink, sex, and food for themselves" (389d–e); none of the "headstrong things that private individuals say to their rulers in works of prose or poetry" (390a); no imitators except "the pure imitator of the good person" (397d); no musical harmonies except the Dorian and Phrygian (399a); no music played on flutes, triangular lutes, harps, or no "multi-stringed or polyharmonic instruments" (399c); no rhythms except those appropriate to "a life that is ordered and courageous" (399d).

The way the philosopher reaches these patterns, moreover, is clear. He looks at the effects that various kinds of poetry have on a guardian's soul. He determines what kind of soul the guardians should have by looking to the role of guardians in the good city (500b–501c, 618b–e). And he determines what that role should be by looking to the good itself, since it is only through knowing it that he knows any other kind of good at all (534b–c).

The patterns the philosopher reaches in this way are forms. But they are, as we have seen, quite unspecific: they are not detailed blueprints for actual poems. All they determine are the features that a *good* poem must have. The same, presumably, is true of the forms of other things. Thus the philosopher's pattern of an F simply specifies the features an F must have, or must lack, *if it is to be good*.

To see more clearly what such a form or pattern is, we turn to the allegory of the sun:

> What gives truth to the things known and the power to know to the knower is the form of the good. And as the cause of knowledge and truth, you must think of it as an object of knowledge. Both knowledge and truth are beautiful things. But if you are to think correctly, you must think of the good as other and more beautiful than they. In the visible realm, light and sight are rightly thought to be sunlike, but wrongly thought to be the sun. So, here it is right to think of knowledge and truth as goodlike, but wrong to think that either of them is the good—for the state of the good is yet more honored. (508e–509a)

The form of the good, then, is something like a self-illuminating object that can shed the intelligible analogue of light on other objects of knowledge—other paradigms—in such a way as to render them intelligible: it is an intelligible object that is somehow a condition of the intelligibility of other things. This suggests that the "light" the good itself gives off is something like rational or logical order, and that it itself is a paradigm of such order.

A second side of the sun allegory is about reality and its nature:

> The sun, I think you would say, not only gives visible things the power to be seen but also provides for their coming-to-be, growth, and nourishment—although it is not itself coming to be. . . . Therefore, you

> should also say that not only do the objects of knowledge owe their
> being known to the good, but their existence and being are also due to
> it; although the good is not being, but something yet beyond being,
> superior to it in rank and power. (509b)

Visible things—including the sun—are components of the visible realm.
But the sun has a very special role therein: without it there would be no
such realm. The same holds of the form of the good considered as a paradigm of rational order: it is a component of the intelligible realm, without
which there would be no such realm. Hence its superior rank.

The form of the good is a standard or paradigm, then, that enables the
philosopher to determine what poetical, political, or any other kind of
goodness is. That is why other types of expertise need philosophy. Consider
shoemaking, for example. The shoemaker knows how to make a shoe—he
has access to the form of a shoe (596b). But he does not, qua shoemaker,
know how to make a good shoe—one that reliably contributes to human
happiness. For that he must turn to the philosopher, since only he can
judge the goodness of the cities of which shoemakers, and all other experts,
must form a part if human happiness is to be reliably achieved. That, and
the philosopher's need for the sustenance and protection these experts provide, is what makes the good city possible in Plato's view (369b ff.).

SPECIALIZATION AND THE STRUCTURE OF KALLIPOLIS

We might expect that Socrates' first step would be to draft a set of laws for
Kallipolis. Instead, he focuses almost exclusively on designing a social structure that will dispose all the citizens to virtue. The reason for this is ulti-
mately psychological. Socrates thinks that unless socialization (including
education) makes people's appetites and emotions as responsive as possible to
reason, so that they acquire civic virtue, no system of laws will be effective,
but that once they have acquired such virtue, legislation by philosopher-
kings is a routine matter (422e–427d). Put the other way around, he believes
that the threat posed to political good order by lawless or unnecessary appetites is the greatest political evil of all. It is this belief that explains so much
that we are likely to find most abhorrent in the *Republic*, such as the lies of
the rulers, the critique of the family and private property, and the censorship
of art. Of more immediate relevance, it is also what explains the sort of labor
specialization that Socrates claims must be mandatory in Kallipolis.

In *Republic* 2 through 5, Socrates accepts *unique aptitudes*—a descriptive
principle according to which each person is born with a natural aptitude
for a unique craft (454d, 455e). On the basis of it, he also accepts *strong specialization*—a normative principle requiring everyone in Kallipolis to practice exclusively throughout life the unique craft for which he has a natural
aptitude, on the grounds that better products will be produced in greater

abundance, ensuring greater well-being (370a–b, 374a–c, 394e, 423c–d, 433a, 443b–c, 453b). Nonetheless, he eventually seems to abandon these views, or to accept them only in a much more restricted form.

What Socrates does finally accept is the *upper-bound doctrine,* according to which a person's ruling desires set a unique upper limit to his cognitive development. Indeed, this doctrine, as we saw in the allegory of the cave, is the very cornerstone of his psychological theory. Moreover, because he accepts it, he also accepts *weak specialization,* which states that each person in Kallipolis must practice exclusively, throughout life, whichever of the three crafts—producing, guardianship, or ruling—demands of him the highest level of cognitive development of which he is capable: money-lovers must be producers of some kind; honor-lovers must be guardians; philosophers must be kings (434a–b).

That is why, as we learn in *Republic* 4, *strong specialization* was merely a provisional first stab at its weaker analogue and is explicitly replaced by it. If *all* the practitioners of the various ordinary crafts exchanged tools, that would not do "any great harm to the city" (434a). If the producers, guardians, and rulers did the same, on the other hand, it would "destroy the city" (434a–b). For *strong specialization* was never anything more than "a sort of image of justice" (443c), whereas *weak specialization* is its very essence: a soul is just if its three constituent parts (reason, spirit, appetite) obey this doctrine, as is a city when its parts (rulers, guardians, producers) do the same (434c, 443c–d).

THE LIES OF THE RULERS

On a couple of occasions, Socrates tells us that the rulers of Kallipolis will often find it necessary or useful to lie to the guardians and producers. The specter of Thrasymachean false ideology and exploitation is immediately raised. In this section, we shall try to determine how large an obstacle it poses to the ethical acceptability of Plato's politics.

At the end of *Republic* 2, Socrates distinguishes between two types of lies or falsehoods. A "true lie," or a "real lie" (382a, 382c), is a lie told by someone "about the most important things to what is most important in himself" (382a–b). A real lie, therefore, must so mislead reason, which is the most important part of the soul, as to prevent the soul from achieving its overall good (441e–442c). A "lie in words," by contrast, is a "sort of imitation" of a genuine lie (382b–c) that can be used to prevent people from doing something bad out of ignorance or insanity (382c–d).

What we have to imagine, then, is something like this: *B* is attempting to do *x,* falsely believing, because he is mad or ignorant, that it is good to do it. *A* knows that it is not good for *B* to do *x,* and so tells *B* something that he himself knows to be false in order to prevent *B* from doing it. *A* has lied to *B.* But *B* does not come to have a false belief about the good in the rational part of his soul as a result. Indeed, he is steered toward the good, not away from it.

A genuine lie misleads reason about the good. A verbal lie may seem to do the same—especially to the person (*B* in our example) who discovers he has been misled. For *B*, of course, believes that doing *x is* a good thing to do. That is why a verbal lie is a "sort of imitation" of a genuine lie. But it is not a pure lie because it does not in fact mislead reason about the good. The verbal lie comes "after" the genuine lie (382b–c), because *A* cannot reliably lie in words until he knows the form of the good and is in a position to tell genuine lies that mislead reason about it. That is why everyone except the philosopher-kings must avoid lies altogether (389b–c).

That the lies of the rulers are all intended to be verbal rather than genuine is made clear by Socrates' examples. One of these is the well-known myth of the metals (414b–415d). Since it is referred to as "one of those useful lies we were talking about a while ago" (414b–c), it is clearly intended to be verbal. Its function is to tie the members of Kallipolis to one another by bonds of love or friendship (415d). But their friendship is in fact well founded in mutual self-interest. So, this lie fits our account. Those who believe it do not come to believe a genuine lie, for the belief benefits them and leads them toward the good, not away from it.

We last hear about the lies of the rulers in *Republic* 5 in connection with the lottery secretly rigged by the rulers to ensure that the best men have sex with the best women as frequently as possible (459c–460a). Here again the lie that luck, not planning, controls the sexual lottery is intended to be verbal, since it is supposed to benefit the city as a whole by preserving the quality of the guardian class. One cannot help feeling, however, that Plato's intentions are less than well realized here. For sex is something even honor-loving guardians enjoy—that is why getting to have it often is a reward for them (460b, 468b–c). Consequently, the loss of it, which inferior guardians suffer in Kallipolis, is a real loss—one, moreover, for which they are not compensated.

This defect in Kallipolis is surely a minor one, however. Plato has, for contingent historical reasons, simply chosen a less than optimum solution to the problem at hand. For he has no objection to sex per se—when guardians are beyond the age of reproduction, they are allowed to have sex with anyone they want, provided they avoid incest (461b–c). Hence contraception would provide a better solution to the eugenics problem than rigged lotteries.

To grasp the philosophical significance of all this, we need to draw a few rough and ready distinctions. If the subjects in a society falsely believe they are happier there than elsewhere, in part because the worldview they have been taught is false and known to be false by their rulers, they are the victims of *false ideology*. If, on the other hand, they believe truly that they are happier, but do so because they have been taught to accept a worldview that is false and known to be false by their rulers, their ideology is *falsely sustained*. Finally, if they believe they are happier there and their belief is both true and sustained by a true worldview, they and their society are *ideology-free*. Because the lies of the rulers are verbal lies, it is clear that the producers and guardians who believe them are not the victims of false ideology. But because what they believe is false, and known by the philosopher-kings to be false, their ideology is falsely sustained.

The worldviews available to the producers and guardians in Kallipolis are intended to be as close to the truth, however, as their natural abilities and ruling desires allow. So, although the producers and guardians do not see their values or their place in Kallipolis with complete clarity, their vision is as undistorted as their natures—fully developed by education—allow.

It is obvious that everyone has a self-interested reason to avoid a society in which he is the victim of false ideology. That, after all, is the gist of Thrasymachus' argument. But it is not so clear that everyone has a reason to avoid one in which his ideology is falsely sustained—especially if the degree of falsehood involved is minimal. Indeed, it may be rational for him to prefer such a society to one that is altogether ideology-free. It all depends on what his natural abilities are and what he most wants in life. If what he most wants is the pleasure of making money or the pleasure of being honored, for example, he has every reason to trade some truth in his worldview for more of his own favorite pleasure. Indeed, if he lacks the natural ability to escape ideology altogether, he may have no choice in the matter.

So, the fact that the ideologies of the guardians and producers are falsely sustained while the philosopher-kings are ideology-free seems to be a strength in Kallipolis, rather than a weakness. There, and only there, do honor-lovers and money-lovers get the benefits of the freedom from ideology of which they are themselves incapable.

PRIVATE LIFE AND PRIVATE PROPERTY

On his return in *Republic* 5 to the topic of the way of life appropriate to the guardians, Socrates raises the question of how female guardians should be trained and educated. Should they reduce the amount of work required of the males by sharing their duties, or should they "stay indoors and look after the house" (451d)? It is argued by Socrates' critic, as it has been throughout the ages, that a difference in reproductive roles does indeed entail a difference in social ones. Socrates sees through this, however, pointing out that it is not clear that one's role in reproduction has anything to do with one's aptitude for a type of work or occupation (454d–e). Hence, in Kallipolis, women will not be confined to the house but trained in the craft for which their natural aptitude is highest.

These provisions are certainly enlightened, even by our own standards, but because they form a part of the discussion of guardian women, it may seem that they are intended to apply only to female *guardians,* not to female producers. Stray remarks that have clear application to the latter, however, suggest that this may not be the case. *Specialization,* for example, is said to apply to "every child, woman, free person, craftsman, ruler, and subject" (433d1–5). The implication is that female producers will be trained in the occupation for which they are naturally best suited. Since Socrates implies that there are women with a natural aptitude for carpentry (454d), explicitly mentions female physicians, and claims that natural aptitudes for each occupation are to be found in both sexes (455d–e), it seems that female producers are intended to be apprenticed in an appropriate occupation in precisely the same way as the males.

It must be conceded, however, that Plato is not a feminist. He shows no interest in liberating women as such and implies that they are generally inferior to men (455c–d). Moreover, his casual remarks reveal a streak of unregenerate sexism and misogyny (431b–c, 469d, 557c, 563b). But these are relatively small matters and do not affect the general point that in Kallipolis men and women with the same natural assets will receive the same education and have access to the same careers. Still, Plato is regrettably vague about the producers, whether male or female, and has left us somewhat in the dark on the important question of who will do the housework and rear the children if both parents are employed full-time outside the household.

In the case of the guardians, he is more forthcoming, although what he describes may not appeal to us. If the guardians and producers were in competition for the same social goods, producers would fare very badly, since the guardians are armed and trained for warfare in a way that the producers are not (419a). Hence the guardians are segregated from the producers and denied both private property and private family life (the objects of the producers' ruling appetitive desires), on the grounds that "if they acquire private land, houses, and money themselves, they will be household managers and farmers, instead of guardians—hostile masters of the other citizens instead of their allies" (417a–b). The result is all the things that are likely to estrange us most from the *Republic:* sex by lottery as part of a state-sponsored eugenics program; state-run "rearing pens" for guardian offspring (451c–461e); and the totalitarian domination of the private sphere by the public.

Part of what has led Plato in this unattractive direction, to be sure, is his profound suspicion of the appetites and the politically destructive potential of greed and self-interest. Removing the things that stimulate them therefore becomes appealing. Even so, it is difficult not to see the cure as at least as bad as—if not worse than—the disease.

CENSORSHIP

The most important political institutions in Kallipolis, or in any other society, in Socrates' view, are educational. The "one great thing," he says, is education and upbringing. Hence "what the overseers of our city must cling to, not allow to become corrupted without their noticing it, and guard against everything, is this: there must be no innovation in musical or physical training that goes against the established order" (423d–424c). It should come as no surprise, therefore, that having completed the account of his own revolutionary educational proposals, and having justified them by showing that they promote both maximal justice and maximal happiness in those who receive them, Socrates should turn in *Republic* 10 to attack his competition—the poets and playwrights who were the purveyors of traditional Greek ethical education. The philosophers, not the poets, he argues, are the true teachers of virtue.

The reasons he gives are these: first of all, being able to imitate virtue or virtuous people in rhythms and rhymes that please and entertain most people does not qualify one to teach human beings how to live. The poet or dramatist writes for a nonspecialist audience. Hence he must employ a conceptual framework similar to theirs. Character, motive, plot—all must be drawn from folk psychology; not, say, from cognitive science or whatever the true theory of the soul turns out to be. This means that art represents people and their motives and actions, not necessarily as they really are, but only as they seem to people without specialist training. The languages of art are not, then, the technical mathematics-like language of Platonic truth. The scientist, or philosopher-king, by contrast, is free of this constraint, since his is primarily an audience of fellow specialists (601a–b, 603b–605c).

Second, poetry and drama, like all art, aim to provide a certain characteristic pleasure or satisfaction (606b), which on Plato's view, as on Freud's, is related to repression. Art enables us to satisfy without reproach or shame the very desires we must repress in real life. These are characteristically appetitive desires, especially sexual ones. This might plausibly be taken to entail that representations of ethically good people do not provide the kind of satisfaction art typically provides and are not what a poet needs to know how to produce (604e–605a). If we suppose, as Plato does (485d), that even artistic indulgence of repressed desires strengthens them and weakens the repressive mechanisms, we will see reason here to mistrust art in general (605b, 606b).

Finally, we must look at the poet himself, and why he writes. Plato is confident that no one would be satisfied merely to represent life if he knew how to live it well, or could teach others how to do so (599b–601a). If we think again of the characteristic pleasure art provides, his view becomes intelligible and, again, rather like a view of Freud's. A life devoted to making things that provide a fantasy satisfaction for unnecessary appetites could not rank very highly among lives.

These arguments are unlikely simply to command our assent. But even if we find them inconclusive, they extend the right invitation to philosophers who think that art has something to teach us about how to live: develop metaphysics, epistemology, psychology, and politics, on the basis of which it will be clear that the knowledge a good poet or dramatist needs is relevant to ethics. It is precisely as such an invitation, indeed, that Plato himself seems to understand them (607d–e).

FREEDOM AND AUTONOMY

A person's needs, wants, and interests are determined by the natural genetic lottery, by education and upbringing, and by actual circumstances. They also depend on his beliefs, which in turn depend to some extent on the same factors as do his needs, wants, and interests themselves. His *real interests* are those he would form under optimal conditions—those in which his needs are satisfied, he is neither maltreated nor coerced nor the victim of false ideology, and he is as aware as possible of his actual circumstances and the real alternatives to them. Happiness is optimal satisfaction of real interests in the long term.

The relevance of this picture to the *Republic* is no doubt clear. For Kallipolis has emerged as a community intended by Plato to provide optimal conditions of the type in question. Each of its members has his needs satisfied, is neither maltreated nor coerced nor the victim of false ideology, and is educated and trained so as to develop a conception of the world and his place in it that is as close to the truth as his nature—fully developed with an eye to his maximal happiness—permits. Each has his ruling desires satisfied throughout life. Thus each develops his real interests and is made really happy.

Even when we bear all that in mind, the *Republic* is still likely to feel authoritarian and repressive. Some of that is due to controversial beliefs we bring to it. For example, we are inclined to presuppose that no amount of knowledge of the way the world is validates or underwrites a unique conception of the good (we cannot derive ought from is, value from fact). Different conceptions are determined by what different individuals happen to want or prefer. The state exists, not to judge among these conceptions, but to allow each individual to realize his own conception as far as is compatible with others' realizing theirs to the same extent. In this way, the state at once respects the individuality of its members and treats them equally. An activity, institution, or issue is paradigmatically political for us, indeed, if it pertains to disputes between people who may have different conceptions of the good, yet must coexist and have dealings with one another in the same community or the same world. Individual freedom, on this broadly liberal conception, is freedom to do what one wants; freedom to live in accordance with a conception of the good that is rooted in one's own desires, preferences, or choices. And a state is free to the extent that it limits individual freedom only to guarantee equal freedom to all its members. It is not surprising, then, that when in imagination we project ourselves into Kallipolis, *we* do feel repressed and unfree.

This conception of political freedom is not the only one, however. Freedom to do what we want—*instrumental* freedom—is certainly important. But its importance can be undermined by the very desires on which it depends. For if we would not have the desires we are free to satisfy had we engaged in a process of ideal, rational deliberation, then being free to satisfy them seems less worth caring about. If our desires, like those of a drug addict, can make us unfree, instrumental freedom seems insufficient for real freedom or autonomy.

Perhaps, then, we should think instead in terms of *deliberative* freedom, which is the freedom to have and to satisfy those desires we would choose to have if we were aware of the relevant facts, were thinking clearly, and were free from distorting influences. If so, we can see at once that a state that guaranteed deliberative freedom might look and feel very repressive to someone solely concerned about instrumental freedom. It would very much depend on what his desires happened to be. Since the psychological and political cost of repression is high, however, we can well imagine that an enlightened state, committed to deliberative freedom, would want to devote much of its resources to education and training so as to ensure that its members are as close to being deliberatively rational as possible. Such a state would already begin to look a little like Kallipolis, and to share some of its priorities.

In any case, it seems clear that Kallipolis is intended to provide its members with as much deliberative freedom as their natures, fully developed in optimal conditions, permit:

> Why do you think someone is reproached for menial work or handicraft? Or shall we say that it is for no other reason than because the best element is naturally weak in him, so that it cannot rule the beasts within him, but can only serve them and learn what flatters them? . . . In order to ensure, then, that someone like that is also ruled by something similar to what rules the best person, we say that he should be the slave of that best person who has the divine ruler within himself. It is not to harm the slave that we say he should be ruled, as Thrasymachus supposed was true of all subjects, but because it is better for everyone to be ruled by a divine and wise ruler—preferably one that is his own and that he has inside himself—otherwise one imposed on him from outside, so that we may all be as alike and as friendly as possible, because we are all captained by the same thing. (590c–d; also 395b–c)

Thus, even if we retain our liberal suspicion about the possibility of a science of values, we might still, by coming to see merit in the idea of deliberative freedom, also come to see the *Republic,* not as predominantly a totalitarian hymn to the benefits of repression and unfreedom, but as an attempt to design a city whose members enjoy as much real happiness, and as much real freedom, as possible.

Select Bibliography

Adam, J. *The* Republic *of Plato*. Cambridge: Cambridge University Press, 1902. (Critical edition of the Greek text, with notes and commentary.)

Annas, J. *An Introduction to Plato's* Republic. Oxford: Clarendon Press, 1981.

Bobonich, C. *Plato's Utopia Recast: His Later Ethics and Politics*. Oxford: Clarendon Press, 2002.

Burnyeat, M. "Platonism and Mathematics: A Prelude to Discussion." In *Mathematics and Metaphysics in Aristotle,* edited by A. Graeser, pp. 213–40. Bern: Paul Haupt, 1987.

———. "Plato on Why Mathematics is Good for the Soul." In *Mathematics and Necessity,* edited by T. Smiley, pp. 1–81. Oxford: Oxford University Press, 2000.

———. "Plato." *Proceedings of the British Academy* 111 (2000): 1–22.

Cooper, J. M. "The Psychology of Justice in Plato." *American Philosophical Quarterly* 14 (1977): 151–7. Reprinted in his *Reason and Emotion,* pp. 138–50. Princeton: Princeton University Press, 1999.

———. "Plato's Theory of Human Motivation." *History of Philosophy Quarterly* 1 (1984): 3–21. Reprinted in his *Reason and Emotion,* pp. 118–37. Princeton: Princeton University Press, 1999.

Ferrari, G. *City and Soul in Plato's* Republic. Sankt Augustin: Academia Verlag, 2003.

Fine, G., ed. *Plato 1: Metaphysics and Epistemology.* Oxford: Oxford University Press, 1999.

———. *Plato 2: Ethics, Politics, Religion, and the Soul.* Oxford: Oxford University Press, 1999.

Irwin, T. *Plato's Ethics.* New York: Oxford University Press, 1995.

Kraut, R., ed. *The Cambridge Companion to Plato.* Cambridge: Cambridge University Press, 1992.

———, ed. *Plato's* Republic: *Critical Essays.* Lanham, Md.: Rowman and Littlefield, 1997.

Moravcsik, J., and P. Temko, eds. *Plato on Beauty, Wisdom, and the Arts.* Totowa, N.J.: Rowman and Littlefield, 1982.

Murdoch, I. *The Fire and the Sun: Why Plato Banished the Artists.* Oxford: Oxford University Press, 1977.

Popper, K. *The Open Society and Its Enemies,* vol. 1. Princeton: Princeton University Press, 1971.

Reeve, C. *Philosopher-Kings: The Argument of Plato's* Republic. Princeton: Princeton University Press, 1988.

Sachs, D. "A Fallacy in Plato's *Republic.*" *Philosophical Review* 72 (1963): 141–58.

Vlastos, G. "The Theory of Social Justice in the *Polis* in Plato's *Republic.*" In *Interpretations of Plato: A Swarthmore Symposium,* edited by H. North, pp. 1–40. Leiden: Brill, 1977.

———. "Elenchus and Mathematics: A Turning-point in Plato's Philosophical Development." *American Journal of Philology* 109 (1988): 362–96.

Wagner, E., ed. *Essays on Plato's Psychology.* Lanham, Md.: Lexington Books, 2001.

White, N. *A Companion to Plato's* Republic. Indianapolis: Hackett Publishing Company, 1979.

———. *Individual and Conflict in Greek Ethics.* Oxford: Clarendon Press, 2002.

Synopsis

BOOK 1

On his way home from a religious festival, Socrates meets Polemarchus and accompanies him to the house of his aged father, Cephalus. • Socrates and Cephalus discuss the burdens of old age. Cephalus claims that, while these burdens are eased by wealth, it is people's characters and habits, not their ages, that determine what their lives are like. Wealth is mostly important, he claims, because it reduces the likelihood of being tempted into injustice by poverty and so lessens the fear of what will happen after death. This leads to a discussion of justice, which will itself culminate—many books later—in a myth about the afterlife (Book 10). • Cephalus claims that justice consists in speaking the truth and paying one's debts. Before he can respond to Socrates' criticism of his definition, Polemarchus interrupts. Cephalus hands over the argument to him and goes off to attend to a sacrifice to the gods. An examination of Polemarchus follows, in the course of which he is forced to abandon a number of different views about justice that he has adopted along the way. • Thrasymachus demands that Socrates give his own positive account of justice but is persuaded to give an account himself instead. Justice, he claims, is what is advantageous for the stronger. Thrasymachus defends it with two separate arguments (338d–341a, 343a–344c), which Socrates then attempts to refute.

BOOK 2

Unsatisfied with the outcome of Book 1, Glaucon and Adeimantus renew Thrasymachus' views. In response, Socrates must show that justice is choiceworthy (a) because of itself, and (b) because of its consequences (357a–358a). Socrates does not complete his argument for (a) until the end of Book 9. • Socrates shifts the debate from individual justice to political justice. He will describe an ideal or completely good city—Kallipolis. Having located justice in it, he will then look for it in the soul. • The first city he describes is dismissed by Glaucon as fit only for pigs, not for sophisticated Athenians. • The second city is more luxurious. But the presence in it of appetites for more than the necessities provided in its simpler predecessor leads to civil faction and war. To prevent these from destroying the city, soldier-police are needed. These are the guardians. • The natural assets they need and the education they must have are next described. Since musical training begins before physical training, its content—more specifically the sorts of stories that the future guardians should hear about gods and heroes—is the first item of business (377e).

Book 3

The discussion of these stories continues. Once complete, Socrates turns to the content of stories about human beings, only to postpone his discussion until Book 10. (He explains why at 392a–c.) • The appropriate *style* for these stories to have and the appropriate harmonies and rhythms for lyric odes and songs are characterized. • Physical training is next. • The final topic is the selection of rulers (including the "myth of the metals"), and the housing and lifestyles of the guardians (412b–417b).

Book 4

A question from Adeimantus about the happiness of the guardians leads Socrates to clarify the goal of Kallipolis, which is not to make any one group of citizens outstandingly happy at the expense of others, but to make everyone as happy as his nature allows (421c). This goal will be achieved, he argues, if the guardians protect the system of elementary education described in Books 2 and 3. For it is what provides the training in political virtue without which no system of laws or constitution can hope to achieve anything worthwhile (423c–427a). • The place of religion in Kallipolis is then very briefly discussed (427b–c). • Kallipolis is pronounced complete (427d). Since it is completely good (427e), it must have all the virtues of a city (see 352d–354a): wisdom, courage, temperance, and justice. By the time that search for them is concluded (434d), they have all been identified with distinct structural features of Kallipolis. • This leads to the argument for the division of the soul into three elements—appetitive, spirited, and rational—that correspond to the three major classes in Kallipolis—producers, guardians, and rulers (435c–441c). Once this argument is in place, it remains to find the virtues in the soul and to show that they are the same structural features of it as of Kallipolis (441c–444e). • Glaucon is ready at this point to pronounce justice more choiceworthy than injustice, but Socrates is not (445a–b). In his view, the question cannot be answered until much more work has been done on virtue and vice.

Book 5

The discussion of that topic is interrupted by Polemarchus and the other interlocutors, all of whom want Socrates to explain the remark he made (423e4–424a2) about the guardians sharing their women and children. Socrates' lengthy response occupies the majority of the book. In it, he makes the revolutionary proposal that children should be brought up by the city rather than by their biological parents, and that men and women with the same natural abilities should receive the same education and training and do the same kind of work, including guarding and ruling. • The smallest change that would transform an already existing city into Kallipolis, Socrates now argues, is for its kings or rulers to become philosophers, or vice versa. The remainder of Book 5 is the beginning of Socrates' portrait of philosophers, which continues until the end of Book 7. It consists of a complex argument intended to show that only they can have access to forms, and that without such access knowledge is impossible (474c4–480a13).

Book 6

Real philosophers are contrasted with those popularly called philosophers. • The former must master the most important subjects (503e), the ones that lead to knowledge of the form of the good (504e–505b). • Socrates cannot explain directly what this is, but in the sun and line analogies he tries to give an indirect account of them (507a–511e).

Book 7

Book 7 begins with the famous allegory of the cave, which is intended to fit together with the sun and line (517b), by illustrating the effects of education on the soul (514a). • The discussion of the education of the philosophers continues. Primary education in musical and physical training and elementary mathematics (535a–537b) is followed by two or three years of compulsory physical training (537b–c), ten years of education in the mathematical sciences (537c–d, 522c–531d), five years of training in dialectic (537d–540a, 531e–535a), and fifteen years of practical political training (539e–540a). After such education, its recipients are ready to see the good itself and to be philosopher-kings (540a).

Book 8

The description of Kallipolis and the person whose character resembles it—the philosopher-king—is now complete. So, Socrates returns to the argument interrupted at the beginning of Book 5. He describes four types of people and four types of constitutions that result when people of these types rule a city. He presents these as four stages in the increasing corruption or decline of Kallipolis, explaining why Kallipolis will decline by appeal to the Muses' story of the "geometrical number" (546a–547a). • The first of the defective cities Socrates describes is a timocracy, which is ruled by people who are themselves ruled by the spirited element in their souls. • The second is an oligarchy, which is ruled by people ruled by their necessary appetites. • The third is a democracy, which is ruled by people ruled by their unnecessary appetites. • The worst city of all is a tyranny, which is ruled by someone ruled by his lawless unnecessary appetites.

BOOK 9

A lengthy description of the tyrant begins the book. Socrates is then ready to respond to the challenge Glaucon raised in Book 2. • His response consists of three complex arguments. The first (580a–c) appeals to the description of the five cities and the five corresponding character types. It concludes that a philosopher-king is the happiest and most just of people, a timocrat second, an oligarch third, a democrat fourth, and a tyrant least happy and least just. The second argument (580d–583b) appeals to the triadic division of the soul. Socrates argues that a philosopher's assessment of the relative pleasantness of his life and those of money-lovers and honor-lovers is more reliable than their assessments of the relative pleasantness of his life and theirs. The third argument (583b–588a) uses the metaphysical theory developed in Books 5 through 7, together with the psychological theory of Book 4, to develop a complex theory of pleasure. It concludes that a philosopher's pleasures are truer and purer than those of a money-lover or an honor-lover.

BOOK 10

The kind of poetry about human beings permitted in Kallipolis—postponed in Book 3 (392a–c)—can now be revisited. Given the importance attributed to musical and physical training (424b–425a), this topic is not anticlimactic, but rather the moment at which Socrates' new, philosophy-based education confronts the traditional, poetry-based one. Central to the discussion is a new account of *mimesis*—imitation—based on the metaphysical theories of Books 5 through 7. • The next topic is the immortality of the soul. • Finally, by appeal to the myth of Er, Socrates argues that the good consequences of justice, both in this life and the next, far outweigh those of injustice. This completes the argument that justice is choiceworthy both for its own sake and for its consequences, and so belongs in the best of the three classes of goods that Glaucon distinguished.

Note to the Reader

All proper names and place names are listed, most of them with brief iden-
tifications, in the Glossary and Index of Names. Unfamiliar concepts are
defined in the Glossary of Terms. Marginal page numbers, known as
"Stephanus" page numbers (after an earlier editor of Plato's works), are
standardly used in scholarly citations. Line numbers, which are approximate
in translations (including this one), refer to John Burnet, *Platonis Opera,*
vols. I–V (Oxford: Clarendon Press, 1900–1907). The basis for the present
translation is S. R. Slings, *Platonis Rempublicam* (Oxford: Clarendon Press,
2003).

Book 1

SOCRATES' NARRATION BEGINS: *I went down to the Piraeus yesterday with Glaucon, the son of Ariston, to say a prayer to the goddess,[1] and also because I wanted to see how they would manage the festival, since they were holding it for the first time. I thought the procession of the local residents was beautiful, but the show put on by the Thracians was no less so, in my view. After we had said our prayer and watched the procession, we started back toward town.[2] Then Polemarchus, the son of Cephalus, saw us from a distance as we were hurrying homeward, and told his slave boy to run and ask us to wait for him. The boy caught hold of my cloak[3] from behind.*

SLAVE: Polemarchus wants you to wait.

I turned around and asked where he was.

SLAVE: He is coming up behind you; please wait for him.

GLAUCON: All right, we will.

Shortly after that, Polemarchus caught up with us. Adeimantus, Glaucon's brother, was with him, and so were Niceratus, the son of Nicias, and some others, all of whom were apparently on their way from the procession.

POLEMARCHUS: It looks to me, Socrates, as if you two are hurrying to get away to town.

SOCRATES: That isn't a bad guess.

POLEMARCHUS: But do you see how many we are?

SOCRATES: Certainly.

POLEMARCHUS: Well, then, either you must prove yourselves stronger than all these people or you will have to stay here.

---

[1] *Hê theos:* Most probably—as 354a10–11 implies—the Thracian goddess Bendis, whose cult had recently been introduced in Piraeus. However, for Athenians, Athena is *hê theos.*

[2] See Glossary of Terms s.v. city.

[3] See Glossary of Terms s.v. cloak.

10 SOCRATES: Isn't there another alternative still: that we persuade you that you should let us go?

POLEMARCHUS: But could you persuade us, if we won't listen?

GLAUCON: There is no way we could.

POLEMARCHUS: Well, we won't listen; you had better make up your mind to that.

328a ADEIMANTUS: You mean to say you don't know that there is to be a torch race on horseback for the goddess tonight?

SOCRATES: On horseback? That is something new. Are they going to race
5 on horseback and hand the torches on in relays, or what?

POLEMARCHUS: In relays. And, besides, there will be an all-night celebration that will be worth seeing. We will get up after dinner and go to see the festivities. We will meet lots of young men there and have a discussion. So
b stay and do as we ask.

GLAUCON: It looks as if we will have to stay.

SOCRATES: If you think so, we must.

*So, we went to Polemarchus' house, and there we found Lysias and Euthyde-
5 mus, the brothers of Polemarchus, and what is more, Thrasymachus of Chalcedon was there too, and Charmantides of Paeania, and Clitophon, the son
of Aristonymus. Polemarchus' father, Cephalus, was also inside, and I
thought he looked quite old. You see, I hadn't seen him for some time. He
c was sitting on a sort of chair with cushions and had a wreath on his head, as
he had been offering a sacrifice in the courtyard. We sat down beside him,
since some chairs were arranged in a circle there. As soon as he saw me, Ceph-
5 alus greeted me:*

Socrates, you don't often come down to the Piraeus to see us. Yet you should. If it were still easy for me to make the trip to town, you wouldn't have to come here. On the contrary, we would come to you. But as it is,
d you ought to come here more often. I want you to know, you see, that in my case at least, as the other pleasures—the bodily ones—wither away, my appetites for discussions and their pleasures grow stronger.[4] So please do as I
5 ask: have your conversation with these young men, and stay here with us, as you would with your close friends and relatives.

SOCRATES: I certainly will, Cephalus. In fact, I enjoy engaging in discus-
e sion with the very old. I think we should learn from them—since they are like people who have traveled a road that we too will probably have to fol-low—what the road is like, whether rough and difficult or smooth and easy.

[4] See 485d6–e1.

2

And I would be particularly glad to find out from you what you think about it, since you have reached the point in life the poets call old age's threshold.[5] Is it a difficult time of life? What have you to report about it?

CEPHALUS: By Zeus, Socrates, I will tell you exactly what I think. You see, a number of us who are more or less the same age often get together, so as to preserve the old saying.[6] When they meet, the majority of our members lament, longing for the lost pleasures of their youth and reminiscing about sex, drinking parties, feasts, and the other things that go along with them. They get irritated, as if they had been deprived of important things, and had lived well then but are not living now. Some others, too, even moan about the abuse heaped on old people by their relatives, and for *that* reason recite a litany of all the evils old age has caused them. But I don't think they blame the real cause, Socrates. After all, if that were the cause, I too would have had the same experiences, at least as far as old age is concerned, and so would everyone else of my age. But as it is, I have met others in the past who don't feel that way—in particular, the poet Sophocles. I was once present when he was asked by someone, "How are you as far as sex goes, Sophocles? Can you still make love to a woman?" "Quiet, man," he replied, "I am very glad to have escaped from all that, like a slave who has escaped from a deranged and savage master." I thought at the time what he said was sensible, and I still do. You see, old age brings peace and freedom from all such things. When the appetites cease to stress and importune us, everything Sophocles said comes to pass, and we escape from many insane masters. But in these matters, and in those concerning one's relatives, the real cause isn't old age, Socrates, but the way people live. If they are orderly and contented, old age, too, is only moderately onerous; if they aren't, both old age, Socrates, *and* youth are hard to bear.

I admired him for saying that, and I wanted him to tell me more, so I urged him on.

I imagine when you say that, Cephalus, the masses[7] do not accept it. On the contrary, they think you bear old age more easily, not because of the way you live, but because you are wealthy. For the wealthy, they say, have many consolations.

CEPHALUS: That's true, they are not convinced. And there is something in their objection, though not as much as they think. Themistocles' retort is relevant here. When someone from Seriphus insulted him by saying his high reputation was due to his city, not to himself, he replied that, had he

---

[5] Namely, death.

[6] "God ever draws together like to like."

[7] See Glossary of Terms s.v. masses.

been a Seriphian, he would not be famous; but nor would the other, had he been an Athenian.[8] The same account applies to those who are not rich and find old age hard to bear: a good person would not easily bear old age

5   if it were coupled with poverty, but one who wasn't good would not be at peace with himself even if he were wealthy.

SOCRATES: Did you inherit most of your wealth, Cephalus, or did you make it yourself?

CEPHALUS: What did I make for myself, Socrates, you ask. As a money-

b   maker I am in between my grandfather and my father. You see, my grandfather and namesake inherited about the same amount of wealth as I possess and multiplied it many times. However, my father, Lysanias, diminished

5   that amount to even less than I have now. As for me, I am satisfied to leave my sons here no less, but a little more, than I inherited.

SOCRATES: The reason I asked is that you do not seem particularly to love

c   money. And those who have not made it themselves are usually like that. But those who have made it themselves love it twice as much as anyone else. For just as poets love their poems and fathers their children, so those who have made money take their money seriously both as something they

5   have made themselves and—just as other people do—because it is useful. This makes them difficult even to be with, since they are unwilling to praise anything except money.

CEPHALUS: That's true.

d   SOCRATES: Indeed, it is. But tell me something else. What do you think is the greatest good you have enjoyed as a result of being very wealthy?

CEPHALUS: What I have to say probably would not persuade the masses.

5   But you are well aware, Socrates, that when someone thinks his end is near, he becomes frightened and concerned about things he did not fear before. It is then that the stories told about Hades, that a person who has been unjust here must pay the penalty there—stories he used to make fun of—

e   twist his soul this way and that for fear they are true. And whether because of the weakness of old age, or because he is now closer to what happens in Hades and has a clearer view of it, or whatever it is, he is filled with foreboding and fear, and begins to calculate and consider whether he has been

5   unjust to anyone. If he finds many injustices in his life, he often even awakes from sleep in terror, as children do, and lives in anticipation of evils

331a   to come. But someone who knows he has not been unjust has sweet good hope as his constant companion—a nurse to his old age, as Pindar says. For he puts it charmingly, Socrates, when he says that when someone lives a

5   just and pious life,

[8] A slightly different version of the story appears in Herodotus 8.125.

Sweet hope is in his heart
Nurse and companion to his age
Hope, captain of the ever-twisting
Mind of mortal men.

How amazingly well he puts that. It is in this connection I would say the 10
possession of wealth is most valuable, not for every man, but for a good and
orderly one. Not cheating someone even unintentionally, not lying to him, b
not owing a sacrifice to some god or money to a person, and as a result
departing for that other place in fear—the possession of wealth makes no
small contribution to this. It has many other uses, too, but putting one 5
thing against the other, Socrates, I would say that for a man with any sense,
that is how wealth is most useful.

SOCRATES: A fine sentiment, Cephalus. But speaking of that thing itself,
justice,[9] are we to say it is simply speaking the truth and paying whatever c
debts one has incurred? Or is it sometimes just to do these things, sometimes unjust? I mean this sort of thing, for example: everyone would surely 5
agree that if a man borrows weapons from a sane friend, and if he goes mad
and asks for them back, the friend should not return them, and would not
be just if he did. Nor should anyone be willing to tell the whole truth to
someone in such a state.

CEPHALUS: That's true. d

SOCRATES: Then the following is not the definition of justice: to speak
the truth and repay what one has borrowed.

Polemarchus interrupted:

It certainly is, Socrates, if indeed we are to trust Simonides at all. 5

CEPHALUS: Well, then, I will hand over the discussion to you, since it is
time for me to look after the sacrifices.

POLEMARCHUS: Am I, Polemarchus, not heir of all your possessions?

Cephalus replied with a laugh:

Certainly.

And off he went to the sacrifice.

SOCRATES: Then tell us, heir to the discussion, just what Simonides said e
about justice that you think is correct.

[9] See Glossary of Terms s.v. justice.

POLEMARCHUS: He said it is just to give to each what is owed to him. And a fine saying it is, in my view.

SOCRATES: Well, now, it is not easy to disagree with Simonides, since he is a wise and godlike man. But what exactly does he mean? Perhaps you know, Polemarchus, but I do not understand. Clearly, he does not mean what we said a moment ago—namely, giving back to someone whatever he has lent to you, even if he is out of his mind when he asks for it. And yet what he has lent to you is surely something that is owed to him, isn't it?

332a

POLEMARCHUS: Yes.

SOCRATES: But when he is out of his mind, it is, under no circumstances, to be given to him?

POLEMARCHUS: True.

SOCRATES: Then it seems Simonides must have meant something else when he says that to return what is owed is just.

POLEMARCHUS: Something else indeed, by Zeus! He meant friends owe something good to their friends, never something bad.

SOCRATES: I understand. You mean someone does not give a lender what he is owed by giving him gold, when the giving and taking would be harmful, and both he and the lender are friends. Isn't that what you say Simonides meant?

b

POLEMARCHUS: It certainly is.

SOCRATES: Now what about this? Should one also give to one's enemies whatever is owed to them?

POLEMARCHUS: Yes, by all means. What is *in fact* owed to them. And what an enemy owes an enemy, in my view, is also precisely what is appropriate—something bad.

SOCRATES: It seems, then, Simonides was speaking in riddles—just like a poet!—when he said what justice is. For what he meant, it seems, is that it is just to give to each *what is appropriate to him,* and this is what he called giving him *what he is owed.*

c

POLEMARCHUS: What else did you think he meant?

SOCRATES: Then what, in the name of Zeus, do you think he would answer if someone asked him: "Simonides, what owed or appropriate things does the craft[10] we call medicine give, and to which things?"

POLEMARCHUS: Clearly, he would say it gives drugs, food, and drink to bodies.

[10] See Glossary of Terms s.v. craft.

SOCRATES: And what owed or appropriate things does the craft we call cooking give, and to which things?

POLEMARCHUS: It gives pleasant flavors to food.   d

SOCRATES: Good. Now what does the craft we would call justice give, and to whom or what does it give it?

POLEMARCHUS: If we are to follow the previous answers, Socrates, it gives benefit to friends and harm to enemies.   5

SOCRATES: Does Simonides mean, then, that treating friends well and enemies badly is justice?

POLEMARCHUS: I believe so.

SOCRATES: And who is most capable of treating sick friends well and ene-   10
mies badly in matters of disease and health?

POLEMARCHUS: A doctor.

SOCRATES: And who can do so best in a storm at sea?   e

POLEMARCHUS: A ship's captain.[11]

SOCRATES: What about the just person? In what actions and what work is he most capable of benefiting friends and harming enemies?

POLEMARCHUS: In wars and alliances, I imagine.   5

SOCRATES: All right. Now when people are not sick, Polemarchus, a doctor is useless to them.

POLEMARCHUS: True.

SOCRATES: And so is a ship's captain to those who are not sailing?

POLEMARCHUS: Yes.   10

SOCRATES: So to people who are not at war, a just man is useless?

POLEMARCHUS: No, I don't think that at all.

SOCRATES: So justice is also useful in peacetime?

POLEMARCHUS: Yes, it is useful.   333a

SOCRATES: And so is farming, isn't it?

POLEMARCHUS: Yes.

SOCRATES: For providing produce?

POLEMARCHUS: Yes.   5

SOCRATES: And shoemaking as well, of course?

POLEMARCHUS: Yes.

---

[11] See Glossary of Terms s.v. captain.

SOCRATES: For the acquisition of shoes, I suppose you would say?

POLEMARCHUS: Of course.

10 SOCRATES: Tell me, then, what is justice useful for using or acquiring in peacetime?

POLEMARCHUS: Contracts, Socrates.

SOCRATES: And by contracts you mean partnerships, or what?

POLEMARCHUS: Partnerships, of course.

b SOCRATES: So is it a just man who is a good and useful partner in a game of checkers, or an expert checkers player?

POLEMARCHUS: An expert checkers player.

SOCRATES: And in laying bricks and stones, is a just person a better and
5 more useful partner than a builder?

POLEMARCHUS: Not at all.

SOCRATES: Well, in what kind of partnership, then, is a just person a better partner than a builder or a lyre player, in the way a lyre player is better than a just person at hitting the right notes?

10 POLEMARCHUS: In money matters, I think.

SOCRATES: Except, I presume, Polemarchus, in using money. You see, whenever one needs to buy or sell a horse jointly, I think a horse breeder is
c a more useful partner. Isn't he?

POLEMARCHUS: Apparently.

SOCRATES: And when it is a boat, a boat builder or a ship's captain?

POLEMARCHUS: It would seem so.

5 SOCRATES: In what joint use of silver or gold, then, is a just person a more useful partner than anyone else?

POLEMARCHUS: When yours must be deposited for safekeeping, Socrates.

SOCRATES: You mean whenever there is no need to use it, but only to keep it?

10 POLEMARCHUS: Of course.

SOCRATES: So when money is not being used, that is when justice is use-
d ful for it?

POLEMARCHUS: It looks that way.

SOCRATES: And when one needs to keep a pruning knife safe, justice is useful both in partnerships and for the individual. When you need to use it, however, it is the craft of vine pruning that is useful?

5 POLEMARCHUS: Apparently.

8

SOCRATES: And would you also say that when one needs to keep a shield and a lyre safe and not use them, justice is a useful thing, but when you need to use them it is the soldier's craft or the musician's that is useful?

POLEMARCHUS: I would have to.

SOCRATES: And so in all other cases, too, justice is useless when they are in use, but useful when they are not?   10

POLEMARCHUS: It looks that way.

SOCRATES: Then justice cannot be something excellent, can it, my friend,   e
if it is only useful for useless things. But let's consider the following point.
Isn't the person who is cleverest at landing a blow, whether in boxing or
any other kind of fight, also cleverest at guarding against it?

POLEMARCHUS: Of course.   5

SOCRATES: And the one who is clever at guarding against disease is also
cleverest at producing it unnoticed?

POLEMARCHUS: That is my view, at any rate.

SOCRATES: And the one who is a good guardian of an army is the very   334a
one who can steal the enemy's plans and dispositions?

POLEMARCHUS: Of course.

SOCRATES: So whenever someone is a clever guardian of something, he is
also clever at stealing it.   5

POLEMARCHUS: It seems so.

SOCRATES: So if a just person is clever at guarding money, he must also be
clever at stealing it.

POLEMARCHUS: So the argument suggests, at least.

SOCRATES: It seems, then, that a just person has turned out to be a kind of
thief. You probably got that idea from Homer. For he loves Autolycus, the   10
maternal grandfather of Odysseus, whom he describes as better than every-   b
one at stealing and swearing false oaths.[12] According to you, Homer, and
Simonides, then, justice seems to be some sort of craft of stealing—one that
benefits friends and harms enemies. Isn't that what you meant?   5

POLEMARCHUS: No, by Zeus, it isn't. But I do not know anymore what I
meant. I still believe this, however, that benefiting one's friends and harming one's enemies is justice.

SOCRATES: Speaking of friends, do you mean those a person believes to be   c
good and useful, or those who actually are good and useful, even if he does
not believe they are, and similarly with enemies?

[12] *Odyssey* 19.392–8.

POLEMARCHUS: Probably, one loves those one considers good and useful
and hates those one considers bad.

SOCRATES: But don't people make mistakes about this, so that lots of those
who seem to them to be good and useful aren't, and vice versa?

POLEMARCHUS: They do.

SOCRATES: So, for them, good people are enemies and bad ones friends?

POLEMARCHUS: Of course.

SOCRATES: All the same, it is then just for them to benefit bad people and
harm good ones?

POLEMARCHUS: Apparently.

SOCRATES: Yet good people are just and are not the sort to do injustice.

POLEMARCHUS: True.

SOCRATES: According to your account, then, it is just to do bad things to
those who do no injustice.

POLEMARCHUS: Not at all, Socrates. It is *my account* that seems to be bad.

SOCRATES: It is just, then, is it, to harm unjust people and benefit just
ones?

POLEMARCHUS: That seems better than the other view.

SOCRATES: Then it follows, Polemarchus, that it is just for many people—
the ones who are mistaken in their judgment—to harm their friends, since
they are bad for them, and benefit their enemies, since they are good. And
so we will find ourselves claiming the very opposite of what we said Simonides meant.

POLEMARCHUS: Yes, that certainly follows. But let's change our definition.
For it looks as though we did not define friends and enemies correctly.

SOCRATES: How did we define them, Polemarchus?

POLEMARCHUS: We said that a friend is someone who is believed to be
good.

SOCRATES: And how are we to change that now?

POLEMARCHUS: Someone who is both believed to be good and is good is
a friend; someone who is believed to be good, but is not, is believed to be a
friend but is not. And the same goes for enemies.

SOCRATES: According to that account, then, a good person will be a
friend and a bad one an enemy.

POLEMARCHUS: Yes.

SOCRATES: So you want us to add something to what we said before about
the just man. Then we said that it is just to treat friends well and enemies

10

badly. Now you want us to add to this: to treat a friend well, *provided he is good,* and to harm an enemy, *provided he is bad?*

POLEMARCHUS: Yes, that seems well put to me.

SOCRATES: Should a just man really harm anyone whatsoever?

POLEMARCHUS: Of course. He should harm those who are both bad and enemies.

SOCRATES: When horses are harmed, do they become better or worse?

POLEMARCHUS: Worse.

SOCRATES: With respect to the virtue[13] that makes dogs good, or to the one that makes horses good?

POLEMARCHUS: With respect to the one that makes horses good.

SOCRATES: And when dogs are harmed, they become worse with respect to the virtue that makes dogs, not horses, good?

POLEMARCHUS: Necessarily.

SOCRATES: And what about human beings, comrade; shouldn't we say that, when they are harmed, they become worse with respect to human virtue?

POLEMARCHUS: Of course.

SOCRATES: But isn't justice human virtue?

POLEMARCHUS: Yes, that's necessarily so, too.

SOCRATES: Then, my dear Polemarchus, people who have been harmed are bound to become more unjust.

POLEMARCHUS: So it seems.

SOCRATES: Now, can musicians use music to make people unmusical?

POLEMARCHUS: No, they can't.

SOCRATES: Or can horsemen use horsemanship to make people unhorse-manlike?

POLEMARCHUS: No.

SOCRATES: Well, then, can just people use justice to make people unjust? In a word, can good people use their virtue or goodness to make people bad?

POLEMARCHUS: No, they can't.

SOCRATES: For it isn't the function of heat to cool things down, I imagine, but that of its opposite.

POLEMARCHUS: Yes.

[13] See Glossary of Terms s.v. virtue.

SOCRATES: Nor the function of dryness to make things wet, but that of its
5   opposite.

POLEMARCHUS: Of course.

SOCRATES: So the function of a good person isn't to harm, but that of his
opposite.

POLEMARCHUS: Apparently.

SOCRATES: And a just person is a good person?

10   POLEMARCHUS: Of course.

SOCRATES: So it isn't the function of a just person to harm a friend or
anyone else, Polemarchus, but that of his opposite, an unjust person.

POLEMARCHUS: I think you are absolutely right, Socrates.

e   SOCRATES: So if someone tells us it is just to give to each what he is owed,
and understands by this that a just man should harm his enemies and benefit his friends, the one who says it is not wise. I mean, what he says is not
5   true. For it has become clear to us that it is never just to harm anyone.

POLEMARCHUS: I agree.

SOCRATES: You and I will fight as partners, then, against anyone who tells
us that Simonides, Bias, Pittacus, or any of our other wise and blessedly
happy men said this.

10   POLEMARCHUS: I, for my part, am willing to be your partner in the battle.

336a   SOCRATES: Do you know whose saying I think it is, that it is just to benefit friends and harm enemies?

POLEMARCHUS: Whose?

5   SOCRATES: I think it is a saying of Periander, or Perdiccas, or Xerxes, or
Ismenias of Thebes, or some other wealthy man who thought he had great
power.

POLEMARCHUS: That's absolutely true.

SOCRATES: All right. Since it has become apparent, then, that neither justice nor the just consists in benefiting friends and harming enemies, what
10   else should one say it is?

b   *Now, while we were speaking, Thrasymachus had tried many times to take
over the discussion but was restrained by those sitting near him, who wanted to
hear our argument to the end. When we paused after what I had just said,
however, he could not keep quiet any longer: crouched up like a wild beast
5   about to spring, he hurled himself at us as if to tear us to pieces. Polemarchus
and I were frightened and flustered as he roared into our midst:*

What nonsense you two have been talking all this time, Socrates! Why do you act like naïve people, giving way to one another? If you really want to know what justice is, don't just ask questions and then indulge your love of honor by refuting the answers. You know very well it is easier to ask questions than to answer them. Give an answer yourself and tell us what *you* say the just is. And don't tell me it is the right, the beneficial, the profitable, the gainful, or the advantageous, but tell me clearly and exactly what you mean. For I won't accept such nonsense from you.

His words startled me and, looking at him, I was afraid. And I think if I had not seen him before he looked at me, I would have been dumbstruck.[14] But as it was, I happened to look at him just as he began to be exasperated by our argument, so I was able to answer; and trembling a little, I said:

Do not be too hard on us, Thrasymachus. If Polemarchus and I made an error in our investigation of the accounts, you may be sure we did so involuntarily. If we were searching for gold, we would never voluntarily give way to each other, if by doing so we would destroy our chance of finding it. So do not think that in searching for justice, a thing more honorable than a large quantity of gold, we would foolishly give way to one another or be less than completely serious about finding it. You surely must not think that, my friend, but rather—as I do—that we are incapable of finding it. Hence it is surely far more appropriate for us to be pitied by you clever people than to be given rough treatment.

When he heard that, he gave a loud sarcastic laugh:

By Heracles! That is Socrates' usual irony[15] for you! I knew this would happen. I even told these others earlier that you would be unwilling to answer, that you would be ironic and do anything rather than give an answer, if someone questioned *you*.

SOCRATES: That is because you are a wise fellow, Thrasymachus. You knew very well if you ask someone how much twelve is, and in putting the question you warn him, "Don't tell me, man, that twelve is twice six, or three times four, or six times two, or four times three; for I won't accept such nonsense from you"—it was obvious to you, I imagine, that no one could respond to a person who inquired in that way. But suppose he said to you: "What do you mean, Thrasymachus; am I not to give any of the answers you mention, not even if twelve happens to be one of those things? You are amazing. Do you want me to say something other than the truth? Or do you mean something else?" What answer would you give him?

[14] In Greek superstition, anyone seen by a wolf before he sees it is struck dumb.

[15] See Glossary of Terms s.v. irony.

13

THRASYMACHUS: Well, so you think the two cases are alike?

SOCRATES: Why shouldn't I? But even if they are not alike, yet seem so to the person you asked, do you think he is any less likely to give the answer that seems right to him, whether we forbid him to do so or not?

THRASYMACHUS: Is that what you are going to do, give one of the forbidden answers?

SOCRATES: I would not be surprised—provided it is the one that seems right to me after I have investigated the matter.

THRASYMACHUS: What if I show you another answer about justice, one that is different from all these and better than any of them? What penalty would you deserve then?

SOCRATES: The very one that is appropriate for someone who does not know—what else? And what is appropriate is to learn from the one who does know. That, therefore, is what I deserve to suffer.

THRASYMACHUS: What a pleasant fellow you are! But in addition to learning, you must pay money.

SOCRATES: I will if I ever have any.

GLAUCON: He has it already. If it is a matter of money, speak, Thrasymachus. We will all contribute for Socrates.

THRASYMACHUS: Oh yes, sure, so that Socrates can carry on as usual: he gives no answer himself, and if someone else does, he takes up his account and refutes it.

SOCRATES: How can someone give an answer, my excellent man, when, first of all, he does not know and does not claim to know, and then, even if he does have some opinion about the matter, is forbidden by no ordinary man to express any of the things he thinks? No, it is much more appropriate for you to answer, since you say you do know and can tell us. Don't be obstinate. Give your answer as a favor to me and do not begrudge your teaching to Glaucon and the others.

While I was saying this, Glaucon and the others begged him to do as I asked. Thrasymachus clearly wanted to speak in order to win a good reputation, since he thought he had a very good answer. But he pretended to want to win a victory at my expense by having me do the answering. However, he agreed in the end, and then said:

That is Socrates' wisdom for you: he himself isn't willing to teach but goes around learning from others and isn't even grateful to them.

SOCRATES: When you say I learn from others, you are right, Thrasymachus; but when you say I do not give thanks, you are wrong. I give as much as I can. But I can give only praise, since I have no money. And just how enthusiastically I give it, when someone seems to me to speak well, you will know as soon as you have answered, since I think you will speak well.

THRASYMACHUS: Listen, then. I say justice is nothing other than what is advantageous for the stronger. Well, why don't you praise me? No, you are unwilling.   c

SOCRATES: First, I must understand what you mean. For, as things stand, I do not. What is advantageous for the stronger, you say, is just. What on   5 earth do you mean, Thrasymachus? Surely you do not mean something like this: Polydamas, the pancratist,[16] is stronger than we are. Beef is advantageous for his body. So, this food is also both advantageous and just for us who are weaker than he?   d

THRASYMACHUS: You disgust me, Socrates. You interpret my account in the way that does it the most evil.

SOCRATES: That's not it at all, my very good man; I only want you to make your meaning clearer.   5

THRASYMACHUS: Don't you know, then, that some cities are ruled by a tyranny, some by a democracy, and some by an aristocracy?

SOCRATES: Of course I do.

THRASYMACHUS: And that what is stronger in each city is the ruling element?   10

SOCRATES: Certainly.

THRASYMACHUS: And each type of rule makes laws that are advantageous for itself: democracy makes democratic ones, tyranny tyrannical ones, and   e so on with the others. And by so legislating, each declares that what is just for its subjects is what is advantageous for itself—the ruler—and it punishes anyone who deviates from this as lawless and unjust. That, Socrates, is what   5 I say justice is, the same in all cities: what is advantageous for the established rule. Since the established rule is surely stronger, anyone who does the   339a rational calculation correctly will conclude that the just is the same everywhere—what is advantageous for the stronger.

SOCRATES: Now I see what you mean. Whether it is true or not, I will try   5 to find out. But you yourself have answered that what is just is what is advantageous, Thrasymachus, whereas you forbade me to answer that. True, you have added *for the stronger* to it.

THRASYMACHUS: And I suppose you think that is an insignificant addition.   b

SOCRATES: It isn't clear yet whether it is significant. What *is* clear is that we must investigate whether or not it is true. I agree that what is just is

---

[16] See Glossary of Terms s.v. pancration.

something advantageous. But you add *for the stronger.* I do not know about
that. We will have to look into it.

THRASYMACHUS: Go ahead and look.

SOCRATES: That is just what I am going to do. Tell me, then, you also
claim, don't you, that it is just to obey the rulers?

THRASYMACHUS: I do.

SOCRATES: And are the rulers in each city infallible, or are they liable to
error?

THRASYMACHUS: No doubt, they are liable to error.

SOCRATES: So, when they attempt to make laws, they make some correctly, others incorrectly?

THRASYMACHUS: I suppose so.

SOCRATES: And a law is correct if it prescribes what is advantageous for
the rulers themselves, and incorrect if it prescribes what is disadvantageous
for them? Is that what you mean?

THRASYMACHUS: It is.

SOCRATES: And whatever laws the rulers make must be obeyed by their
subjects, and that is what is just?

THRASYMACHUS: Of course.

SOCRATES: According to your account, then, it isn't only just to do what
is advantageous for the stronger, but also the opposite: what is not advantageous.

THRASYMACHUS: What is that you are saying?

SOCRATES: The same as you, I think. But let's examine it more closely.
Haven't we agreed that the rulers are sometimes in error as to what is best
for themselves when they give orders to their subjects, and yet that it is just
for their subjects to do whatever their rulers order? Wasn't that agreed?

THRASYMACHUS: I suppose so.

SOCRATES: You will also have to suppose, then, that you have agreed that
it is just to do what is disadvantageous for the rulers and those who are
stronger, whenever they unintentionally order what is bad for themselves.
But you say, too, that it is just for the others to obey the orders the rulers
gave. You are very wise, Thrasymachus, but doesn't it necessarily follow that
it is just to do the opposite of what you said, since the weaker are then
ordered to do what is disadvantageous for the stronger?

POLEMARCHUS: By Zeus, Socrates, that's absolutely clear.

And Clitophon interrupted:

16

Of course it is, if you are to be his witness, at any rate.

POLEMARCHUS: Who needs a witness? Thrasymachus himself agrees that the rulers sometimes issue orders that are bad for them, and that it is just for the others to obey them.

CLITOPHON: That, Polemarchus, is because Thrasymachus maintained that it is just to obey the orders of the rulers.

POLEMARCHUS: Yes, Clitophon, and he also maintained that what is advantageous for the stronger is just. And having maintained both principles, he went on to agree that the stronger sometimes order the weaker, who are subject to them, to do things that are disadvantageous for the stronger themselves. From these agreements it follows that what is advantageous for the stronger is no more just than what is not advantageous.

CLITOPHON: But what he meant by what is advantageous for the stronger is what the stronger *believes* to be advantageous for him. That is what he maintained the weaker must do, and that is what he maintained is what is just.

POLEMARCHUS: But it is not what he said.

SOCRATES: It makes no difference, Polemarchus. If Thrasymachus wants to put it that way now, let's accept it. But tell me, Thrasymachus, is that what you intended to say, that what is just is what the stronger believes to be advantageous for him, whether it is in fact advantageous for him or not? Is that what we are to say you mean?

THRASYMACHUS: Not at all. Do you think I would call someone who is in error stronger at the very moment he errs?

SOCRATES: I did think you meant that, when you agreed that the rulers are not infallible but sometimes make errors.

THRASYMACHUS: That is because you are a quibbler in arguments, Socrates. I mean, when someone makes an error in the treatment of patients, do you call him a doctor in virtue of the fact that he made that very error? Or, when someone makes an error in calculating, do you call him an accountant in virtue of the fact that he made that very error in calculation? I think we express ourselves in words that, taken literally, do say that a doctor is in error, or an accountant, or a grammarian. But each of these, to the extent that he is what we call him, never makes errors, so that, according to the precise account (and you are a stickler for precise accounts), no craftsman ever makes errors. It is when his knowledge fails him that he makes an error, and, in virtue of the fact that he made that error, he is no craftsman. No craftsman, wise man, or ruler makes an error at the moment when he is ruling, even though everyone will say that a physician or a ruler makes errors. It is in this loose way that you must also take the answer I gave just now. But the most precise answer is this: a ruler,

17

341a to the extent that he is a ruler, never makes errors and unerringly decrees what is best for himself, and that is what his subject must do. Thus, as I said from the first, it is just to do what is advantageous for the stronger.

5 SOCRATES: Well, Thrasymachus, so you think I quibble, do you?

THRASYMACHUS: Yes, I do.

SOCRATES: And you think that I asked the questions I did in a premeditated attempt to do you evil in the argument?

THRASYMACHUS: I am certain of it. But it won't do you any good. You
b will never be able to do me evil by covert means, and without them, you will never be able to overpower me by argument.

SOCRATES: Bless you, Thrasymachus; I would not so much as try! But to prevent this sort of confusion from happening to us again, would you define whether you mean the ruler and stronger in the ordinary sense or in
5 what you were just now calling the precise sense, when you say that it is just for the weaker to do what is advantageous for him, since he is the stronger?

THRASYMACHUS: I mean the ruler in the most precise sense. Now do *that* evil, if you can, and practice your quibbling on it—I ask no favors. But you
10 will find there is nothing you can do.

SOCRATES: Do you think that I am crazy enough to try to shave a lion[17]
c and quibble with Thrasymachus?

THRASYMACHUS: Well, you certainly tried just now, although you were a good-for-nothing at it, too!

SOCRATES: That's enough of that! Tell me: is a doctor—in the precise
5 sense, the one you mentioned before—a moneymaker or someone who treats the sick? Tell me about the one who is really a doctor.

THRASYMACHUS: Someone who treats the sick.

SOCRATES: What about a ship's captain? Is the true captain a ruler of sail-
10 ors, or a sailor?

THRASYMACHUS: A ruler of sailors.

SOCRATES: In other words, we should not take any account of the fact
d that he sails in a ship, and he should not be called a sailor for that reason. For it is not because he is sailing that he is called a ship's captain, but because of the craft he practices and his rule over sailors?

THRASYMACHUS: True.

5 SOCRATES: And is there something that is advantageous for each of these?[18]

---

[17] Proverbial characterization of an almost impossible task.

[18] I.e., for sailors and bodies.

18

THRASYMACHUS: Certainly.

SOCRATES: And isn't it also the case that the natural aim of the craft is to consider and provide what is advantageous for each?

THRASYMACHUS: Yes, that is its aim.

SOCRATES: And is anything advantageous for each of the crafts themselves besides being as perfect as possible?

THRASYMACHUS: How do you mean?

SOCRATES: It is like this: suppose you asked me whether it is satisfactory for a body to be a body, or whether it needs something else. I would answer, "Of course it needs something. In fact, that is why the craft of medicine has been discovered—because a body is deficient and it is not satisfactory for it to be like that.[19] To provide what is advantageous, that is what the craft was developed for." Do you think I am speaking correctly in saying this, or not?

THRASYMACHUS: Correctly.

SOCRATES: What about medicine itself? Is it deficient? Does a craft need some further virtue, as the eyes are in need of sight and the ears of hearing, so that another craft is needed to consider and provide what is advantageous for them?[20] Does a craft have some similar deficiency itself, so that each craft needs another to consider what is advantageous for it? And does the craft that does the considering need still another, and so on without end? Or does each consider by itself what is advantageous for it? Does it need neither itself nor another craft to consider what—in light of its own deficiency—is advantageous for it? Indeed, is there no deficiency or error in any craft? And is it inappropriate for any craft to consider what is advantageous for anything besides that with which it deals? And since it is itself correct, is it without fault or impurity so long as it is wholly and precisely the craft it is? Consider this with that precision of language you mentioned. Is it so or not?

THRASYMACHUS: It appears to be so.

SOCRATES: Doesn't it follow that medicine does not consider what is advantageous for medicine, but for the body?

THRASYMACHUS: Yes.

SOCRATES: And horse breeding does not consider what is advantageous for horse breeding, but for horses? Indeed, no other craft considers what is

---

[19] See 608d13–610d3.

[20] Sight is the virtue or excellence of the eyes. Without it, the eyes cannot achieve what is advantageous to them: namely, sight. But Socrates assumes throughout Book 1 that virtues are types of craft (see 332d). Hence he can conclude that the eyes need a further craft in order to achieve what is advantageous to them.

advantageous for itself—since it has no further needs—but what is advantageous for that with which it deals?

THRASYMACHUS: Apparently so.

SOCRATES: Now surely, Thrasymachus, the various crafts rule over and are
stronger than that with which they deal?

He gave in at this point as well, very reluctantly.

SOCRATES: So no kind of knowledge considers or enjoins what is advantageous for itself, but what is advantageous for the weaker, which is subject
to it.

*He finally agreed to this too, although he tried to fight it. When he had
agreed, however, I said:*

Surely then, no doctor, to the extent that he is a doctor, considers or
enjoins what is advantageous for himself, but what is advantageous for his
patient? For we agreed that a doctor, in the precise sense, is a ruler of bodies, not a moneymaker. Isn't that what we agreed?

THRASYMACHUS: Yes.

SOCRATES: So a ship's captain, in the precise sense, is a ruler of sailors, not
a sailor?

THRASYMACHUS: That is what we agreed.

SOCRATES: Doesn't it follow that a ship's captain and ruler won't consider
and enjoin what is advantageous for a captain, but what is advantageous for
a sailor and his subject?

He reluctantly agreed.

SOCRATES: So then, Thrasymachus, no one in any position of rule, to the
extent that he is a ruler, considers or enjoins what is advantageous for himself, but what is advantageous for his subject—that on which he practices
his craft. It is to his subject and what is advantageous and proper for it that
he looks, and everything he says and does, he says and does for it.

*When we reached this point in the argument and it was clear to all that his
account of justice had turned into its opposite, instead of answering, Thrasymachus said:*

Tell me, Socrates, do you still have a wet nurse?

SOCRATES: What is that? Shouldn't you be giving answers rather than asking such things?

20

THRASYMACHUS: Because she is letting you run around sniveling and doesn't wipe your nose when you need it, since it is her fault that you do not know the difference between sheep and shepherds.

SOCRATES: What exactly is it I do not know? 10

THRASYMACHUS: You think that shepherds and cowherds consider what is b good for their sheep and cattle, and fatten them and take care of them with some aim in mind other than what is good for their master and themselves. Moreover, you believe that rulers in cities—true rulers, that is—think about their subjects in a different way than one does about sheep, and that 5 what they consider night and day is something other than what is advantageous for themselves. You are so far from understanding justice and what is c just, and injustice and what is unjust, that you do not realize that justice is really the good of another, what is advantageous for the stronger and the ruler, and harmful to the one who obeys and serves. Injustice is the oppo- 5 site, it rules those simpleminded—for that is what they really are—just people, and the ones it rules do what is advantageous for the other who is stronger; and they make the one they serve happy, but they do not make themselves the least bit happy.

You must consider it as follows, Socrates, or you will be the most naïve d of all: a just man must always get less than does an unjust one. First, in their contracts with one another, when a just man is partner to an unjust, you will never find, when the partnership ends, that the just one gets 5 more than the unjust, but less. Second, in matters relating to the city, when taxes are to be paid, a just man pays more on an equal amount of property, an unjust one less; but when the city is giving out refunds, a just man gets nothing while an unjust one makes a large profit. Finally, when each of them holds political office, a just person—even if he is not penal- e ized in other ways—finds that his private affairs deteriorate more because he has to neglect them, that he gains no advantage from the public purse because of his justice, and that he is hated by his relatives and acquaintances because he is unwilling to do them an unjust favor. The opposite is 5 true of an unjust man in every respect. I mean, of course, the person I described before: the man of great power who does better[21] than everyone else. He is the one you should consider if you want to figure out how 344a much more advantageous it is for the individual to be unjust than just. You will understand this most easily if you turn your thoughts to injustice of the most complete sort, the sort that makes those who do injustice happiest, and those who suffer it—those who are unwilling to do injustice— 5 most wretched. The sort I mean is tyranny, because it uses both covert means and force to appropriate the property of others—whether it is sacred or secular, public or private—not little by little, but all at once. If

---

[21] See Glossary of Terms s.v. do better.

21

b someone commits a part of this sort of injustice and gets caught, he is punished and greatly reproached—temple robbers,[22] kidnappers, house-breakers, robbers, and thieves are what these partly unjust people are called when they commit those harms. When someone appropriates the
5 possessions of the citizens, on the other hand, and then kidnaps and enslaves the possessors as well, instead of these shameful names he is called
c happy and blessed: not only by the citizens themselves, but even by all who learn that he has committed the whole of injustice. For it is not the fear of doing injustice, but of suffering it, that elicits the reproaches of those who revile injustice.

5 So you see, Socrates, injustice, if it is on a large enough scale, is stronger, freer, and more masterful than justice. And, as I said from the beginning, justice is what is advantageous for the stronger, while injustice is profitable and advantageous for oneself.

d *Having, like a bath attendant, emptied this great flood of words into our ears all at once, Thrasymachus was thinking of leaving. But those present wouldn't let him. They made him stay and give an account of what he had said. And I*
5 *myself was particularly insistent:*

You are marvelous, Thrasymachus; after hurling such a speech at us, you surely cannot be thinking of leaving before you have adequately instructed us—or learned yourself—whether you are right or not. Or do you think it
e is a trivial matter you are trying to determine, and not rather a way of life—the one that would make living life that way most profitable for each of us?

THRASYMACHUS: Do you mean that I do not think it is a serious matter?

5 SOCRATES: Either that, or you care nothing for us and so are not worried about whether we will live better or worse lives because of our ignorance of what you claim to know. No, be a good fellow and show some willing-ness to teach us—you won't do badly for yourself if you help a group as
345a large as ours. For my own part, I will tell you that I am not persuaded. I do not believe that injustice is more profitable than justice, not even if you should give it full scope to do what it wants. Suppose, my good fellow, that
5 there *is* an unjust person, and suppose he *does* have the power to do injus-tice, whether by covert means or open warfare; nonetheless, he does not persuade me that injustice is more profitable than justice. Perhaps someone here besides myself feels the same as I do. So, blessed though you are, you
b are going to have to fully persuade us that we are wrong to value justice more highly than injustice in deliberating.

---

[22] The temples served as public treasuries, so that a temple robber is the equivalent of a present-day bank robber.

THRASYMACHUS: And how am I to persuade you? If you are not persuaded by what I said just now, what more can I do? Am I to take my argument and pour it into your very soul?

SOCRATES: No, by Zeus, do not do that! But first, stick to what you have said, or, if you change your position, do it openly and do not try to deceive us. You see, Thrasymachus, having defined the true doctor—to continue examining the things you said before—you did not consider it necessary to maintain the same level of exactness when you later turned to the true shepherd. You do not think a shepherd—to the extent that he is a shepherd—fattens sheep with the aim of doing what is best for them. But you think that, like a guest about to be entertained at a feast, his aim is to eat well or to make a future sale—as if he were a moneymaker rather than a shepherd. But of course, the only concern of the craft of shepherding is to provide what is best for that with which it deals, since it itself is adequately provided with all it needs to be at its best, as we know, when it does not fall short in any way of being the craft of shepherding. That is why I, at any rate, thought it necessary for us to agree before[23] that every kind of rule— to the extent that it is a kind of rule—does not seek anything other than what is best for the thing it rules and cares for, and this is true both in political and in private rule. But do you think that those who rule cities—the ones who are truly rulers—rule willingly?

THRASYMACHUS: I do not think it, by Zeus, I know it.

SOCRATES: But, Thrasymachus, don't you realize that in other kinds of rule there is no willing ruler? On the contrary, they demand to be paid on the assumption that their ruling will benefit not themselves, but their subjects. For tell me, don't we say that each craft differs from every other in what it is capable of doing? Blessed though you are, please don't answer contrary to your belief, so that we can come to some definite conclusion.

THRASYMACHUS: Yes, that is what differentiates them.

SOCRATES: And doesn't each craft provide us with a particular benefit, different from the others? For example, medicine provides us with health, captaincy with safety at sea, and so on with the others?

THRASYMACHUS: Certainly.

SOCRATES: And doesn't wage-earning provide us with wages, since that is what it is capable of doing? Or would you call medicine the same craft as captaincy? Indeed, if you want to define matters precisely, as you proposed, even if someone who is a ship's captain becomes healthy because what is advantageous for him is sailing on the sea, you would not for that reason call what he does medicine, would you?

[23] See 341e–342e above.

THRASYMACHUS: Of course not.

SOCRATES: Nor would you call wage-earning medicine, even if someone becomes healthy while earning wages?

THRASYMACHUS: Of course not.

SOCRATES: Nor would you call medicine wage-earning, even if someone
10 earns pay while healing?

c THRASYMACHUS: No.

SOCRATES: We are agreed then, aren't we, that each craft brings its own special benefit?

THRASYMACHUS: Yes, we are.

5 SOCRATES: So whatever benefit all craftsmen jointly receive must clearly derive from their joint practice of some additional craft that is the same for each of them.

THRASYMACHUS: It seems so.

SOCRATES: And we say that the additional craft in question, which bene-
10 fits the craftsmen by earning them wages, is the craft of wage-earning?

He reluctantly agreed.

SOCRATES: Then this very benefit, receiving wages, is not provided to
d each of them by his own craft. On the contrary, if we are to examine the matter precisely, medicine provides health and wage-earning provides a wage; house-building provides a house, and wage-earning, which accompanies it, provides a wage; and so on with the other crafts. Each of them
5 does its own work and benefits that with which it deals. So, wages aside, is there any benefit that craftsmen get from their craft?

THRASYMACHUS: Apparently not.

SOCRATES: But he still provides a benefit, even when he works for
e nothing?

THRASYMACHUS: Yes, I think he does.

SOCRATES: Then, it is clear now, Thrasymachus, that no type of craft or rule provides what is beneficial for itself; but, as we have been saying for
5 some time, it provides and enjoins what is beneficial for its subject, and aims at what is advantageous for *it*—the weaker, not the stronger. That is why I said just now, my dear Thrasymachus, that no one chooses to rule voluntarily and take other people's troubles in hand and straighten them out, but each asks for wages. You see, anyone who is going to practice his
347a type of craft well never does or enjoins what is best for himself—at least not when he is acting as his craft prescribes—but what is best for his subject. It

24

is because of this, it seems, that wages must be provided to a person if he is going to be willing to rule, whether they are in the form of money or honor or a penalty if he refuses.

GLAUCON: What do you mean, Socrates? I am familiar with the first two kinds of wages, but I do not understand what penalty you mean, or how you can call it a wage.

SOCRATES: Then you do not understand the sort of wages for which the best people rule, when they are willing to rule. Don't you know that those who love honor and those who love money are despised, and rightly so?

GLAUCON: I do.

SOCRATES. Well, then, that is why good people won't be willing to rule for the sake of money or honor. You see, if they are paid wages openly for ruling, they will be called hirelings, and if they take them covertly as the fruits of their rule, they will be called thieves. On the other hand, they won't rule for the sake of honor either, since they are not ambitious honor-lovers. So, if they are going to be willing to rule, some compulsion or punishment must be brought to bear on them—that is probably why wanting to rule when one does not have to is thought to be shameful. Now, the greatest punishment for being unwilling to rule is being ruled by someone worse than oneself. And I think it is fear of that that makes good people rule when they do rule. They approach ruling, not as though they were going to do something good or as though they were going to enjoy themselves in it, but as something necessary, since it cannot be entrusted to anyone better than—or even as good as—themselves. In a city of good men, if it came into being, the citizens would fight in order *not to rule,* just as they now do in order to rule. There it would be quite clear that anyone who is really and truly a ruler does not naturally seek what is advantageous for himself, but what is so for his subject. As a result, anyone with any sense would prefer to be benefited by another than to go to the trouble of benefiting him. So I cannot at all agree with Thrasymachus that justice is what is advantageous for the stronger. But we will look further into that another time. What Thrasymachus is now saying—that the life of an unjust person is better than that of a just one—seems to be of far greater importance. Which life would you choose, Glaucon? And which of our views do you think is closer to the truth?

GLAUCON: I think the life of a just person is more profitable.

SOCRATES: Did you hear all the good things Thrasymachus attributed a moment ago to the unjust man?

GLAUCON: I did, but I am not persuaded.

SOCRATES: Then do you want us to persuade him, if we can find a way, that what he says is not true?

5
10
b
5
c
5
d
5
e
5
348a
5

GLAUCON: Of course I do.

SOCRATES: Well, if we oppose him with a speech parallel to his speech enumerating in turn the many good things that come from being just, and he replies, and then we do, we will have to count and measure the good things mentioned on each side, and we will need a jury to decide the case.

b   But if, on the other hand, we investigate the question, as we have been doing, by seeking agreement with each other, we ourselves can be both jury and advocates at once.

5   GLAUCON: Certainly.

SOCRATES: Then which approach do you prefer?

GLAUCON: The second.

SOCRATES: Come on then, Thrasymachus, answer us from the beginning. You say, don't you, that complete injustice is more profitable than complete

10   justice?

c   THRASYMACHUS: I certainly have said that. And I have told you why.

SOCRATES: Well, then, what do you say about this? Do you call one of the two a virtue and the other a vice?

THRASYMACHUS: Of course.

5   SOCRATES: That is to say, you call justice a virtue and injustice a vice?

THRASYMACHUS: Is that likely, sweetest one, when I say that injustice is profitable and justice is not?

SOCRATES: Then what exactly do you say?

10   THRASYMACHUS: The opposite.

SOCRATES: That justice is a vice?

THRASYMACHUS: No, just very noble naiveté.[24]

d   SOCRATES: So you call injustice deviousness?

THRASYMACHUS: No, I call it being prudent.

SOCRATES: Do you also consider unjust people to be wise and good, Thrasymachus?

THRASYMACHUS: Yes, if they do complete injustice and can bring cities

5   and whole nations under their power. Perhaps, you thought I meant pickpockets? Not that such crimes aren't also profitable, if they are not found out. But they are not worth discussing by comparison to what I described.

---

[24] *Euêtheia, kakoêtheia:* Thrasymachus uses *euêtheia* in the bad sense, to mean stupidity. Socrates takes him to mean it in the good sense of being straightforward, and so contrasts it with *kakoêtheia*—deviousness. See 400e1.

SOCRATES: Yes, I am not unaware of what you mean. But this did surprise   e
me: that you include injustice with virtue and wisdom, and justice with
their opposites.

THRASYMACHUS: Nevertheless, that is where I put them.

SOCRATES: That is now a harder problem, comrade, and it is not easy to   5
know what to say in response. If you had declared that injustice is more profitable, but agreed that it is a vice or shameful, as some others do, we could be
discussing the matter on the basis of conventional views. But now, obviously,
you will say that injustice is fine and strong and apply to it all the attributes we   10
used to apply to justice, since you dare to include it with virtue and wisdom.   349a

THRASYMACHUS: You have guessed my views exactly.

SOCRATES: All the same, we must not shrink from pursuing the argument
and looking into this, just as long as I take you to be saying what you really   5
think. You see, I believe that you really are not joking now, Thrasymachus,
but saying what you believe to be the truth.

THRASYMACHUS: What difference does it make to you, whether *I* believe
it or not? Isn't it *my account* you are supposed to be refuting?   10

SOCRATES: It makes no difference. But here is a further question I would
like you to try to answer: do you think that a just person wants to do bet-   b
ter[25] than another just person?

THRASYMACHUS: Not at all. Otherwise, he would not be the civilized and
naïve person he actually is.   5

SOCRATES: What about than the just action?

THRASYMACHUS: No, not than that, either.

SOCRATES: And does he claim that he deserves to do better than an unjust
person and believe that it is just for him to do so, or doesn't he believe that?

THRASYMACHUS: He would want to do better than him, and he would
claim to deserve to do so, but he would not be able.   10

SOCRATES: That is not what I am asking, but whether a just person wants,
and claims to deserve, to do better than an unjust person, but not than a   c
just one?

THRASYMACHUS: He does.

SOCRATES: What about an unjust person? Does he claim that he deserves
to do better than a just person or a just action?   5

THRASYMACHUS: Of course he does; he thinks he deserves to do better
than everyone.

[25] See Glossary of Terms s.v. do better.

SOCRATES: Then will an unjust person also do better than an *unjust* person or an *unjust* action, and will he strive to get the most he can for himself from everyone?

10 THRASYMACHUS: He will.

SOCRATES: Then let's put it this way: a just person does not do better than someone like himself, but someone unlike himself, whereas an unjust per-
d son does better than those who are like *and* those who are unlike him.

THRASYMACHUS: Very well put.

SOCRATES: Now, an unjust person is wise and good, and a just one is neither?

5 THRASYMACHUS: That is well put, too.

SOCRATES: So isn't an unjust person also *like* a wise and good person, while the just person is not?

THRASYMACHUS: Of course. How could he fail to be like people who have such qualities, when he has them himself? But the unjust person is not like them.

10 SOCRATES: Fine. Then each of them has the qualities of the people he is like?

THRASYMACHUS: What else could he have?

SOCRATES: All right, Thrasymachus. Do you call one person musical and
e another non-musical?

THRASYMACHUS: I do.

SOCRATES: Which of them is wise in music and which is not?

THRASYMACHUS: The musical one is wise, presumably, and the other not
5 wise.

SOCRATES: And in the things in which he is wise, he is good; and in the things in which he is not wise, he is bad?

THRASYMACHUS: Yes.

SOCRATES: Isn't the same true of a doctor?

THRASYMACHUS: It is.

SOCRATES: Do you think, then, Thrasymachus, that a man who is a musi-
10 cian, when he is tuning his lyre and tightening and loosening the strings, wants to do better than another musician, and does he claim that that is what he deserves?[26]

---

[26] What Socrates has in mind is explained at 350a. All expert musicians try to get the same result, perfect harmony, so they tighten and loosen their strings to exactly the same degree: namely, the one that will produce the right pitch. In the same way, all doctors who are masters of medicine prescribe the same diet for people with the same diseases: namely, the one that will best restore them to health.

THRASYMACHUS: I do not.

SOCRATES: But he does want to do better than a non-musician? 15

THRASYMACHUS: Necessarily.

SOCRATES: What about a doctor? When he is prescribing food and drink, 350a
does he want to do better than another doctor or than medical practice?

THRASYMACHUS: Certainly not.

SOCRATES: But he does want to do better than a non-doctor?

THRASYMACHUS: Yes. 5

SOCRATES: In any branch of knowledge or ignorance, do you think that a
knowledgeable person would intentionally try to take more for himself
than another knowledgeable person, or to do or say more, and not rather
exactly what the one like himself would do in the same situation?

THRASYMACHUS: No, I imagine it must be as you say. 10

SOCRATES: And what about an ignorant person? Doesn't he want to do
better than both a knowledgeable person and an ignorant one? b

THRASYMACHUS: I suppose so.

SOCRATES: A knowledgeable person is wise?

THRASYMACHUS: I agree.

SOCRATES: And a wise one is good? 5

THRASYMACHUS: I agree.

SOCRATES: So, a good and wise person does not want to do better than
someone like himself, but someone both unlike and opposite to him.

THRASYMACHUS: So it seems.

SOCRATES: But a bad and ignorant person wants to do better than both his
like and his opposite. 10

THRASYMACHUS: Apparently.

SOCRATES: Well, Thrasymachus, we found that an unjust person tries to
do better than those like him and those unlike him. Didn't you say that?

THRASYMACHUS: I did. 15

SOCRATES: And that a just person won't do better than those like him, but c
those unlike him?

THRASYMACHUS: Yes.

SOCRATES: Then a just person is like a wise and good person, and an
unjust person is like an ignorant and bad one. 5

THRASYMACHUS: It looks that way.

SOCRATES: Moreover, we agreed that each has the qualities of the one he resembles.

THRASYMACHUS: Yes, we did.

10 SOCRATES: A just person has turned out to be good and wise, then, and an unjust one ignorant and bad.

d *Thrasymachus agreed to all this, not easily as I am telling it, but reluctantly, with toil, trouble, and—since it was summer—a quantity of sweat that was amazing to behold. And then I saw something I had never seen before— Thrasymachus blushing. But in any case, after we had agreed that justice is*
5 *virtue and wisdom and that injustice is vice and ignorance, I said:*

All right, let's take that as established. But we also said that injustice is a strong thing, or don't you remember that, Thrasymachus?

THRASYMACHUS: I remember. But I am not satisfied with what you are
10 now saying. I could make a speech about it, but if I did, I know that you would say I was engaging in demagoguery. So, either allow me to say as
e much as I want to say or, if you want to keep on asking questions, go ahead and ask them, and I shall say to you—as one does to old women telling stories—"All right," and nod or shake my head.

5 SOCRATES: No, don't do that; not contrary to your own belief.

THRASYMACHUS: Then I will answer to please you, since you won't let me make a speech. What else do you want?

SOCRATES: Nothing, by Zeus. But if that is what you are going to do, do it, and I will ask the questions.

10 THRASYMACHUS: Ask them, then.

SOCRATES: All right, I will ask precisely what I asked before, so that we may proceed in an orderly fashion with our argument about what sort of
351a thing justice is, as opposed to injustice. For it was claimed, I believe, that injustice is stronger and more powerful than justice. But now, if justice is indeed wisdom and virtue, it will be easy to show, I suppose, that it is stron-
5 ger than injustice, since injustice is ignorance—no one could now be ignorant of that. However, I, at any rate, do not want to consider the matter in such simple terms, Thrasymachus, but to look into it in some such way as this: would you say that a city may be unjust and try to enslave other cities
b unjustly, and succeed at enslaving them,[27] and hold them in subjection which it enslaved in the past?

THRASYMACHUS: Of course. And that is what the best city will especially
5 do, the one that is most completely unjust.

[27] Reading καταδουλώσασθαι.

SOCRATES: I understand that that is your argument, but the point I want to examine is this: will the city that becomes stronger than another achieve this power without justice, or will it need the help of justice?

THRASYMACHUS: If what you said a moment ago stands, and justice is wisdom, it will need the help of justice; but if things are as I stated, it will need the help of injustice.   c

SOCRATES: I am impressed, Thrasymachus, that you are not merely nodding or shaking your head, but giving these fine answers.   5

THRASYMACHUS: That is because I am trying to please you.

SOCRATES: You are doing well at it, too. So please me some more by answering this question: do you think that a city, an army, a band of robbers or thieves, or any other group with a common unjust purpose would be able to achieve it if its members were unjust to each other?   10

THRASYMACHUS: Of course not.   d

SOCRATES: What if they were not unjust to one another? Would they achieve more?

THRASYMACHUS: Certainly.

SOCRATES: Because, Thrasymachus, injustice causes factions, hatreds, and quarrels among them, while justice brings friendship and a sense of common purpose. Isn't that so?   5

THRASYMACHUS: I will say it is, in order not to disagree with you.

SOCRATES: You are still doing well on that front, which is very good of you. So tell me this: if the function of injustice is to produce hatred wherever it occurs, then whenever it arises, whether among free men or slaves, won't it make them hate one another, form factions, and be unable to   10
achieve any common purpose?   e

THRASYMACHUS: Of course.

SOCRATES: What if it arises between two people? Won't they be at odds, hate each other, and be enemies both to one another and to just people?

THRASYMACHUS: They will.   5

SOCRATES: Well, then, my amazing fellow, if injustice arises within a single individual, will it lose its power or will it retain it undiminished?

THRASYMACHUS: Let's say that it retains it undiminished.

SOCRATES: Apparently, then, its power is such that whenever it comes to exist in something—whether in a city, a family, an army, or anything else   10
whatsoever—it makes that thing, first of all, incapable of acting in concert
with itself, because of the faction and difference it creates; and, second of   352a
all, an enemy to itself, and to what is in every way its opposite: namely, justice. Isn't that so?

31

THRASYMACHUS: Of course.

SOCRATES: And in a single individual, too, I presume, it will produce the very same effects that it is in its nature to produce. First, it will make him incapable of acting because of inner faction and not being of one mind with himself; second, it will make him his own enemy as well as the enemy of just people. Isn't that right?

THRASYMACHUS: Yes.

SOCRATES: But, my dear fellow, aren't the gods also just?

THRASYMACHUS: Let's say they are.

SOCRATES: Then an unjust person will also be an enemy of the gods, Thrasymachus, while a just person will be their friend?

THRASYMACHUS: Feast yourself confidently on the argument! Don't worry, I won't oppose you, so as not to arouse the enmity of our friends here.

SOCRATES: Come on, then, complete the banquet for me by continuing to answer as you have been doing now. We have shown that just people are wiser and better and more capable of acting, while unjust ones are not even able to act together. For whenever we speak of men who are unjust acting together to effectively achieve a common goal, what we say is not altogether true. They would never have been able to keep their hands off each other if they were completely unjust. But clearly there must have been some sort of justice in them that at least prevented them from doing injustice among themselves at the same time as they were doing it to others. And it was this that enabled them to achieve what they did. When they started doing unjust things, they were only halfway corrupted by their injustice. For those who are wholly bad and completely unjust are also completely incapable of acting. All this I now see to be the truth, and not what you first maintained. However, we must now examine the question, as we proposed to do before,[28] of whether just people also live better and are happier than unjust ones. I think it is clear even now from what we have said that this is so, but we must consider it further. After all, the argument concerns no ordinary topic, but the way we ought to live.

THRASYMACHUS: Go ahead and consider.

SOCRATES: I will. Tell me, do you think there is such a thing as the function of a horse?

THRASYMACHUS: I do.

SOCRATES: And would you take the function of a horse or of anything else to be that which one can do only with it, or best with it?

[28] 347e.

THRASYMACHUS: I don't understand.

SOCRATES: Let me put it this way: is it possible for you to see with anything except eyes?

THRASYMACHUS: Certainly not.

SOCRATES: Or for you to hear with anything except ears?

THRASYMACHUS: No.

SOCRATES: Would it be right, then, for us to say that these things are their functions?

THRASYMACHUS: Of course.

SOCRATES: Again, couldn't you use a dagger, a carving knife, or lots of other things in pruning a vine?

THRASYMACHUS: Certainly.

SOCRATES: But nothing would do a better job than a pruning knife designed for the purpose?

THRASYMACHUS: That's true.

SOCRATES: Shall we take pruning to be its function, then?

THRASYMACHUS: Yes.

SOCRATES: Now I think you will understand better what I was asking earlier when I asked whether the function of each thing is what it alone can do or what it can do better than anything else.

THRASYMACHUS: I do understand, and I think that that is the function of anything.

SOCRATES: All right. Does there seem to you also to be a virtue[29] for each thing to which some function is assigned? Let's go over the same ground again. We say that eyes have some function?

THRASYMACHUS: They do.

SOCRATES: So eyes also have a virtue?

THRASYMACHUS: They do.

SOCRATES: And ears have a function?

THRASYMACHUS: Yes.

SOCRATES: So they also have a virtue?

THRASYMACHUS: They have a virtue too.

SOCRATES: What about everything else? Doesn't the same hold?

THRASYMACHUS: It does.

[29] See Glossary of Terms s.v. virtue.

33

SOCRATES: Well, then. Could eyes perform their function well if they lacked their proper virtue but had the vice instead?

THRASYMACHUS: How could they? For don't you mean if they had blindness instead of sight?

SOCRATES: Whatever their virtue is. You see, I am not now asking about that, but about whether it is by means of their own proper virtue that their function performs the things it performs well, and by means of vice badly?

THRASYMACHUS: What you say is true.

SOCRATES: So, if ears are deprived of their own virtue, they too perform their function badly?

THRASYMACHUS: Of course.

SOCRATES: And the same argument applies to everything else?

THRASYMACHUS: So it seems to me, at least.

SOCRATES: Come on, then, and let's next consider this: does the soul have some function that you could not perform with anything else—for example, taking care of things, ruling, deliberating, and all other such things? Is there anything else besides a soul to which you could rightly assign these and say that they special to it?

THRASYMACHUS: No, there is nothing else.

SOCRATES: Then what about living? Don't we say that it is a function of a soul?

THRASYMACHUS: Absolutely.

SOCRATES: And don't we also say that a soul has a virtue?

THRASYMACHUS: We do.

SOCRATES: Will a soul ever perform its functions well, then, Thrasymachus, if it is deprived of its own proper virtue, or is that impossible?

THRASYMACHUS: It is impossible.

SOCRATES: It is necessary, then, that a bad soul rules and takes care of things badly, and that a good soul does all these things well?

THRASYMACHUS: It is necessary.

SOCRATES: Now, didn't we agree that justice is a soul's virtue and injustice its vice?

THRASYMACHUS: Yes, we did agree.

SOCRATES: So a just soul and a just man will live well and an unjust one badly.

THRASYMACHUS: Apparently so, according to your argument.

SOCRATES: And surely anyone who lives well is blessed and happy, and anyone who does not is the opposite. 354a

THRASYMACHUS: Of course.

SOCRATES: Therefore, a just person is happy and an unjust one wretched.

THRASYMACHUS: Let's say so. 5

SOCRATES: But surely it is profitable, not to be wretched, but to be happy.

THRASYMACHUS: Of course.

SOCRATES: So then, blessed Thrasymachus, injustice is never more profitable than justice.

THRASYMACHUS: Let that be your banquet, Socrates, at the feast of Bendis. 10

SOCRATES: Given by you, Thrasymachus, after you became gentle with me and ceased to be difficult. Yet I have not had a good banquet. But that is my fault, not yours. I seem to have behaved like those gluttons who snatch at every dish that passes and taste it before having properly savored the preceding one. Before finding the first thing we inquired about—namely, what justice is—I let that go, and turned to investigate whether it is a kind of vice and ignorance or a kind of wisdom and virtue. Then an argument came up about injustice being more profitable than justice, and I could not refrain from abandoning the previous one and following up on it. Hence the result of the discussion, so far as I am concerned, is that I know nothing. For when I do not know what justice is, I will hardly know whether it is a kind of virtue or not, or whether a person who has it is happy or unhappy.

b

5

c

Book 2

SOCRATES' NARRATION CONTINUES: *When I had said this, I thought I had done with the discussion. But it all turned out to be only a prelude, as it were. You see, Glaucon, who is always very courageous in everything, refused on this occasion, too, to accept Thrasymachus' capitulation. Instead, he said:*

Do you want to *seem* to have persuaded us, Socrates, that it is better in every way to be just rather than unjust, or do you want to *really* persuade us of this?

SOCRATES: I want to really persuade you, if I can.

GLAUCON: Well, then, you certainly are not doing what you want. Tell me, do you think there is a sort of good we welcome, not because we desire its consequences, but because we welcome it for its own sake—enjoying, for example, and all the harmless pleasures from which nothing results afterward beyond enjoying having them?

SOCRATES: Certainly, I think there is such a thing.

GLAUCON: And is there a sort of good we love for its own sake, and also for the sake of its consequences—knowing, for example, and seeing, and being healthy? For we welcome such things, I imagine, on both counts.

SOCRATES: Yes.

GLAUCON: And do you also recognize a third kind of good, such as physical training, medical treatment when sick, medicine itself, or ways of making money generally? We would say that these are burdensome but beneficial to us, and we would not choose them for their own sake, but for the sake of their rewards and other consequences.

SOCRATES: Yes, certainly, there is also this third kind. But what of it?

GLAUCON: In which of them do you place justice?

SOCRATES: I myself put it in the finest one—the one that anyone who is going to be blessed with happiness must love both because of itself and because of its consequences.

GLAUCON: That is not what the masses think. On the contrary, they think it is of the burdensome kind: the one that must be practiced for the sake of the rewards and the popularity that are the consequences of a good reputation, but that is to be avoided as intrinsically burdensome.

SOCRATES: I know that is the general view. Thrasymachus has been fault-ing justice and praising injustice on these grounds for some time. But it seems that I am a slow learner.

GLAUCON: Come on, then, listen to what I have to say as well, and see whether you still have that problem. You see, I think Thrasymachus gave up before he had to, as if he were a snake you had charmed. Yet, to my way of thinking, there was still no demonstration on either side. For I want to hear what justice and injustice are, and what power each has when it is just by itself in the soul. I want to leave out of account the rewards and the conse-quences of each of them.

So, if you agree, I will renew the argument of Thrasymachus. First, I will state what sort of thing people consider justice to be, and what its ori-gins are. Second, I will argue that all who practice it do so unwillingly, as something necessary, not as something good. Third, I will argue that they have good reason to act as they do. For the life of the unjust person is, they say, much better than that of the just one.

It isn't, Socrates, that I believe any of that myself. I am perplexed, indeed, and my ears are deafened listening to Thrasymachus and countless others. But I have yet to hear anyone defend justice in the way I want, as being better than injustice. I want to hear it praised *on its own,* and I think that I am most likely to learn this from you. That is why I am going to speak at length in praise of the unjust life: by doing so, I will be showing you the way I want to hear you praising justice and denouncing injustice. But see whether you want me to do what I am saying or not.

SOCRATES: I want it most of all. Indeed, what subject could a person with any sense enjoy talking and hearing about more often?

GLAUCON: Excellent sentiments. Now, listen to what I said I was going to discuss first—what justice is like and what its origins are. People say, you see, that to do injustice is naturally good and to suffer injustice bad. But the badness of suffering it far exceeds the goodness of doing it. Hence, those who have done and suffered injustice and who have tasted both—the ones who lack the power to do it and avoid suffering it—decide that it is profit-able to come to an agreement with each other neither to do injustice nor to suffer it. As a result, they begin to make laws and covenants; and what the law commands, they call lawful and just. That, they say, is the origin and very being[1] of justice. It is in between the best and the worst. The best is to do injustice without paying the penalty; the worst is to suffer it with-out being able to take revenge. Justice is in the middle between these two extremes. People love it, not because it is a good thing, but because they are too weak to do injustice with impunity. Someone who has the power to do

[1] See Glossary of Terms s.v. being.

it, however—someone who is a real man—would not make an agreement with anyone, neither to do injustice nor to suffer it. For him, that would be insanity. That is the nature of justice, according to the argument, Socrates, and those are its natural origins.

We can see most clearly that those who practice it do so unwillingly, because they lack the power to do injustice, if we imagine the following thought-experiment. Suppose we grant to the just and the unjust person the freedom to do whatever they like. We can then follow both of them and see where their appetites would lead. And we will catch the just person red-handed, traveling the same road as the unjust one. The reason for this is the desire to do better[2] than others. This is what every natural being naturally pursues as good. But by law and force, it is made to deviate from this path and honor equality.

They would especially have the freedom I am talking about if they had the power that the ancestor of Gyges of Lydia is said to have possessed.[3] The story goes that he was a shepherd in the service of the ruler of Lydia. There was a violent thunderstorm, and an earthquake broke open the ground and created a chasm at the place where he was tending his sheep. Seeing this, he was filled with amazement and went down into it. And there, in addition to many other amazing things of which we are told stories, he saw a hollow, bronze horse. There were windowlike openings in it and, peeping in, he saw a corpse, which seemed to be of more than human size, wearing nothing but a gold ring on its finger. He took off the ring and came out of the chasm. He wore the ring at the usual monthly meeting of shepherds that reported to the king on the state of the flocks. And as he was sitting among the others, he happened to turn the setting of the ring toward himself, toward the inside of his hand. When he did this, he became invisible to those sitting near him, and they went on talking as if he had gone. He was amazed at this and, fingering the ring, he turned the setting outward again and became visible. So, he experimented with the ring to test whether it indeed had this power—and it did. If he turned the setting inward, he became invisible; if he turned it outward, he became visible again. As soon as he realized this, he arranged to become one of the messengers sent to report to the king. On arriving there, he seduced the king's wife, attacked the king with her help, killed him, and in this way took over the kingdom.

Let's suppose, then, that there were two such rings, one worn by the just person, the other by the unjust. Now no one, it seems, would be so incorruptible that he would stay on the path of justice, or bring himself to keep away from other people's possessions and not touch them, when he could take whatever he wanted from the marketplace with impunity, go

---

[2] See Glossary of Terms s.v. do better.

[3] At 612b4, the ring is assigned to Gyges himself, not his ancestor.

into people's houses and have sex with anyone he wished, kill or release
from prison anyone he wished, and do all the other things that would
make him like a god among humans. And in so behaving, he would do no
differently than the unjust person, but both would pursue the same course.

This, some would say, is strong evidence that no one is just willingly, but
only when compelled. No one believes justice to be a good thing when it
is kept private, since whenever either person thinks he can do injustice
with impunity, he does it. Indeed, all men believe that injustice is far more
profitable to themselves than is justice. And what they believe is true, so the
exponent of this argument will say. For someone who did not want to do
injustice, given this sort of opportunity, and who did not touch other people's property, would be thought most wretched and most foolish by everyone aware of the situation. Though, of course, they would praise him in
public, deceiving each other for fear of suffering injustice. So much for my
second topic.

As for decision itself about the life of the two we are discussing, if we
contrast the extremes of justice and injustice, we shall be able to make the
decision correctly; but if we don't, we won't. What, then, is the contrast I
have in mind? It is this: we will subtract nothing from the injustice of the
unjust person, and nothing from the justice of the just one. On the contrary, we will take each to be perfect in his own pursuit. First, then, let the
unjust person act like a clever craftsman. An eminent ship's captain or doctor, for example, knows the difference between what his craft can and cannot do. He attempts the first but lets the second go by. And if he happens to
slip, he can put things right. In the same way, if he is to be completely
unjust, let the unjust person correctly attempt unjust acts and remain undetected. The one who is caught should be thought inept. For the extreme of
injustice is to be believed to be just without actually being so. And our
completely unjust person must be given complete injustice—nothing must
be subtracted from it. We must allow that, while doing the greatest injustice, he has nonetheless provided himself with the greatest reputation for
justice. If he does happen to slip up, he must be able to put it right, either
through his ability to speak persuasively if any of his unjust activities are discovered, or to use force if force is needed, because he is courageous and
strong and has provided himself with wealth and friends.

Having hypothesized such a person, let's now put the just man next to
him in our argument—someone who is simple and noble and who, as
Aeschylus says, does not want to be believed to be good, but to be so.[4] We
must take away his reputation. For a reputation for justice would bring him
honor and rewards, so that it would not be clear whether he is being just

---

[4] In *Seven against Thebes* 592–4, it is said of Amphiaraus that "he did not wish to be
believed to be the best but to be it." The passage continues with the words Glaucon
quotes below at 362a–b.

for the sake of justice, or for the sake of those honors and rewards. We must strip him of everything except justice, and make his situation the opposite of the unjust person's. Though he does no injustice, he must have the greatest reputation for it, so that he may be tested with regard to justice by seeing whether or not he can withstand a bad reputation and its consequences. Let him stay like that, unchanged, until he is dead—just, but all his life believed to be unjust. In this way, both will reach the extremes, the one of justice and the other of injustice, and we will be able to judge which of them is happier.

SOCRATES: Whew! My dear Glaucon, how vigorously you have scoured each of the men in our competition, just as you would a pair of statues for an art competition.

GLAUCON: I am doing the best I can. Since the two are as I have described, in any case, it should not be difficult to complete the account of the sort of life that awaits each of them, but it must be done. And if what I say sounds crude, Socrates, remember that it is not *I* who speak, but those who praise injustice at the expense of justice. They will say that the just person in such circumstances will be whipped, stretched on a rack, chained, blinded with a red-hot iron, and, at the end, when he has suffered every sort of bad thing, he will be impaled, and will realize then that one should not want to be just, but to be believed to be just. Indeed, Aeschylus' words are far more correctly applied to the unjust man. For people will say that it is really the unjust person who does not want to be believed to be unjust, but actually to be so, because he bases his practice on the truth about things and does not allow reputation to regulate his life. He is the one who "harvests a deep furrow in his mind, where wise counsels propagate." First, he rules his city because of his reputation for justice. Next, he marries into any family he wishes, gives his children in marriage to anyone he wishes, has contracts and partnerships with anyone he wants, and, besides benefiting himself in all these ways, he profits because he has no scruples about doing injustice. In any contest, public or private, he is the winner and does better than his enemies. And by doing better than them, he becomes wealthy, benefits his friends, and harms his enemies. He makes adequate sacrifices to the gods and sets up magnificent offerings to them, and takes much better care of the gods—and, indeed, of the human beings he favors—than the just person. So he may reasonably expect that the gods, in turn, will love him more than the just person. That is why they say, Socrates, that gods and humans provide a better life for the unjust person than for the just one.

When Glaucon had said this, I had it in mind to respond, but his brother Adeimantus intervened:

You surely do not think that the argument has been adequately stated?

SOCRATES: Why shouldn't I?

ADEIMANTUS: The most important point has not been mentioned.   5

SOCRATES: Well, then, as the saying goes, a man's brother must stand by
him.[5] So if Glaucon has omitted something, you must help him. Though,
for my part at any rate, what he has already said is quite enough to throw
me to the canvas and make me incapable of coming to the aid of justice.

ADEIMANTUS: Nonsense. But listen to what more I have to say, as well.   e
You see, in order to clarify what Glaucon has in mind, we should also fully
explore the arguments that are opposed to the ones he gave—those that
praise justice and disparage injustice.

As you know, when fathers speak to their sons to give them advice, they
say that one must be just, as do all those who have others in their charge.   5
But they do not praise justice itself, only the good reputation it brings: the 363a
inducement they offer is that if we are reputed to be just, then, as a result of
our reputation, we will get political offices, good marriages, and all the
things that Glaucon recently said that the just man would get as a result of
having a good reputation.

But these people have even more to say about the consequences of reputation. For by throwing in being well thought of by the gods, they have   5
plenty of good things to talk about—all the ones the gods are said to give to
those who are pious. For example, the noble Hesiod and Homer say such
things. For Hesiod says that the gods make the oak trees "bear acorns at the   b
top, bees in the middle, and fleecy sheep heavy laden with wool" for those
who are just, and tells of many other good things akin to these.[6] And
Homer says pretty much the same: 5

> When a good king, in his piety,
> Upholds justice, the black earth bears
> Wheat and barley for him, and his trees are heavy with fruit,   c
> His sheep bear lambs unfailingly and the sea yields up its fish.[7]

Musaeus and his son claim that the gods give just people even more excit-
ing goods than these. In their account, they lead the just to Hades, seat
them on couches, provide them with a symposium of pious people, crown   5
them with wreaths, and make them spend all their time drinking—as if
they thought eternal drunkenness was the finest wage of virtue. Others   d
stretch even further the wages that virtue receives from the gods. For they
say that someone who is pious and keeps his promises leaves his children's
children and a whole race behind him.

[5] See Homer, *Odyssey* 16.97–8.

[6] Hesiod, *Works and Days* 332–3.

[7] Homer, *Odyssey* 19.109.

5   In these and other similar ways, they praise justice. But the impious and unjust they bury in mud in Hades, and they force them to carry water in a sieve. They bring them into bad repute while they are still alive. And all those penalties that Glaucon gave to just people who are thought to be

e   unjust, they give to the unjust ones. But they have nothing else to say.

    That, then, is the praise and blame given to each. But in addition,

5   Socrates, there is another kind of argument about justice and injustice for you to consider—one that is used both by private individuals and by poets.

364a   With one voice they all chant the hymn that justice and temperance are fine things, but difficult and onerous, while intemperance and injustice are sweet and easy to acquire and are only shameful by repute and convention. They also say that unjust deeds are, for the most part, more profitable than

5   just ones; and whereas they are perfectly willing to bestow public and private honors on bad people—provided they have wealth and other types of power—and to declare them to be happy, they dishonor and disregard those who happen to be in any way weak or poor, even though they admit that

b   they are better than the others.

    But most amazing of all are the accounts they give of the gods and virtue, and how it is that the gods, too, assign misfortune and a bad life to many good people, and the opposite fate to their opposites. Begging priests and

5   prophets go to the doors of rich people and persuade them that, through sacrifices and incantations, they have acquired a god-given power: if the rich

c   person or any of his ancestors has committed an injustice, they can fix it with pleasant rituals. And if he wishes to injure an enemy, he will be able to harm a just one or an unjust one alike at little cost, since by means of spells and enchantments they can persuade the gods to do their bidding.

5   And the poets are brought forward as witnesses to all these accounts. Some harp on the ease of vice, on the grounds that

>   Vice in abundance is easy to get,

d   The road is smooth and begins beside you,

>   But the gods have put sweat between us and virtue

and a road that is long, rough, and steep.[8] Others quote Homer to bear wit-

5   ness that the gods can be influenced by humans, since he too said:

>   Even the gods themselves can be swayed by prayer.
>   And with sacrifices and soothing promises,
>   Incense and libation-drinking, human beings turn them from

e   their purpose,

>   When someone has transgressed and sinned.[9]

---

[8] *Works and Days* 287–9, with minor alterations.

[9] *Iliad* 9.497–501, with minor alterations.

And they present a noisy throng of books by Musaeus and Orpheus—who are the offspring, they claim, of Selene and the Muses—on which they base their rituals. And they persuade not only private individuals, but whole cities, that there are in fact absolutions and purifications for unjust deeds. For the living, these consist of ritual sacrifices and pleasant games. But there are also special rites for the dead. These initiations, as they call them, free people from evils hereafter, while terrible things await those who have not performed the rituals.

With so many things of this sort, my dear Socrates, being said about virtue and vice, and about how human beings and gods honor them, what effect do we suppose they have on the souls of young people? I mean those who are naturally gifted and able to flit, so to speak, from one of these sayings to another and gather from them an impression of what sort of people they should be, and of how best to travel the road of life. He would surely ask himself Pindar's question: "Is it by justice or by crooked tricks that I will scale the higher wall," and so live out my life surrounded by secure defenses? And he will answer: "As for what people say, they say that there is no advantage in my being just if I am not also thought just, whereas the troubles and penalties of being just are apparent; but the unjust person, who has secured for himself a reputation for justice, lives the life of a god. Since, then, 'opinion forcibly overcomes truth,' and 'controls happiness,' as the wise men say, I must surely turn entirely to it.[10] I should create an illusionist painting[11] of virtue around me to deceive those who come near, but keep behind it the wise Archilochus' greedy and cunning fox."

"But surely," someone will object, "it is not easy for evil to remain always hidden." We will reply that nothing great is easy. And, in any case, if we are to be happy, we must go where the tracks of the arguments lead. To remain undiscovered we will form secret societies and political clubs. And there are teachers of persuasion to make us clever in dealing with assemblies and law courts. Therefore, partly by persuasion, partly by force, we will contrive to do better than other people, without paying the penalty.

"But surely we cannot hide from the gods or overpower them by force!" Well, if the gods do not exist, or do not concern themselves with human affairs, why should we worry at all about hiding from them? On the other hand, if they do exist, and do care about us, we know nothing about them except what we have learned from the laws and from the poets who give their genealogies. But these are the very people who tell us that the gods can be persuaded and influenced by sacrifices, gentle prayers, and offerings. Hence, we should believe them on both matters, or on neither. If we

[10] The quotation is attributed to Simonides, who is cited by Polemarchus in Book 1.

[11] See Glossary of Terms s.v. illusionistic painting.

43

believe them, we should be unjust and offer sacrifices from the fruits of our injustice. For if we are just, our only gain is not to be punished by the gods, but we will lose the profits of our injustice. But if we are unjust, we will get those profits, and afterward we will entreat the gods and, persuading them, escape with our crimes and transgressions unpunished.

"But in Hades, won't we pay the penalty for crimes committed here, either ourselves or through our children's children?" "My friend," the young man will say as he does his rational calculation, "mystery rites and the gods of absolution have great power. The greatest cities tell us this, as do those children of the gods who have become the gods' poets and prophets and reveal it to be so."

On the basis of what further argument, then, should we choose justice over the greatest injustice? For if we possess such injustice with a false façade, we will do as we have a mind to among gods and humans, both while we are living and when we are dead, as both the masses and the eminent claim. So given all that has been said, Socrates, what device could get someone with any power—whether of mind, wealth, body, or family—to be willing to honor justice, and not laugh aloud when he hears it praised?

Indeed, if anyone can show that what we have said is false, and has adequate knowledge that justice is best, what he feels for unjust people won't be anger, but a large measure of forgiveness. After all, he knows that apart from someone of godlike character who is disgusted by doing injustice, or someone who has gained knowledge and avoids injustice for that reason, no one is just willingly. Through cowardice or old age or some other weakness, people do indeed object to injustice. But it is obvious that they do so only because they lack the power to do injustice. For the first of them to gain that power is the first to do as much injustice as he can.

And all this has no other cause than the one that led to the whole of Glaucon's and my argument with you, Socrates. "Socrates, you amazing man," we said, "of all of you who claim to praise justice, beginning from the earliest heroes of old whose accounts survive up to the men of the present day, not one has ever blamed injustice or praised justice except by mentioning the reputations, honors, and rewards that are their consequences. No one has ever adequately described what each does itself, through its own power, by its presence in the soul of the person who possesses it, even if it remains hidden from gods and humans. No one, whether in poetry or in private discussions, has adequately argued that injustice is the greatest evil a soul can have in it, and justice the greatest good. If all of you had spoken in this way and had tried to persuade us from our earliest youth, we would not now be guarding against one another's injustice, but each would be his own best guardian, afraid that by doing injustice he would be living on intimate terms with the worst thing possible."

That, Socrates, and probably other things in addition, are what Thrasymachus (or possibly someone else) might say in discussing justice and injustice—crudely inverting their power, in my view. But *I*—for I have no reason to hide anything from you—want to hear the opposite from you, and that is why I am speaking with all the force I can muster. So do not merely demonstrate to us by argument that justice is stronger than injustice, but tell us what each one itself does, because of itself, to someone who possesses it, that makes the one bad and the other good. Follow Glaucon's advice and do not take reputations into account.[12] For if you do not deprive justice and injustice of their true reputations and attach false ones to them, we will say that it is not justice you are praising, but its reputation; nor injustice you are condemning, but its reputation; and that you are encouraging us to be unjust but keep it secret. In that case, we will say that you agree with Thrasymachus that justice is the good of another, the advantage of the stronger, while injustice is one's own advantage and profit, though not the advantage of the weaker.

You agree that justice is one of the greatest goods, the ones that are worth having for the sake of their consequences, but much more so for their own sake—such as seeing, hearing, knowing, being healthy, of course, and all the others that are genuine goods by nature and not simply by repute. This is what I want you to praise about justice. How does it—because of its very self—benefit its possessor, and how does injustice harm him? Leave wages and reputations for others to praise.

I can put up with other people praising justice and blaming injustice in that way—extolling the reputations and wages of the one and denigrating those of the other. But I won't put up with that from you (unless you insist on it). For you have spent your whole life investigating this and nothing else. So do not merely demonstrate to us by argument that justice is stronger than injustice, but show what effect each one itself has, because of itself, on the person who has it—the one for good, the other for bad—whether it remains hidden from gods and human beings or not.

Now, I had always admired the natural characters of Glaucon and Adeimantus, but I was especially pleased when I heard what they had to say on this occasion, and I replied:

Sons of that man,[13] Glaucon's lover was not wrong to begin the elegy he wrote, when you distinguished yourselves at the battle of Megara, by

---

[12] At 361b–c.

[13] *Ekeinou tou andros:* Sometimes taken to be a facetious, indexical reference to Thrasymachus, whose heirs (sons) in the argument Glaucon and Adeimantus self-confessedly are. It is more likely, however, that it is an honorific expression equivalent in meaning to "that well-known man."

addressing you as "Sons of Ariston, godlike family of a famous man."[14] That, my dear friends, was well said, in my view. For something altogether god-like must have affected you if you are not convinced that injustice is better than justice and yet can speak like that on its behalf. And I do believe that you really are unconvinced by your own words. I infer this from your general character, since if I had only your arguments to go on, I would not trust you. The more I trust you, however, the more I am at a loss as to what to do. I do not see how I can be of help. Indeed, I believe I am incapable of it. And here is my evidence: I thought that what I said to Thrasymachus showed that justice is better than injustice, but you won't accept that from me as a proof. On the other hand, I do not see how I can refuse my help. For I fear that it may even be impious to have breath in one's body and the ability to speak, and yet stand idly by and not defend justice when it is being prosecuted. The best thing, then, is to give justice any assistance I can.

Glaucon and the others begged me not to abandon the argument but to help in every way to track down what justice and injustice each is, and the truth about their respective benefits. So I told them what I had in mind:

The investigation we are undertaking is not an easy one, in my view, but requires keen eyesight. So, since we are not clever people, I think we should adopt the method of investigation that we would use if, lacking keen eyesight, we were told to identify small letters from a distance, and then noticed that the same letters existed elsewhere in a larger size and on a larger surface. We would consider it a godsend, I think, to be allowed to identify the larger ones first, and then to examine the smaller ones to see whether they are really the same.

ADEIMANTUS: Of course we would. But how is this case similar to our investigation of justice in your view?

SOCRATES: I will tell you. We say, don't we, that there is a justice that belongs to a single man, and also one that belongs to a whole city?

ADEIMANTUS: Certainly.

SOCRATES: And a city is larger than a single man?

ADEIMANTUS: Yes, it is larger.

SOCRATES: Perhaps, then, there will be more justice in the larger thing, and it will be easier to discern. So, if you are willing, let's first find out what sort of thing justice is in cities, and afterward look for it in the individual, to see if the larger entity is similar in form to the smaller one.

---

[14] Homosexual relations between older men and late-adolescent boys were an acceptable part of Athenian social life, especially among the upper classes. See K. J. Dover, *Greek Homosexuality* (Cambridge, Mass.: Harvard University Press, 1978).

ADEIMANTUS: I think that is a fine idea.

SOCRATES: If, in our discussion, we could look at a city coming to be, wouldn't we also see its justice coming to be, and its injustice as well?

ADEIMANTUS: We probably would.

SOCRATES: And once that process is completed, could we expect to find what we are looking for more easily?

ADEIMANTUS: Yes, much more easily.

SOCRATES: Do you think we should try to carry it out then? It is no small task, in my view. So, think it over.

ADEIMANTUS: It has been thought over. Don't do anything besides try.

SOCRATES: Well, then, a city comes to exist, I believe, because none of us is individually self-sufficient, but each has many needs he cannot satisfy. Or do you think that a city is founded on some other principle?

ADEIMANTUS: No, none.

SOCRATES: Then because we have many needs, and because one of us calls on another out of one need, and on a third out of a different need, we gather many into a single settlement as partners and helpers. And we call such a shared settlement a city. Isn't that so?

ADEIMANTUS: Yes, indeed.

SOCRATES: And if they share things with one another—if they give something to one another, or take something from one another—don't they do so because each believes that this is better for himself?

ADEIMANTUS: Of course.

SOCRATES: Come on, then, let's, in our discussion, create a city from the beginning. But its real creator, it seems, will be our need.

ADEIMANTUS: Certainly.

SOCRATES: Now, the first and greatest of our needs is to provide food in order to sustain existence and life.

ADEIMANTUS: Yes, absolutely.

SOCRATES: The second is for shelter, and the third is for clothes and things of that sort.

ADEIMANTUS: That's right.

SOCRATES: Tell me, then, how will a city be able to provide all this? Won't one person have to be a farmer, another a builder, and another a weaver? And shouldn't we add a shoemaker to them, or someone else to take care of our bodily needs?

ADEIMANTUS: Of course.

SOCRATES: A city with the barest necessities, then, would consist of four or five men?

e   ADEIMANTUS: Apparently.

SOCRATES: Well, then, should each of them contribute his own work for the common use of all? I mean, should a farmer, although he is only one person, provide food for four people, and spend quadruple the time and labor to provide food to be shared by them all? Or should he not be concerned about everyone else? Should he produce one quarter the food in one quarter the time for himself alone? Should he spend the other three quarters providing a house, a cloak, and shoes? Should he save himself the bother of sharing with other people and mind his own business on his own?

5   ADEIMANTUS: The first alternative, Socrates, is perhaps easier.

SOCRATES: There is nothing strange in that, by Zeus. You see, it occurred to me while you were speaking that, in the first place, we are not all born alike. On the contrary, each of us differs somewhat in nature from the others, one being suited to one job, another to another. Or don't you think so?

ADEIMANTUS: I do.

SOCRATES: Well, then, would one person do better work if he practiced many crafts or if he practiced one?

ADEIMANTUS: If he practiced one.

SOCRATES: And it is also clear, I take it, that if one misses the opportune moment in any job, the work is spoiled.

ADEIMANTUS: It is clear.

10   SOCRATES: That, I take it, is because the thing that has to be done won't wait until the doer has the leisure to do it. No, instead the doer must, of necessity, pay close attention to what has to be done and not leave it for his idle moments.

ADEIMANTUS: Yes, he must.

SOCRATES: The result, then, is that more plentiful and better-quality goods are more easily produced, if each person does one thing for which he is naturally suited and does it at the opportune moment, because his time is freed from all the others.

ADEIMANTUS: Absolutely.

SOCRATES: Then, Adeimantus, we are going to need more than four citizens to provide the things we have mentioned. For a farmer won't make his own plow, it seems, if it is going to be a good one, nor his hoe, nor any of his other farm implements. Nor will a carpenter—and he, too, needs lots of tools. And the same is true of a weaver and a shoemaker, isn't it?

ADEIMANTUS: It is.

SOCRATES: So carpenters, metalworkers, and many other craftsmen of that sort will share our little city and make it bigger.

ADEIMANTUS: Yes, indeed.

SOCRATES: Yet it still would not be a very large settlement, even if we added cowherds, shepherds, and other herdsmen, so that the farmers would have cows to do their plowing, the builders oxen to share with the farmers in hauling their materials, and the weavers and shoemakers hides and fleeces to use.

ADEIMANTUS: It would not be a small city either, if it had to hold all that.

SOCRATES: Moreover, it is almost impossible, at any rate, to establish the city itself in the sort of place where it will need no imports.

ADEIMANTUS: Yes, that is impossible.

SOCRATES: Then we will need still other people who will import whatever is needed from another city.

ADEIMANTUS: We will.

SOCRATES: And if our servant goes empty-handed to another city, without any of the things needed by those from whom he is trying to get what his own people need, he will come away empty-handed, won't he?

ADEIMANTUS: I should think so.

SOCRATES: Our citizens, then, must produce not only enough for themselves at home, but also goods of the right quality and quantity to satisfy the needs of others.

ADEIMANTUS: Yes, they must.

SOCRATES: So we will need more farmers and other craftsmen in our city.

ADEIMANTUS: Yes.

SOCRATES: And also other servants, I imagine, who are to take care of imports and exports. These are merchants, aren't they?

ADEIMANTUS: Yes.

SOCRATES: We will need merchants too, then.

ADEIMANTUS: Of course.

SOCRATES: And if the trade is carried on by sea, we will need a great many others who have expert knowledge of the business of the sea.

ADEIMANTUS: A great many, indeed.

SOCRATES: Again, within the city itself, how will people share with one another the things they each produce? It was in order to *share*, after all, that we associated with one another and founded a city.

49

ADEIMANTUS: Clearly, they must do it by buying and selling.

SOCRATES: Then we will need a marketplace and a currency for such exchange.

ADEIMANTUS: Yes, indeed.

SOCRATES: So if a farmer or any other craftsman brings some of his prod-
c   ucts to the marketplace, and he does not arrive at the same time as those who want to exchange things with him, is he to sit idly in the marketplace, neglecting his own craft?

ADEIMANTUS: Not at all. On the contrary, there will be people who notice
5   this situation and provide the requisite service—in well-organized cities, they are generally those whose bodies are weakest and who are not fit to do any other sort of work. Their job is to wait there in the marketplace and
d   exchange money for the goods of those who have something to sell, and then to exchange goods for the money of those who want to buy them.

5 SOCRATES: This need, then, causes retailers to be present in our city. Those who wait in the marketplace, and provide this service of buying and selling, are called retailers, aren't they, whereas those who travel between cities are merchants?

ADEIMANTUS: Yes, that's right.

SOCRATES: There are also other servants, I think, whose minds would not
e   altogether qualify them for membership in our community, but whose bodies are strong enough for hard labor. So they sell the use of their strength for a price called a wage, and that is why they are called wage-
5   earners. Isn't that so?

ADEIMANTUS: Yes.

SOCRATES: So the wage-earners too, it seems, serve to complete our city?

ADEIMANTUS: I think so.

SOCRATES: Well, then, Adeimantus, has our city now grown to com-
10 pleteness?

ADEIMANTUS: Maybe it has.

SOCRATES: Then where are justice and injustice to be found in it? With which of the people we considered did they come in?

372a ADEIMANTUS: I have no idea, Socrates, unless it is somewhere in some need that these people have of one another.

SOCRATES: Perhaps what you say is right. We must look into it and not back off. First, then, let's see what sort of life people will lead who have
5 been provided for in this way. They will make food, wine, clothes, and shoes, won't they? And they will build themselves houses. In the summer,

they will mostly work naked and barefoot, but in the winter they will wear adequate clothing and shoes. For nourishment, they will provide themselves with barley meal and wheat flour, which they will knead and bake into noble cakes and loaves and serve up on a reed or on clean leaves. They will recline on couches strewn with yew and myrtles and feast with their children, drink their wine, and, crowned with wreaths, hymn the gods. They will enjoy having sex with one another, but they will produce no more children than their resources allow, lest they fall into either poverty or war.

At this point Glaucon interrupted and said:

It seems that you make your people feast without any relishes.[15]

SOCRATES: True enough, I was forgetting that they will also have relishes—salt, of course, and olives and cheese, and they will boil roots and vegetables the way they boil them in the country. We will give them desserts too, I imagine, consisting of figs, chickpeas, and beans. And they will roast myrtles and acorns before the fire and drink in moderation. And so they will live in peace and good health, it seems, and when they die at a ripe old age, they will pass on a similar sort of life to their children.

GLAUCON: If you were founding a city of pigs, Socrates, isn't that just what you would provide to fatten *them?*

SOCRATES: What, then, would you have me do, Glaucon?

GLAUCON: Just what is conventional. If they are not to suffer hardship, they should recline on proper couches, I suppose, dine at tables, and have the relishes and desserts that people have nowadays.

SOCRATES: All right, I understand. It isn't merely the origins of a city that we are considering, it seems, but those of a city that is *luxurious,* too. And that may not be a bad idea. For by examining such a city, we might perhaps see how justice and injustice grow up in cities. Yet the true city, in my view, is the one we have described: the healthy one, as it were. But if you also want to look at a feverish city, so be it. There is nothing to stop us. You see, the things I mentioned earlier, and the way of life I described, won't satisfy some people, it seems; but couches, tables, and other furniture will have to be added to it, and relishes, of course, and incense, perfumes, prostitutes, pastries—and the multifariousness of each of them. In particular, we cannot just provide them with the necessities[16] we mentioned at first, such as houses, clothes, and shoes; no, instead we will have to get painting and embroidery going, and procure gold and ivory and all sorts of everything of that sort. Isn't that so?

[15] See Glossary of Terms s.v. relish.
[16] See 558d8–559d2.

b   GLAUCON: Yes.

SOCRATES: Then we will have to enlarge our city again: the healthy one is no longer adequate. On the contrary, we must now increase it in size and population and fill it with a multitude of things that go beyond what is necessary for a city—hunters, for example, and all those imitators. Many of the

5   latter work with shapes and colors; many with music—poets and their assistants, rhapsodes,[17] actors, choral dancers, theatrical producers. And there will have to be craftsmen of multifarious devices, including, among other things, those needed for the adornment of women. In particular, then, we

c   will need more servants—don't you think—such as tutors, wet nurses, nannies, beauticians, barbers, and relish cooks and meat cooks, too? Moreover, we will also need people to farm pigs. This animal did not exist in our ear-

5   lier city, since there was no need for it, but we will need it in this one. And we will also need large numbers of other meat-producing animals, won't we, if someone is going to eat them?

GLAUCON: We certainly will.

SOCRATES: And if we live like that, won't we have a far greater need for

d   doctors than we did before?

GLAUCON: Yes, far greater.

SOCRATES: And the land, I take it, that used to be adequate to feed the population we had then will now be small and inadequate. Or don't you

5   agree?

GLAUCON: I do.

SOCRATES: Won't we have to seize some of our neighbors' land, then, if we are to have enough for pasture and plowing? And won't our neighbors want to seize part of ours in turn, if they too have abandoned themselves to the endless acquisition of money and overstepped the limit of their neces-

10 sary desires?

e   GLAUCON: Yes, that is quite inevitable, Socrates.

SOCRATES: And the next step will be war, Glaucon, don't you agree?

GLAUCON: I do.

SOCRATES: Now, let's not say yet whether the effects of war are good or

5   bad, but only that we have now found the origin of war: it comes from those same factors, the occurrence of which is the source of the greatest evils for cities and the individuals in them.

GLAUCON: Indeed, it does.

SOCRATES: The city must be further enlarged, then, my dear Glaucon, and not just a little, but by the size of a whole army. It will do battle with

---

[17] See Glossary of Terms s.v. rhapsode.

the invaders in defense of the city's wealth, and of all the other things we just described.   374a

GLAUCON: Why so? Aren't the inhabitants themselves adequate for that purpose?

SOCRATES: No, not, at any rate, if the agreement that you and the rest of us made when we were founding the city was a good one. I think we agreed, if you remember, that it is impossible for a single person to practice   5 many crafts well.

GLAUCON: True, we did say that.

SOCRATES: Well, then, don't you think that warfare is a craft?   b

GLAUCON: It is, indeed.

SOCRATES: So, should we be more concerned about the craft of shoemaking than the craft of warfare?

GLAUCON: Not at all.   5

SOCRATES: Well, now, we prevented a shoemaker from trying to be a farmer, weaver, or builder at the same time, instead of just a shoemaker, in order to ensure that the shoemaker's job was done well. Similarly, we also assigned just the one job for which he had a natural aptitude to each of the other people, and said that he was to work at it his whole life, free from having to do any of the other jobs, so as not to miss the opportune   c moments for performing it well. But isn't it of the greatest importance that warfare be carried out well? Or is fighting a war so easy that a farmer, a shoemaker, or any other artisan can be a soldier at the same time, even   5 though no one can become so much as a good checkers player or dice player if he considers it only as a sideline and does not practice it from childhood? Can someone just pick up a shield, or any other weapon or instrument of war and immediately become a competent fighter in an   d infantry battle or whatever other sort of battle it may be, even though no other tool makes someone who picks it up a craftsman or an athlete, or is even of any service to him unless he has acquired knowledge of it and has   5 had sufficient practice?

GLAUCON: If tools could do that, they would be valuable indeed.

SOCRATES: Then to the degree that the guardians' job is most important,   e it requires the most freedom from other things, as well as the greatest craft and practice.

GLAUCON: I should think so.

SOCRATES: And doesn't it also require a person whose nature is suited to that very practice?

GLAUCON: Certainly.   5

53

SOCRATES: Then our task, it seems, is to select, if we can, which natures, which sorts of natures, suit people to guard the city.

GLAUCON: Yes, that is our task.

10 SOCRATES: By Zeus, it is no trivial task that we have taken on, then. All the same, we must not shrink from it, but do the best we can.

375a GLAUCON: No, we must not.

SOCRATES: Do you think that there is any difference, when it comes to the job of guarding, between the nature of a noble hound and that of a well-bred youth?

GLAUCON: What do you mean?

5 SOCRATES: I mean that both of them have to be sharp-eyed, quick to catch what they see, and strong, too, in case they have to fight what they capture.

GLAUCON: Yes, they need all these things.

SOCRATES: And they must be courageous, surely, if indeed they are to fight well.

10 GLAUCON: Of course.

SOCRATES: Now, will a horse, a dog, or any other animal be courageous if it is not spirited? Or haven't you noticed just how invincible and unbeatable

b spirit is, so that its presence makes the whole soul fearless and unconquerable in any situation?

GLAUCON: I have noticed that.

SOCRATES: Then it is clear what physical qualities the guardians should

5 have.

GLAUCON: Yes.

SOCRATES: And as far as their souls are concerned, they must, at any rate, be spirited.

GLAUCON: That too.

SOCRATES: But with natures like that, Glaucon, how will they avoid

10 behaving like savages to one another and to the other citizens?

GLAUCON: By Zeus, it won't be easy for them.

c SOCRATES: But surely they must be gentle to their own people and harsh to their enemies. Otherwise, they will not wait around for others to destroy them, but will do it themselves first.

5 GLAUCON: That's true.

SOCRATES: What are we to do, then? Where are we to find a character that is both gentle and high-spirited at the same time? For, of course, a gentle nature is the opposite of the spirited kind.

54

GLAUCON: Apparently.

SOCRATES: But surely if someone lacks either of these qualities, he cannot   10
be a good guardian. Yet the combination of them seems to be impossible.
And so it follows, then, that a good guardian is impossible.   d

GLAUCON: I am afraid so.

I could not see a way out, and on reexamining what had gone before, I said:

We deserve to be stuck, my dear Glaucon. For we have lost track of the
analogy we put forward.   5

GLAUCON: How do you mean?

SOCRATES: We have overlooked the fact that there *are* natures of the sort
we thought impossible, ones that include these opposite qualities.

GLAUCON: Where?

SOCRATES: You can see the combination in other animals, too, but espe-   10
cially in the one to which we compared the guardian. For you know, of
course, that noble hounds naturally have a character of that sort. They are as   e
gentle as can be to those they are familiar with and know, but the opposite
to those they do not know.

GLAUCON: Yes, I do know that.   5

SOCRATES: So the combination we want *is* possible, after all, and what we
are seeking in a good guardian is not contrary to nature.

GLAUCON: No, I suppose not.

SOCRATES: Now, don't you think that our future guardian, besides being
spirited, must also be, by nature, philosophical?[18]   10

GLAUCON: How do you mean? I don't understand.   376a

SOCRATES: It too is something you see in dogs, and it should make us
wonder at the merit of the beast.

GLAUCON: In what way?

SOCRATES: In that when a dog sees someone it does not know, it gets
angry even before anything bad happens to it. But when it knows some-   5
one, it welcomes him, even if it has never received anything good from
him. Have you never wondered at that?

GLAUCON: I have never paid it any mind until now. But it is clear that a
dog does do that sort of thing.   10

SOCRATES: Well, that seems to be a naturally refined quality, and one that
is truly philosophical.   b

[18] *Philosophos:* used here in its general sense to refer to intellectual curiosity or wanting knowledge for its own sake.

GLAUCON: In what way?

SOCRATES: In that it judges anything it sees to be either a friend or an enemy on no other basis than that it knows the one and does not know the other. And how could it be anything besides a lover of learning[19] if it defines what is its own and what is alien to it in terms of knowledge and ignorance?

GLAUCON: It surely could not be anything but.

SOCRATES: But surely the love of learning and philosophy are the same, aren't they?

GLAUCON: Yes, they are the same.

SOCRATES: Then can't we confidently assume that the same holds for a human being too—that if he is going to be gentle to his own and those he knows, he must be, by nature, a lover of learning and a philosopher?

GLAUCON: We can.

SOCRATES: Philosophy, then, and spirit, speed, and strength as well, must all be combined in the nature of anyone who is going to be a really fine and good guardian of our city.

GLAUCON: Absolutely.

SOCRATES: Then that is what he would have to be like at the outset. But how are we to bring these people up and educate them? Will inquiring into that topic bring us any closer to the goal of our inquiry, which is to discover the origins of justice and injustice in a city? We want our account to be adequate, but we do not want it to be any longer than necessary.

And Glaucon's brother replied:

I for one certainly expect that this inquiry will help us.

SOCRATES: By Zeus, in that case, my dear Adeimantus, we must not abandon it, even if it turns out to be a somewhat lengthy affair.

ADEIMANTUS: No, we must not.

SOCRATES: Come on, then, and like people in a fable telling stories at their leisure, let's in our discussion educate these men.

ADEIMANTUS: Yes, let's.

SOCRATES: What, then, will the education be? Or is it difficult to find a better one than the one that has been discovered over a long period of time—physical training for bodies and musical training for the soul?[20]

---

[19] *Philomathês.*

[20] See Glossary of Terms s.v. physical training, musical training.

ADEIMANTUS: Yes, it is. 5

SOCRATES: Now, won't we start musical training before physical training?

ADEIMANTUS: Of course.

SOCRATES: And you include stories under musical training, don't you?

ADEIMANTUS: I do. 10

SOCRATES: But aren't there two kinds of stories, one true and the other false?

ADEIMANTUS: Yes.

SOCRATES: And education must make use of both, but first of the false ones? 377a

ADEIMANTUS: I do not understand what you mean.

SOCRATES: Don't you understand that we first begin by telling stories to children? And surely they are false on the whole, though they have some 5 truth in them. And we use stories on children before physical training.

ADEIMANTUS: That's true.

SOCRATES: That, then, is what I meant by saying that musical training should be taken up before physical training. 10

ADEIMANTUS: And you were right.

SOCRATES: Now, you know, don't you, that the beginning of any job is the most important part, especially when we are dealing with anything young and tender? For that is when it is especially malleable and best takes b on whatever pattern one wishes to impress on it.

ADEIMANTUS: Precisely so.

SOCRATES: Shall we carelessly allow our children to hear any old stories 5 made up by just anyone, then, and to take beliefs into their souls that are, for the most part, the opposite of the ones we think they should hold when they are grown up?

ADEIMANTUS: We certainly won't allow that at all.

SOCRATES: So our first task, it seems, is to supervise the storytellers: if they make up a good story, we must accept it; if not, we must reject it. We will persuade nurses and mothers to tell the acceptable ones to their chil- c dren, and to spend far more time shaping their souls with these stories than they do shaping their bodies by handling them. Many of the stories they tell now, however, must be thrown out. 5

ADEIMANTUS: Which sorts?

SOCRATES: In the more significant stories, we will see the less significant ones as well. For surely the more significant ones and the less significant

ones both follow the same pattern and have the same effects. Don't you
think so?

ADEIMANTUS: Indeed, I do. But I do not understand at all what more significant ones you mean.

SOCRATES: The ones Homer, Hesiod, and other poets tell us. After all, they
surely composed false stories, which they told and are still telling to people.

ADEIMANTUS: Which stories do you mean? And what is the fault you find
in them?

SOCRATES: The first and most important fault that one ought to find,
especially if the falsehood has no good features.

ADEIMANTUS: Yes, but what *is* it?

SOCRATES: Using a story to create a bad image of what the gods and
heroes are like, just as a painter might paint a picture that is not at all like
the things he is trying to paint.

ADEIMANTUS: Yes, you are right to find fault with that. But what cases in
particular, what sorts of cases, do you mean?

SOCRATES: First, the biggest falsehood about the most important things
has no good features—I mean Hesiod telling us about how Uranus
behaved, how Cronus punished him for it, and how he was in turn punished by his own son.[21] But even if these stories were true, they should be
passed over in silence, I would think, and not told so casually to the foolish
and the young. And if, for some reason, they must be told, only a very few
people should hear them—people who are pledged to secrecy and have had
to sacrifice not just a pig, but something so large and scarce that the number of people who hear them is kept as small as possible.

ADEIMANTUS: Yes, those stories are certainly troubling.

SOCRATES: And they should not be told in our city, Adeimantus. No
young person should hear it said that if he were to commit the worst
crimes, he would be doing nothing amazing, or that if he were to inflict
every sort of punishment on an unjust father, he would only be doing the
same as the first and greatest of the gods.

ADEIMANTUS: No, by Zeus, I do not think myself that these stories are fit
to be told.

[21] Uranus prevented his wife, Gaia, from giving birth to his children by blocking
them up inside her. Gaia gave a sickle to one of these children, Cronus, which he
used to castrate his father when the latter next had intercourse with her. Cronus ate
the children he had by his wife, Rhea, until, by deceiving him with a stone, she was
able to save Zeus from suffering this fate. Zeus then overthrew his father. See
Hesiod, *Theogony* 154–210, 453–506.

SOCRATES: Indeed, we must not allow *any* stories about gods warring, fighting, or plotting against one another if we want the guardians of our city to think that it is shameful to be easily provoked into mutual hatred. After all, those stories are not true either. Still less should battles between gods and giants, or the many other multifarious hostilities of gods and heroes toward their families and friends, occur in the stories the guardians hear or in the embroidered pictures they see. On the contrary, if we are somehow going to persuade our people that no citizen has ever hated another, and that it is impious to do so, then *those* are the things their male and female elders should tell them from childhood on. And the poets they listen to as they grow older should be compelled to tell them the same sort of thing. Stories about Hera being chained by her son, on the other hand, or about Hephaestus being hurled from heaven by his father when he tried to save his mother from a beating, or about the battle of the gods in Homer, should not be admitted into our city, either as allegories or non-allegories. For the young cannot distinguish what is allegorical from what is not. And the beliefs they absorb at that age are difficult to erase and tend to become unalterable. For these reasons, then, we should probably take the utmost care to ensure that the first stories they hear about virtue are the best ones for them to hear.

ADEIMANTUS: Yes, that makes sense. But if, at this point too,[22] someone were once again to ask us what stories these are, how should we reply?

SOCRATES: You and I are not poets at present, Adeimantus, but we *are* founding a city. And it is appropriate for the founders to know the patterns on which the poets must base their stories, and from which they must not deviate. But they should not themselves make up any poems.

ADEIMANTUS: That's right. But what precisely are the patterns that stories about the gods must follow?[23]

SOCRATES: Something like this: whether in epic, lyric, or tragedy, a god must always be represented as he is.

ADEIMANTUS: Yes, he must.

SOCRATES: Now, gods,[24] of course, are really good, aren't they, and must be described as such?

ADEIMANTUS: Certainly.

SOCRATES: And surely nothing good is harmful, is it?

---

[22] As at 377d10.

[23] *Theologia:* theology.

[24] *Ho theos:* literally, "the god." But the definite article is almost certainly functioning as a universal quantifier, as in "The swallow is a migratory bird," which means (all) swallows migrate.

ADEIMANTUS: I suppose not.

5   SOCRATES: Well, can what is not harmful do any harm?

ADEIMANTUS: No, never.

SOCRATES: And can what does no harm do anything bad?

ADEIMANTUS: No, it can't do that either.

SOCRATES: But what does nothing bad could not be the cause of anything bad, could it?

10   ADEIMANTUS: No, it could not.

SOCRATES: What about what is good? Is it beneficial?

ADEIMANTUS: Yes.

SOCRATES: So, it is the cause of doing well?

ADEIMANTUS: Yes.

SOCRATES: What is good is not the cause of all things, then. Instead, it is
15   the cause of things that are good, while of bad ones it is not the cause.

c   ADEIMANTUS: Exactly.

SOCRATES: So, since gods are good, they are not—as the masses claim—the
cause of everything. Instead, they are a cause of only a few things that happen to human beings, while of most they are not the cause. For good things
are fewer than bad ones in our lives. Of the good things, they alone are the
5   cause, but we must find some other cause for the bad ones, not the gods.

ADEIMANTUS: That's absolutely true in my view.

SOCRATES: Then we won't accept from Homer—or from anyone else—
d   the foolish mistake he makes about the gods when he says: "There are two
urns at the threshold of Zeus, one filled with good fates, the other with bad
5   ones," and the person to whom Zeus gives a mixture of these "sometimes
meets with a bad fate, sometimes with a good one." But the one who
receives his fate entirely from the second urn, "evil famine drives over the
e   divine earth." Nor will we tolerate the saying that "Zeus is the dispenser of
both good and bad to mortals." As for the breaking of the oaths and the
truce by Pandarus, if anyone tells us that it was brought about by Athena
and Zeus, or that Themis and Zeus were responsible for strife and conten-
5   tion among the gods, we won't praise him. Nor will we allow the young to
380a   hear the words of Aeschylus: "A god makes mortals guilty, when he wants
to destroy a house utterly."[25] And if anyone composes a poem, such as the
5   one those lines are from, about the sufferings of Niobe, or about the house

---

[25] The first three quotations are from *Iliad* 24.527–32. The sources for the fourth,
and for the quotation from Aeschylus, are unknown. The story of Athena urging
Pandarus to break the truce is told at *Iliad* 4.73–126.

of Pelops, or the tale of Troy, or anything else of that sort, he should be required to say that these things are not the works of a god. Or, if they are the works of a god, then the poet must look for roughly the sort of account of them we are now seeking: he must say that the actions of the gods are good and just, and that the people they punish are benefited by them. We won't allow him to say that those who are punished are made wretched, and that it was a god who made them so; but we will allow him to say that bad people are wretched because they are in need of punishment, and that in paying the penalty they are benefited by that god. But as for saying that a god, who is himself good, is the cause of evils, we will fight that in every way. We won't allow anyone to say it in his own city, if it is to be well governed, or anyone to hear it either—whether young or old, whether with meter or without meter. For these stories are impious, disadvantageous to us, and not in concord with one another.

ADEIMANTUS: I like your law, and I will vote with you for it.

SOCRATES: This, then, will be one of the laws or patterns relating to gods that speakers and poets will have to follow: that gods are not the cause of all things, but only of good ones.

ADEIMANTUS: And an entirely satisfactory one it is.

SOCRATES: Now, what about this second law? Do you think that gods are sorcerers who deliberately take different forms at different times, sometimes by changing on their own and altering their own form into a large number of shapes, sometimes by deceiving us into thinking they have done so? Or are they simple beings, and least of all likely to abandon their own form?

ADEIMANTUS: I can't say offhand.

SOCRATES: Well, if something abandons its own form, mustn't it either cause the change itself or be changed by something else?

ADEIMANTUS: It must.

SOCRATES: Now, the best things are least liable to alteration or change, aren't they? For example, a body is altered by food, drink, and labors, and all plants by sun, winds, and other similar affections—but the healthiest and strongest is least altered, isn't that so?

ADEIMANTUS: Of course.

SOCRATES: And wouldn't a soul that is most courageous and most knowledgeable be least disturbed or altered by any outside influence?

ADEIMANTUS: Yes.

SOCRATES: And the same account surely also applies even to manufactured items, such as implements, houses, and clothes: those that are good and well made are least altered by time or any other influences.

10 ADEIMANTUS: That's right.

SOCRATES: So whatever is in good condition—whether due to nature or
b   craft or both—is least subject to change by something else.

ADEIMANTUS: It seems so.

SOCRATES: But gods, of course, as well as the things belonging to them,
are best in every way.

5   ADEIMANTUS: They certainly are.

SOCRATES: So, on this view, gods would be least likely to have many
forms.

ADEIMANTUS: Least likely, indeed.

SOCRATES: Then would they change or alter themselves?

ADEIMANTUS: Clearly so, if indeed they are altered at all.

SOCRATES: Do they change themselves into something better and more
10   beautiful, or into something worse and uglier, than themselves?

ADEIMANTUS: It would have to be into something worse, if indeed they
c   are altered at all. For surely we won't say that gods are deficient in either
beauty or virtue.

SOCRATES: You are absolutely right. And do you think, Adeimantus, that
anyone, whether god or human, would deliberately make himself worse in
5   any way?

ADEIMANTUS: No, that is impossible.

SOCRATES: It is also impossible, then, for a god to want to alter himself.
On the contrary, since each god is, it seems, as beautiful and as good as possible, he must always unqualifiedly retain his own form.

ADEIMANTUS: In my view, at least, that is absolutely necessary.

d   SOCRATES: None of our poets, then, my very good man, is to say that
"The gods, like strangers from foreign lands, assume many disguises when
5   they visit our cities."[26] Nor must they tell lies about Proteus and Thetis, or
present Hera, in their tragedies or other poems, disguised as a priestess collecting alms for "the life-giving sons of the Argive river Inachus,"[27] or tell us
e   any of the many other such lies. Nor should mothers, influenced by these
stories, which terrify children, tell bad tales about gods who go wandering
around at night in the guises of many strange and multifarious beings, lest
5   they blaspheme the gods and, at the same time, make their children too
cowardly.

[26] *Odyssey* 17. 485–6.

[27] Inachus was the father of Io, who was persecuted by Hera because Zeus was in
love with her. The source for the part of the story Plato quotes is unknown.

ADEIMANTUS: Indeed, they should not.

SOCRATES: But, though the gods themselves are the sorts of things that cannot change, do they make us think that they appear in multifarious guises, deceiving us and using sorcery on us?   10

ADEIMANTUS: Perhaps they do.

SOCRATES: What? Would a god be willing to lie by presenting in word or   382a
deed what is only an illusion?

ADEIMANTUS: I don't know.

SOCRATES: Don't you know that all gods and humans hate a *true* lie, if one may call it that?   5

ADEIMANTUS: What do you mean?

SOCRATES: I mean that no one intentionally wants to lie about the most important things to what is most important in himself. On the contrary, he fears to hold a lie there more than anything.

ADEIMANTUS: I still don't understand.   10

SOCRATES: That is because you think I am saying something deep. I simply mean that to lie and to have lied to the soul about the things that are,[28]   b
and to be ignorant, and to have and hold a lie there, is what everyone would least of all accept; indeed, they especially hate it there.   5

ADEIMANTUS: They certainly do.

SOCRATES: But surely, as I was saying just now, it would be most correct to say that it is truly speaking a lie—the ignorance in the soul of the one to whom the lie was told. For a lie in words is a sort of imitation of this affection in the soul, an image of it that comes into being after it, and not an altogether   10
pure lie. Isn't that so?   c

ADEIMANTUS: Yes, it is.

SOCRATES: A real lie, then, is hated not only by the gods, but also by human beings.

ADEIMANTUS: I think it is.   5

SOCRATES: What about a lie in words? Aren't there times when it is useful, and so does not merit hatred? What about when we are dealing with enemies, or with so-called friends who, because of insanity or ignorance, are attempting to do something bad? Isn't it a useful drug for preventing them?   10
And consider the case of those stories we were talking about just now—
those we tell because we do not know the truth about those ancient events.   d
by making the lies that they contain as much like the truth as possible, don't we make them useful?

---

[28] See Glossary of Terms s.v. thing that is.

ADEIMANTUS: We most certainly do.

5   SOCRATES: In which of these ways, then, could a lie be useful to a god? Would he lie by making likenesses of the truth about ancient events because of his ignorance of them?

ADEIMANTUS: It would be ridiculous to think that.

SOCRATES: Then there is nothing of the lying poet in a god?

10   ADEIMANTUS: Not in my view.

SOCRATES: Would he lie, then, through fear of his enemies?

e   ADEIMANTUS: Hardly.

SOCRATES: Because of the foolishness or insanity of his family or friends, then?

ADEIMANTUS: No one who is foolish or mad is a friend of the gods.

SOCRATES: So a god has no reason to lie?

5   ADEIMANTUS: None.

SOCRATES: So both what is daimonic[29] and what is divine are entirely free of lies.

ADEIMANTUS: Absolutely.

SOCRATES: A god, then, is altogether simple, true in both word and deed. He does not change himself or deceive others by means of images, by

10   words, or by sending signs, whether they are awake or dreaming.

ADEIMANTUS: That is my view—at any rate, now that I have heard what

383a   you have to say.

SOCRATES: You agree, then, that this is the second pattern people must follow when speaking or composing poems about the gods: the gods are not sorcerers who change themselves, nor do they mislead us by telling lies

5   in word or deed.

ADEIMANTUS: I agree.

SOCRATES: Even though we praise many things in Homer, then, we won't approve of Zeus' sending the dream to Agamemnon, nor of Aeschylus

b   when he makes Thetis say that Apollo sang, in prophecy at her wedding:

> About the good luck my children would have,
> Free of disease throughout their long lives,
> And of all the blessings the friendship of the gods would bring
>   me.
> I hoped that Phoebus' divine mouth would be free of lies,

---

[29] See Glossary of Terms s.v. daimon.

Endowed as it is with the craft of prophecy.
But the very god who sang, the one at the feast,
The one who said all that, he himself it is
Who killed my son.[30]

Whenever anyone says such things about a god, we will be angry with him, refuse him a chorus,[31] and not allow teachers to use what he says for the education of the young—not if our guardians are going to be as god-fearing and godlike as human beings can be.

ADEIMANTUS: I agree completely about these patterns, and I would use them as laws.

c

5

---

[30] At *Iliad* 2.1–34, Zeus sends a dream to Agamemnon to promise success if he attacks Troy immediately. The promise is false. The source for the quotation from Aeschylus is unknown.

[31] I.e., deny him the funding necessary to hire a chorus of actors and produce his play.

Book 3

386a SOCRATES: Where the gods are concerned, then, it seems that those are the sorts of stories the future guardians should and should not hear from childhood on, if they are to honor the gods and their parents, and not treat lightly their friendship with one another.

5 ADEIMANTUS: I am sure we are right about that.

SOCRATES: What about if they are to be courageous? Shouldn't they be told stories that will make them least likely to fear death? Or do you think b that anyone ever becomes courageous if he has that fear in his heart?

ADEIMANTUS: No, by Zeus, I do not.

SOCRATES: What about if someone believes that Hades exists and is full of 5 terrible things? Can anyone with that fear be unafraid of death and prefer it to defeat in battle and slavery?

ADEIMANTUS: Not at all.

SOCRATES: Then we must also supervise those who try to tell such stories, it seems, and ask them not to disparage the life in Hades in this undiscriminating way, but to speak well of it, since what they now tell us is neither c true nor beneficial to future warriors.

ADEIMANTUS: Yes, we must.

SOCRATES: We will start with the following lines, then, and expunge everything like them: "I would rather labor on earth in another man's service, a man who is landless, with little to live on, than be king over all the dead";[1] and this: "He feared that his home should be revealed to mortals d and immortals as dreadful, dank, and hated even by the gods;"[2] and: "Alas, there survives in the Halls of Hades a soul, a mere phantasm, with its wits completely gone";[3] and this: "He alone can think others to be flitting

---

[1] *Odyssey* 11.489–91. Odysseus is being addressed by Achilles in Hades.

[2] *Iliad* 20.64–5. Hades is afraid that the earth will split open and reveal what his home is like.

[3] *Iliad* 23.103–4. Achilles speaks these lines as the soul of the dead Patroclus leaves for Hades.

shadows";[4] and: "The soul, leaving his limbs, made its way to Hades, lamenting its fate, leaving manhood and youth behind";[5] and this: "His soul went below the earth like smoke, screeching as it went";[6] and: 387a

> As when bats in an awful cave
> Fly around screeching if one of them falls
> From the cluster on the ceiling, all clinging to one another,
> so their souls went screeching.[7]

We will beg Homer and the rest of the poets not to be angry if we delete these and all similar passages—not because they are not poetic and pleasing to the masses when they hear them, but because the more poetic they are, the more they should be kept away from the ears of children and men who are to be free and to fear slavery more than death.   b

   5

ADEIMANTUS: Absolutely.

SOCRATES: Then, in addition, we must also get rid of the terrible and frightening names that occur in such passages: Cocytus, Styx,[8] "those below," "the sapless ones," and all the other names of the same pattern that supposedly make everyone who hears them shudder. Perhaps they are useful for other purposes, but our fear is that all that shuddering will make our guardians more emotional and soft than they ought to be.   c

   5

ADEIMANTUS: And our fear is justified.

SOCRATES: Should we remove them, then?

ADEIMANTUS: Yes.

SOCRATES: And follow the opposite pattern in speech and poetry?

ADEIMANTUS: Clearly.   10

SOCRATES: Shall we also remove the lamentations and pitiful speeches of famous men?   d

ADEIMANTUS: If what we did before was necessary, so is that.

SOCRATES: Consider, though, whether we will be right to remove them or not. What we claim is that a good man won't think that death is a terrible thing for another good one to suffer—even if the latter happens to be his friend.   5

---

[4] *Odyssey* 10.493–5. Circe speaking to Odysseus about the prophet Tiresias.

[5] *Iliad* 16.856–7. The words refer to Patroclus, who has just been mortally wounded by Hector.

[6] *Iliad* 23.100. The soul referred to is that of Patroclus.

[7] *Odyssey* 14.6–9. The souls are those of Penelope's suitors, whom Odysseus has killed.

[8] "Cocytus" means river of wailing or lamenting; "Styx," river of hatred.

ADEIMANTUS: Yes, we do claim that.

SOCRATES: So, he won't mourn for him as if he had suffered a terrible fate.

10   ADEIMANTUS: Certainly not.

SOCRATES: But we also claim this: a good person is most self-sufficient when it comes to living well, and is distinguished from other people by
e   having the least need of anyone or anything else.

ADEIMANTUS: True.

SOCRATES: So it is less terrible for him than for anyone else to be deprived of a son, brother, possessions, or the like.

5   ADEIMANTUS: Yes, much less.

SOCRATES: So, he will lament it the least and bear it the most calmly when some such misfortune overtakes him.

ADEIMANTUS: Of course.

SOCRATES: We would be right, then, to remove the lamentations of
10   famous men. We would leave them to women (provided they are not excel-
388a   lent women) and cowardly men, so that those we say we are training to guard our land will be ashamed to do such things.

ADEIMANTUS: That's right.

SOCRATES: In addition, then, we will have to ask Homer and the other
5   poets not to represent Achilles, who was the son of a goddess, as:

> Lying now on his side, now on his back, now again
> On his belly; then standing up to wander distracted
> This way and that on the shore of the unharvested sea;[9]

b   or to make him pick up ashes with both hands and pour them over his head, weeping and lamenting to the extent and in the manner Homer describes;[10]
5   or to represent Priam, a close descendant of the gods, as "begging and roll-ing around in dung, as he calls upon each of his men by name."[11] And yet more insistently than that, we will ask them at least not to make *the gods* lament and say: "Woe is me, unfortunate that I am, wretched mother of a
c   great son."[12] But, if they do make the gods do such things, at least they must not dare to represent *the greatest of the gods* in so unlikely a fashion as to make him say: "Alas, with my own eyes I see a man who is most dear to me being

---

[9] *Iliad* 24.3–12.

[10] *Iliad* 18.23–4.

[11] *Iliad* 22.414–5.

[12] *Iliad* 18.54. Thetis, the mother of Achilles, is mourning his fate among the Nereids.

chased around the city, and my heart laments";[13] or "Woe is me, that Sarpedon, who is most dear to me, should be fated to be killed by Patroclus, the son of Menoetius."[14] You see, my dear Adeimantus, if our young people listen seriously to these stories without ridiculing them as not worth hearing, none of them is going to consider such things to be unworthy of a mere human being like himself, or rebuke himself if it occurred to him to do or say any of them. On the contrary, without shame or perseverance, he would chant many dirges and laments at the slightest sufferings.

ADEIMANTUS: That's absolutely true.

SOCRATES: But that must not happen, as our argument has shown—and we must remain persuaded by it until someone shows us a better one.

ADEIMANTUS: No, it must not.

SOCRATES: Moreover, they must not be lovers of laughter either. For whenever anyone gives in to violent laughter, a violent reaction pretty much always follows.

ADEIMANTUS: I agree.

SOCRATES: So, if someone represents worthwhile people as overcome by laughter, we must not accept it, and we will accept it even less if they represent the gods in that way.

ADEIMANTUS: Much less.

SOCRATES: Then we must not accept the following sorts of sayings about the gods from Homer: "And unquenchable laughter arose among the blessed gods as they saw Hephaestus limping through the hall."[15] According to your argument, they must be rejected.

ADEIMANTUS: Yes, if you want to attribute it to me, but they must be rejected in any case.

SOCRATES: Moreover, we have to be concerned about truth as well. For if what we said just now is correct and a lie is really useless to the gods, but useful to human beings as a form of drug, it is clear that it must be assigned to doctors, whereas private individuals must have nothing to do with it.

ADEIMANTUS: It is clear.

SOCRATES: It is appropriate for the rulers, then, if anyone, to lie because of enemies or citizens for the good of the city. But no one else may have anything to do with it. On the contrary, we will say that for a private individual to lie to such rulers is as bad a mistake as for a sick person not to tell

---

[13] *Iliad* 22.168–9. Zeus is watching Hector being pursued by Achilles.

[14] *Iliad* 16.433–4.

[15] *Iliad* 1.599–600.

his doctor or an athlete his trainer the truth about his physical condition, or for someone not to tell the captain the things that are true about the ship and the sailors, or about how he himself or one of his fellow sailors is far-ing—indeed, it is a worse mistake.

ADEIMANTUS: That's absolutely true.

SOCRATES: So, if anyone else is caught telling lies in the city—"any of the craftsmen, whether a prophet, a doctor who heals the sick, or a carpenter who works in wood"[16]—he will be punished for introducing a practice that is as subversive and destructive of a city as of a ship.

ADEIMANTUS: Indeed it is, at any rate, if what people do is influenced by what he says.

SOCRATES: What about temperance?[17] Won't our young people also need that?

ADEIMANTUS: Of course.

SOCRATES: And aren't the most important aspects of temperance for the majority of people, at any rate, to obey the rulers and to rule over the pleasures of drink, sex, and food for themselves?

ADEIMANTUS: That is my view, anyway.

SOCRATES: So we will claim, I imagine, that it is fine to say the sort of thing that Diomedes says in Homer: "Sit down in silence, my friend, and be persuaded by my story";[18] and what follows it: "The Achaeans went in silently, breathing valor, afraid of their commanders";[19] and anything else of that sort.

ADEIMANTUS: Yes, it is fine.

SOCRATES: But what about things like, "You drunkard, with the eyes of a dog and the heart of a deer," and what follows it?[20] Are they, then, fine things to say? And what about all the other headstrong things that private individuals say to their rulers in works of prose or poetry?

ADEIMANTUS: No, they are not fine.

SOCRATES: That, I imagine, is because they are not suitable for inculcating temperance in the young people who hear them. But it would not be surprising if they were found pleasant in some other context. What do you think?

---

[16] *Odyssey* 17.384.

[17] *Sôphrosunê.*

[18] *Iliad* 4.412. Agamemnon has unfairly rebuked Diomedes for cowardice. Diomedes' squire protests, but Diomedes quiets him with these words. By obeying, the squire exhibits the kind of moderation that most people can come to possess.

[19] A mix of *Iliad* 3.8 and 4.431.

[20] *Iliad* 1.225. Achilles is insulting his commander, Agamemnon.

ADEIMANTUS: The same as you.

SOCRATES: What about making the wisest man say that the best thing of all, as it seems to him, is when "the tables are well laden with bread and meat, and the wine-bearer draws wine from the mixing bowl, brings it, and pours it in the cups"?[21] Do you think that hearing things like that is suitable for inculcating self-mastery in young people? Or that "death by starvation is the most pitiful fate"?[22] Or about how Zeus stayed awake alone deliberating, when all the other gods and mortals were asleep, and then easily forgot all his plans because of his sexual appetite, and was so overcome by the sight of Hera that he did not even want to go to their bedroom, but to possess her there on the ground, saying that his appetite for her was even greater than it was when they first made love to one another "without their parents' knowledge"?[23] Or what about the chaining together of Ares and Aphrodite by Hephaestus[24] for similar reasons?

ADEIMANTUS: No, by Zeus, that does not seem suitable to me.

SOCRATES: On the other hand, if there are any words or deeds of famous men that express perseverance in the face of everything, surely they must be seen and heard. For example, "He struck his chest and spoke to his heart: 'Bear up, my heart, you have suffered more shameful things than this.'"[25]

ADEIMANTUS: Absolutely.

SOCRATES: And we must not, of course, allow our men to be bribable with gifts or to be money-lovers.

ADEIMANTUS: Certainly not.

SOCRATES: Then they must not sing: "Gifts persuade gods, and gifts persuade revered kings."[26] Nor must we praise Phoenix, the tutor of Achilles, for being moderate, when he advises Achilles to take the gifts and defend the Achaeans, but not to lay aside his anger without gifts.[27] Nor should we agree that Achilles himself was such a money-lover as to accept the gifts of Agamemnon, or to release a corpse when he got paid for it, but otherwise to refuse.[28]

ADEIMANTUS: No, it certainly is not right to praise such things.

---

[21] *Odyssey* 9.8–10.

[22] *Odyssey* 12.342. Eurylochus urges the men to slay the cattle of Helios in Odysseus' absence.

[23] *Iliad* 14.294–341.

[24] *Odyssey* 8.266ff.

[25] *Odyssey* 20.17–8. The speaker is Odysseus.

[26] The source of the passage is unknown. Cf. Euripides, *Medea* 964.

[27] *Iliad* 9.602–3.

[28] *Iliad* 19.278ff., 24.594.

SOCRATES: It is only out of respect for Homer, indeed, that I hesitate to say that it is positively impious to accuse Achilles of such things, or to believe them when others say them. Or to believe that he said to Apollo: "You have injured me, Farshooter, most deadly of the gods; And I would punish you, if only I had the power."[29] Or that he disobeyed the river—a god—and was ready to fight it.[30] Or that he consecrated hair to the dead Patroclus, which he had already consecrated to the other river, Sphercheius: "To the hero, Patroclus, I give my hair to take with him."[31] We must not believe that he did that. Nor is it true that he dragged the dead Hector around the tomb of Patroclus[32] or massacred the captives on his pyre.[33] So we will deny these things. Nor will we allow our people to believe that Achilles—the son of a goddess and of Peleus (who was himself the most temperate of men and the grandson of Zeus), and the pupil of the most wise Cheiron—was so full of inner disorder as to have two opposite diseases within him: illiberality accompanied by the love of money on the one hand, and arrogance toward gods and humans on the other.

ADEIMANTUS: That's right.

SOCRATES: Moreover, we will neither believe nor allow it to be said that Theseus, the son of Poseidon, and Peirithous, the son of Zeus, ever attempted those terrible rapes,[34] nor that any other child of a god and hero dared to do any of the terrible and impious deeds that are now falsely attributed to them. We will compel the poets either to deny that they did such things, or else to deny that they were children of the gods. But they must not say both or attempt to persuade our young people that the gods produce evils, nor that heroes are no better than humans. After all, as we were saying earlier, these things are neither pious nor true. For we demonstrated, I take it, that it is impossible for the gods to produce evils.[35]

ADEIMANTUS: We certainly did.

SOCRATES: And they are also positively harmful to those who hear them. You see, everyone will be ready to excuse himself when he is bad, if he has been persuaded that similar things are done and were done by "close descendants of the gods, near kin of Zeus, whose ancestral altar is in the ether on Ida's peak," and "in whom the blood of daimons has not

[29] *Iliad* 22.15, 20.
[30] *Iliad* 21.232ff.
[31] *Iliad* 23.151–2.
[32] *Iliad* 14.14–8.
[33] *Iliad* 23.175.
[34] According to some legends, Theseus and Peirithous abducted Helen and tried to abduct Persephone from Hades.
[35] See 380b8–383c7.

[Handwritten margin note: Socrates is building a city of ignorance (70–73+) – we will not tell the young ones that Gods can do bad or else they will excuse their own bad behaviour – No critical thinking]

weakened."[36] That is why we must put a stop to such stories; if we do not, they will produce in our young people a very casual attitude to evil. 392a

ADEIMANTUS: Exactly.

SOCRATES: What kind of stories are still left, then, about which we must determine whether or not they may be told? I mean, we have discussed how gods, heroes, daimons, and things in Hades should be portrayed. 5

ADEIMANTUS: We have.

SOCRATES: Then wouldn't stories about human beings be left?

ADEIMANTUS: Obviously so.

SOCRATES: But it is not possible, my friend, to discuss them here. 10

ADEIMANTUS: Why not?

SOCRATES: Because what we are going say, I imagine, is that poets and prose writers get the most important things about human beings wrong. They say that many unjust people are happy and many just ones wretched, b that doing injustice is profitable if it escapes detection, and that justice is another's good but one's own loss. We will forbid them to say such things, I imagine, and order them to sing and tell the opposite. Don't you think so? 5

ADEIMANTUS: No, I *know* so.

SOCRATES: Well, then, if you agree that what I said is correct, won't I say to you that you have conceded the point we were investigating all along?

ADEIMANTUS: And your claim would be correct.

SOCRATES: Then we won't come to an agreement about what stories should be told about human beings until we have discovered what sort of c thing justice is, and how, given its nature, it profits the one who has it, whether he is believed to be just or not.

ADEIMANTUS: That's absolutely right. 5

SOCRATES: Our discussion of the content of stories is complete, then. Our next task, I take it, is to investigate their style. And then we will have completely investigated both what they should say and how they should say it.

ADEIMANTUS: I don't understand what you mean. 10

SOCRATES: Well, we must see that you do. Maybe this will help you to grasp it better: isn't everything said by poets and storytellers a narration of d past, present, or future events?

ADEIMANTUS: Of course.

SOCRATES: And don't they proceed by narration alone, narration through imitation, or both? 5

[36] Thought to be from Aeschylus' lost play *Niobe*.

ADEIMANTUS: I need a still clearer understanding of that, too.

SOCRATES: What a ridiculously unclear teacher I seem to be! So, I will do what incompetent speakers do: I won't try to deal with the subject as a whole. Instead, I will take up a particular example and use that to explain what I mean. Tell me, do you know the beginning of the *Iliad* where the poet tells us that Chryses begged Agamemnon to release his daughter, that Agamemnon got angry, and that Chryses, having failed to get what he wanted, prayed to his god[37] to punish the Achaeans?

ADEIMANTUS: I do.

SOCRATES: You know, then, that up to the lines, "He begged all the Achaeans, but especially the commanders of the army, the two sons of Atreus,"[38] the poet himself is speaking and is not trying to make us think that the speaker is anyone but himself. After that, however, he speaks as if he himself were Chryses, and tries as hard as he can to make us think that the speaker is not Homer, but the priest himself, who is an old man. And all the rest of his narration of the events in Ilium and Ithaca, and all of the *Odyssey,* are written in pretty much the same way.

ADEIMANTUS: Yes, they are.

SOCRATES: Now, each of the speeches, as well as the material between them, is narration, isn't it?

ADEIMANTUS: Of course.

SOCRATES: But when he makes a speech as if he were someone else, won't we say that he makes his own style as much like that of the person he tells us is about to speak?

ADEIMANTUS: We certainly will.

SOCRATES: Now, to make oneself like someone else in voice or appearance is to imitate the person one makes oneself like, isn't it?

ADEIMANTUS: Of course.

SOCRATES: Then in a passage of that sort, it seems, he, and the rest of poets as well, produce their narration through imitation.

ADEIMANTUS: Yes, indeed.

SOCRATES: But if the poet never disguised himself, his entire poem would be narration without imitation. To prevent you from saying that you still do not understand, I will tell you what that would be like. If Homer said that Chryses came with a ransom for his daughter to supplicate the Achaeans, especially the kings, and if after that Homer had gone on speaking, not as if

---

[37] Apollo.
[38] *Iliad* 1.15ff.

he had become Chryses, but still as Homer, you know that it would not be imitation but narration pure and simple. It would have gone something like this—I will speak without meter since I am not a poet: the priest came and prayed that the gods would grant it to the Achaeans to capture Troy and have a safe return home, and he entreated them to accept the ransom and free his daughter, out of reverence for the god.[39] When he had said this, the others approved of it and consented. But Agamemnon was angry and ordered him to leave and never return, or else his priestly wand and the wreaths of the god would not protect him. He said that the priest's daughter would grow old in Argos by his side sooner than be freed. He ordered Chryses to leave and not make him angry if he wanted to get home safely. When the old man heard this, he was frightened and went off in silence. And once he had left the camp, he prayed at length to Apollo, invoking the cult names of the god, reminding him of his past gifts, and asking to be repaid for any that had found favor with him, whether they were temples he had built or victims he had sacrificed. He prayed that, in return for these things, the arrows of the god would make the Achaeans pay for his tears. That, comrade, is how we get pure narration without any imitation.

ADEIMANTUS: I understand.

SOCRATES: Also understand, then, that the opposite occurs when one omits the words between the speeches and leaves the speeches on their own.

ADEIMANTUS: I understand that, too; it is what happens in tragedies, for example.

SOCRATES: You have got it absolutely right. And now I think I can make clear to you what I could not before. One sort of poetry and storytelling employs only imitation—tragedy, as you said, and comedy. Another sort, which you find primarily in dithyrambs,[40] employs only narration by the poet himself. A third sort, which uses both, is what we find in epic poetry and many other places. Do you follow me?

ADEIMANTUS: Yes, now I understand what you meant.

SOCRATES: And before that, as you remember, we said that we had already dealt with *content,* but that we had yet to investigate *style.*

ADEIMANTUS: Yes, I remember.

SOCRATES: What I meant, then, was just this: we need to come to an agreement about whether to allow our poets to narrate as imitators, or as imitators of some things, but not others—and what sorts of things these are; or not to allow them to imitate at all.

[39] Apollo as at 393a1 and 394a3.
[40] See Glossary of Terms s.v. dithyramb.

ADEIMANTUS: I imagine that you are considering whether we will admit
tragedy and comedy into our city or not.

SOCRATES: Perhaps so, but it may be an even wider question than that. I
really do not know yet. But wherever the wind of argument blows us, so to
speak, that is where we must go.

ADEIMANTUS: Yes, well put.

SOCRATES: What I want you to consider, then, Adeimantus, is whether
our guardians should be imitators or not. Or does the answer follow from
what we have said already—namely, that whereas each individual can practice one pursuit well, he cannot practice many well, and if he tried to do
this and dabbled in many things, he would surely fail to achieve distinction
in all of them?

ADEIMANTUS: Of course. Why wouldn't it?

SOCRATES: Then doesn't the same principle also apply to imitation—
namely, that a single individual cannot imitate many things as well as he can
imitate one?

ADEIMANTUS: No, he cannot.

SOCRATES: Then he will hardly be able to practice any pursuit worth talking about while at the same time imitating lots of things and being an imitator. For, as you know, even when two sorts of imitation are thought to be
closely akin, the same people are not able to practice both of them well
simultaneously. The writing of tragedy and comedy is an example. Didn't
you just call both of these imitations?

ADEIMANTUS: I did, and you are quite right; the same people cannot do
both.

SOCRATES: Nor can they be both rhapsodes and actors simultaneously.

ADEIMANTUS: True.

SOCRATES: Indeed, the same men cannot be used as both tragic and comic
actors. And all these are imitations, aren't they?

ADEIMANTUS: They are.

SOCRATES: And human nature, Adeimantus, seems to me to be minted in
even smaller coins than this, so that an individual can neither imitate many
things well nor perform well the actions themselves of which those imitations are likenesses.

ADEIMANTUS: That's absolutely true.

SOCRATES: So, if we are to preserve our first argument, that our guardians
must be kept away from all other crafts so as to be the most exact craftsmen
of the city's freedom, and practice nothing at all except what contributes to
this, then they must neither do nor imitate anything else. But if they imitate

76

anything, they must imitate right from childhood what is appropriate for them—that is to say, people who are courageous, temperate, pious, free, and everything of that sort. On the other hand, they must not be clever at doing or imitating illiberal or shameful actions, so that they won't acquire a taste for the real thing from imitating it. Or haven't you noticed that imitations, if they are practiced much past youth, get established in the habits and nature of body, tones of voice, and mind?

ADEIMANTUS: I have indeed.

SOCRATES: Since those we claim to care about are *men,* then, and men who must become good, we won't allow them to imitate a *woman,* young or old, as she abuses her husband, quarrels with the gods, brags because she thinks herself happy, or suffers misfortune and is possessed by sorrows and lamentations—and still less a woman who is ill, passionately in love, or in labor.

ADEIMANTUS: Absolutely not.

SOCRATES: Nor must they imitate either male or female slaves doing servile actions.

ADEIMANTUS: No, they must not.

SOCRATES: Nor cowardly, bad men, it seems, or those whose actions are the opposite of what we described just now—men who libel and ridicule each other, and use shameful language when drunk or even when sober, or who wrong themselves and others by word or deed in the other ways that are typical of such people. And they must not get into the habit, I take it, of acting or talking like madmen. They must *know,* of course, about mad and evil men and women, but they must not do or imitate anything they do.

ADEIMANTUS: That's absolutely true.

SOCRATES: What about metalworkers or other craftsmen, or those who row in triremes, or their coxswains, or the like—should they imitate them?

ADEIMANTUS: No, they should not, since they are not allowed even to pay any mind to those pursuits.

SOCRATES: And what about neighing horses, bellowing bulls, roaring rivers, the crashing sea, thunder, or the like—will they imitate them?

ADEIMANTUS: No, they have already been forbidden to be mad or to imitate madmen.

SOCRATES: So you are saying, if I understand you, that there is one kind of style and narration that a really good and fine person would use whenever he had to say something, and another kind, unlike that one, which his opposite by nature and education would always favor, and in which he would narrate his story.

ADEIMANTUS: What kinds are they?

SOCRATES: In my view, when a moderate man comes upon the words or actions of a good man in the course of a narration, he will be willing to report them as if he were that man himself, and he won't be ashamed of that sort of imitation. He will be most willing to imitate the good man when he is acting in a faultless and intelligent manner, but less willing and more reluctant to do so when he is upset by disease, passion, drunkenness, or some other misfortune. When he comes upon a character who is beneath him, however, he will be unwilling to make himself resemble this inferior character in any serious way—except perhaps for a brief period in which he is doing something good. On the contrary, he will be ashamed to do something like that, both because he is unpracticed in the imitation of such people, and also because he cannot stand to shape and mold himself on an inferior pattern. In his mind he despises that, except when it is for the sake of amusement.

ADEIMANTUS: Probably so.

SOCRATES: Won't he use the sorts of narration, then, that we described in dealing with the Homeric epics a moment ago? And though his style of speaking will involve both imitation and the other sort of narration, won't imitation play a small part even in a long story? Or am I talking nonsense?

ADEIMANTUS: Not at all. That must indeed be the pattern followed by that sort of speaker.

SOCRATES: As for the other sort of speaker, the more inferior he is, the more willing he will be to narrate anything and to consider nothing beneath him. Hence he will undertake to imitate, before a large audience and in a serious way, all the things we just mentioned: thunder and the sounds of winds, hail, axles, and pulleys; trumpets, flutes, pipes, and all the other instruments; and even the cries of dogs, sheep, and birds. And his style will consist entirely of imitation in voice and gesture, won't it, with possibly a small bit of plain narration thrown in?

ADEIMANTUS: Yes, that must be so, too.

SOCRATES: Well, then, that is what I meant when I said that there are two kinds of style.

ADEIMANTUS: And you were right; there are.

SOCRATES: Now, one of them involves little variation.[41] Hence if an appropriate harmony and rhythm are provided for this style, won't anyone who speaks in it correctly come close to speaking in a single harmony and, what is more, in a rhythm of pretty much the same sort, since the variations involved in it are slight?

[41] *Metabolê:* variation in general, but also a technical term in music for the transition from one harmony to another.

The city is being created by Socrates yet he calls it divine law – at same time look a method – immanent critique – elenchus

Guardian Education

ADEIMANTUS: Yes, that's precisely what he will do.

SOCRATES: What about the other kind of style? Won't it need the opposite: namely, every harmony and every rhythm, if it, too, is going to be spoken in properly, since it is multifarious in the forms of its variations? 5

ADEIMANTUS: Yes, that's very much what it is like.

SOCRATES: Now, doesn't every poet and speaker adopt a style that fits one or the other of these patterns, or a mixture of both? 10

ADEIMANTUS: Necessarily.

SOCRATES: What are we to do, then? Shall we admit all of these into our city, or one of the pure sorts, or the mixed one? d

ADEIMANTUS: If my view prevails, we will admit only the pure imitator of the good person. 5

SOCRATES: And yet, Adeimantus, the mixed style *is* pleasing. And the one that is most pleasing to children, their tutors, and the vast majority of people is the opposite of the one you chose.

ADEIMANTUS: Yes, it is the most pleasing.

SOCRATES: But perhaps you would say that it does not harmonize with our constitution, because there is no twofold or manifold man among us, e since each does only one job.

ADEIMANTUS: Indeed, it does not harmonize with it.

SOCRATES: And isn't that the reason that it is only in a city like ours that we will find a shoemaker who is a shoemaker, not a ship's captain who also 5 makes shoes; and a farmer who is a farmer, not a juror who also farms; and a soldier who is a soldier, not a moneymaker who also soldiers, and so on?

ADEIMANTUS: True, it is.

SOCRATES: Suppose, then, that a man whose wisdom enabled him to become multifarious and imitate everything were to arrive in person in our 398a city and want to give a performance of his poems. It seems that we would bow down before him as someone holy, amazing, and pleasing. But we would tell him that there is no man like him in our city, and that it is not in 5 accord with divine law for there to be one. Then we would anoint his head with perfumes, crown him with a woolen wreath,[42] and send him away to another city. But, for our own benefit, we would employ a more austere and less pleasant poet and storyteller ourselves—one who would imitate the b speech of a good person and make his stories fit the patterns we laid down at the beginning, when we undertook to educate our soldiers.

ADEIMANTUS: Yes, that is certainly what we would do, if it were up to us. 5

---

[42] As was traditionally done to statues of the gods.

79

SOCRATES: And now, my friend, it looks to me as though we have completed our discussion of the branch of musical training that deals with speech and stories. After all, we have discussed both what is to be said and how it is to be said.

ADEIMANTUS: Yes, it seems that way to me, too.

SOCRATES: Wouldn't what is left for us to discuss next, then, be lyric odes and songs?

ADEIMANTUS: Clearly.

SOCRATES: And couldn't anyone discover by now what to say about what they must be like, if indeed it is going to be concordant with what has already been said?

And Glaucon laughed and said:

I am afraid, Socrates, that "anyone" does not include me. You see, it is not sufficiently clear to me at the moment what we are to say, though I have my suspicions.

SOCRATES: Nonetheless, you are sufficiently clear about this: first, that a song consists of three elements—speech, harmony, and rhythm.

GLAUCON: Yes, I do know that, at least.

SOCRATES: Now, as far as speech is concerned, at any rate, it is no different, is it, from speech that is not part of a song, in that it must still be spoken in conformity to the patterns we established just now?

GLAUCON: True.

SOCRATES: Further, the harmony and rhythm must fit the speech.

GLAUCON: Of course.

SOCRATES: But we said that there is no longer a need for dirges and lamentations in words.[43]

GLAUCON: No, there is not.

SOCRATES: What are the lamenting harmonies, then? You tell me; you are musical.

GLAUCON: The mixo-Lydian, the syntono-Lydian, and some others of that sort.

SOCRATES: Shouldn't we exclude them, then? After all, they are even useless for helping women to be as good as they should be, let alone men.

GLAUCON: We certainly should.

[43] 387d–388e.

SOCRATES: Now, surely drunkenness is also entirely inappropriate for our guardians, and softness and idleness as well.

GLAUCON: Of course. 5

SOCRATES: What, then, are the soft harmonies, and the ones suitable for drinking parties?

GLAUCON: There are some Ionian ones that are called "relaxed," and also some Lydian ones. 10

SOCRATES: Could you use any of them, my friend, on men who are warriors? 399a

GLAUCON: No, never. So it looks as though you have got the Dorian and Phrygian left.

SOCRATES: I do not know the harmonies, so just leave me that harmony 5 that would appropriately imitate the vocal sounds and tones[44] of a courageous person engaged in battle or in other work that he is forced to do, and who—even when he fails and faces wounds or death or some other misfortune—always grapples with what chances to occur, in a disciplined and res- b olute way. And also leave me another harmony for when he is engaged in peaceful enterprises, or in those he is not forced to do but does willingly; or for when he is trying to persuade someone of something, or entreating a god though prayer, or a human being through instruction and advice; or for when he is doing the opposite—patiently listening to someone else, 5 who is entreating or instructing him, or trying to change his mind through persuasion. Leave me the harmony that will imitate him, when he does not behave arrogantly when these things turn out as he intends; but, on the contrary, is temperate and moderate in all these enterprises, and satisfied with their outcomes. Leave me these two harmonies, then—the forced and c the willing—that will best imitate the voices of temperate and courageous men in good fortune and in bad.

GLAUCON: You are asking to be left with the very ones I just mentioned. 5

SOCRATES: Well, then, we will have no need for multi-stringed or poly-harmonic instruments to accompany our odes and songs.

GLAUCON: No, it seems to me we won't.

SOCRATES: Then we won't maintain craftsmen who make triangular lutes, 10 harps, and all other such multi-stringed and polyharmonic instruments. d

GLAUCON: Apparently not.

[44] *Phthongos, prosôdia: phthongos* is a human voice, an animal cry, or more generally a sound of some sort; *prosôdia* is the tone or accent of a syllable, or a song accompanied by music.

SOCRATES: What about flute-makers and flute players? Will you allow them into the city? Or isn't the flute the most multi-stringed of all?[45] And aren't polyharmonic instruments all imitations of it?

GLAUCON: Clearly, they are.

SOCRATES: You have the lyre and the cithara left, then, as useful in our city; and in the countryside, by contrast, there would be a sort of pipe for the herdsman to play.

GLAUCON: That is what our argument suggests, anyway.

SOCRATES: Well we are certainly not doing anything new, my friend, in preferring Apollo and his instruments to Marsyas and his.[46]

GLAUCON: No, by Zeus, I suppose we aren't.

SOCRATES: And, by the dog,[47] we have certainly been unwittingly re-purifying the city we described as luxurious a while ago.

GLAUCON: That just shows how temperate we are.

SOCRATES: Then let's complete the purification. Now, the next topic after harmonies is the discussion of rhythms. We should not chase after complexity or multifariousness in the basic elements.[48] On the contrary, we should try to discover the rhythms of a life that is ordered and courageous, and then adapt the metrical foot and the melody to the speech characteristic of it, not the speech to them. What rhythms these would be is for you to say, just as you did in the case of the harmonies.

GLAUCON: No, by Zeus, I cannot tell you that. However, I can tell you from observation that there are three kinds of metrical feet[49] out of which the others are constructed, just as there are four, in the case of voices, from which come all the harmonies.[50] But I cannot tell you which sort imitates which sort of life.

SOCRATES: Well, then, we will also have to consult with Damon, on this point, and ask him which metrical feet suit illiberality, arrogance, madness,

---

[45] See Glossary of Terms s.v. flute. It is characterized as multi-stringed because of the number of different notes it is capable of producing.

[46] After Athena had invented the flute, she discarded it because playing it distorted her features. It was picked up by the satyr Marsyas, who was foolish enough to challenge Apollo (inventor of the lyre) to a musical contest. He was defeated, and Apollo flayed him alive. Satyrs were bestial in their behavior and desires—especially their sexual desires.

[47] *Nê ton kuna:* probably the dog-headed Egyptian god Anubis, as at *Gorgias* 428b5.

[48] Rhythm is poetic meter, and the elements are the metrical feet.

[49] Probably those in which the foot is divided in the ratio of: (1) 2:2—e.g., the dactyl (ˉ ˘ ˘) or the spondee (ˉ ˉ); (2) 3:2—e.g., the paeon (ˉ ˘ ˘ ˘); (3) 1:2 or 2:1—e.g., the iamb (˘ ˉ) or the trochee (ˉ ˘).

[50] The precise reference is unclear.

and the other vices, and which their opposites. I think I have heard him using the unclear terms "warlike," "complex," "fingerlike,"[51] and "heroic" to describe one foot, which he arranged, I do not know how, to be equal up and down in the interchange of long and short.[52] And I think he called one foot an iamb and another a trochee, and assigned long and short quantities to them. In the case of some of these, I think he approved or disapproved of the tempo of the foot as much as of the rhythm itself, or of some combination of the two—I cannot tell you which. But, as I said, we will leave these things to Damon, since to decide them would take a long discussion. Or do you think we should try it?

GLAUCON: No, by Zeus, I do not.

SOCRATES: But you are able to decide this, at least, aren't you: that grace goes along with good rhythm and lack of grace with bad rhythm?

GLAUCON: Of course.

SOCRATES: Furthermore, good rhythm goes along with fine speaking and is similar to it, while bad rhythm goes along with the opposite sort, and the same goes for harmony and disharmony; since, as we said just now, rhythm and harmony must conform to speech, and not vice versa.

GLAUCON: Yes, they certainly must conform to speech.

SOCRATES: And what about the style of speaking and what is said? Don't they go along with the character of the speaker's soul?

GLAUCON: Of course.

SOCRATES: And don't all the rest go along with the style of speaking?

GLAUCON: Yes.

SOCRATES: Fine speech, then, as well as harmony, grace, and rhythm, go along with naiveté. I do not mean the stupidity for which naiveté[53] is a euphemism, but the quality a mind has when it is equipped with a truly good and fine character.

GLAUCON: Absolutely.

SOCRATES: And mustn't our young people try to achieve these on every occasion, if they are going to do the job that is really theirs?

---

[51] Reading δακτυλικόν with Jackson and Waterfield.

[52] The foot being described is probably the dactyl (‾ ˘ ˘): it is warlike and heroic, because Greek heroic poetry was written in dactylic hexameter; complex, because it consists of a long syllable and two short ones; equal up and down in the interchange of long and short, because a long syllable is equal in length to two short ones; and fingerlike, because the first joint on a finger is roughly equal in length to the other two.

[53] See 348c12 note.

GLAUCON: Yes, they must indeed.

SOCRATES: Now, surely painting and all the crafts similar to it are full of
401a these qualities—weaving is full of them, as are embroidery, architecture,
and likewise the manufacture of implements generally; and so, furthermore,
is the nature of bodies and that of the other things that grow. For in all
5 these there is grace or the lack of it. And lack of grace, bad rhythm, and disharmony are akin to bad speech and bad character, while their opposites are
akin to and imitate their opposite—a character that is temperate and good.

GLAUCON: Absolutely.

b SOCRATES: Is it only poets we have to supervise, then, compelling them
either to embody the image of a good character in their poems or else not
to practice their craft among us? Or mustn't we also supervise all the other
craftsmen, and forbid them to represent a character that is bad, intemperate,
5 illiberal, and graceless, in their images of living beings, in their buildings, or
in any of the other products of their craft? And mustn't the one who finds
this impossible be prevented from practicing in our city, so that our guard-
c ians will not be brought up on images of evil as in a meadow of bad grass,
where they crop and graze every day from all that surrounds them until, little by little, they unwittingly accumulate a large amount of evil in their
souls? Instead, mustn't we look for craftsmen who are naturally capable of
5 pursuing what is fine and graceful in their work, so that our young people
will live in a healthy place and be benefited on all sides as the influence
exerted by those fine works affects their eyes and ears like a healthy breeze
from wholesome regions, and imperceptibly guides them from earliest
d childhood into being similar to, friendly toward, and concordant with the
beauty of reason?

GLAUCON: Yes, that would be by far the best education for them.

SOCRATES: Then aren't these the reasons, Glaucon, that musical training is
5 most important? First, because rhythm and harmony permeate the inner-
most element of the soul, affect it more powerfully than anything else, and
bring it grace, such education makes one graceful if one is properly trained,
e and the opposite if one is not. Second, because anyone who has been properly trained will quickly notice if something has been omitted from a thing,
or if that thing has not been well crafted or well grown. And so, since he
feels distaste correctly, he will praise fine things, be pleased by them, take
5 them into his soul, and, through being nourished by them, become fine
402a and good. What is ugly or shameful, on the other hand, he will correctly
condemn and hate while he is still young, before he is able to grasp the reason. And, because he has been so trained, he will welcome the reason when
it comes and recognize it easily because of its kinship with himself.

5 GLAUCON: Yes, it seems to me that these are the goals of musical training.

SOCRATES: It is like learning to read, then. We became adequately proficient only when the few letters that there are did not escape us in any of the different words in which they are scattered about; and when we did not disregard them, either in a small word or a big one, as if they were not worth noticing; but tried hard to distinguish them wherever they occur, knowing   b that we would not be competent readers until we knew our letters.

GLAUCON: True.

SOCRATES: And isn't it also true that if there are images of letters reflected in water or mirrors, we won't know them until we know the letters them   5 selves, for both abilities are parts of the same craft and discipline?

GLAUCON: Absolutely.

SOCRATES: Then, by the gods, aren't I right in saying that neither we nor the guardians we claim to be educating will be musically trained until   c we know the different forms of temperance, courage, generosity, highmindedness, and all their kindred, and their opposites, too, which are carried around everywhere; and see them in the things in which they are,   5 both themselves and their images; and do not disregard them, either in small things or in large, but accept that the knowledge of both belongs to the same craft and discipline?

GLAUCON: Yes, that necessarily follows.

SOCRATES: Then, if the fine habits in someone's soul and those in his   d physical form agree and are in concord with one another, so that both share the same pattern, wouldn't that be the most beautiful sight for anyone capable of seeing it?

GLAUCON: By far.   5

SOCRATES: And surely the most beautiful is also the most loveable, isn't it?

GLAUCON: Of course.

SOCRATES: A really musical person, then, would passionately love people who are most like that. But a disharmonious person, he would not passionately love.

GLAUCON: No, he would not—at least, not if the defect were in the soul. If it were only in the body, however, he would put up with it and still be   10 willing to embrace the boy who had it.   e

SOCRATES: I understand that you love or have loved such a boy yourself, and I agree with you. But tell me this: does excessive pleasure share anything in common with temperance?

GLAUCON: How can it? It surely drives one no less mad than pain does.   5

SOCRATES: What about with any other virtue?

403a GLAUCON: Never.

SOCRATES: Then, what about with arrogance and intemperance?

GLAUCON: Yes, with them most of all.

SOCRATES: Can you think of any pleasure that is greater or keener than
5 sexual pleasure?

GLAUCON: No, I cannot—or of a more insane one either.

SOCRATES: But isn't the right sort of passion a naturally moderate and
musically educated passion for order and beauty?

GLAUCON: Yes.

10 SOCRATES: Then nothing insane and nothing akin to dissoluteness can be
involved in the right love?

GLAUCON: No, they cannot.

b SOCRATES: Then sexual pleasure must not be involved, must it, and the
lover and the boy who passionately love and are loved in the right way must
have no share in it?

GLAUCON: No, by Zeus, Socrates, it must not be involved.

SOCRATES: It seems, then, that you will lay it down as a law in the city we
are founding that a lover—if he can persuade his boyfriend to let him—
5 may kiss him, be with him, and touch him, as a father would a son, for the
sake of beautiful things. But in all other respects, his association with the
c one he cares about must never seem to go any further than this. Otherwise,
he will be reproached as untrained in music, and as lacking in appreciation
for beautiful things.

GLAUCON: That's right.

SOCRATES: Do you agree, then, that our account of musical training has
5 come to an end? At any rate, it ought to end where it has ended; for surely
training in the musical crafts ought to end in a passion for beauty.

GLAUCON: I agree.

SOCRATES: Now, after musical training, our young people must be given
physical training.

10 GLAUCON: Of course.

SOCRATES: And in this, too, they must have a careful training, which starts
in childhood and continues throughout life. It would, I believe, be some-
d thing like this—but you should consider what you think, too. You see, I, for
my part, do not believe that a healthy body, by means of its own virtue,
makes the soul good. On the contrary, I believe that the opposite is true: a
good soul, by means of its own virtue, makes the body as good as possible.
5 What do you think?

GLAUCON: I think so, too.

SOCRATES: Then if we give adequate care to the mind, entrust it with the detailed supervision of the body, and content ourselves with indicating the general patterns to be followed rather than going on at great length, wouldn't we be proceeding in the right way?

e

GLAUCON: Yes, indeed.

SOCRATES: Now, we said that our prospective guardians must avoid drunkenness.[54] For surely a guardian is the last person who should get so drunk that he does not know where on earth he is.

5

GLAUCON: Yes, it would be ridiculous for a *guardian* to need a guardian himself!

SOCRATES: What about food? These men are athletes in the greatest contest, aren't they?

GLAUCON: Yes.

10

SOCRATES: Then would the regimen of ordinary, trained athletes be suitable for them?

404a

GLAUCON: Maybe.

SOCRATES: But it seems to be a soporific sort of regimen and unreliable as regards health. Or haven't you noticed that these athletes sleep their lives away, and that if they deviate even a little from their orderly regimen, they become seriously and violently ill?

5

GLAUCON: I have noticed that.

SOCRATES: Then we need a more refined sort of training for our warrior-athletes, since they must be like sleepless hounds, as it were, who have the keenest possible sight and hearing, and whose health is not so precarious that it cannot sustain the frequent changes of water and diet generally, and the heat waves and winter storms typical of war.

10

b

GLAUCON: I agree.

SOCRATES: Wouldn't the best physical training, then, be akin to the simple musical training we described a moment ago?

5

GLAUCON: How do you mean?

SOCRATES: I mean a simple and good physical training, and one that is especially adapted to the conditions of war.

GLAUCON: In what way?

SOCRATES: You could learn *that* even from Homer. For you know that when his heroes are at war, he does not portray them banqueting on

---

[54] 398e6.

c   fish[55]—even though they are by the sea in the Hellespont—or boiled meat, but roasted meat only, which is the sort most easily available to soldiers. For it is pretty much always easier to use an open fire than to carry pots and pans around everywhere.

5   GLAUCON: Quite right.

SOCRATES: Nor, I believe, does Homer mention rich sauces anywhere. In fact, isn't everyone else who is in training also aware that if he is planning to stay in good physical condition, he must avoid such things altogether?

GLAUCON: Yes, and they are certainly right to be aware of it and to avoid them.

SOCRATES: If you think they are right to do that, my dear Glaucon, you
d   apparently do not approve of Syracusan cuisine or complex Sicilian relishes.

GLAUCON: I suppose not.

5   SOCRATES: Then you also object to men having a Corinthian girlfriend, if they are planning to be in good physical condition.[56]

GLAUCON: Absolutely.

SOCRATES: And also to their enjoying the reputed delights of Attic pastries?

10   GLAUCON: I would have to.

SOCRATES: And the reason for that, I take it, is that we would be right to compare this sort of diet, and this lifestyle, to the polyharmonic songs and
e   lyric odes that make use of every sort of rhythm.

GLAUCON: Of course.

SOCRATES: There complexity engendered intemperance, didn't it, and here it engenders illness; whereas simplicity in musical training engenders
5   temperance in the soul, and in physical training health in the body?

GLAUCON: That's absolutely true.

405a   SOCRATES: And as intemperance and disease breed in a city, aren't many law courts and surgeries opened? And don't the legal and medical professions give themselves airs when even free men in large numbers take them very seriously?

5   GLAUCON: How could it be otherwise?

SOCRATES: Could you find better evidence that a city's education is in a bad and shameful state than when eminent doctors and lawyers are needed, not only by inferior people and handicraftsmen, but by those who claim to

---

[55] Fish was a luxury item in Plato's Athens. See James Davidson, *Courtesans and Fishcakes: The Consuming Passions of Classical Athens* (New York: St. Martin's, 1998).

[56] Corinthian prostitutes enjoyed an international reputation in the Classical period.

have been brought up in the manner of free men? Indeed, don't you think it is shameful and strong evidence of lack of education to be forced to make use of a justice imposed by others, as if they were one's masters and judges, because one lacks such qualities oneself?

GLAUCON: That is the most shameful thing of all.

SOCRATES: Do you really think so? Isn't it even more shameful not just to spend a good part of one's life in court defending oneself and prosecuting someone else, but to be so vulgar that one is persuaded to take pride in this and regard oneself as amazingly clever at doing injustice, and as so accomplished at every trick and turn that one can wiggle through any loophole, and avoid punishment—and to do all that for the sake of little worthless things, and because one is ignorant of how much better and finer it is to arrange one's own life so that one won't need to find a judge[57] who is asleep?

GLAUCON: Yes, that is even more shameful.

SOCRATES: What about needing the craft of medicine for something besides wounds or some seasonal illnesses? What about needing it because idleness and the regimen we described has filled one full of gasses and phlegm, like a stagnant swamp, so that sophisticated Asclepiad doctors are forced to come up with names like "flatulence" and "catarrh" to describe one's diseases? Don't you think that is shameful?

GLAUCON: Yes, it is; and those truly are strange new names for diseases.

SOCRATES: And of a sort that I do not imagine even existed in the time of Asclepius himself. My evidence for this is that his sons at Troy did not criticize the woman who treated the wounded Eurypylus with Pramneian wine that had lots of barley meal and grated cheese sprinkled on it, even though such treatment is now thought to cause inflammation. Moreover, they did not criticize Patroclus, who prescribed the treatment.[58]

GLAUCON: Yet, surely it *was* a strange drink for someone in that condition.

SOCRATES: Not if you recall that the sort of modern medicine that coddles the disease was not used by the Asclepiads before the time of Herodicus. Herodicus was a physical trainer who became ill and, through a combination of physical training and medicine, tormented first and foremost himself, and then lots of other people as well.

GLAUCON: How did he do that?

SOCRATES: By making his death a lengthy process. You see, although he was always tending his illness, he was not able to cure it, since it was terminal.

---

[57] See Glossary of Terms s.v. judge.

[58] At *Iliad* 11.580ff. Eurypylus is wounded, but not treated in this way (see 11.828–36). However, Machaon, the son of Asclepius, does receive this treatment at 11.624–50.

And so he spent his life under medical treatment, with no free time for anything else whatsoever. He suffered torments if he departed even a little from his accustomed regimen; but, thanks to his wisdom, he struggled against death and reached old age.

GLAUCON: A fine reward for his craft that was!

c

SOCRATES: And appropriate for someone who did not know that it was not because of ignorance or inexperience of this kind of medicine that Asclepius failed to teach it to his sons, but because he knew that everyone in a well-regulated city has his own work to do, and that no one has the

5 time to be ill and under treatment all his life. We see how ridiculous this would be in the case of craftsmen, but we do not see it in the case of those who are supposedly happy—the rich.

GLAUCON: What do you mean?

SOCRATES: When a carpenter is ill, he expects to get a drug from his doc-

d tor that will make him throw up what is making him sick or evacuate it through his bowels; or to get rid of his disease through surgery or cautery. If anyone prescribes a lengthy regimen for him and tells him that he should rest with his head bandaged and so on, he quickly replies that he has no

5 time to be ill, and that it is not profitable for him to live like that, always

e minding his illness and neglecting the work at hand. After that, he says goodbye to his doctor, resumes his usual regimen, lives doing his own job, and recovers his health; alternatively, if his body cannot withstand the illness, he dies and escapes his troubles.

GLAUCON: That does seem to be the correct way for someone like that to

5 use the craft of medicine.

SOCRATES: Isn't that because he had a job to do, and that if he could not

407a do it, it would not profit him to go on living?

GLAUCON: Clearly.

SOCRATES: But a rich person, it is said, has no job assigned to him of the

5 sort that would make his life not worth living if he had to keep away from it.

GLAUCON: So it is said, at least.

SOCRATES: What, have you not heard the saying of Phocylides that once one has the means of life, one must practice virtue?[59]

GLAUCON: And even earlier, in my view.

10 SOCRATES: Let's not quarrel with him about that. But let's try to find out for ourselves whether this virtue is something a rich person must practice, and if his life is not worth living if he does not practice it; or whether

[59] Phocylides of Miletus was a mid-sixth–century elegiac and hexameter poet best known for his epigrams.

nursing an illness, while an obstacle to putting your mind to carpentry and other crafts, is no obstacle whatever to taking Phocylides' advice.

GLAUCON: But, by Zeus, it is: excessive care of the body that goes beyond simple physical training is pretty much the biggest obstacle of all. For it's a nuisance in household management, in military service, and even in sedentary political office.

SOCRATES: And most important of all, surely, is that it makes any sort of learning, thought, or private meditation difficult, by forever causing imaginary headaches or dizziness and accusing philosophy of causing them. Hence, wherever this sort of virtue is practiced and submitted to philosophical scrutiny, excessive care of the body hinders it. For it is constantly making you imagine that you are ill and never lets you stop agonizing about your body.

GLAUCON: Yes, probably so.

SOCRATES: Then won't we say that Asclepius knew this, too, and that he invented the craft of medicine for people whose bodies are healthy in nature and habit, but have some specific disease in them? That is the type of person and condition for which he invented it. He rid them of their disease by means of drugs or surgery, and then prescribed their normal regimen, so that affairs of politics would not be harmed. However, he did not attempt to prescribe regimens for those whose bodies were riddled with disease, so that by drawing off a little here and pouring in a little there, he could make their life a prolonged misery and enable them to produce offspring in all probability like themselves. He did not think that he should treat someone who could not live a normal life, since such a person would profit neither himself nor his city.

GLAUCON: Asclepius was a true man of politics, in your view.

SOCRATES: Clearly so. And it was because he was like that, don't you see, that his sons, too, turned out to be good men in the war at Troy, and practiced the craft of medicine as I say they did. Don't you remember that they "sucked out the blood and applied gentle drugs" to the wound Pandarus inflicted on Menelaus? But they no more prescribed what he should eat or drink after that than they did for Eurypylus?[60] That was because they assumed that their drugs were sufficient to cure men who were healthy and living an orderly life before being wounded, even if they happened to drink wine mixed with barley and cheese right afterward. But they thought that the lives of naturally sick and intemperate people were profitable neither to themselves nor to anyone else, that the craft of medicine shouldn't be practiced on them, and that they should not be given treatment, not even if they were richer than Midas.

[60] *Iliad* 4.218–9. In the extant text, Machaon is acting alone.

GLAUCON: The sons of Asclepius were indeed very sophisticated, in your view.

SOCRATES: It is the right view to hold of them. And yet it is on just this point that Pindar and the tragedians are not persuaded by us. They say that Asclepius, even though he was the son of Apollo, was bribed with gold to heal a rich man who was already dying, and that that is why he was struck by lightning. But, in view of what we said before, we won't accept both claims from them. On the contrary, we will say that if Asclepius was the son of a god, he was not a money-grubber; and that if he was a money-grubber, he was not the son of a god.

GLAUCON: That's absolutely right. But what do you say about the following, Socrates? Won't we need to have good doctors in our city? And the best, I take it, will be those who have treated the greatest number of healthy and diseased people. In the same way, the best judges[61] will be those who have associated with people with multifarious natures.

SOCRATES: I certainly agree that we need good ones. But do you know which ones I regard as such?

GLAUCON: I will, if you will tell me.

SOCRATES: Well, I will try. However, you ask about things that are not alike in the same question.

GLAUCON: What do you mean?

SOCRATES: Doctors, it is true, would become cleverest if, in addition to learning the craft of medicine, they associated with the greatest possible number of the most diseased bodies right from childhood,[62] had themselves experienced every illness, and were not, by nature, very healthy. After all, they do not treat a body with a body. If they did, we would not allow their bodies to be or become bad. But it is with a soul that a body is treated, and it is not possible for a soul to treat anything well if it is or has become bad itself.

GLAUCON: That's right.

SOCRATES: But a *judge,* my friend, does rule a soul with a soul. And it is not possible for a soul to be nurtured among bad souls from childhood, to have associated with them, and to have itself indulged in every sort of injustice, so as to be able to draw exact inferences from itself about the injustices of others, as in the case of diseases of the body. On the contrary, it itself must have no experience of, and be uncontaminated by, bad characters while it is young, if as a fine and good soul itself, it is going to make judgments about what is just in a healthy way. That is precisely the reason, indeed, that good people are thought to be naïve when they are young and

[61] See Glossary of Terms s.v. judge.
[62] See 341e4–6.

easily deceived by unjust ones: they do not have models within themselves   b
of the behavior of bad ones.

GLAUCON: Yes, indeed, that is precisely what happens to them.

SOCRATES: That is why a good judge must not be young, but old—a late
learner of what sort of thing injustice is, who has become aware of it, not as   5
something at home in his own soul, but as an alien thing present in other
people's souls. He must have trained himself over many years to discern
how naturally bad it is by using his theoretical knowledge, not his own intimate experience of it.   c

GLAUCON: At any rate, it would seem that *the noblest* judge would be like
that.

SOCRATES: And so is the *good* one you asked about, since the one who has
a good soul is good. The clever and suspicious person, on the other hand,
who has committed many injustices himself and thinks of himself to be
unscrupulous and wise, appears clever when he associates with those like   5
himself, because he is on his guard and looks to the models within himself.
But when he meets with good people who are older, he is seen to be stupid, distrustful at the wrong time, and ignorant of what a healthy character
is, since he has no model of this within himself. But because he meets bad   d
people more often than good ones, he seems more wise than foolish, both
to himself and to them as well.

GLAUCON: That's absolutely true.   5

SOCRATES: Then we must not look for a good judge among people like
that, but among the sort we described earlier. For while a bad person could
never come to know either vice or virtue, a naturally virtuous person,
when educated, will in time acquire knowledge of both virtue and vice.
And it is someone like that, and not a bad person, who becomes a wise
judge in my view.   e

GLAUCON: And I share your view.

SOCRATES: Then won't you establish by law in your city both the craft of
medicine we mentioned and this craft of judging along with it? And these
crafts will care for such of your citizens as have naturally good bodies and   5
souls; but those whose bodies are not like that they will allow to die, while   410a
those whose souls are naturally and incurably bad they will themselves put
to death. Capital punishment?

GLAUCON: Yes, we have seen that that is best both for those who receive
such treatment and for the city.   5

SOCRATES: And so it is clear that *your* young people will be wary of coming to need a judge, since they employ that simple sort of musical training,
which we said engenders temperance.

10 GLAUCON: Of course.

b SOCRATES: And won't a person who is musically trained hunt for a type of physical training by following these same tracks, and catch it, if he chooses? And won't the result be that he will have no need of the craft of medicine, except when absolutely necessary?

GLAUCON: That's my view, at any rate.

5 SOCRATES: And he will undertake even the regimens and exertions of physical training with an eye less to strength than to arousing the spirited part of his nature, unlike all other athletes who use diets and exertions only to gain muscle power.

GLAUCON: That's absolutely right.

10 SOCRATES: Then, doesn't it follow, Glaucon, that those who established musical training and physical training did not establish them with the aim

c that some people attribute to them: namely, to treat the body with the former and the soul with the latter?

GLAUCON: What was it then?

5 SOCRATES: It looks as though they established both chiefly for the sake of the soul.

GLAUCON: How so?

SOCRATES: Have you never noticed the mind-set of those who have a life-long association with physical training but stay away from musical training?

10 Or, again, that of those who do the opposite?

GLAUCON: What do you mean?

d SOCRATES: Savagery and toughness, in the one case; softness and over-cultivation, in the other.

GLAUCON: I have certainly noticed that people who devote themselves exclusively to physical training turn out to be more savage than they should, while those who devote themselves to musical training turn out to

5 be softer than is good for them.

SOCRATES: And surely the savageness derives from the spirited element of their nature, which, if rightly nurtured, becomes courageous, but, if over-strained, is likely to become hard and harsh.

10 GLAUCON: So it seems.

SOCRATES: What about the cultivation? Wouldn't it derive from the philo-

e sophic element of their nature, which, if relaxed too much, becomes softer than it should, but, if well nurtured, is cultivated and orderly?

GLAUCON: That's right.

SOCRATES: Now, we said that our guardians must have both these natures.[63]

GLAUCON: Yes, they must.

SOCRATES: And mustn't the two be harmonized with one another?

GLAUCON: Of course.

SOCRATES: And isn't the soul of the person thus harmonized temperate and courageous?

GLAUCON: Certainly.

SOCRATES: And that of the inharmonious person, cowardly and savage?

GLAUCON: Exactly.

SOCRATES: So when someone gives himself over to musical training and lets the flute pour into his soul through his ears, as through a funnel, those sweet, soft, and plaintive harmonies we mentioned; and when he spends his whole life humming, entranced by song, the first result is that whatever spirit he had, he softens the way he would iron and makes useful, rather than useless and brittle. But when he keeps at it unrelentingly and charms his spirit, the next result is that he melts it and dissolves it completely until he has cut out, so to speak, the very sinews of his soul and makes himself "a feeble warrior."[64]

GLAUCON: Yes, indeed.

SOCRATES: And if he has a spiritless nature to begin with, this happens quickly. But if he has a spirited one, his spirit becomes weak and unstable, quickly inflamed by trivial things and quickly extinguished. As a result, people like that become quick-tempered and prone to anger, instead of spirited, and filled with peevishness.

GLAUCON: Absolutely.

SOCRATES: On the other hand, what about someone who works hard at physical training, eats very well, and never touches musical training or philosophy? At first, because his body is in good strong condition, isn't he full of pride and spirit, and more courageous than he was before?

GLAUCON: He certainly is.

SOCRATES: But what happens if he does nothing but this and never enters into partnership with a Muse? Even if there was some love of learning in his soul, because it never tastes any sort of instruction or investigation, and never participates in any discussion or in any of the rest of musical training,

---

[63] 375c6–8.
[64] *Iliad* 17.588.

5 doesn't it become weak, deaf, and blind, because it never receives any stimulation or nourishment, and its senses are never purified?

GLAUCON: Yes, it does.

SOCRATES: Then a person like that, I take it, becomes an unmusical hater of argument[65] who no longer uses argument to persuade people, but force

e and savagery, behaves like a wild beast, and lives in awkward ignorance without rhythm or grace.

GLAUCON: That's exactly how it is.

SOCRATES: So I, for one, would claim that it is to deal with *these* two things, so it seems, that a god has given two crafts to human beings—musi-

5 cal training and physical training—to deal with the philosophical and spirited elements, and not, except as a byproduct, with the soul and the body; but with these two, so that they might be harmonized with one another by

412a being stretched and relaxed to the appropriate degree.

GLAUCON: Yes, it seems so.

SOCRATES: Then it is the person who makes the best blend of musical and physical training, and applies them in the most perfect proportion to his

5 soul, that we would be most correct to describe as completely trained in music and as most in harmony—far more so than the one who merely attunes his strings to one another.

GLAUCON: Probably so, Socrates.

SOCRATES: Then won't we also need this sort of person in our city, Glau-

10 con, as a permanent overseer, if indeed its constitution is to be preserved?

b GLAUCON: Yes, we will need him most of all.

SOCRATES: Those, then, would be the patterns of their education and upbringing. For why should we enumerate their dances, hunts, chases with hounds, athletic contests, and horse races? After all, it is pretty much clear

5 that they should be consistent with these patterns, and so there should no longer be any difficulty in discovering them.

GLAUCON: No, presumably there should not.

SOCRATES: All right. Now, what is the next question we have to settle? Isn't it which of these same people will rule and which be ruled?

c GLAUCON: Of course.

SOCRATES: Well, isn't it clear that the older ones must rule, whereas the younger ones must be ruled?

GLAUCON: Yes, it is clear.

---

[65] *Misologos:* the opposite of a philosopher, who is a *philologos,* a lover of argument. See *Laches* 188c4–189b7, *Phaedo* 89d1–91b7.

- Rulers come from the guardians
- Remember city built for individuals not groups
- Truth held up here but earlier guardians were taught ignorance

SOCRATES: And that the rulers must be the best among them?   5

GLAUCON: Yes, that's clear, too.

SOCRATES: And aren't the best farmers the ones who are best at farming?

GLAUCON: Yes.

SOCRATES: In the present case, then, since the rulers must be the best of
the guardians, mustn't they be the ones who are best at guarding the city?   10

GLAUCON: Yes.

SOCRATES: Then mustn't they be knowledgeable and capable in this matter, and, in addition, mustn't they care for the city?

GLAUCON: Yes, they must.   d

SOCRATES: But a person would care most for what he loved.

GLAUCON: Necessarily.

SOCRATES: And he would love something most if he thought that the
same things were advantageous both for it and for himself, and if he
thought that when it did well, he would do well, too; and that if it didn't,   5
the opposite would happen.

GLAUCON: That's right.

SOCRATES: Then we must choose from among our guardians the sort of
men who seem on the basis of our observation to be most inclined,
throughout their entire lives, to do what they believe to be advantageous
for the city, and most unwilling to do the opposite.   e

GLAUCON: Yes, they would be suitable for the job.

SOCRATES: I think, then, that we will have to observe them at every stage
of their lives to make sure that they are good guardians of this conviction,   5
and that neither compulsion nor sorcery will cause them to discard or forget their belief that they must do what is best for the city.

GLAUCON: What do you mean by discarding?

SOCRATES: I will tell you. It seems to me that the departure of a belief
from someone's mind is either voluntary or involuntary—voluntary when   10
he learns that the belief is false; involuntary in the case of all true beliefs.   413a

GLAUCON: I understand the voluntary sort, but I still need instruction
about the involuntary.

SOCRATES: What? Don't you know that people are involuntarily deprived
of good things, but voluntarily deprived of bad ones? And isn't being   5
deceived about the truth a bad thing, whereas possessing the truth is a good
one? Or don't you think that to believe things that are is to possess the
truth?

97

GLAUCON: No, you are right. And I do think that people are involuntarily deprived of true beliefs.

SOCRATES: Then isn't it through theft, sorcery, and compulsion that this happens?

GLAUCON: Now I do not understand again.

SOCRATES: I suppose I am making myself as clear as a tragic poet![66] By those who have their beliefs stolen from them, I mean those who are over-persuaded, or those who forget; because argument, in the one case, and time, in the other, takes away their beliefs without their noticing. You understand now, don't you?

GLAUCON: Yes.

SOCRATES: Well then, by those who are compelled, I mean those who are made to change their beliefs by some suffering or pain.

GLAUCON: I understand that, too, and you are right.

SOCRATES: And the victims of sorcery, I think you would agree, are those who change their beliefs because they are charmed by pleasure or terrified by some fear.

GLAUCON: It seems to me that all deception is a form of sorcery.

SOCRATES: Well then, as I was just saying, we must discover which of them are best at safeguarding within themselves the conviction that they must always do what they believe to be best for the city. We must watch them right from childhood, and set them tasks in which a person would be most likely to forget such a conviction or be deceived out of it. And we must select the ones who remember and are difficult to deceive, and reject the others. Do you agree?

GLAUCON: Yes.

SOCRATES: And we must also subject them to labors, pains, and contests, and watch for the same things there.

GLAUCON: That's right.

SOCRATES: Then we must also set up a third kind of competition for sorcery. Like those who lead colts into noise and tumult to see if they are afraid, we must subject our young people to fears and then plunge them once again into pleasures, so as to test them much more thoroughly than people test gold in a fire. And if any of them seems to be immune to sorcery, preserves his composure throughout, is a good guardian of himself and

---

[66] *Tragikôs:* The participles Socrates has used at 413b1–2—*klapentes* (theft), *goê-teuthentes* (sorcery), *biasthentes* (compulsion)—are, like much tragic poetry, both metaphorical and grand.

of the musical training he has received, and proves himself to be rhythmical and harmonious in all these trials—he is the sort of person who would be most useful, both to himself and to the city. And anyone who is tested as a child, youth, and adult, and always emerges as being without impurities, should be established as a ruler of the city as well as a guardian, and should be honored in life and receive the most prized tombs and memorials after his death. But those who do not should be rejected. That is the sort of way, Glaucon, that I think rulers and guardians should be selected and established. Though I have provided only a pattern, not the precise details.

GLAUCON: I also think much the same.

SOCRATES: Then wouldn't it really be most correct to call these people complete guardians—the ones who guard against external enemies and internal friends, so that the former will lack the power, and the latter the desire, to do any evil; but to call the young people to whom we were referring as guardians just now, *auxiliaries* and supporters of the guardians' convictions?

GLAUCON: Yes, I think it would.

SOCRATES: How, then, could we devise one of those useful lies we were talking about a while ago,[67] a single noble lie that would, preferably, persuade even the rulers themselves; but, failing that, the rest of the city?

GLAUCON: What sort of lie?

SOCRATES: Nothing new, but a sort of Phoenician story[68] about something that happened in lots of places prior to this—at least, that is what the poets say and have persuaded people to believe. It has not happened in our day, and I do not know if it could happen. It would take a lot of persuasion to get people to believe it.

GLAUCON: You seem hesitant to tell the story.

SOCRATES: You will realize that I have every reason to hesitate, when I do tell it.

GLAUCON: Out with it. Do not be afraid.

SOCRATES: All right, I will—though I do not know where I will get the audacity or the words to tell it. I will first be trying to persuade the rulers and the soldiers, and then the rest of the city, that the upbringing and the education we gave them were like dreams; that they only imagined they were undergoing all the things that were happening to them, while in fact

---

[67] 382a4–d3.

[68] Apparently a reference, first, to the legend of the Phoenician hero, Cadmus, who sowed the earth with dragon's teeth from which giants grew; and, second, to the *Odyssey,* and the tales Odysseus tells to the Phaeacians.

they themselves were at that time down inside the earth being formed and nurtured, and that their weapons and the rest of their equipment were also manufactured there. When they were entirely completed, the earth, their mother, sent them up, so that now, just as if the land in which they live were their mother and nurse, they must deliberate on its behalf, defend it if anyone attacks it, and regard the other citizens as their earthborn brothers.

GLAUCON: It is not for nothing that you were ashamed to tell your lie earlier.

SOCRATES: No, it was only to be expected. But all the same, you should listen to the rest of the story. "Although all of you in the city are brothers," we will say to them in telling our story, "when the god was forming you, he mixed gold into those of you who are capable of ruling, which is why they are the most honorable; silver into the auxiliaries; and iron and bronze into the farmers and other craftsmen. For the most part, you will produce children like yourselves; but, because you are all related, a silver child will occasionally be born to a golden parent, a golden child to a silver parent, and so on. Therefore, the first and most important command from the god to the rulers is that there is nothing they must guard better or watch more carefully than the mixture of metals in the souls of their off-spring. If an offspring of theirs is born with a mixture of iron or bronze, they must not pity him in any way, but assign him an honor appropriate to his nature and drive him out to join the craftsmen or the farmers. On the other hand, if an offspring of the latter is found to have a mixture of gold or silver, they will honor him and take him up to join the guardians or the auxiliaries. For there is an oracle that the city will be ruined if it ever has an iron or a bronze guardian." So, have you a device that will make them believe this story?

GLAUCON: No, none that would make this group believe it themselves. But I do have one for their sons, for later generations, and for all other people who come after them.

SOCRATES: Well, even that would have a good effect, by making them care more for the city and for each other. For I think I understand what you mean—namely, that all this will go where *tradition* leads. What *we* can do, however, when we have armed our earthborn people, is lead them forth with their rulers at their head. They must go and look for the best place in the city for a military encampment, a site from which they can most easily control anyone in the city who is unwilling to obey the laws, or repel any outside enemy who, like a wolf, attacks the fold. And when they have established their camp and sacrificed to the appropriate gods, they must make their sleeping quarters, mustn't they?

GLAUCON: Yes.

[Margin note: Social mobility— seems to have a rather weird/crude darwinian thinking in terms of best will beget best. But then the noble lie suggests that, if naturally suited for a higher station they should be mobile, but how to derive this "natural" state]

SOCRATES: And mustn't these provide adequate shelter against the storms of winter and the heat of summer?

GLAUCON: Yes, of course. After all, I assume you are talking about their living quarters.

SOCRATES: Yes, but ones for *soldiers,* not moneymakers.

GLAUCON: What difference do you think there is between the two, again?   416a

SOCRATES: I will try to tell you. You see, it is surely the most terrible and most shameful thing in the world for shepherds to rear dogs as auxiliaries to help them with their flocks in such a way that those dogs themselves— because of intemperance, hunger, or some other bad condition—try to do   5 evil to the sheep, acting not like sheepdogs but like wolves.

GLAUCON: Of course, that is terrible.

SOCRATES: So, mustn't we use every safeguard to prevent our auxiliaries   b from treating the citizens like that—because they are stronger—and becoming savage masters rather than gentle allies?

GLAUCON: Yes, we must.

SOCRATES: And wouldn't they have been provided with the greatest safe- guard possible if they have been really well educated?   5

GLAUCON: But surely they have been.

SOCRATES: That is not something that deserves to be asserted so confi- dently, my dear Glaucon. But what does deserve it is what we were saying just now, that they must have the right education, whatever it is, if they are going to have what will do most to make them gentle to one another and   c to the ones they are guarding.

GLAUCON: That's right.

SOCRATES: But anyone with any sense will tell us that, besides this educa- tion, they must be provided with living quarters and other property of the   5 sort that will neither prevent them from being the best guardians nor encourage them to do evil to the other citizens.   d

GLAUCON: And he would be right.

SOCRATES: Consider, then, whether or not they should live and be housed in some such way as this, if they are going to be the sort of men we described. First, none of them should possess any private property that is not wholly necessary. Second, none should have living quarters or store-   5 rooms that are not open for all to enter at will. Such provisions as are required by temperate and courageous men, who are warrior-athletes, they should receive from the other citizens as a salary for their guardianship, the   e amount being fixed so that there is neither a shortfall nor a surplus at the end of the year. They should have common messes to go to, and should live

together like soldiers in a camp. We will tell them that they have gold and
silver of a divine sort in their souls as a permanent gift from the gods, and
have no need of human gold in addition. And we will add that it is impious
for them to defile this divine possession by possessing an admixture of mortal gold, because many impious deeds have been done for the sake of the
currency of the masses, whereas their sort is pure. No, they alone among
the city's population are forbidden by divine law to handle or even touch
gold and silver. They must not be under the same roof as these metals, wear
them as jewelry, or drink from gold or silver goblets. And by behaving in
that way, they would save both themselves and the city. But if they acquire
private land, houses, and money themselves, they will be household managers and farmers instead of guardians—hostile masters of the other citizens, instead of their allies. They will spend their whole lives hating and
being hated, plotting and being plotted against, much more afraid of internal than of external enemies—already rushing, in fact, to the brink of their
own destruction and that of the rest of the city as well. For all these reasons,
let's declare that *that* is how the guardians must be provided with housing
and the rest, and establish it as a law. Or don't you agree?

GLAUCON: Of course I do.

Book 4

How will you defend yourself, Socrates, *he said,* if someone objects that   419a
you are not making these men very happy and, furthermore, that it is their
own fault that they are not? I mean, the city really belongs to them, yet
they derive no good from the city. Others own land, build fine, big houses,   5
acquire furnishings to go along with them, make their own private sacrifices to the gods, entertain guests, and also, of course, possess what you
were talking about just now: gold and silver and all the things that those
who are going to be blessedly happy are thought to require. Instead of that,
he might say, they seem simply to be paid auxiliaries established in the city   10
as a garrison, and nothing else.   420a

SOCRATES: Yes, and what is more, they do it just for upkeep and get no
wages in addition to their upkeep, as other men do. So, they won't even be
able to take a personal trip out of town if they want to, or give presents to
their girlfriends, or spend money in whatever other ways they might wish,   5
as people do who are considered happy. You have omitted these and a host
of other similar facts from your list of charges.

ADEIMANTUS: Well, let them too be added to the charges.

SOCRATES: How will we defend ourselves? Is that what you are asking?   b

ADEIMANTUS: Yes.

SOCRATES: I think we will discover what to say if we follow the same path
as before. You see, our reply will be this: it would not be at all surprising if
these people were happiest just as they are. However, in establishing our   5
city, we are not looking to make any one group in it outstandingly happy,
but to make the whole city so as far as possible. For we thought that we
would be most likely to find justice in such a city, and injustice, by contrast,
in the one that is governed worst. And we thought that by observing both
cities, we would be able to decide the question we have been inquiring into
for so long. At the moment, then, we take ourselves to be forming a happy   c
city—not separating off a few happy people and putting them in it, but
making the city as a whole happy. (We will look at the opposite city soon.)[1]

---

[1] This discussion begins at 445c, but is interrupted and does not resume again until
Book 8.

Suppose, then, that we were painting a statue[2] and someone came up to us and started to criticize us, saying that we had not applied the most beautiful colors to the most beautiful parts of the statue; because the eyes, which are the most beautiful part, had been painted black rather than purple. We would think it reasonable to offer the following defense: "My amazing fellow, you must not expect us to paint the eyes so beautifully that they no longer look like eyes at all, nor the other parts either. On the contrary, you must look to see whether, by dealing with each part appropriately, we are making the whole thing beautiful. Similarly, in the present case, you must not force us to give our guardians the sort of happiness that would make them something other than guardians. You see, we know how to clothe the farmers in purple robes, festoon them with gold jewelry, and tell them to work the land whenever they please. We know we could have our potters recline on couches from right to left in front of the fire,[3] drinking and feasting with their wheel beside them for whenever they have a desire to make pots. And we can make all the others happy in the same way, so that the whole city is happy. But please do not urge us to do this. For if we are persuaded by you, a farmer won't be a farmer, nor a potter a potter, nor will any of the others from which a city is constituted remain true to type. But for most of the others, it matters less: cobblers who become inferior and corrupt, and claim to be what they are not, do nothing terrible to the city. But if the guardians of our laws and city are not really what they seem to be, you may be sure that they will destroy the city utterly and, on the other hand, that they alone have the opportunity to govern it well and make it happy."

Now, if we are making genuine guardians, the sort least likely to do the city evil, and if our critic is making pseudo-farmers—feasters happy at a festival, so to speak, not in a city—he is not talking about a city, but about something else. What we have to consider, then, is whether our aim in establishing the guardians is the greatest possible happiness for them, or whether—since our aim is to see this happiness develop for the whole city—we should compel or persuade the auxiliaries and guardians to ensure that they, and all the others as well, are the best possible craftsmen at their own work; and then, with the whole city developing and being governed well, leave it to nature to provide each group with its share of happiness.

ADEIMANTUS: Yes, I think what you say is right.

SOCRATES: Well, then, will you also think me reasonable if I say something closely related?

[2] Ancient Greek statues were painted and gilded.

[3] At formal drinking parties (*sumposia*), the toastmaster (*sumposiarchos*) sat at the head of the table. The others sat in order of their importance, from his right counterclockwise around the table to his left.

ADEIMANTUS: What exactly? 10

SOCRATES: Take the rest of the craftsmen again, and consider whether these things corrupt them to such an extent that they actually become bad. d

ADEIMANTUS: What things?

SOCRATES: Wealth and poverty.

ADEIMANTUS: What do you mean? 5

SOCRATES: This: do you think that a potter who has become wealthy will still be willing to devote himself to his craft?

ADEIMANTUS: Not at all.

SOCRATES: Won't he become idler and more careless than he was?

ADEIMANTUS: Much more. 10

SOCRATES: Then won't he become a worse potter?

ADEIMANTUS: Yes, much worse.

SOCRATES: And surely if poverty prevents him from providing himself with tools, or any of the other things he needs for his craft, he will make poorer products himself and worse craftsmen of his sons or anyone else he teaches. e

ADEIMANTUS: Of course.

SOCRATES: So poverty and wealth make the products and the practitioners of the crafts worse. 5

ADEIMANTUS: Apparently.

SOCRATES: It seems, then, that we have found other things that our guardians must prevent in every way from slipping into the city undetected.

ADEIMANTUS: What things?

SOCRATES: Wealth and poverty. For the former makes for luxury, idleness, 422a and revolution; and the latter for illiberality, bad work, and revolution as well.

ADEIMANTUS: That's right. But consider this, Socrates: how will our city be able to fight a war if it has acquired no wealth—especially if it has to 5 fight a great and wealthy city?

SOCRATES: Obviously, it will be harder to fight one such city, but easier to fight two. b

ADEIMANTUS: How do you mean?

SOCRATES: First of all, if our city has to fight a city of the sort you mention, won't it be a case of warrior-athletes fighting rich men?

ADEIMANTUS: Yes, it will. 5

SOCRATES: Well, then, Adeimantus, don't you think that a single boxer who has had the best possible training could easily fight two non-boxers who are rich and fat?

ADEIMANTUS: Maybe not at the same time.

c SOCRATES: Not even if he could start to run away and then turn and hit the one who caught up with him first, and could do this often, out in the stifling heat of the sun? Couldn't a man like that overcome even more than two such enemies?

ADEIMANTUS: It certainly would not be surprising if he could.

SOCRATES: Well, don't you think that rich people have more knowledge 5 and experience of boxing than of how to fight a war?

ADEIMANTUS: I do.

SOCRATES: In all likelihood, then, our athletes will easily be able to fight two or three times their number.

ADEIMANTUS: I will have to grant you that, since I think what you say is 10 right.

d SOCRATES: Well, then, what if they sent an envoy to another city with the following true message: "We use no gold or silver. It is against divine law for us to do so, but not for you. So join us in this war and you can have the property of our enemy." Do you think that anyone who heard this message 5 would choose to fight hard, lean hounds, rather than to join the hounds in fighting fat and tender sheep?

ADEIMANTUS: No, I do not. But if the wealth of all other cities were e amassed by a single one, don't you think that would endanger your non-wealthy city?

SOCRATES: You are happily innocent if you think that any city besides the 5 one we are constructing deserves to be called *a* city.

ADEIMANTUS: What should we call them, then?

SOCRATES: We will have to find a "greater" title for the others because each of them is a great many cities, but not *a* city, as they say in the game.[4] They contain two, at any rate, which are at war with one another: the city 423a of the poor and that of the rich. And within each of these, there are a great many more. So if you treat them as one city, you will be making a big mistake. But if you treat them as many and offer one the money, power, and the very inhabitants of another, you will always find many allies and few

---

[4] The reference is obscure; it may be to a saying or proverb, or to a game like checkers called *poleis,* or cities, in which the set of pieces on each side, or perhaps any subset of them, were called cities, while the individual members of the sets were called dogs.

enemies. And as long as your own city is temperately governed in the way we just arranged, it will be the greatest one—not in reputation; I do not mean that; but the greatest in fact—even if it has only a thousand soldiers to defend it. For you won't easily find one city so great among either Greeks or barbarians, though you will find many that are reputed to be many times greater. Or do you disagree?

ADEIMANTUS: No, by Zeus, I do not.

SOCRATES: This, then, would also provide our rulers with the best limit for determining the proper size of the city, and how much land they should mark off for a city that size, letting the rest go.

ADEIMANTUS: What limit is that?

SOCRATES: I think it is this: as long as it is willing to remain *one* city, it may continue to grow, but not beyond that point.

ADEIMANTUS: And it is a good one.

SOCRATES: Then we will also give our guardians this further order, that they are to guard in every possible way against the city's being either small in size or great in reputation, rather than adequate in size and one in number.

ADEIMANTUS: No doubt, *that* will be a trivial instruction for them to follow!

SOCRATES: Here is another that is even more trivial. We mentioned it earlier as well.[5] We said that if an offspring of the guardians is inferior, he must be sent off to join the other citizens, and that if the others have an excellent offspring, he must join the guardians. This was meant to make clear that every other citizen, too, must be assigned to what naturally suits him, with one person assigned to one job so that, practicing his own pursuit, each of them will become not many but one, and the entire city thereby naturally grow to be one, not many.

ADEIMANTUS: Oh, yes, that is a more minor one!

SOCRATES: Really, my good Adeimantus, the orders we are giving them are neither as numerous nor as difficult as one would think. Indeed, they are all insignificant provided, as the saying goes, they safeguard the one great thing—or rather not great but adequate.[6]

ADEIMANTUS: What's that?

SOCRATES: Their education and upbringing. For if a good education makes them moderate men, they will easily discover all this for themselves—and everything else that we are now omitting, such as the possession of women, marriages, and the procreation of children, and how all

[5] 415a–c.
[6] See 423c4.

424a these must be governed as far as possible by the old proverb that friends share everything in common.

ADEIMANTUS: Yes, that would be best.

SOCRATES: And surely once our constitution is well started, it will, as it
5 were, go on growing in a circle. For good education and upbringing, if
they are kept up, produce good natures; and sound natures, which in turn
receive such an education, grow up even better than their predecessors in
every respect—but particularly with respect to their offspring, as in the case
b of all the other animals.

ADEIMANTUS: Yes, probably so.

SOCRATES: To put it briefly, then, what the overseers of our city must
cling to, not allow to become corrupted without their noticing it, and
5 guard against everything, is this: there must be no innovation in musical or
physical training that goes against the established order. On the contrary,
they must guard against that as much as they can. And they should dread to
hear anyone say that "people think most of the song that floats newest from
10 the singer's lips,"[7] in case someone happens to suppose that the poet means
c not new *songs,* but a new *way of singing,* and praises that. We should not
praise such a claim, however, or take it to be what the poet meant. You see,
a change to a new kind of musical training is something to beware of as
wholly dangerous. For one can never change the ways of training people in
5 music without affecting the greatest political laws. That is what Damon
says, and I am convinced he is right.

ADEIMANTUS: You can also count me among those who are convinced.

d SOCRATES: It seems, then, that it is in musical training that the guardhouse
of our guardians must surely be built.

ADEIMANTUS: At any rate, this sort of lawlessness easily inserts itself undetected.

SOCRATES: Yes, because it is supposed to be only part of a game that, as
5 such, can do no harm.

ADEIMANTUS: And it does not do any—except, of course, that when it has
established itself there, it slowly and silently flows over into people's habits
and practices. From these it travels forth with greater vigor into private
10 contracts, and then from private contracts it advances with the utmost inso-
e lence into the laws and constitution, Socrates, until in the end it overthrows
everything public and private.

SOCRATES: Well, is that so?

ADEIMANTUS: I think it is.

---

[7] *Odyssey* 1.351–2. Our text of Homer is slightly different.

SOCRATES: Then, as we were saying at the beginning, our children must take part in games that are more law-abiding right from the start, since, if their games become lawless and the children follow suit, isn't it impossible for them to grow up into excellent and law-abiding men?

ADEIMANTUS: Of course.

SOCRATES: So whenever children play in a good way right from the start and absorb lawfulness from musical training, there is the opposite result: lawfulness follows them in everything and fosters their growth, correcting anything in the city that may have been neglected before.

[handwritten margin note: what about the virtue of respecting laws?]

ADEIMANTUS: That's true.

SOCRATES: And so such people rediscover the seemingly insignificant conventional views their predecessors had destroyed.

ADEIMANTUS: Which sort?

SOCRATES: Those dealing with things like this: the silence appropriate for younger people in the presence of their elders; the giving up of seats for them and standing up in their presence; the care of parents; hairstyles; clothing; shoes; the general appearance of the body; and everything else of that sort. Don't you agree?

ADEIMANTUS: I do.

SOCRATES: To legislate about such things is naïve, in my view, since verbal or written decrees will never make them come about or last.

ADEIMANTUS: How could they?

SOCRATES: At any rate, Adeimantus, it looks as though the start of someone's education determines what follows. Or doesn't like always encourage like?

ADEIMANTUS: It does.

SOCRATES: And the final outcome of education, I imagine we would say, is a single, complete, and fresh product that is either good or the opposite.

ADEIMANTUS: Of course.

SOCRATES: That is why I, for my part, would not try to legislate about such things.

ADEIMANTUS: And with good reason.

SOCRATES: Then, by the gods, what about all that marketplace business, the contracts people make with one another in the marketplace, for example, and contracts with handicraftsmen, and slanders, injuries, indictments, establishing juries, paying or collecting whatever dues are necessary in marketplace and harbors, and, in a word, the entire regulation of marketplace, city, harbor, or what have you—dare we legislate about any of these?

ADEIMANTUS: No, it would not be appropriate to dictate to men who are fine and good. For they will easily find out for themselves whatever needs to be legislated about such things.

SOCRATES: Yes, my friend, provided that a god grants that the laws we have already described are preserved intact.

ADEIMANTUS: If not, they will spend their lives continually enacting and amending such laws in the hope of finding what is best.

SOCRATES: You mean they will live like those sick people who, because they are intemperate, are not willing to abandon their bad way of life.

ADEIMANTUS: That's right.

SOCRATES: Such people really do lead a charming life! Their medical treatment achieves nothing, except to make their illnesses worse and more complex, and they are always hoping that someone will recommend some new drug that will make them healthy.

ADEIMANTUS: Yes, that's exactly what happens to invalids of this sort.

SOCRATES: And isn't it another charming feature of theirs that they think their worst enemy of all is the one who tells them the truth—that until they give up drunkenness, overeating, sexual indulgence, and idleness, then no drug, cautery, or surgery, no charms, amulets, or anything else of that sort will do them any good?

ADEIMANTUS: It is not charming at all. Being harsh to someone who tells the truth is not charming.

SOCRATES: You do not approve of such men, apparently.

ADEIMANTUS: No, by Zeus, I do not.

SOCRATES: Then nor will you approve of an entire city that behaves in the way we were just describing. Or don't you think that such invalids behave in the very same way as cities where the following occurs? Because they are badly governed politically, the citizens are warned not to change the city's whole political system, and the one who does is threatened with the death penalty. But the one who serves these cities most pleasantly, while they remain politically governed in that way; who indulges them, flatters them, anticipates their wishes, and is clever at fulfilling them; isn't he, on that account, honored by them as a good man who is wise in the most important matters?

ADEIMANTUS: Yes, I think their behavior is the same and I do not approve of it at all.

SOCRATES: What about those who are willing and eager to provide treatment for such cities? Don't you approve of their courage and also their lighthearted irresponsibility?

110

ADEIMANTUS: I do indeed—except for those who are actually deluded and suppose themselves to be true men of politics because they are praised by the masses.

SOCRATES: What do you mean? Have you no sympathy for these men? Or do you think it is possible for a man who does not know how to measure anything not to believe that he is four cubits tall[8] when many others, who are similarly ignorant, tell him that he is?

ADEIMANTUS: No, I do not think that.

SOCRATES: Then do not be too hard on them. You see, such people are surely the most charming of all. They pass and amend the sorts of laws we have just been describing, and are always expecting that they will find a way to put a stop to cheating on contracts, and the other evildoings I mentioned just now, not realizing that they are really just cutting off a Hydra's head.[9]

ADEIMANTUS: Yet that is all they are really doing.

SOCRATES: I would have thought, then, that a true lawgiver should not bother with laws or constitutions of this kind, whether in a politically badly governed or in a politically well-governed city—in the one because it is useless and accomplishes nothing; in the other because some of them are discoverable by anyone, while the others follow automatically from the practices already described.

ADEIMANTUS: What remains for us to legislate, then?

SOCRATES: For us, nothing; but for the Delphic Apollo, there remain the greatest, finest, and first of legislations.

ADEIMANTUS: What are they about?

SOCRATES: The establishing of temples and sacrifices, and other forms of service to gods, daimons, and heroes; the burial of the dead, and the services that ensure the favor of those who have gone to the other world. For we, of course, have no knowledge of these things and so, when we are founding a city, we won't take anyone else's advice, if we have any sense, or employ any interpreter except our ancestral one. And in fact, this god—as he delivers his interpretations from his seat at the navel of the earth[10]—is the ancestral guide on these matters for the whole human race.

ADEIMANTUS: Well put. That is what we must do.

[8] Roughly seven feet. A cubit is between seventeen and twenty-two inches long.

[9] The Hydra was a mythical monster. When one of its heads was cut off, two or three new heads grew in its place. Heracles (or Hercules) had to slay the Hydra as one of his labors.

[10] The oracle of Apollo at Delphi was traditionally consulted by all Greeks on religious and other such matters. A stone there marked the supposed center of the earth.

111

SOCRATES: So then, son of Ariston, your city would now seem to be founded. As the next step, look inside it, having got hold of an adequate light somewhere. Look yourself and invite your brother and Polemarchus and the rest of us to help you, to see where justice and injustice might be in it, how they differ from one another, and which of the two must be possessed by the person who is going to be happy, whether that fact is hidden from all gods and humans or not.

And Glaucon said:

That's nonsense! You promised you would look for them yourself, because you said it was impious for you not to defend justice in every way you could.[11]

SOCRATES: You are right to remind me, and I must do what I promised. But you will have to help.

GLAUCON: We will.

SOCRATES: I expect, then, to find justice in the following way. I think our city, if indeed it has been correctly founded, is completely good.

GLAUCON: Yes, it must be.

SOCRATES: Clearly, then, it is wise, courageous, temperate, and just.

GLAUCON: Clearly.

SOCRATES: Then if we find any of these in it, what remains will be what we have not found?

GLAUCON: Of course.

SOCRATES: Therefore, as in the case of any other four things, if we were looking for one of them in something and recognized it first, that would be enough to satisfy us. But if we recognized the other three first, that itself would enable us to recognize what we were looking for, since clearly it could not be anything other than the one that remains.

GLAUCON: That's right.

SOCRATES: So, since there also happen to be four things we are interested in, mustn't we look for them in the same way?

GLAUCON: Clearly.

SOCRATES: Now, the first thing I think I can see clearly in the city is wisdom. And there seems to be something odd about it.

GLAUCON: What?

---

[11] 368b7–c3.

SOCRATES: I think that the city we described is really wise. And that is because it is prudent,[12] isn't it?

GLAUCON: Yes.   5

SOCRATES: And surely it is clear that this very thing, prudence, is some sort of knowledge. I mean, it certainly is not through *ignorance* that people do the prudent thing, but through knowledge.

GLAUCON: Clearly.

SOCRATES: But there are, of course, many multifarious sorts of knowledge in the city.   10

GLAUCON: Certainly.

SOCRATES: So, is it because of the knowledge possessed by the carpenters that the city deserves to be described as wise and prudent?

GLAUCON: Not at all. It is called skilled in carpentry because of that.   c

SOCRATES: So a city shouldn't be called wise because it has the knowledge that deliberates about how wooden things can be best.

GLAUCON: Certainly not.

SOCRATES: What about this, then? What about the knowledge of things made of bronze, or anything else of that sort?   5

GLAUCON: Not anything of that sort either.

SOCRATES: And not the knowledge of how to produce crops from the soil. On the contrary, it is skilled in farming because of that.

GLAUCON: That's my view.   10

SOCRATES: Then is there some knowledge in the city we have just founded, which some of its citizens have, that does not deliberate about some particular thing in the city, but about the city as a whole, and about how its internal relations and its relations with other cities will be the best possible.   d

GLAUCON: There is indeed.

SOCRATES: What is it and who has it?   5

GLAUCON: It is the craft of guardianship. And the ones who possess it are those rulers we just now called complete guardians.[13]

SOCRATES: Because it has this knowledge, then, how do you describe the city?

---

[12] *Euboulos*: In Greek cities, the *boule* was the council that had day-to-day responsibility for public affairs. In kingships it served as an advisory body to the kings; in democratic Athens it served as an advisory body and steering committee for the assembly of all the adult male citizens.

[13] 414b1–6.

10 GLAUCON: As prudent and really wise.

SOCRATES: Now, do you think that there will be more metalworkers in
e the city, or more of these true guardians?

GLAUCON: There will be far more metalworkers.

SOCRATES: Of all those who are called by a certain name because they
have some sort of knowledge, wouldn't the true guardians be the fewest in
5 number?

GLAUCON: By far.

SOCRATES: So, it is because of the smallest group or part of itself, and the
knowledge that is in it—the part that governs and rules—that a city
founded according to nature would be wise as a whole. And this class—
which seems to be, by nature, the smallest—is the one that inherently pos-
429a sesses a share of the knowledge that alone among all the other sorts of
knowledge should be called wisdom.

GLAUCON: That's absolutely true.

5 SOCRATES: So we have found—though I do not know how—this one of
the four and its place in the city, too.

GLAUCON: It seems to me, at least, that it has been well and truly found.

SOCRATES: But surely courage and the part of the city it is in, and because
of which the city is described as courageous, is not very difficult to spot.

10 GLAUCON: How so?

b SOCRATES: Who would describe a city as cowardly or courageous by
looking at anything other than that part which defends it and wages war on
its behalf?

GLAUCON: No one would look at anything else.

5 SOCRATES: Because, I take it, whether the others are courageous or cowardly doesn't make it one or the other.

GLAUCON: No, it doesn't.

SOCRATES: So courage, too, belongs to a city because of a part of itself—
because it has in that part the power to preserve through everything its
belief that the things, and the sorts of things, that should inspire terror are
c the very things, and sorts of things, that the lawgiver declared to be such in
the course of educating it. Or don't you call that courage?

GLAUCON: I do not completely understand what you said. Would you
mind repeating it?

5 SOCRATES: I mean that courage is a sort of preservation.

GLAUCON: What sort of preservation?

SOCRATES: The preservation of the belief, inculcated by the law through education, about what things, and what sorts of things, inspire terror. And by its preservation "through everything," I mean preserving it though pains, pleasures, appetites, and fears and not abandoning it. I will compare it to something I think it resembles, if you like.

d

GLAUCON: I would like that.

SOCRATES: You know, then, that when dyers want to dye wool purple, they first select from wools of many different colors the ones that are naturally white. Then they give them an elaborate preparatory treatment, so that they will accept the color as well as possible. And only at that point do they dip them in the purple dye. When something is dyed in this way, it holds the dye fast, and no amount of washing, whether with or without detergent, can remove the color. But you also know what happens when things are not dyed in this way, when one dyes wools of other colors, or even these white ones, without preparatory treatment.

5

e

5

GLAUCON: I know they look washed out and ridiculous.

SOCRATES: You should take it, then, that we too were trying as hard as we could to do something similar when we selected our soldiers and educated them in musical and physical training. It was contrived, you should suppose, for no purpose other than to ensure that—persuaded by us—they would absorb the laws in the best possible way, just like wool does a dye; that as a result, their beliefs about what things should inspire terror, and about everything else, would hold fast because they had the proper nature and rearing; so fast that the dye could not be washed out even by those detergents that are so terribly effective at scouring—pleasure, which is much more terribly effective at this than any chalestrian[14] or alkali, and pain and fear and appetite, which are worse than any detergent. This power, then, to preserve through everything the correct and law-inculcated belief about what should inspire terror and what should not is what I, at any rate, call courage. And I will assume it is this, unless you object.

430a

5

b

5

GLAUCON: No, I have no objection. For I presume that the sort of correct belief about these same matters that you find in animals and slaves, which is not the result of education and has nothing at all to do with law, is called something other than courage.

SOCRATES: You are absolutely right.

c

GLAUCON: Well, then, I accept your account of courage.

SOCRATES: Yes, do accept it, at any rate, as my account of *political* courage, and you will be right to accept it. If you like, we will discuss that more fully some other time. You see, at the moment, our inquiry is not about courage

[14] Carbonate of soda from Chalestra, a town and lake in Macedonia.

5   but about justice. And for the purpose of that inquiry, I think that what we have said is sufficient.

GLAUCON: You are right.

SOCRATES: Two things, then, remain for us to find in the city: temper-
d   ance[15] and—the goal of our entire inquiry—justice.

GLAUCON: Yes, indeed.

SOCRATES: How could we find justice, then, so we won't have to bother
5   with temperance any further?

GLAUCON: Well I, for my part, do not know of any, nor would I want justice to appear first if that means that we are not going to investigate temperance any further. So if you want to please me, look for it before the
other.

e   SOCRATES: Of course I want to. It would be wrong not to.[16]

GLAUCON: Go ahead and look, then.

SOCRATES: I will. And seen from here, it is more like a sort of concord and
harmony than the previous ones.

5   GLAUCON: How so?

SOCRATES: Temperance is surely a sort of order, the mastery of certain
sorts of pleasures and appetites. People indicate as much when they use the
term "self-mastery"—though I do not know in what way. This and other
similar things are like tracks that temperance has left. Isn't that so?

10   GLAUCON: Absolutely.

SOCRATES: Isn't the term "self-mastery" ridiculous, though? For, of
course, the one who is master of himself is also the one who is weaker, and
the one who is weaker is also the one who masters. After all, the same per-
431a   son is referred to in all these descriptions.

GLAUCON: Of course.

SOCRATES: It seems to me, however, that what this term is trying to indicate is that within the same person's soul, there is a better thing and a worse
5   one. Whenever the naturally better one masters the worse, this is called
being master of oneself. At any rate, it is praised. But whenever, as a result
of bad upbringing or associating with bad people, the smaller and better
one is mastered by the inferior majority, this is blamed as a disgraceful thing
b   and is called being weaker than oneself, or being intemperate.

GLAUCON: Yes, that seems plausible.

---

[15] See Glossary of Terms s.v. temperance.
[16] See 427d8–e4.

SOCRATES: Now, then, take a look at our new city and you will find one of these conditions present in it. For you will say that it is rightly described as master of itself, if indeed anything in which the better rules the worse is to be described as temperate and master of itself.

GLAUCON: I am looking, and what you say is true.

SOCRATES: Furthermore, pleasures, pains, and appetites that are numerous and multifarious are things one would especially find in children, women, household slaves, and in the so-called free members of the masses—that is, the inferior people.

GLAUCON: Yes.

SOCRATES: But the pleasures, pains, and appetites that are simple and moderate, the ones that are led by rational calculation with the aid of understanding and correct belief, you would find in those few people who are born with the best natures and receive the best education.

GLAUCON: That's true.

SOCRATES: Don't you see, then, that this too is present in your city, and that the appetites of the masses—the inferior people—are mastered there by the wisdom and appetites of the few—the best people?

GLAUCON: I do.

SOCRATES: So, if any city is said to be master of its pleasures and appetites and of itself, it is this one.

GLAUCON: Absolutely.

SOCRATES: So isn't it also temperate because of all this?

GLAUCON: Yes, indeed.

SOCRATES: And moreover, if there is any city in which rulers and subjects share the same belief about who should rule, it is this one. Or don't you agree?

GLAUCON: Yes, I certainly do.

SOCRATES: And in which of them do you say temperance is located when they are in this condition? In the rulers or the subjects?

GLAUCON: In both, I suppose.

SOCRATES: Do you see, then, that the hunch we had just now—that temperance is like a sort of harmony—was quite plausible?

GLAUCON: Why is that?

SOCRATES: Because its operation is unlike that of courage and wisdom, each of which resides in one part and makes the city either courageous or wise. Temperance does not work like that, but has literally been stretched

117

throughout the whole, making the weakest, the strongest, and those in between all sing the same song in unison—whether in wisdom, if you like, or in physical strength, if you prefer; or, for that matter, in numbers, wealth, or anything else. Hence we would be absolutely right to say that this unanimity is temperance—this concord between the naturally worse and the naturally better, about which of the two should rule both in the city and in each individual.

GLAUCON: I agree completely.

SOCRATES: All right. We have now spotted three kinds of virtue in our city. What kind remains, then, that would give the city yet another share of virtue? For it is clear that what remains is justice.

GLAUCON: It is clear.

SOCRATES: So then, Glaucon, we must now station ourselves like hunters surrounding a wood and concentrate our minds, so that justice does not escape us and vanish into obscurity. For it is clear that it is around here somewhere. Keep your eyes peeled and do your best to catch sight of it, and if you happen to see it before I do, show it to me.

GLAUCON: I wish I could help. But it is rather the case that if you use me as a follower who can see only what you point out to him, you will be using me in a more reasonable way.

SOCRATES: Pray for success, then, and follow me.

GLAUCON: I will. You have only to lead.

SOCRATES: And it truly seems to be an impenetrable place and full of shadows. It is dark, at any rate, and difficult to search through. But all the same, we must go on.

GLAUCON: Yes, we must.

And then I caught sight of something and shouted:

SOCRATES: Ah ha![17] Glaucon, it looks as though there is a track here, and I do not think our quarry will altogether escape us.

GLAUCON: That's good news.

SOCRATES: Oh dear, what a stupid condition in which to find ourselves!

GLAUCON: How so?

SOCRATES: It seems, blessed though you are, that the thing has been rolling around at our feet from the very beginning, and yet, like ridiculous fools, we could not see it. For just as people who are holding something in their hands sometimes search for the very thing they are holding, we did

---

[17] *Iou iou:* usually a cry of woe in tragedy, not (like *iô iô*) a cry of joy.

not look in the right direction but gazed off into the distance, and perhaps   e
that is the very reason we did not notice it.

GLAUCON: What do you mean?

SOCRATES: This: I think we have been talking and hearing about it all this   5
time without understanding ourselves, or realizing that we were, in a way,
talking about it.

GLAUCON: That was a long prelude! Now I want to hear what you mean!

SOCRATES: Listen, then, and see whether there is anything in what I say.
You see, what we laid down at the beginning when we were founding our   433a
city, about what should be done throughout it—that, I think, or some form
of that, is justice. And surely what we laid down and often repeated, if you
remember, is that each person must practice one of the pursuits in the city,
the one for which he is naturally best suited.   5

GLAUCON: Yes, we did say that.

SOCRATES: Moreover, we have heard many people say, and have often said
ourselves, that justice is doing one's own work and not meddling with what
is not one's own.   b

GLAUCON: Yes, we have.

SOCRATES: This, then, my friend, provided it is taken in a certain way,
would seem to be justice—this doing one's own work. And do you know
what I take as evidence of that?

GLAUCON: No, tell me.   5

SOCRATES: After our consideration of temperance, courage, and wisdom,
I think that what remains in the city is the power that makes it possible for
all of these to arise in it, and that preserves them when they have arisen for
as long as it remains there itself. And we did say that justice would be what   c
remained when we had found the other three.[18]

GLAUCON: Yes, that must be so.

SOCRATES: Yet, surely, if we had to decide which of these will most contribute to making our city good by being present in it, it would be difficult   5
to decide. Is it the agreement in belief between the rulers and the subjects?
The preservation among the soldiers of the law-inculcated belief about
what should inspire terror and what should not? The wisdom and guardianship of the rulers? Or is what most contributes to making it good the fact   d
that every child, woman, slave, free person, craftsman, ruler, and subject
each does his own work and does not meddle with what is not?   5

GLAUCON: Of course it's a difficult decision.

[18] 428a2–9.

contra early to defn of justice?

exchange blw classes does the most harm

SOCRATES: It seems, then, that this power—which consists in everyone's doing his own work—rivals wisdom, temperance, and courage in its contribution to the city's virtue.

10 GLAUCON: It certainly does.

SOCRATES: And wouldn't you say that justice is certainly what rivals them
e in contributing to the city's virtue?

GLAUCON: Absolutely.

SOCRATES: Look at it this way, too, if you want to be convinced. Won't you assign to the rulers the job of judging lawsuits in the city?

5 GLAUCON: Of course.

SOCRATES: And will they have any aim in judging other than this: that no citizen should have what is another's or be deprived of what is his own?

GLAUCON: No, they will have none but that.

10 SOCRATES: Because that is just?

GLAUCON: Yes.

SOCRATES: So from that point of view, too, having and doing of one's
434a own, of what belongs to one, would be agreed to be justice.

GLAUCON: That's right.

SOCRATES: Now, see whether you agree with me about this: if a carpenter attempts to do the work of a shoemaker, or a shoemaker that of a carpenter, or they exchange their tools or honors with one another, or if the same
5 person tries to do both jobs, and all other such exchanges are made, do you think that does any great harm to the city?

GLAUCON: Not really.

SOCRATES: But I imagine that when someone who is, by nature, a craftsman or some other sort of moneymaker is puffed up by wealth, or by hav-
b ing a majority of votes, or by his own strength, or by some other such thing, and attempts to enter the class of soldiers; or when one of the soldiers who is unworthy to do so tries to enter that of judge and guardian, and these exchange their tools and honors; or when the same person tries
5 to do all these things at once, then I imagine you will agree that these exchanges and this meddling destroy the city.

GLAUCON: Absolutely.

SOCRATES: So, meddling and exchange among these three classes is the
c greatest harm that can happen to the city and would rightly be called the worst evil one could do to it.

GLAUCON: Exactly.

SOCRATES: And wouldn't you say that the worst evil one could do to one's own city is injustice?

GLAUCON: Of course.

SOCRATES: That, then, is what injustice is. But let's put it in reverse: the opposite of this—when the moneymaking, auxiliary, and guardian class each do their own work in the city—is justice, isn't it, and makes the city just?

GLAUCON: That's exactly what I think too.

SOCRATES: Let's not state it as fixedly established just yet. But if this kind of thing is agreed by us to be justice in the case of individual human beings as well, then we can assent to it. For what else will there be for us to say? But if it is not, we will have to look for something else. For the moment, however, let's complete the inquiry in which we supposed that if we first tried to observe justice in some larger thing that possessed it, that would make it easier to see what it is like in an individual human being.[19] We agreed that this larger thing is a city, and so we founded the best city we could, knowing well that justice would of course be present in one that was good. So, let's apply what has come to light for us there to an individual, and if it is confirmed, all will be well. But if something different is found in the case of the individual, we will go back to the city and test it there. And perhaps by examining them side by side and rubbing them together like fire-sticks, we can make justice blaze forth and, once it has come to light, confirm it in our own case.

GLAUCON: Well, the road you describe is the right one, and we should follow it.

SOCRATES: Well, then, if you call a bigger thing and a smaller thing by the same name, are they unalike in the respect in which they are called the same, or alike?

GLAUCON: Alike.

SOCRATES: So a just man won't differ at all from a just city with respect to the form of justice but will be like it.

GLAUCON: Yes, he will be like it.

SOCRATES: But now, the city, at any rate, was thought to be just because each of the three natural classes within it did its own job; and to be temperate, courageous, and wise, in addition, because of certain other conditions or states of these same classes.

GLAUCON: That's true.

[19] 368c7–369a3.

SOCRATES: Then, my friend, we would expect an individual to have these same kinds of things in his soul, and to be correctly called by the same names as the city because the same conditions are present in them both.

c

GLAUCON: Inevitably.

SOCRATES: Well, you amazing fellow, here is another trivial investigation[20] we have stumbled into: does the soul have these three kinds of things in it or not?

5

GLAUCON: It does not look at all trivial to me. Perhaps, Socrates, there is some truth in the old saying that everything beautiful is difficult.

SOCRATES: Apparently so. In fact, you should be well aware, Glaucon, that it is my belief we will never ever grasp this matter precisely by methods of the sort we are now using in our discussions. However, there is in fact another longer and more time-consuming road that does lead there.[21] But perhaps we can manage to come up to the standard of our previous statements and inquiries.

d

5

GLAUCON: Shouldn't we be content with that? It would be enough for me, at least for now.

SOCRATES: Well, then, it will be quite satisfactory for me, too.

GLAUCON: Then do not weary, but go on with the inquiry.

SOCRATES: Well, isn't it absolutely necessary for us to agree to this much: that the very same kinds of things and conditions exist in each one of us as exist in the city? After all, where else would they come from? You see, it would be ridiculous for anyone to think that spiritedness did not come to be in cities from the private individuals who are reputed to have this quality, such as the Thracians, Scythians, and others who live to the north of us; or that the same is not true of the love of learning, which is mostly associated with our part of the world; or of the love of money, which is said to be found not least among the Phoenicians and Egyptians.

e

5

436a

GLAUCON: It certainly would.

SOCRATES: We may take that as being so, then, and it was not at all difficult to discover.

5

GLAUCON: No, it certainly was not.

SOCRATES: But this, now, *is* difficult. Do we do each of them with the same thing or, since there are three, do we do one with one and another with another: that is to say, do we learn with one, feel anger with another, and with yet a third have an appetite for the pleasures of food, sex, and

10

---

[20] See 423c5–e2.

[21] See 504b1–c4 for an explanation.

those closely akin to them? Or do we do each of them with the whole of our soul, once we feel the impulse? *That* is what is difficult to determine in a way that is up to the standards of our argument.

GLAUCON: I think so, too.

SOCRATES: Well, then, let's try in this way to determine whether they are the same as one another or different.

GLAUCON: What way?

SOCRATES: It is clear that the same thing cannot do or undergo opposite things; not, at any rate, in the same respect, in relation to the same thing, at the same time. So, if we ever find that happening here, we will know that we are not dealing with one and the same thing, but with many.

GLAUCON: All right.

SOCRATES: Consider, then, what I am about to say.

GLAUCON: Say it.

SOCRATES: Is it possible for the same thing, at the same time, and in the same respect, to be standing still and moving?

GLAUCON: Not at all.

SOCRATES: Let's come to a more precise agreement, in order to avoid disputes later on. You see, if anyone said of a person who is standing still but moving his hands and head, that the same thing is moving and standing still at the same time, we would not consider, I imagine, that he should say that; but rather that in one respect the person is standing still, while in another he is moving. Isn't that so?

GLAUCON: It is.

SOCRATES: Then, if the one who said this became still more charming and made the sophisticated point that spinning tops, at any rate, stand still as a whole at the same time as they are also in motion, when, with the peg fixed in the same place, they revolve, or that the same holds of anything else that moves in a circle on the same spot—we would not agree, on the grounds that in such situations it is not in the same respects that these objects are both moving and standing still. On the contrary, we would say that these objects have both a straight axis and a circumference in them, and that with respect to the straight axis they stand still—since they do not wobble to either side—whereas with respect to the circumference they move in a circle. But if their straight axis wobbles to the left or right or front or back at the same time as they are spinning, we will say that they are not standing still in any way.

GLAUCON: And we would be right.

123

SOCRATES: No such objection will disturb us, then, or make us any more likely to believe that the same thing can—at the same time, in the same respect, and in relation to the same thing—undergo, be, or do opposite 437a things.

GLAUCON: They won't have that effect on me at least.

SOCRATES: All the same, in order to avoid going through all these objec-
5 tions one by one and taking a long time to prove them all untrue, let's hypothesize that what we have said is correct and carry on—with the understanding that if it should ever be shown to be incorrect, all the conse-quences we have drawn from it will be invalidated.

10 GLAUCON: Yes, that's what we should do.

b SOCRATES: Now, wouldn't you consider assent and dissent, wanting to have something and rejecting it, taking something and pushing it way, as all being pairs of mutual opposites—whether of opposite doings or of opposite
5 undergoings does not matter?

GLAUCON: Yes, they are pairs of opposites.

SOCRATES: What about thirst, hunger, and the appetites as a whole, and also wishing and willing? Would you include all of them somewhere among
c the kinds of things we just mentioned? For example, wouldn't you say that the soul of someone who has an appetite wants the thing for which it has an appetite, and draws toward itself what it wishes to have; and, in addition, that insofar as his soul wishes something to be given to it, it nods assent to
5 itself as if in answer to a question, and strives toward its attainment?

GLAUCON: I would.

SOCRATES: What about not-willing, not-wishing, and not-having an appetite? Wouldn't we include them among the very opposites, cases in which the soul pushes and drives things away from itself?

d GLAUCON: Of course.

SOCRATES: Since that is so, won't we say that there is a kind consisting of appetites, and that the most conspicuous examples of them are what we call hunger and thirst?

5 GLAUCON: We will.

SOCRATES: Isn't the one for food, the other for drink?

GLAUCON: Yes.

SOCRATES: Now, insofar as it is thirst, is it an appetite in the soul for more than what we say it is for? I mean, is thirst a thirst for hot drink or cold, or
10 much drink or little, or—in a word—for drink of a certain sort? Or isn't it rather that if heat is present in addition to thirst, it causes the appetite to be
e for something cold as well, whereas the addition of cold makes it an appetite

for something hot? And if there is much thirst, because of the presence of muchness, won't it cause the desire to be for much drink, and where little for little? But thirst itself will never be for anything other than the very thing that it is in its nature to be an appetite for: namely, drink itself; and, similarly, hunger is for food.

GLAUCON: That's the way it is. By itself, at any rate, each appetite is for its natural object only, while an appetite for an object of this or that sort depends on additions.

SOCRATES: No one should catch us unprepared, then, or disturb us by claiming that no one has an appetite for drink but rather for good drink, nor for food but rather for good food, since everyone's appetite is for good things. And so, if thirst is an appetite, it will be an appetite for good drink or good whatever, and similarly for the other appetites.

GLAUCON: Yes, there might seem to be something in that objection.

SOCRATES: But surely, whenever things are related to something, those that are of a particular sort are related to a particular sort of thing, as it seems to me, whereas those that are just themselves are related only to a thing that is just itself.

GLAUCON: I do not understand.

SOCRATES: Don't you understand that the greater is such as to be greater than something?

GLAUCON: Of course.

SOCRATES: Than the less?

GLAUCON: Yes.

SOCRATES: And the much greater than the much less. Isn't that so?

GLAUCON: Yes.

SOCRATES: And the once greater than the once less? And the going-to-be greater than the going-to-be less?

GLAUCON: Certainly.

SOCRATES: And doesn't the same hold of the more in relation to the fewer, the double to the half, and everything of that sort; and also of heavier to lighter and faster to slower; and, in addition, of hot to cold, and all other similar things?

GLAUCON: Yes, indeed.

SOCRATES: What about the various kinds of knowledge? Aren't they the same way? Knowledge itself is of what can be learned itself (or of whatever we should take the object of knowledge to be), whereas a particular knowledge of a particular sort is of a particular thing of a particular sort. I mean

125

something like this: when knowledge of building houses was developed, it

d differed from the other kinds of knowledge, and so was called knowledge of building. Isn't that so?

GLAUCON: Of course.

SOCRATES: And wasn't that because it was a different sort of knowledge

5 from all the others?

GLAUCON: Yes.

SOCRATES: And wasn't it because it was of a particular sort of thing that it itself became a particular sort of knowledge? And isn't this true of all the crafts and sciences?

10 GLAUCON: It is.

SOCRATES: Well, then, you should think of that as what I wanted to get across before—if you understand it now—when I said that whenever things are related to something, those that are just themselves are related to things that are just themselves, whereas those of a particular sort are related to things of a particular sort. And I do not at all mean that the sorts in question

e have to be the same for them both—that the knowledge of health and disease is healthy and diseased, or that that of good and bad things is good and bad. On the contrary, I mean that when knowledge occurred that was not just knowledge of the thing itself that knowledge is of, but of something of

5 a particular sort, which in this case was health and disease, the result was that it itself became a particular sort of knowledge; and this caused it to be no longer called simply knowledge but, with the addition of the particular sort, medical knowledge.

GLAUCON: I understand and I think you are right.

SOCRATES: Returning to thirst, then, wouldn't you include it among the

439a things that are related to something just by being what they are? Surely thirst is related to. . . .

GLAUCON: I would. It is related to drink.

SOCRATES: So a particular sort of thirst is for a particular sort of drink.

5 Thirst itself, however, is not for much or little, good or bad, or, in a word, for drink of a particular sort; rather, thirst itself is, by nature, just for drink itself. Right?

GLAUCON: Absolutely.

SOCRATES: Hence the soul of the thirsty person, insofar as it is simply thirsty, does not want anything else except to drink, and this is what it

b longs for and is impelled to do.

GLAUCON: Clearly.

SOCRATES: Then if anything in it draws it back when it is thirsty, wouldn't it be something different from what thirsts and, like a beast, drives it to drink? For surely, we say, the same thing, in the same respect of itself, in relation to the same thing, and at the same time, cannot do opposite things.

GLAUCON: No, it cannot.

SOCRATES: In the same way, I imagine, it is not right to say of the archer that his hands at the same time push the bow away and draw it toward him. On the contrary, we should say that one hand pushes it away, while the other draws it toward him.

GLAUCON: Absolutely.

SOCRATES: Now, we would say, wouldn't we, that some people are thirsty sometimes, yet unwilling to drink?

GLAUCON: Many people often are.

SOCRATES: What, then, should one say about them? Isn't it that there is an element in their soul urging them to drink, and also one stopping them— something different that masters the one doing the urging?

GLAUCON: I certainly think so.

SOCRATES: Doesn't the element doing the stopping in such cases arise— when it does arise—from rational calculation, while the things that drive and drag are present because of feelings and diseases?

GLAUCON: Apparently so.

SOCRATES: It would not be unreasonable for us to claim, then, that there are two elements, different from one another; and to call the element in the soul with which it calculates, the rationally calculating element; and the one with which it feels passion, hungers, thirsts, and is stirred by other appetites, the irrational and appetitive element, friend to certain ways of being filled and certain pleasures.

GLAUCON: No, it would not. Indeed, it would be a very natural thing for us to do.

SOCRATES: Let's assume, then, that we have distinguished these two kinds of elements in the soul. Now, is the spirited element—the one with which we feel anger—a third kind of thing, or is it the same in nature as one of these others?

GLAUCON: As the appetitive element, perhaps.

SOCRATES: But I once heard a story and I believe it. Leontius, the son of Aglaeon, was going up from the Piraeus along the outside of the North Wall when he saw some corpses with the public executioner nearby. He had an appetitive desire to look at them, but at the same time he was disgusted and

10
440a turned himself away. For a while he struggled and put his hand over his eyes, but finally, mastered by his appetite, he opened his eyes wide and rushed toward the corpses, saying: "Look for yourselves, you evil wretches; take your fill of the beautiful sight."[22]

GLAUCON: I have also heard that story myself.

5 SOCRATES: Yet, surely, the story suggests that anger sometimes makes war against the appetites as one thing against another.

GLAUCON: Yes, it does suggest that.

SOCRATES: And don't we often notice on other occasions that when
b appetite forces someone contrary to his rational calculation, he reproaches himself and feels anger at the thing in him that is doing the forcing; and just as if there were two warring factions, such a person's spirit becomes the ally of his reason? But spirit partnering the appetites to do what reason has
5 decided should not be done—I do not imagine you would say that you had ever seen that, either in yourself or in anyone else.

GLAUCON: No, by Zeus, I would not.

SOCRATES: And what about when a person thinks he is doing some injus-
c tice? Isn't it true that the nobler he is, the less capable he is of feeling angry if he suffers hunger, cold, or the like at the hands of someone whom he believes to be inflicting this on him justly; and won't his spirit, as I say,
5 refuse to be aroused?

GLAUCON: It is true.

SOCRATES: But what about when a person believes he is being unjustly treated? Doesn't his spirit boil then, and grow harsh and fight as an ally of what he holds to be just? And even if it suffers hunger, cold, and every imposition of that sort, doesn't it stand firm and win out over them, not
d ceasing its noble efforts until it achieves its purpose, or dies, or, like a dog being called to heel by a shepherd, is called back by the reason alongside it and becomes gentle?

GLAUCON: Your simile is perfect. And, in fact, we did put the auxiliaries
5 in our city to be like obedient sheepdogs for the city's shepherdlike rulers.

SOCRATES: You have understood what I was trying to say very well. But have you also noticed something else about it?

e GLAUCON: What?

[22] A fragment of the comedy *Kapêlides* by Theopompus (410–370 BCE) tells us that a certain Leontinus (emended to Leontius because of Plato's reference here) was known for his love of boys as pale as corpses. So his desire is probably sexual in origin, and for that reason appetitive. The North and South Walls enclosed an area connecting Athens to Piraeus.

128

SOCRATES: That it is the opposite of what we recently thought about the kind of thing spirit is. You see, then we thought of it as something appetitive.[23] But now, far from saying that, we say that in the faction that takes place in the soul, it is far more likely to take arms on the side of the rationally calculating element.

GLAUCON: Absolutely.

SOCRATES: Is it also different from this, then, or is it some kind of rationally calculating element, so that there are not three kinds of things in the soul, but two—the rationally calculating element and the appetitive one? Or rather, just as there were three classes in the city that held it together— the moneymaking, the auxiliary, and the deliberative—is there also this third element in the soul, the spirited kind, which is the natural auxiliary of the rationally calculating element, if it has not been corrupted by bad upbringing?

GLAUCON: There must be a third.

SOCRATES: Yes, provided, at any rate, that it can be shown to be as distinct from the rationally calculating element as it was shown to be from the appetitive one.

GLAUCON: But it is not difficult to show that. After all, one can see it even in small children: they are full of spirit right from birth, but as for rational calculation, some of them seem to me never to possess it, while the masses do so quite late.

SOCRATES: Yes, by Zeus, you put that really well. Besides, one can see in animals that what you say is true. But, in addition to that, our earlier quotation from Homer also bears it out: "He struck his chest and spoke to his heart."[24] You see, in it Homer clearly presents what has calculated about better and worse, rebuking what is irrationally angry as though it were something different.

GLAUCON: That's exactly right.

SOCRATES: Well, we have had a difficult swim through all that, and we are pretty much agreed that the same classes as are in the city are in the soul of each individual, and an equal number of them too.

GLAUCON: That's true.

SOCRATES: Then doesn't it already necessarily follow that the private individual is wise in the same way and because of the same element as is the city?

GLAUCON: Of course.

[23] 439e5.

[24] *Odyssey* 20.17. See 390d.

SOCRATES: And that the city is courageous in the same way and because
of the same element as is the private individual? And that in everything else
that pertains to virtue, both are alike?

GLAUCON: Necessarily.

SOCRATES: And so, Glaucon, I take it we will also say that a man is just in
exactly the same way as is a city.

GLAUCON: That too follows with absolute necessity.

SOCRATES: But we surely have not forgotten that the city was just because
each of the three classes in it does its own work.

GLAUCON: I do not think we have.

SOCRATES: We should also bear in mind, then, that in the case of each one
of us as well, the one in whom each of the elements does its own job will
be just and do his own job.

GLAUCON: Certainly.

SOCRATES: Then isn't it appropriate for the rationally calculating element
to rule, since it is really wise and exercises foresight on behalf of the whole
soul; and for the spirited kind to obey it and be its ally?

GLAUCON: Of course.

SOCRATES: Now, as we were saying, isn't it a mixture of musical and physical training that makes these elements concordant, tightening and nurturing the first with fine words and learning, while relaxing, soothing, and
making gentle the second by means of harmony and rhythm?

GLAUCON: Yes, exactly.

SOCRATES: And these two elements, having been trained in this way and
having truly learned their own jobs and been educated, will be put in
charge of the appetitive element—the largest one in each person's soul and,
by nature, the most insatiable for money. They will watch over it to see that
it does not get so filled with the so-called pleasures of the body that it
becomes big and strong, and no longer does its own job but attempts to
enslave and rule over the classes it is not fitted to rule, thereby overturning
the whole life of anyone in whom it occurs.

GLAUCON: Yes, indeed.

SOCRATES: And wouldn't these two elements also do the finest job of
guarding the whole soul and body against external enemies—the one by
deliberating, the other by fighting, following the ruler, and using its courage to carry out the things on which the former had decided?

GLAUCON: Yes, they would.

SOCRATES: I imagine, then, that we call each individual courageous because of the latter part—that is, when the part of him that is spirited in kind preserves through pains and pleasures the pronouncements of reason[25] about what should inspire terror and what should not.

GLAUCON: That's right.

SOCRATES: But we call him wise, surely, because of the small part that rules in him, makes those pronouncements, and has within it the knowledge of what is advantageous—both for each part and for the whole, the community composed of all three.

GLAUCON: Yes, indeed.

SOCRATES: What about temperance? Isn't he temperate because of the friendly and concordant relations between these same things: namely, when both the ruler and its two subjects share the belief that the rationally calculating element should rule, and do not engage in faction against it?

GLAUCON: Temperance in a city and in a private individual is certainly nothing other than that.

SOCRATES: But surely, now, a person will be just because of what we have so often described and in the way we have so often described.

GLAUCON: Necessarily.

SOCRATES: Well, then, has our justice become in any way blurred? Does it look like anything other than the very thing we found in the city?

GLAUCON: It doesn't seem so to me, at least.

SOCRATES: We could make perfectly sure, if there is still anything in our souls that disputes this, by applying everyday tests to it.

GLAUCON: Which ones?

SOCRATES: For example, if we had to come to an agreement about whether a man similar in nature and training to this city of ours had embezzled gold or silver he had accepted for deposit, who do you think would consider him more likely to have done so rather than men of a different sort?

GLAUCON: No one.

SOCRATES: And would he have anything to do with temple robberies,[26] thefts, or betrayals of friends in private life or of cities in public life?

GLAUCON: No, nothing.

SOCRATES: And he would be in no way untrustworthy when it came to promises or other agreements.

---

[25] Reading τοῦ λόγου with Adam.

[26] See 344b3 note.

GLAUCON: How could he be?

SOCRATES: And surely adultery, disrespect for parents, and neglect of the gods would be more characteristic of any other sort of person than of this one.

GLAUCON: Of any other sort, indeed.

SOCRATES: And isn't the reason for all this the fact that each element within him does its own job where ruling and being ruled are concerned?

GLAUCON: Yes, that and nothing else.

SOCRATES: Are you still looking for justice to be something besides this power that produces men and cities of the sort we have described?

GLAUCON: No, by Zeus, I am not.

SOCRATES: The dream we had has been completely fulfilled, then—I mean the suspicion we expressed that right from the beginning, when we were founding the city, we had, with the help of some god, chanced to hit upon the origin and pattern of justice.[27]

GLAUCON: Absolutely.

SOCRATES: So, Glaucon, it really was—which is why it was so helpful—a sort of image of justice, this principle that it is right for someone who is, by nature, a shoemaker to practice shoemaking and nothing else, for a carpenter to practice carpentry, and the same for all the others.

GLAUCON: Apparently so.

SOCRATES: And in truth, justice is, it seems, something of this sort. Yet it is not concerned with someone's doing his own job on the outside. On the contrary, it is concerned with what is inside; with himself, really, and the things that are his own. It means that he does not allow the elements in him each to do the job of some other, or the three sorts of elements in his soul to meddle with one another. Instead, he regulates well what is really his own, rules himself, puts himself in order, becomes his own friend, and harmonizes the three elements together, just as if they were literally the three defining notes of an octave—lowest, highest, and middle—as well as any others that may be in between. He binds together all of these and, from having been many, becomes entirely one, temperate and harmonious. Then and only then should he turn to action, whether it is to do something concerning the acquisition of wealth or concerning the care of his body, or even something political, or concerning private contracts. In all these areas, he considers and calls just and fine the action that preserves this inner harmony and helps achieve it,[28] and wisdom the *knowledge* that oversees such

[27] 432d2–433b4.
[28] Cf. 338e1–339a4.

action; and he considers and calls unjust any action that destroys this harmony, and ignorance the *belief* that oversees it.[29]   444a

GLAUCON: That's absolutely true, Socrates.

SOCRATES: Well, then, if we claim to have found the just man, the just
city, and what justice really is in them, we won't, I imagine, be thought to   5
be telling a complete lie.

GLAUCON: No, by Zeus, we certainly won't.

SOCRATES: Shall we claim it, then?

GLAUCON: Yes, let's.

SOCRATES: So be it, then. I take it we must look for injustice next.   10

GLAUCON: Clearly.

SOCRATES: Mustn't it, in turn, be a kind of faction among those three—   b
their meddling and interfering with one another's jobs; the rebellion of a
part of the soul against the whole in order to rule in it inappropriately, since
its nature suits it to be a slave of the ruling class.[30] We will say something   5
like that, I imagine, and that their disorder and wandering is injustice,
licentiousness, cowardice, ignorance, and, in a word, the whole of vice.

GLAUCON: That is precisely what they are.

SOCRATES: Doing unjust actions, then, and being unjust; and, the oppo-   c
site, doing just ones—they all surely become clear at once, don't they, provided that both injustice and justice are also clear?

GLAUCON: What do you mean?

SOCRATES: That they do not differ in any way from healthy actions and   5
unhealthy ones, that what the latter are in the body, they are in the soul.

GLAUCON: In what respect?

SOCRATES: Surely, healthy actions engender health, unhealthy ones disease.

GLAUCON: Yes.

SOCRATES: Well, doesn't doing just actions also engender justice, unjust
ones injustice?   d

GLAUCON: Necessarily.

SOCRATES: But to produce health is to put the elements that are in the
body in their natural relations of mastering and being mastered by one
another; while to produce disease is to establish a relation of ruling and
being ruled by one another that is contrary to nature   5

---

[29] The difference between knowledge (*epistêmê*) and belief (*doxa*) is explored at
475d1–480a13.

[30] Reading δουλεύειν τῷ τοῦ ἀρχικοῦ γένους with Adam.

GLAUCON: That's right.

SOCRATES: Doesn't it follow, then, that to produce justice is to establish the elements in the soul in a natural relation of mastering and being mastered by one another, while to produce injustice is to establish a relation of ruling and being ruled by one another that is contrary to nature?

GLAUCON: Absolutely.

SOCRATES: Virtue, then, so it seems, is a sort of health, a fine and good state of the soul; whereas vice seems to be a shameful disease and weakness.

GLAUCON: That's right.

SOCRATES: And don't fine practices lead to the possession of virtue, shameful ones to vice?

GLAUCON: Necessarily.

SOCRATES: So it now remains, it seems, for us to consider whether it is more profitable to do just actions, engage in fine practices, and be just, whether one is known to be so or not; or to do injustice and be unjust, provided that one does not have to pay the penalty and become a better person as a result of being punished.

GLAUCON: But, Socrates, that question seems to me, at least, to have become ridiculous, now that the two have been shown to be as we described. Life does not seem worth living when the body's natural constitution is ruined, not even if one has food and drink of every sort, all the money in the world, and every political office imaginable. So how—even if one could do whatever one wished, except what would liberate one from vice and injustice and make one acquire justice and virtue—could it be worth living when the natural constitution of the very thing by which we live[31] is ruined and in turmoil?

SOCRATES: Yes, it is ridiculous. All the same, since in fact we have reached a point from which we can see with the utmost clarity, as it were, that these things are so, we must not give up.

GLAUCON: That's absolutely the last thing we should do.

SOCRATES: Come up here, then, so that you can see how many kinds of vice there are—the ones, at any rate, that are worth seeing.

GLAUCON: I am following. Just tell me.[32]

SOCRATES: Well, from the vantage point, so to speak, that we have reached in our argument, it seems to me that there is one kind of virtue and an unlimited number of kinds of vice, four of which are worth mentioning.

---

[31] I.e., the soul. See 353d9–10.
[32] See 432c3–4.

GLAUCON: What do you mean?

SOCRATES: It seems likely that there are as many types of soul as there are types of political constitution of a specific kind.

GLAUCON: How many is that?

SOCRATES: Five types of constitution, and five of soul.

GLAUCON: Tell me what they are.

SOCRATES: I will tell you that one type would be the constitution we have been describing. However, there are two ways of referring to it: if one outstanding man emerges among the rulers, it is called a kingship; if more than one, it is called an aristocracy.

GLAUCON: That's true.

SOCRATES: Well, then, that is one of the kinds I had in mind. You see, whether many arise or just one, they won't change any of the laws of the city that are worth mentioning, since they will have been brought up and educated in the way we described.

GLAUCON: No, they probably won't.

Book 5

449a SOCRATES: That, then, is the sort of city and constitution—and the sort of man—I call good and correct. And if indeed this one is correct, all the others are bad and mistaken, both as city governments and as ways of organizing the souls of private individuals. The deficient ones fall into four kinds.

GLAUCON: What are they?

I was going to describe them in the order in which I thought they developed
b *out of one another.[1] But Polemarchus, who was sitting not far from Adeimantus, extended his hand, gripped the latter's cloak by the shoulder from above, drew Adeimantus toward him, and, leaning forward himself, said some things*
5 *in his ear. We overheard nothing of what he said, other than this:*

Shall we let it go, then, or what?

ADEIMANTUS: (*Now speaking aloud.*) Certainly not.

SOCRATES: What is it exactly you won't let go?

ADEIMANTUS: You!

c SOCRATES: Why exactly?

ADEIMANTUS: We think you are being lazy, that you are robbing us of a whole important section of the argument in order to avoid having to explain it. You thought we would not notice when you said—as though it were something inconsequential—that, as regards women and children, anyone
5 could see that it will be a case of friends sharing everything in common.[2]

SOCRATES: But isn't that correct, Adeimantus?

ADEIMANTUS: Yes, it is. But it is just like all the rest we have discussed; its correctness requires an explanation of how the sharing will be arranged, since there are many ways to bring it about. So, do not omit to tell us about
d the particular one you have in mind. We have all been waiting for a long time in the expectation that you would surely discuss how procreation will be handled, how the children that are born will be reared, and the whole

[1] This task is taken up in Book 8.
[2] See 423e4–424a2.

subject of what you mean by sharing women and children. You see, we think that this makes a considerable difference—indeed, all the difference—to whether a constitution is correct or incorrect. So now that you are beginning to describe another constitution without having analyzed this matter adequately, we are resolved, as you overheard, not to let you go until you explain all this just as you did the rest.

GLAUCON: Include me, too, as having a share in this vote.

And Thrasymachus said:

In fact, you can take it as the resolution of *all* of us, Socrates.

SOCRATES: What a thing to do, attacking me like that. You have started up a huge discussion about the constitution—it will be like starting from the beginning. I was delighted to think I had already completed its description by this time and was satisfied to have what I had said earlier be accepted as is. You do not realize what a swarm of arguments you are now stirring up by making this demand. It was because I could see it that I left the topic aside, to avoid all the trouble it would cause us.

THRASYMACHUS: What of it? Don't you think these people have come here now to listen to arguments, not to smelt ore?[3]

SOCRATES: Yes—within moderation, at least.

GLAUCON: But surely it is within moderation, Socrates, for people with any sense to listen to such arguments their whole life long. So never mind about *us*. Don't *you* get tired of explaining your views on what we asked about: namely, what the sharing of children and women will amount to for our guardians, and how the children will be brought up while they are still small. After all, the time between birth and the beginning of formal education seems to be the most troublesome period of all. So, try to tell us in what way it should be handled.

SOCRATES: It is not easy to explain, my happy fellow. It raises even more doubts than the topics we have discussed so far. One might, in fact, doubt whether what we proposed is possible, and, even if one granted that it is entirely so, one might still have doubts about whether it would be for the best. That, then, is why I was somewhat hesitant to bring it up: I was afraid, my dear comrade, that our argument might seem to be no more than wishful thinking.

GLAUCON: Do not hesitate at all. You see, your audience won't be inconsiderate, or incredulous, or hostile.

---

[3] A proverbial expression applied to those who neglect the task at hand for an uncertain profit. Thrasymachus is reminding Socrates of his own words at 336e4–9.

SOCRATES: My very good fellow, are you saying that because you want to encourage me?

GLAUCON: I am.

SOCRATES: Well, you are having precisely the opposite effect. If I were confident that I was speaking with knowledge, your encouragement would be all very well. When one is among knowledgeable and beloved friends, and one is speaking what one knows to be the truth about the most important and most beloved things, one can feel both secure and confident. But to produce arguments when one is uncertain and searching, as I am doing, is a frightening thing and makes one feel insecure. I am not afraid of being ridiculed—that would be childish, indeed—but I am afraid that if I fail to secure the truth, just where it is most important to do so, I will not only fall myself but drag my friends down as well. So I bow to Adrasteia, Glaucon, for what I am about to say. You see, I suspect that involuntary homicide is a lesser crime than misleading people about beautiful, good, and just conventions. That is a risk it would be better to run among enemies than among friends. So you have well and truly encouraged me.

Glaucon laughed and said:

Well, Socrates, if we suffer from any false note you strike in the argument, we will release you, as we would in a homicide case, as guiltless and no deceiver of us. So you may speak with confidence.

SOCRATES: Well, it is true; the one who is acquitted in that situation is guiltless, so the law says. And if it is true there, it is probably true here, too.

GLAUCON: On these grounds, then, tell us.

SOCRATES: I will have to go back again, then, and say now what perhaps I should have said then in the proper place. But maybe it is all right, after having completed a male drama, to perform a female one next[4]—especially when you demand it in this way. For people born and educated as we have described, then, there is, I believe, no correct way to acquire and employ children and women other than to follow the path on which we first set them. Surely, in our argument, we tried to establish the men as guard-dogs of their flock.

GLAUCON: Yes.

SOCRATES: Then let's proceed by giving corresponding rules for birth and rearing, and see whether they suit us or not.

---

[4] This may be an allusion to the mimes of Sophron of Syracuse (c. 470–400 BCE), which were divided into male mimes, in which men were represented, and female ones, in which women were represented.

GLAUCON: How?

SOCRATES: As follows. Do we think that the females of our guard-dogs should join in guarding precisely what the males guard, hunt with them, and share everything with them? Or do we think that they should stay indoors and look after the house,[5] on the grounds that they are incapable of doing this because they must bear and rear the puppies, while the males should work and have the entire care of the flock?

GLAUCON: They should share everything—except that we employ the females as we would weaker animals, and the males as we would stronger ones.

SOCRATES: Is it possible, then, to employ an animal for the same tasks as another if you do not give it the same upbringing and education?

GLAUCON: No, it is not.

SOCRATES: Then if we employ women for the same tasks as men, they must also be taught the same things.

GLAUCON: Yes.

SOCRATES: Now, we gave the latter musical and physical training.

GLAUCON: Yes.

SOCRATES: So, we must also give these two crafts, as well as military training, to the women, and employ them in the same way.

GLAUCON: That seems reasonable, given what you say.

SOCRATES: But perhaps many of the things we are now saying, because they are contrary to custom, would seem ridiculous if they were put into practice.

GLAUCON: Indeed, they would.

SOCRATES: What do you see as the most ridiculous aspect of them? Isn't it obvious that it is the idea of the women exercising stripped in the palestras alongside the men?[6] And not just the young women, but the older ones too—like the old men we see in gymnasiums who, even though their bodies are wrinkled and not pleasant to look at, still love physical training.

---

[5] Respectable, well-to-do women lived secluded lives in most Greek states: they were confined to the household (see 579b8) and to domestic work and were largely excluded from the public spheres of culture, politics, and warfare. See John Gould, "Law, Custom and Myth: Aspects of the Social Position of Women in Classical Athens," *Journal of Hellenic Studies* 100 (1980): 38–59.

[6] The women will be *gumnozomenas,* which can mean stripped naked, but often also means wearing a tunic, or undergarment, without a cloak (see 457a6–7). A palestra was a wrestling school and training ground.

GLAUCON: Yes, by Zeus, that *would* look really ridiculous, at least under present conditions.

SOCRATES: Yet, since we have started to discuss the matter, we must not be afraid of the various jokes that the wits will make both about this sort of change in musical and physical training and—even more so—about the change in the bearing of arms and the mounting of cavalry horses.[7]

GLAUCON: You are right.

SOCRATES: But since we have started, we must move on to the rougher part of the law, and ask these wits *not* to do their own job, but to be serious. And we will remind them that it is not long since the *Greeks* thought it shameful and ridiculous (as many barbarians still do) for *men* to be seen stripped, and that when first the Cretans and then the Lacedaemonians began the gymnasiums, the wits of the time had the opportunity to make a comedy of it all. Or don't you think so?

GLAUCON: I certainly do.

SOCRATES: But when it became clear, I take it, to those who employed these practices, that it was better to strip than to cover up all such parts, the laughter in the eyes faded away because of what the arguments had proved to be best. And this showed that it is a fool who finds anything ridiculous except what is bad, or tries to raise a laugh at the sight of anything except what is stupid or bad, or—putting it the other way around—who takes seriously any standard of what is beautiful other than what is good.

GLAUCON: Absolutely.

SOCRATES: Well, then, shouldn't we first agree about whether our proposals are viable or not? And mustn't we give anyone who wishes to do so—whether it is someone who loves a joke or someone serious—the opportunity to dispute whether the female human does have the natural ability to share in *all* the tasks of the male sex, or in none at all, or in some but not others; and, in particular, whether this holds in the case of warfare? By making the best beginning in this way, wouldn't one also be likely to reach the best conclusion?

GLAUCON: Of course.

SOCRATES: So, would you like us to dispute with one another on their behalf, so that their side of the argument won't be attacked without defenders?

GLAUCON: Why not?

[7] A reference, perhaps, to Aristophanes, *Assembly Women,* which makes fun of the idea of women having political power and making laws like these. As in English, the term *hoplon* ("weapon" or "tool") was used to refer to the male genitals, and *ocheuein* ("mounting," "riding") to refer to sexual intercourse (as at 454e1).

SOCRATES: Then let's say this on their behalf: "Socrates and Glaucon, you do not need *other people* to dispute you. After all, you yourselves, when you were beginning to found your city, agreed that each one had to do the one job for which he was naturally suited." 5

GLAUCON: We did agree to that, I think. Of course we did.

SOCRATES: "Can it be, then, that a woman is not by nature very different from a man?"

GLAUCON: Of course she is different.

SOCRATES: "Then isn't it also appropriate to assign a different job to each of them, the one for which they are naturally suited?" 10

GLAUCON: Certainly. c

SOCRATES: "How is it, then, that you are not making a mistake now and contradicting yourselves, when you say that men and women must do the same jobs, seeing that they have natures that are most distinct?" Do you 5 have any defense, you amazing fellow, against that attack?

GLAUCON: It is not easy to think of one on the spur of the moment. On the contrary, I shall ask—indeed, I am asking—you to explain the argument on our side as well, whatever it is.

SOCRATES: That, Glaucon, and many other problems of the same sort, which I foresaw long ago, was what I was afraid of when I hesitated to d tackle the law concerning the possession and upbringing of women and children.

GLAUCON: No, by Zeus, it certainly does not seem to be a simple matter.

SOCRATES: No, it is not. But the fact is that whether one falls into a small 5 diving pool or into the middle of the largest sea, one has to swim all the same.

GLAUCON: Of course.

SOCRATES: Then we must swim, too, and try to save ourselves from the sea of argument, hoping for a dolphin to pick us up, or for some other 10 unlikely rescue.[8]

GLAUCON: It seems so. e

SOCRATES: Come on, then, let's see if we can find a way out. We have agreed, of course, that different natures must have different pursuits, and that the natures of a woman and a man are different. But we now say that those different natures must have the same pursuits. Isn't that the charge against us? 5

[8] The story of Arion's rescue by the dolphin is told in Herodotus, *Histories* 1.23–4.

141

GLAUCON: Yes, exactly.

SOCRATES: What a noble power, Glaucon, the craft of disputation⁹ possesses!

GLAUCON: Why is that?

SOCRATES: Because many people seem to me to fall into it even against their wills, and think they are engaging not in eristic,¹⁰ but in discussion. This happens because they are unable to examine what has been said by dividing it up into kinds. Instead, it is on the purely verbal level that they look for the contradiction in what has been said, and employ eristic, not dialectic, on one another.

GLAUCON: Yes, that certainly does happen to many people. But surely it is not pertinent to us at the moment, is it?

SOCRATES: It most certainly is. At any rate, we are in danger of unconsciously dealing in disputation.

GLAUCON: How?

SOCRATES: We are trying to establish the principle that different natures should not be assigned the same pursuits in a bold and eristic manner, *on the verbal level*. But we did not at all investigate what kind of natural difference or sameness we had in mind, or in what regard the distinction was pertinent, when we assigned different pursuits to different natures and the same ones to the same.

GLAUCON: No, we did not investigate that.

SOCRATES: And because we did not, it is open to us, apparently, to ask ourselves whether the natures of bald and long-haired men are the same or opposite. And, once we agree that they are opposite, it is open to us to forbid the long-haired ones to be shoemakers, if that is what the bald ones are to be, or *vice versa*.

GLAUCON: But that would be ridiculous.

SOCRATES: And is it ridiculous for any other reason than that we did not have in mind *every* kind of difference and sameness in nature, but were keeping our eyes only on the kind of difference and sameness that was pertinent to the pursuits themselves? We meant, for example, that a male and female whose souls are suited for medicine have the same nature. Or don't you think so?

GLAUCON: I do.

SOCRATES: But a male doctor and a male carpenter have different ones?

---

⁹ See Glossary of Terms s.v. disputation.

¹⁰ See Glossary of Terms s.v. eristic.

GLAUCON: Of course, completely different.

SOCRATES: In the case of both the male and the female sex, then, if one of them is shown to be different from the other with regard to a particular craft or pursuit, we will say that is the one who should be assigned to it. But if it is apparent that they differ in this respect alone, that the female bears the offspring while the male mounts the female, we will say it has not yet been demonstrated that a woman is different from a man with regard to what we are talking about, and we will continue to believe our guardians and their women should have the same pursuits.

GLAUCON: And rightly so.

SOCRATES: Next, won't we urge our opponent to tell us the precise craft or pursuit, relevant to the organization of the city, for which a woman's nature and a man's are not the same but different?

GLAUCON: That would be a fair question, at least.

SOCRATES: Perhaps, then, this other person might say, just as you did a moment ago,[11] that it is not easy to give an adequate answer on the spur of the moment, but that after reflection it would not be at all difficult.

GLAUCON: Yes, he might say that.

SOCRATES: Do you want us to ask the one who disputes things in this way, then, to follow us to see whether we can somehow show him that there is no pursuit relevant to the management of the city that is peculiar to women?

GLAUCON: Of course.

SOCRATES: Come on, then, we will say to him, give us an answer: "Is this what you meant by one person being naturally well suited for something and another naturally unsuited: that the one learns it easily, the other with difficulty; that the one, after a little instruction, can discover a lot for himself in the subject being studied, whereas the other, even if he gets a lot of instruction and attention, does not even retain what he was taught; that the bodily capacities of the one adequately serve his mind, while those of the other obstruct his? Are there any other factors than these, by which you distinguish a person who is naturally well suited for each pursuit from one who is not?"

GLAUCON: No one will be able to mention any others.

SOCRATES: Do you know of anything practiced by human beings, then, at which the male sex is not superior to the female in all those ways? Or must we make a long story of it by discussing weaving and the preparation of

[11] 453c7–9.

baked and boiled food[12]—the very pursuits in which the female sex is thought to excel, and in which its defeat would expose it to the greatest ridicule of all?

d

GLAUCON: It is true that the one sex shows greater mastery than the other in pretty much every area. Yet there are many women who are better than many men at many things. But on the whole, it is as you say.

5

SOCRATES: Then, my friend, there is no pursuit relevant to the management of the city that belongs to a woman because she is a woman, or to a man because he is a man; but the various natural capacities are distributed in a similar way between both creatures, and women can share by nature in every pursuit, and men in every one, though for the purposes of all of them women are weaker than men.[13]

e

GLAUCON: Of course.

SOCRATES: So shall we assign all of them to men and none to women?

5

GLAUCON: How could we?

SOCRATES: We could not. For we will say, I imagine, that one woman is suited for medicine, another not, and that one is naturally musical, another not.

GLAUCON: Of course.

SOCRATES: Won't one be suited for physical training or war, then, while another is unwarlike and not a lover of physical training?

456a

GLAUCON: I suppose so.

SOCRATES: And one a philosopher (lover of wisdom), another a "misosopher" (hater of wisdom)? And one spirited, another spiritless?

5

GLAUCON: That too.

SOCRATES: So there is also a woman who is suited to be a guardian, and one who is not. Or wasn't that the sort of nature we selected for our male guardians, too?[14]

GLAUCON: It certainly was.

SOCRATES: A woman and a man can have the same nature, then, relevant to guarding the city—except to the extent that she is weaker and he is stronger.

10

GLAUCON: Apparently so.

---

[12] Men were in charge of roasting meat. See 404b10–c4.

[13] *Epi pasi:* The claim is not that no woman is stronger or better than any man in any such pursuit (which would contradict 455d4–5), but that the physical weakness of women is a relevant factor in all of them. See 451e1–2, 456a10–11.

[14] 374e4–376c5.

SOCRATES: Women of that sort, then, must be selected to live and guard
with men of the same sort, since they are competent to do so and are akin
to the men by nature.

GLAUCON: Of course.

SOCRATES: And mustn't we assign the same pursuits to the same natures?

GLAUCON: Yes, the same ones.

SOCRATES: We have come around, then, to what we said before, and we
are agreed that it is not against nature to assign musical and physical training
to the female guardians.

GLAUCON: Absolutely.

SOCRATES: So, we are not legislating impossibilities or mere fantasies, at
any rate, since the law we were proposing is in accord with nature. Rather,
it is the contrary laws that we have now that turn out to be more contrary
to nature, it seems.

GLAUCON: It does seem that way.

SOCRATES: Now, wasn't our inquiry about whether our proposals were
both viable and best?

GLAUCON: Yes, it was.

SOCRATES: And that they are in fact viable has been agreed, hasn't it?

GLAUCON: Yes.

SOCRATES: So, we must next come to an agreement about whether they
are for the best?

GLAUCON: Clearly.

SOCRATES: Now, as regards producing a woman who is equipped for
guardianship, we won't have one sort of education that will produce our
guardian men, will we, and another our women—especially not when it
will have the same nature to work on in both cases?

GLAUCON: No, we won't.

SOCRATES: What is your belief about this, then?

GLAUCON: What?

SOCRATES: The notion that one man is better or worse than another—or
do you think they are all alike?

GLAUCON: Not at all.

SOCRATES: In the city we are founding, who do you think will turn out
to be better men: our guardians, who get the education we have described,
or the shoemakers, who are educated in shoemaking?

GLAUCON: What a ridiculous question!

e

SOCRATES: I realize that. Aren't the guardians the best of the citizens?

GLAUCON: By far.

SOCRATES: And what about the female guardians? Won't they be the best of the women?

5

GLAUCON: Yes, they are by far the best, too.

SOCRATES: Is there anything better for a city than that the best possible men and women should come to exist in it?

GLAUCON: No, there is not.

SOCRATES: And that is what musical and physical training, employed as we have described, will achieve?

457a

GLAUCON: Of course.

SOCRATES: Then the law we were proposing was not only possible, but also best for a city?

5

GLAUCON: Yes.

SOCRATES: Then the female guardians must strip, clothing themselves in virtue instead of cloaks.[15] They must share in warfare, and whatever else guarding the city involves, and do nothing else. But within these areas, the women must be assigned lighter tasks than the men, because of the weak-

10

ness of their sex. And the man who laughs at the sight of women stripped for physical training, when their stripping is for the best, is "plucking the

b

unripe fruit of laughter's wisdom,"[16] and knows nothing, it seems, about what he is laughing at or what he is doing. For it is, and always will be, the

5

finest saying that what is beneficial is beautiful; what is harmful ugly.

GLAUCON: Absolutely.

SOCRATES: May we claim, then, that we are avoiding one wave,[17] as it were, in our discussion of the law about women, so that we are not alto-gether swept away when we declare that our male and female guardians must share all their pursuits, and that our argument is somehow self-consistent

c

when it states that this is both viable and beneficial?

GLAUCON: It is certainly no small wave that you are avoiding.

5

SOCRATES: You won't think it is so big when you see the next one.

GLAUCON: I won't see it unless you tell me about it.[18]

SOCRATES: The law that is consistent with that one, and with the others that preceded it, is this, I take it.

[15] See Glossary of Terms s.v. cloak.

[16] Plato is adapting a phrase of Pindar.

[17] The metaphor begins at 453c10–d7.

[18] See 432c3–4.

GLAUCON: What?

SOCRATES: That all these women should be shared among all the men, that no individual woman and man should live together, and that the children, too, should be shared, with no parent knowing its own offspring, and no child its parent.

GLAUCON: That wave *is* far bigger and more dubitable than the other, both as regards its viability and its benefit.

SOCRATES: As far as its benefit is concerned, at least, I do not think anyone would argue that the sharing of women and children is not the greatest good, if indeed it is viable. But I imagine there would be a lot of dispute about whether or not it is viable.

GLAUCON: No, *both* could very well be disputed.

SOCRATES: You mean I will have to face a coalition of arguments. I thought I had at least escaped one of them—namely, whether you thought the proposal was beneficial—and that I would just be left with the argument about whether it is viable or not.

GLAUCON: Well, you did not escape unnoticed. So you will have to give an argument for both.

SOCRATES: I must pay the penalty. But do me this favor: let me take a holiday and act like those lazy people who make a banquet for themselves of their own thoughts when they are walking alone. People like that, as you know, do not bother to find out how any of their appetites might actually be fulfilled, so as to avoid the trouble of deliberating about what is possible and what is not. They assume that what they want is available, and then proceed to arrange all the rest, taking pleasure in going through everything they will do when they get it—thus making their already lazy souls even lazier. Well, I, too, am succumbing to this weakness at the moment and want to postpone consideration of the viability of our proposals until later. I will assume now that they are viable, if you will permit me to do so, and examine how the rulers will arrange them when they come to pass. And I will try to show that, if they were put into practice, they would be the most beneficial arrangements of all, both for the city and for its guardians. These are the things I will try to examine with you first, leaving the others for later—if indeed you will permit this.

GLAUCON: You have my permission; so proceed with the examination.

SOCRATES: Well, then, I imagine that if indeed our rulers, and likewise their auxiliaries, are worthy of their names, the latter will be prepared to carry out orders, and the former to give orders, obeying our laws in some cases and imitating them in the others that we leave to their discretion.

GLAUCON: Probably so.

SOCRATES: Now, you are their lawgiver, and in just the way you selected these men, you will select as the women to hand over to them those who have natures as similar to theirs as possible. And because they have shared dwellings and meals, and none of them has any private property of that sort, they will live together; and through mixing together in the gymnasia and in the rest of their daily life, they will be driven by innate necessity, I take it, to have sex with one another. Or don't you think I am talking about necessities here?

GLAUCON: Not *geometric* necessities, certainly, but *erotic* ones; and they probably have a sharper capacity to persuade and attract most people.

SOCRATES: They do, indeed. But the next point, Glaucon, is that for them to have unregulated sexual intercourse with one another, or to do anything else of that sort, would not be a pious thing in a city of happy people, and the rulers won't allow it.

GLAUCON: No, it would not be just.

SOCRATES: It is clear, then, that we will next have to make marriages as sacred as possible. And sacred marriages will be those that are most beneficial.

GLAUCON: Absolutely.

SOCRATES: How, then, will the most beneficial ones come about? Tell me this, Glaucon. I see you have hunting dogs and quite a flock of noble birds at home.[19] Have you, by Zeus, noticed anything in particular about their "marriages" and breeding?

GLAUCON: Like what?

SOCRATES: In the first place, though they are all noble animals, aren't there some that are, or turn out to be, the very best?

GLAUCON: There are.

SOCRATES: Do you breed from them all to the same extent, then, or do you try hard to breed as far as possible from the best ones?

GLAUCON: From the best ones.

SOCRATES: And do you breed from the youngest, the oldest, or as far as possible from those in their prime?

GLAUCON: From those in their prime.

SOCRATES: And if they were not bred in this way, do you think that your race of birds and dogs would get much worse?

GLAUCON: I do.

SOCRATES: And what do you think about horses and other animals? Is the situation any different with them?

---

[19] Both hunting dogs and aviaries were common in rich Greek households.

GLAUCON: It would be strange if it were.

SOCRATES: Good heavens, my dear comrade! Then our need for eminent rulers is quite desperate, if indeed the same also holds for the human race.

GLAUCON: Well, it does hold of them. But so what?

SOCRATES: It follows that our rulers will then have to employ a great many drugs. You know that when people do not need drugs for their bodies, and they are prepared to follow a regimen, we regard even an inferior doctor as adequate. But when drugs are needed, we know that a much bolder doctor is required.

GLAUCON: That's true. But what is your point?

SOCRATES: This: it looks as though our rulers will have to employ a great many lies and deceptions for the benefit of those they rule. And you remember, I suppose, we said all such things were useful as a kind of drug.[20]

GLAUCON: And we were correct.

SOCRATES: Well, in the case of marriages and procreation, its correctness is particularly evident.

GLAUCON: How so?

SOCRATES: It follows from our previous agreement that the best men should mate with the best women in as many cases as possible, while the opposite should hold of the worst men and women; and that the offspring of the former should be reared, but not that of the latter, if our flock is going to be an eminent one. And all this must occur without anyone knowing except the rulers—if, again, our herd of guardians is to remain as free from faction as possible.

GLAUCON: That's absolutely right.

SOCRATES: So then, we will have to establish by law certain festivals and sacrifices at which we will bring together brides and bridegrooms, and our poets must compose suitable hymns for the marriages that take place. We will leave the number of marriages for the rulers to decide. That will enable them to keep the number of males as constant as possible, taking into account war, disease, and everything of that sort; so that the city will, as far as possible, become neither too big nor too small.[21]

GLAUCON: That's right.

SOCRATES: I imagine that some sophisticated lotteries will have to be created, then, so that an inferior person of that sort will blame chance rather than the rulers at each mating time.

[20] 382c6–d3. The Noble Lie

[21] See 423b4–c5.

149

GLAUCON: Yes, indeed.

SOCRATES: And presumably, the young men who are good at war or at other things must—among other prizes and awards—be given a greater opportunity to have sex with the women, in order that a pretext may also be created at the same time for having as many children as possible fathered by such men.

GLAUCON: That's right.

SOCRATES: And then, as offspring are born, won't they be taken by the officials appointed for this purpose, whether these are men or women or both—for surely our offices are also open to both women and men.

GLAUCON: Yes.

SOCRATES: And I suppose they will take the offspring of good parents to the rearing pen and hand them over to special nurses who live in a separate part of the city. But those of inferior parents, or any deformed offspring of the others, they will hide in a secret and unknown place, as is fitting.[22]

GLAUCON: Yes, if indeed the race of guardians is going to remain pure.

SOCRATES: And won't these nurses also take care of the children's feeding by bringing the mothers to the rearing pen when their breasts are full, while devising every device[23] to ensure that no mother will recognize her offspring? And won't they provide other women as wet nurses if the mothers themselves have insufficient milk—taking care, however, that the mothers breast-feed the children for only a moderate period of time, and assigning sleepless nights and similar burdens to the nurses and wet nurses?

GLAUCON: You are making childbearing a soft job for the guardians' women.

SOCRATES: Yes, properly so. But let's take up the next thing we proposed. We said, as you know, that offspring should be bred from parents who are in their prime.[24]

GLAUCON: True.

SOCRATES: Do you agree that a woman's prime lasts, on average, for a period of twenty years and a man's for thirty?

GLAUCON: Which years are those?

SOCRATES: A woman should bear children for the city from the age of twenty to that of forty; whereas a man should beget them for the city

[22] Infanticide by exposure was commonly used in ancient Greece as a method of birth control.

[23] See 414b8–c2.

[24] 452b1–3.

from the time that he passes his peak as a runner until he reaches fifty-five.[25]

GLAUCON: At any rate, that is the physical and mental prime for both.   461a

SOCRATES: Then if any male who is younger or older than that engages in reproduction for the community, we will say that his offense is neither pious nor just. For the child he fathers for the city, if it escapes discovery,   5
will be begotten and born without the benefit of sacrifices, or of the prayers that priestesses, priests, and the entire city will offer at every marriage festival, asking that from good and beneficial parents ever better and more beneficial offspring should be produced. On the contrary, it will be   b
born in darkness through a terrible act of lack of self-control.

GLAUCON: That's right.

SOCRATES: The same law will apply if a man who is still of breeding age has sex with a woman in her prime when the rulers have not mated them.   5
We will say that he is imposing an illegitimate, unauthorized, and unholy child on the city.

GLAUCON: That's absolutely right.

SOCRATES: But when women and men have passed breeding age, I imagine we will leave them free to have sex with whomever they wish—except that a man may not have sex with his daughter, mother, daughters' daugh-   c
ters, or mother's female ancestors, or a woman with her son and his descendants or her father and his ancestors. And we will permit all that only after telling them to be very careful not to let even a single fetus see the light of day, if one should happen to be conceived; but if one does force its way   5
out, they must dispose of it on the understanding that no nurture is available for such a child.

GLAUCON: All that sounds reasonable. But how will they recognize one another's fathers, daughters, and the others you mentioned?   d

SOCRATES: They won't. Instead, from the day a man becomes a bridegroom, he will call all offspring born in the tenth month afterward (and in

---

[25] Greek women were often married before they turned twenty. The puzzling characterization of the minimum age for male procreation is, perhaps, explained by a passage from Aristotle's *Politics*: "As to the bodily characteristics in parents that are most beneficial to the offspring being produced. . . . Neither the physical condition of athletes nor that of one who is overly reliant on medical treatment and poorly suited to exertion is useful from the point of view of health or procreation, or is the condition needed in a good citizen. But the condition that is in a mean between these two *is* useful for these purposes. The proper physical condition, therefore, is one that is achieved by exertion, but not by violent exertion, and that promotes not just one thing, as the athletic condition does, but the actions of free people. And these should be provided to women and men alike" (7.16 1335^{b}2–12).

the seventh, of course) his sons,[26] if they are male, and his daughters, if they are female; and they will call him father. Similarly, he will call their children his grandchildren, and they, in turn, will call the group to which he belongs grandfathers and grandmothers. And those who were born at the same time as their mothers and fathers were breeding, they will call their brothers and sisters. Thus, as we were saying just now, they will avoid sexual relations with each other. However, the law *will* allow brothers and sisters to have sex with one another, if the lottery works out that way and the Pythia approves.[27]

GLAUCON: You are absolutely right.

SOCRATES: That, then, Glaucon, or something like it, is how the sharing of women and children by the guardians of your city will be handled. The next point we need to have confirmed by argument, then, is that this arrangement is both consistent with the rest of the constitution and by far the best. Isn't that so?

GLAUCON: Yes, by Zeus, it is.

SOCRATES: As a beginning step toward reaching agreement, shouldn't we ask ourselves what we think is the greatest good for the organization of the city—the one at which the legislator should aim in making its laws—and what the greatest evil? And then examine whether what we have just described is in harmony with the tracks of the good we have found, and in disharmony with those of the bad?

GLAUCON: Absolutely.

SOCRATES: Now, do we know of any greater evil for a city than what tears it apart and makes it many instead of one? Or any greater good than what binds it together and makes it one?

GLAUCON: No, we do not.

SOCRATES: Well, doesn't sharing pleasure and pain bind it together—when, as far as possible, all the citizens feel more or less the same joy or pain at the same gains or losses?

GLAUCON: Absolutely.

SOCRATES: On the other hand, doesn't the privatization of these things dissolve the city—when some are overwhelmed with distress and others overjoyed by the same things happening to the city or some of its inhabitants?

GLAUCON: Of course.

[26] These are lunar months. The period is from roughly seven to roughly nine calendar months. A fetus of less than seven months was considered nonviable.

[27] Greek law did not usually permit marriage between biological siblings, who will be included in the class referred to here. See 427c3.

SOCRATES: And isn't that what happens when people do not apply such phrases as "mine" and "not mine" in unison in the city? And similarly with "someone else's"?

GLAUCON: Precisely.

SOCRATES: Then isn't the city that is best governed the one in which the vast majority of people apply "mine" and "not mine" to the same things on the basis of the same principle?

GLAUCON: Certainly.

SOCRATES: And isn't it the city whose condition is most like that of a single person? I mean, when one of us somehow hurts his finger, you know the entire partnership—the one that binds body and soul together into a single system under the ruling part within it—is aware of this, and all of it as a whole feels the pain in unison with the part that suffers. That is why we say that this person has a pain in his finger. And the same principle applies, doesn't it, to any other part of a person, whether it is suffering pain or relieved by pleasure?

GLAUCON: Yes, the same one. And, to answer your question, the city that manages to come closest to this condition *is* the best-governed one.

SOCRATES: I imagine, then, that whenever one of its citizens has an experience, whether good or bad, such a city will most certainly say that the experience is its own, and all of it together will share his pleasure or pain.

GLAUCON: That must be so, since it is well governed.

SOCRATES: It is time for us to return to our own city, then, to look there for the features we have agreed on and to see whether it, or rather some other city, possesses them to the greatest degree.

GLAUCON: Yes, it is.

SOCRATES: Well, now, what about those other cities? Presumably there are rulers and people in them as well as in ours?

GLAUCON: There are.

SOCRATES: And won't all of them call one another "citizens"?

GLAUCON: Of course.

SOCRATES: But besides "citizens," what do the people in those other cities call the rulers?

GLAUCON: In most, they call them "masters," but in democracies they are called just that—"rulers."[28]

[28] The Athenian democracy had nine rulers (archons) in Plato's time. These included the chief magistrates, the chief military leader, and an important authority in religious matters.

SOCRATES: What about the people in our city? Besides "citizens," what do they call the rulers?

GLAUCON: "Preservers"[29] and "auxiliaries."

SOCRATES: And what do *they* call the people?

GLAUCON: "Paymasters" and "providers."

SOCRATES: What do the rulers in other cities call the people?

GLAUCON: "Slaves."

SOCRATES: And what do the rulers call each other?

GLAUCON: "Co-rulers."

SOCRATES: And ours?

GLAUCON: "Co-guardians."

SOCRATES: Now, can you tell me whether a ruler in other cities could address one of his co-rulers as his kinsman and another as an outsider?

GLAUCON: Many do, at any rate.

SOCRATES: And doesn't he regard and speak of his kinsman as belonging to him, while he regards the outsider as not doing so?

GLAUCON: Yes.

SOCRATES: What about your guardians? Could any of them regard or address a co-guardian as an outsider?

GLAUCON: Certainly not. He will regard everyone he meets as a brother or a sister, a father or a mother, a son or a daughter, or some ancestor or descendant of these.

SOCRATES: Very well put. But tell me this, too: will your laws require them simply to use these terms of kinship, or must they also do all the things that go along with the names? In the case of fathers, for example, must they show them the customary respect, solicitude, and obedience owed to parents? Will they fare worse at the hands of gods or men, as people whose actions are neither pious nor just, if they do otherwise? Will these be the sayings that are chanted by all the citizens, and that sound in their ears right from their earliest childhood? Or will they hear something else about their fathers—or the ones they are told to regard as their fathers—or about their other relatives?

GLAUCON: They will hear those. It would be ridiculous if they only mouthed the terms of kinship, without the actions.

SOCRATES: So, in this city more than in any other, when someone is doing well or badly, they will utter in concord the words we mentioned a

---

[29] See 429c5.

moment ago, and say "*my* such-and-such is doing well" or "*my* so-and-so is doing badly." 5

GLAUCON: That's absolutely true.

SOCRATES: Well, didn't we say that this conviction and way of talking are 464a accompanied by the having of pleasures and pains in common?[30]

GLAUCON: Yes, and we were right to do so.

SOCRATES: Then won't our citizens share to the fullest, and call "mine," the very same thing? And because they share it, won't they experience to 5 the fullest the sharing of pleasures and pains?

GLAUCON: Of course.

SOCRATES: And—in the context of the rest of the political system—isn't the sharing of women and children by the guardians responsible for it?

GLAUCON: Yes, it is by far the most important cause. 10

SOCRATES: But we further agreed that this sharing is the greatest good for a city, when we compared a well-governed city to the way a human body b relates to pain and pleasure in one of its parts.

GLAUCON: And we were right to agree.

SOCRATES: Then we have shown that the cause of the greatest good for our city is the sharing of women and children by the auxiliaries. 5

GLAUCON: Yes, we certainly have.

SOCRATES: And what is more, it is consistent with what we said before. For we said, as you know, that if these people are going to be real guardians, they should not have private houses, land, or any other possession, but should receive their upkeep from the other citizens as a wage for their c guardianship, and should all eat communally.[31]

GLAUCON: That's right.

SOCRATES: So, as I say, doesn't what was said earlier, as well as what is 5 being said now, make them into even better guardians and prevent them from tearing the city apart by applying the term "mine" not to the same thing, but to different ones—with one person dragging into his own house whatever he, apart from the others, can get his hands on, and another into a different house to a different wife and children, who create private plea- d sures and pains at things that are private? Instead of that, don't our guardians share a single conviction about what is their own, aim at the same goal, and, as far as possible, feel pleasure and pain in unison? 5

GLAUCON: Absolutely.

[30] 462b4–c9.
[31] 416d3–417b8.

SOCRATES: What about lawsuits and accusations? Won't they pretty much disappear from among them because they have no private possessions except their own bodies and share all the rest? As a result, won't they be free from faction—at any rate, from the sort of faction that the possession of property, children, and families causes among people?

e

GLAUCON: Yes, they will inevitably be entirely free of it.

SOCRATES: Moreover, lawsuits neither for violence nor for assault should justifiably occur among them. For we will declare, surely, that for people to defend themselves against others of the same age is a fine and just thing, since it will compel them to stay in good physical shape.

5

GLAUCON: That's right.

465a

SOCRATES: This law is also correct for another reason: if a spirited person vents his anger in this way, he will be less likely to move on to more serious sorts of faction.

GLAUCON: He certainly will.

SOCRATES: As for an older person, he will be authorized to rule and pun-ish all the younger ones.

5

GLAUCON: Clearly.

SOCRATES: And, unless the rulers command it, it is unlikely that a younger person will ever employ any sort of violence against an older one, or strike him. And I do not imagine he will fail to show him respect in other ways either, since two guardians—fear and shame—are sufficient to prevent it. Shame will prevent him from laying a hand on his parents, as will the fear that the others would come to his victim's aid—some because they are his sons, some because they are his brothers, and some because they are his fathers.

10

b

GLAUCON: Yes, that is what would happen.

SOCRATES: Then won't the laws induce men to live at peace with one another in all respects?

5

GLAUCON: Very much so.

SOCRATES: And if there is no faction among the guardians, there is no ter-rible danger that the rest of the city will form factions, either against them or among themselves.

10

GLAUCON: No, there is not.

SOCRATES: As for the pettiest of the evils the guardians would escape, they are so unseemly, I hesitate even to mention them: the flatteries of the rich by the poor; the perplexities and sufferings involved in bringing up chil-dren; the need to make the money necessary to feed the household—the borrowings, the defaults, and all the things people have to do to provide an income to hand over to their wives and slaves to spend on housekeeping.

c

5

156

The various troubles men endure in these areas, my dear Glaucon, are obvious, quite demeaning, and not worth discussing.

GLAUCON: They are obvious even to the blind.   d

SOCRATES: They will escape from all these things, then, and live a more blessedly happy life than the most blessedly happy one—that of the victors in the Olympian games.

GLAUCON: How so?

SOCRATES: Surely, these victors are considered happy on account of only a small part of what the guardians possess, since the latter victory is even   5
finer, and their upkeep from public funds more complete.[32] After all, the victory they gain is the salvation of the whole city, and the crown of victory they and their children receive is their upkeep and all the necessities of life. They receive privileges from their own city during their lifetime and a   e
worthy burial after their death.

GLAUCON: Yes, those are very fine rewards.

SOCRATES: Now, do you remember that earlier in our discussion we were rebuked by an argument—I forget whose—to the effect that we had not made our guardians happy, that though it was possible for them to have   5
everything that belongs to the citizens, they actually had nothing? We said,   466a
didn't we, that if this happened to come up at some point, we would look into it then, but that our concern at the time was to make our guardians *guardians,* and to make the *city* the happiest possible, rather than looking to any one group within it and molding it for happiness?[33]   5

GLAUCON: I remember.

SOCRATES: Well, then, if indeed the life of our auxiliaries has been shown to be much finer and better than that of Olympian victors, is there any need to compare it with the lives of shoemakers or any other craftsmen, or   b
with that of the farmers?

GLAUCON: I do not think there is.

SOCRATES: Nevertheless, it is surely right to repeat here what I also said on that earlier occasion: if a guardian tries to become happy in such a way   5
that he is no longer a guardian at all, and is not satisfied with a life that is moderate, stable, and (we claim) best, but is seized by a foolish, adolescent belief about happiness, which incites him to use his power to take every-thing in the city for himself—he will come to realize the true wisdom of   c
Hesiod's saying that, in a sense, "the half is worth more than the whole."[34]

---

[32] Men victorious in the Olympic games were often awarded free meals for life by their cities. See *Apology* 36d5–9.

[33] 419a1–421c6.

[34] *Works and Days* 40.

5 GLAUCON: If he takes my advice, he will keep to the former life.

SOCRATES: Do you agree, then, that the women should share with the men, in the way we described, in the areas of education, children, and guarding the other citizens; that whether they remain in the city or go out to war, they must guard together and hunt together, as hounds do, and

d share everything to the extent possible; and that by behaving in this way, they will be doing what is best, not something contrary to the natural relationship of female to male, and the one they are most naturally fitted to share in with one another?

5 GLAUCON: I do agree.

SOCRATES: Then doesn't it remain for us to determine whether it is also possible among human beings, as it is among other animals, for this sort of sharing to come about, and if so, how?

GLAUCON: You took the words out of my mouth.

SOCRATES: As far as war is concerned, I think it is clear how they will

e wage it.

GLAUCON: How?

SOCRATES: They will go to war together. What is more, they will take the children with them to the war, when they are sturdy enough, so that, like the children of other craftsmen, they can see what they will have to do in their own craft when they are grown up. But in addition to observing, they

467a should help and assist in every aspect of war, and take care of their mothers and fathers. For haven't you noticed in the other crafts how the children of potters, for example, assist and watch for a long time before actually putting

5 their hands to the clay?

GLAUCON: I have, indeed.

SOCRATES: Well, should these people take more care than the guardians in training their children by appropriate experience and observation?

GLAUCON: Of course not. That would be completely ridiculous.

10 SOCRATES: Besides, every animal will fight better in the presence of its

b young.

GLAUCON: That's right. But there is a risk, Socrates, and not a small one either, that in the event of a disaster of the sort that is likely to happen in a war, they will lose their children's lives as well as their own, making it impossible for the rest of the city to recover.

SOCRATES: That's true. But, in the first place, do you think they should arrange for the avoidance of all risk?

GLAUCON: Not at all.

SOCRATES: Well, then, if they must face some risk, shouldn't it be one in which they will be improved by success?

GLAUCON: Clearly.

SOCRATES: But you think, do you, that it makes little difference—and so is not worth the risk—whether or not men who are going to be warriors watch warfare when they are still boys?

GLAUCON: No, it does make a difference to what you are talking about.

SOCRATES: Starting from the assumption, then, that we are to make the children observers of war, we must further devise some way of keeping them safe. Then everything will be fine, won't it?

GLAUCON: Yes.

SOCRATES: Well, in the first place, their fathers won't be ignorant, will they, but rather as knowledgeable as people can be, about which military campaigns are dangerous and which are not?

GLAUCON: Presumably so.

SOCRATES: So, they will take the children on the latter, but be wary of taking them on the former.

GLAUCON: That's right.

SOCRATES: And they will not put the worst people in charge of them, I presume, but those whose experience and age qualifies them to be leaders and tutors.

GLAUCON: Yes, that would be proper.

SOCRATES: But we will say that the unexpected happens to many people and on many occasions.

GLAUCON: Yes, indeed.

SOCRATES: So, with that in mind, my friend, we must provide the young children with wings at the outset, so that, if the need arises, they can fly away and escape.

GLAUCON: What do you mean?

SOCRATES: We must mount them on horses when they are still very young, and when they have been taught to ride, they must be taken to view the fighting, not on spirited or aggressive horses, but on the fastest and most manageable ones. In this way, they will get the best view of their own future job, and will be able to make the safest escape, if the need arises, by following their older leaders.

GLAUCON: I think you are right.

SOCRATES: What about warfare itself? How should your soldiers behave toward one another and the enemy? Are my views correct or not?

GLAUCON: Tell me what they are.

SOCRATES: If one of them leaves his post, throws away his shield, or does anything else of that sort out of cowardice, shouldn't he be demoted to craftsman or farmer?

GLAUCON: Certainly.

SOCRATES: And if anyone is captured alive by the enemy, shouldn't he be presented to his captors as a catch to use however they wish?

GLAUCON: Absolutely.

SOCRATES: But if someone distinguishes himself and earns high honors, do you or don't you think that in the first place, while still on campaign, he should be crowned in turn by each of the adolescents and children who are with the army?

GLAUCON: I do.

SOCRATES: What about shaking him by the right hand?

GLAUCON: That too.

SOCRATES: But I do not imagine you would go so far as this.

GLAUCON: As what?

SOCRATES: That he should kiss, and be kissed by, each of them.

GLAUCON: By all means. And I would add to the law that while they are still on campaign, no one he wants to kiss shall be allowed to refuse, so that if anyone passionately loves another, whether male or female, he will try harder to win the prize for bravery.

SOCRATES: Excellent! For we have already mentioned that more opportunities for marriage will be available for a good man,[35] and that men like him will be selected more often than others for such things, so that as many children as possible may be produced from them.

GLAUCON: Yes, we did mention that.

SOCRATES: Moreover, according to Homer too, it is just to honor in such ways those young people who are good. For Homer says that when Ajax distinguished himself in battle, he "was rewarded with the whole backbone,"[36] since he considered that to be an appropriate honor for a courageous young man because it honored him and built up his strength at the same time.

GLAUCON: That's absolutely right.

SOCRATES: Then we will follow Homer in this matter, at any rate. I mean that at sacrifices and all other such occasions, we too will honor good

[35] 460b1–5.

[36] *Iliad* 7.321.

160

men—insofar as they have exhibited their goodness—not only with hymns and all the other things we mentioned, but also with "seats of honor, cuts of meats, and well-filled cups of wine,"[37] so that while honoring our good men and women, we may train them at the same time.

GLAUCON: That's an excellent idea.

SOCRATES: All right. And if any of those who died while on campaign has had a particularly distinguished death, won't we, in the first place, declare that he belongs to the golden race?[38]

GLAUCON: Absolutely.

SOCRATES: And won't we believe with Hesiod that, whenever any of that race die, they become "unsullied daimons living upon the earth, noble beings, protectors against evil, guardians of articulate mortals?"[39]

GLAUCON: We will certainly believe that.

SOCRATES: Won't we ask the god,[40] then, to tell us how and with what distinction these daimons, these godlike people, should be buried, and perform their burial in whatever way he prescribes?

GLAUCON: Of course.

SOCRATES: And for the remainder of time, won't we regard their graves as those of daimons, and take care of them and worship at them? And won't we follow these same rites whenever anyone who has been judged outstandingly good throughout his life dies of old age, or in some other way?

GLAUCON: It would be just to do so, at any rate.

SOCRATES: Now, what about enemies? How will our soldiers behave toward them?

GLAUCON: In what respect?

SOCRATES: First, as regards enslavement, do you think it is just for Greek cities to enslave other Greeks, or should they try as hard as possible not even to allow other cities to do so, and make a habit of sparing the Greek race as a precaution against being enslaved by barbarians?

GLAUCON: Sparing them is by far the best course.

SOCRATES: So, they should not possess any Greek slaves themselves, and should advise the other Greeks to do the same?

GLAUCON: By all means. In that way, at any rate, they would be more likely to turn against the barbarians and keep their hands off one another.

---

[37] *Iliad* 8.162.

[38] See 415a1–c7.

[39] *Works and Days* 122. See Glossary of Terms s.v. diamon.

[40] Apollo. See 427c2 note.

SOCRATES: What about despoiling the dead? Is it a good thing to strip the dead of anything besides their armor after a victory? Doesn't it give cowards

d a pretext for not facing the enemy, since when they are greedily bending over corpses, they will be performing an important duty? And haven't many armies been lost because of such plundering?

5 GLAUCON: Yes, indeed.

SOCRATES: Don't you think it is illiberal and money-loving to strip a corpse? And isn't it small-minded and womanish to regard a dead body as your enemy, when the enemy himself has flitted away leaving behind only the instrument with which he fought? Do you think that people who do this are any different from dogs who get angry with the stones thrown at

e them but leave the person throwing them alone?

GLAUCON: No different at all.

SOCRATES: So they should not strip corpses, should they, or refuse the

5 enemy permission to pick up their dead?

GLAUCON: No, by Zeus, they certainly should not.

SOCRATES: Moreover, we surely won't take weapons to the temples as offerings, and if we care anything about the goodwill of other Greeks, we

470a especially won't do this with Greek weapons. On the contrary, we would even be afraid of polluting[41] the temples if we brought them such things from our own race, unless, of course, the god ordains otherwise.

GLAUCON: That's absolutely right.

5 SOCRATES: What about ravaging Greek land and burning Greek houses? How will your soldiers behave toward their enemies?

GLAUCON: I would like to hear what *you* believe about that.

SOCRATES: Well, I believe they should do neither of these things, but

b destroy only the year's harvest. Do you want me to tell you why?

GLAUCON: Of course.

SOCRATES: It seems to me that just as we have the two names "war" and "faction," so there are also two things, and the names apply to differences

5 between the two. The two I mean are, on the one hand, what is one's own and kin, and, on the other, what is foreign and strange. "Faction" applies to hostility toward one's own, "war" to hostility toward strangers.

10 GLAUCON: Yes, there is nothing wrong with that claim.

c SOCRATES: Consider, then, whether this too is correct. I say that the Greek race, in relation to itself, is its own and kin, but, in relation to barbarians, is strange and foreign.

[41] Greek views on pollution are discussed in R. Parker, *Miasma* (Oxford: Clarendon Press, 1983).

162

GLAUCON: That's right.

SOCRATES: When Greeks fight with barbarians, then, or barbarians with Greeks, we will say that that is warfare, that they are natural enemies, and that such hostilities should be called war. But when Greeks engage in such things with Greeks, we will say they are natural friends, that Greece is sick and divided into factions in such a situation, and that such hostilities should be called faction.

GLAUCON: I, for one, agree to think that way.

SOCRATES: Now, notice that whenever something of the sort that is currently called faction occurs and a city is divided, if each side devastates the land and burns the houses of the other, the faction is thought abominable and neither party is thought to love the city—otherwise they would never have dared to ravage their own nurse and mother.[42] But it is thought reasonable for the ones who have proved stronger to carry off the weaker ones' crops, and to have the attitude of mind of people who will one day be reconciled and won't always be at war.

GLAUCON: That attitude of mind is far more civilized than the other.

SOCRATES: What about the city you are founding? Won't it be Greek?

GLAUCON: It will have to be.

SOCRATES: So won't its citizens be good and civilized people?

GLAUCON: Indeed, they will.

SOCRATES: Then won't they be lovers of Greeks? Won't they consider Greece as their own and share the same religious festivals as other Greeks?

GLAUCON: Yes, indeed.

SOCRATES: Then won't they regard their conflicts with Greeks—their own people—as faction, and not even use the name "war"?

GLAUCON: No, they won't use it.

SOCRATES: And so, they will quarrel with the aim of being reconciled, won't they?

GLAUCON: Of course.

SOCRATES: They will discipline their foes in a friendly spirit, then, and not punish them with enslavement and destruction, since they are discipliners, not enemies.

GLAUCON: That's right.

SOCRATES: As Greeks, then, they won't devastate Greece or burn its houses, nor will they agree that *all* the inhabitants in any city—men,

---

[42] See 414e1–6.

women, and children—are their enemies, but only those few responsible for the conflict. For all these reasons, they won't be willing to devastate

b   their country, since the majority of the inhabitants are their friends, nor destroy the houses, and they will pursue the conflict only to the point at which those responsible are forced to pay the penalty by the innocent ones

5   who are suffering painfully.

GLAUCON: I agree that this is how our citizens should treat their enemies, but they should treat barbarians the way Greeks currently treat each other.

SOCRATES: Then shall we also establish this law for the guardians, that

c   they should neither ravage Greek land nor burn Greek houses?

GLAUCON: Yes, let's establish it. And let's assume that this law and its predecessors are right. But, Socrates, I think that if you are allowed to go on talking about this sort of thing, you will never remember the topic you set

5   aside in order to say all this—namely, whether it is possible for this constitution to come into existence, and how it could ever do so. I agree that *if* it came into existence, everything would be lovely for the city that had it. I will even add some advantages that you have left out: they would fight excellently against their enemies because they would be least likely to

d   desert each other. After all, they recognize each other as brothers, fathers, and sons, and call each other by those names. And if the women, too, joined in their campaigns, either stationed in the same ranks or in the rear,

5   either to strike terror in the enemy or to provide support should the need ever arise, I know that this would make them quite unbeatable. And I also see all the good things they would have at home that you have omitted.

e   Take it for granted that I agree that all these benefits, as well as innumerable others, would result, *if* this constitution came into existence, and say no more about it. Instead, let's now try to convince ourselves of just this: that it is possible and how it is possible, and let's leave the rest aside.

472a   SOCRATES: All of a sudden, you have practically assaulted my argument and lost all sympathy for my holding back. Perhaps you do not realize that just as I have barely escaped from the first two waves of objections, you are now bringing the biggest and most difficult of the three down upon me.[43]

5   When you see and hear it, you will have complete sympathy and recognize that I had good reason after all for hesitating and for being afraid to state and try to examine so paradoxical an argument.

GLAUCON: The more you talk like that, the less we will let you get away

b   without explaining how this constitution could come into existence. So explain it, and do not delay any further.

SOCRATES: The first thing to recall, then, is that it was our inquiry into

5   the nature of justice and injustice that brought us to this point.

---

[43] The third wave was proverbially the greatest.

GLAUCON: True. But what of it?

SOCRATES: Oh, nothing. However, if we discover the nature of justice, should we also expect the just man not to differ from justice itself in any way, but, on the contrary, to have entirely the same nature it does? Or will we be satisfied if he approximates as closely as possible to it and partakes in it far more than anyone else?

GLAUCON: Yes, we will be satisfied with that.

SOCRATES: So, it was in order to have a model that we were inquiring into the nature of justice itself and of the completely just man, supposing he could exist, and what he would be like if he did; and similarly with injustice and the most unjust man. We thought that by seeing how they seemed to us to stand with regard to happiness and its opposite, we would also be compelled to agree about ourselves as well: that the one who was most like them would have a fate most like theirs. But we were not doing this in order to demonstrate that it is possible for these men to exist.

GLAUCON: That's true.

SOCRATES: Do you think, then, that someone would be any less good a painter if he painted a model of what the most beautiful human being would be like, and rendered everything in the picture perfectly well, but could not demonstrate that such a man could actually exist?

GLAUCON: No, by Zeus, I do not.

SOCRATES: What about our own case, then? Weren't we trying, as we put it, to produce a model in our discussion of a good city?[44]

GLAUCON: Certainly.

SOCRATES: So, do you think that our discussion will be any less satisfactory if we cannot demonstrate that it is possible to found a city that is the same as the one we described in speech?

GLAUCON: Not at all.

SOCRATES: Then that is the truth of the matter. But if, in order to please you, we must do our best to demonstrate how, and under what condition, this would be most possible, you must again grant me the same points for the purposes of that demonstration.

GLAUCON: Which ones?

SOCRATES: Is it possible for anything to be carried out exactly as described in speech, or is it natural for practice to have less of a grasp of truth than speech does, even if some people do not think so? Do you agree with this or not?

[44] See 369a5–c10.

GLAUCON: I do.

SOCRATES: Then do not compel me to demonstrate it as coming about in practice exactly as we have described it in speech. Rather, if we are able to discover how a city that most closely approximates to what we have described could be founded, you must admit that we have discovered how all you have prescribed could come about.[45] Or wouldn't you be satisfied with that? *I* certainly would.

GLAUCON: Me, too.

SOCRATES: Then next, it seems, we should try to discover and show what is badly done in cities nowadays that prevents them from being managed our way, and what the smallest change would be that would enable a city to arrive at our sort of constitution—preferably one change; otherwise, two; otherwise, the fewest in number and the least extensive in effect.

GLAUCON: Absolutely.

SOCRATES: Well, there is one change we could point to that I think would accomplish this. It certainly is not small or easy, but it *is* possible.

GLAUCON: What is it?

SOCRATES: I am now about to confront what we likened to the greatest wave. Yet, it must be stated, even if it is going to drown me in a wave of outright ridicule and contempt, as it were. So listen to what I am about to say.

GLAUCON: Say it.

SOCRATES: Until philosophers rule as kings in their cities, or those who are nowadays called kings and leading men become genuine and adequate philosophers so that political power and philosophy become thoroughly blended together, while the numerous natures that now pursue either one exclusively are forcibly prevented from doing so, cities will have no rest from evils, my dear Glaucon, nor, I think, will the human race. And until that happens, the same constitution we have now described in our discussion will never be born to the extent that it can, or see the light of the sun. It is this claim that has made me hesitate to speak for so long. I saw how very unbelievable it would sound, since it is difficult to accept that there can be no happiness, either public or private, in any other city.

GLAUCON: Socrates, what a speech, what an argument you have let burst with! But now that you have uttered it, you must expect that a great many people—and not undistinguished ones either—will immediately throw off their cloaks and, stripped for action, snatch any available weapon and make a headlong rush at you, determined to do terrible things to you. So, if you

---

[45] As at 458c6 and 473e4–5, Socrates is supposing that Glaucon is designing the ideal city.

do not defend yourself by argument and escape, you really will pay the penalty of general derision.

SOCRATES: But aren't *you* the one who is responsible for this happening to me?

GLAUCON: And I was right to do it. Still, I won't desert you. On the contrary, I will defend you in any way I can. And what I can do is provide good will and encouragement, and maybe give you more careful answers to your questions than someone else. So, with the promise of this sort of assistance, try to demonstrate to the unbelievers that things are as you claim.

SOCRATES: I will have to, especially when you agree to be so great an ally! If we are going to escape from the people you mention, I think we need to define for them who the philosophers are that we dare to say should rule; so that once that is clear, one can defend oneself by showing that some people are fitted by nature to engage in philosophy *and* to take the lead in a city, while there are others who should not engage in it, but should follow a leader.

GLAUCON: This would be a good time to define them.

SOCRATES: Come on, then, follow me on the path I am about to take, to see if it somehow leads to an adequate explanation.

GLAUCON: Lead on.

SOCRATES: Do I have to remind you, or do you recall, that when we say someone loves something, if the description is correct, it must be clear not just that he loves some part of it but not another; but, on the contrary, that he cherishes the whole of it?[46]

GLAUCON: You will have to remind me, it seems. I do not recall the point at all.

SOCRATES: I did not expect you to give that response, Glaucon. A passionate man should not forget that *all* boys in the bloom of youth somehow manage to sting and arouse a passionate lover of boys, and seem to merit his attention and passionate devotion. Isn't that the way you people behave to beautiful boys? One, because he is snub-nosed, you will praise as "cute;" another who is hook-nosed you will say is "regal;" while the one in the middle you say is "well proportioned." Dark ones look "manly," and pale ones are "children of the gods." As for the "honey-colored," do you think that this very term is anything but the euphemistic coinage of a lover who found it easy to tolerate a sallow complexion, provided it was accompanied by the bloom of youth? In a word, you people find any excuse, and use any expression, to avoid rejecting anyone whose flower is in full bloom.

[46] See 437d8–e8, 475b11–c4.

GLAUCON: If you insist on taking *me* as your example of what passionate men do, I will go along with you . . . for the sake of argument!

SOCRATES: What about lovers of wine? Don't you observe them behaving in just the same way? Don't they find any excuse to indulge their passionate devotion to wine of any sort?

GLAUCON: They do, indeed.

SOCRATES: And you also observe, I imagine, that if honor-lovers cannot become generals, they serve as lieutenants,[47] and if they cannot be honored by important people and dignitaries, they are satisfied with being honored by insignificant and inferior ones, since it is honor as a whole of which they are desirers.

GLAUCON: Exactly.

SOCRATES: Then do you affirm this or not? When we say that someone has an appetite for something, are we to say that he has an appetite for everything of that kind, or for one part of it but not another?

GLAUCON: Everything.

SOCRATES: Then in the case of the philosopher, too, won't we say that he has an appetite for *wisdom*—not for one part and not another, but for all of it?

GLAUCON: True.

SOCRATES: So, if someone is choosy about what he learns, especially if he is young and does not have a rational grasp of what is useful and what is not, we won't say that he is a lover of learning or a philosopher—any more than we would say that someone who is choosy about his food is famished, or has an appetite for food, or is a lover of food rather than a picky eater.

GLAUCON: And we would be right not to say it.

SOCRATES: But someone who is ready and willing to taste every kind of learning, who turns gladly to learning and is insatiable for it, *he* is the one we would be justified in calling a philosopher. Isn't that so?

GLAUCON: In that case, many strange people will be philosophers! I mean, all the lovers of seeing are what they are, I imagine, because they take pleasure in learning things. And the lovers of listening are very strange people to include as philosophers: they would never willingly attend a serious discussion or spend their time that way; yet, just as if their ears were under contract to listen to every chorus, they run around to all the Dionysiac festivals, whether in cities or villages, and never miss one. Are we to say that these people—and others who are students of similar things or of petty crafts—are philosophers?

[47] *Trittarchousi:* "command the soldiers in a trittys." A trittys was one third of one of the ten tribes of which Athens consisted.

SOCRATES: Not at all, but they are *like* philosophers.

GLAUCON: Who do you think, then, are the true ones?

SOCRATES: The lovers of seeing the truth.|

GLAUCON: That, too, is no doubt correct,[48] but what exactly do you mean by it? 5

SOCRATES: It would not be easy to explain to someone else. But you, I imagine, will agree to the following.

GLAUCON: What?

SOCRATES: That since beautiful is the opposite of ugly, they are two things.

GLAUCON: Of course. 476a

SOCRATES: And since they are two things, each of them is also one?

GLAUCON: That's true too.

SOCRATES: And the same argument applies, then, to just and unjust, good and bad, and all the forms: each of them is itself one thing, but because they appear all over the place in partnership with actions and bodies, and with one another, each of them appears to be many things. 5

GLAUCON: That's right.

SOCRATES: Well, then, that is the basis of the distinction I draw: on one side are the lovers of seeing, the lovers of crafts, and the practical people you mentioned a moment ago; on the other, those we are arguing about, the only ones it is correct to call philosophers. 10 b

GLAUCON: How do you mean?

SOCRATES: The lovers of listening and seeing are passionately devoted to beautiful sounds, colors, shapes, and everything fashioned out of such things.[49] But their thought is unable to see the nature of the beautiful itself or to be passionately devoted to it. 5

GLAUCON: That's certainly true.

SOCRATES: On the other hand, won't those who *are* able to approach the beautiful itself, and see it by itself, be rare? 10

GLAUCON: Very. c

SOCRATES: What about someone who believes in beautiful things but does not believe in the beautiful itself, and would not be able to follow anyone who tried to lead him to the knowledge of it? Do you think he is living in a dream, or is he awake? Just consider. Isn't it dreaming to think—

---

[48] See 449c6–8.

[49] A poem or play is fashioned out of sounds, a painting out of colors and shapes. See 600e4–601b4.

5 whether asleep or awake—that a likeness is not a likeness, but rather the thing itself that it is like?

GLAUCON: I certainly think that someone who does that is dreaming.

SOCRATES: But what about someone who, to take the opposite case, does believe in the beautiful itself, is able to observe both it and the things that
d participate in it, and does not think that the participants are it, or that it is the participants—do you think he is living in a dream or is awake?

GLAUCON: He is very much awake.

5 SOCRATES: So, because this person knows these things, we would be right to describe his thought as knowledge; but the other's we would be right to describe as belief, because he believes what he does?

GLAUCON: Certainly.

SOCRATES: What if the person we describe as believing but not knowing is angry with us and disputes the truth of what we say? Will we have any
e way of soothing and gently persuading him, while disguising the fact that he is not in a healthy state of mind?

GLAUCON: We certainly need one, at any rate.

SOCRATES: Come on, then, consider what we will say to him. Or—once
5 we have told him that nobody envies him any knowledge he may have— that, on the contrary, we would be delighted to discover that he knows something—do you want us to question him as follows? "Tell us this: does someone who knows know something or nothing?" You answer for him.

GLAUCON: I will answer that he knows something.

10 SOCRATES: Something that is[50] or something that is not?

477a GLAUCON: That is. How could something that is not be known?

SOCRATES: We are adequately assured of this, then, and would remain so, no matter how many ways we examined it: what completely is, is completely an object of knowledge; and what in no way is, is not an object of knowledge at all?

5 GLAUCON: Most adequately.

SOCRATES: Good. In that case, then, if anything is such as to be and also not to be, wouldn't it lie in between what purely is and what in no way is?

GLAUCON: Yes, in between them.

SOCRATES: Then, since knowledge deals with what is, ignorance must deal with what is not, while we must look in between knowledge and
10 ignorance for what deals with what lies in between, if there *is* anything of
b that sort.

---

[50] See Glossary of Terms s.v. thing that is.

170

GLAUCON: Yes.

SOCRATES: So, then, do we think there is such a thing as belief?

GLAUCON: Of course.

SOCRATES: Is it a different power from knowledge, or the same?

GLAUCON: A different one.

SOCRATES: So, belief has been assigned to deal with one thing, then, and knowledge with another, depending on what power each has.

GLAUCON: Right.

SOCRATES: Now, doesn't knowledge naturally deal with what is, to know how what is is? But first I think we had better go through the following.

GLAUCON: What?

SOCRATES: We think powers are a type of thing that enables us—or anything else that has an ability—to do whatever we are able to do. Sight and hearing are examples of what I mean by powers, if you understand the kind of thing I am trying to describe.

GLAUCON: Yes, I do.

SOCRATES: Listen, then, to what I think about them. A power has no color for me to see, nor a shape, nor any feature of the sort that many other things have, and that I can consider in order to distinguish them for myself as different from one another. In the case of a power, I can consider only what it deals with and what it does, and it is on that basis that I come to call each the power it is: those assigned to deal with the same things and do the same, I call the same; those that deal with different things and do different things, I call different. What about you? What do you do?

GLAUCON: The same.

SOCRATES: Going back, then, to where we left off, my very good fellow: do you think knowledge is itself a power? Or to what type would you assign it?

GLAUCON: To that one. It is the most effective power of all.

SOCRATES: What about belief? Shall we include it as a power or assign it to a different kind?

GLAUCON: Not at all. Belief is nothing other than the power that enables us to believe.

SOCRATES: But a moment ago you agreed that knowledge and belief are not the same.

GLAUCON: How could anyone with any sense think a fallible thing is the same as an infallible one?

SOCRATES: Fine. Then clearly we agree that belief is different from knowledge.

171

GLAUCON: Yes, it is different.

SOCRATES: Each of them, then, since it has a different power, deals by nature with something different?

5 GLAUCON: Necessarily.

SOCRATES: Surely knowledge deals with what is, to know what is as it is?

GLAUCON: Yes.

SOCRATES: Whereas belief, we say, believes?

GLAUCON: Yes.

SOCRATES: The very same thing that knowledge knows? Can the object
10 of knowledge and the object of belief be the same? Or is that impossible?

GLAUCON: It is impossible, given what we have agreed. If different powers by nature deal with different things, and both opinion and knowledge are
b powers but, as we claim, different ones, it follows from these that the object of knowledge and the object of belief cannot be the same.

SOCRATES: Then if what is is the object of knowledge, mustn't the object of belief be something other than what is?

5 GLAUCON: Yes, it must be something different.

SOCRATES: Does belief, then, believe what is not? Or is it impossible even to believe what is not? Consider this: doesn't a believer take his belief to deal with something? Or is it possible to believe, yet to believe nothing?

GLAUCON: No, it is impossible.

10 SOCRATES: In fact, there is some single thing that a believer believes?

GLAUCON: Yes.

SOCRATES: But surely what is not is most correctly characterized not as a
c single thing, but as nothing?

GLAUCON: Of course.

SOCRATES: But we had to assign ignorance to what is not and knowledge to what is?

5 GLAUCON: Correct.

SOCRATES: So belief neither believes what is nor what is not?

GLAUCON: No, it does not.

SOCRATES: Then belief cannot be either ignorance or knowledge?

GLAUCON: Apparently not.

10 SOCRATES: Well, then, does it lie beyond these two, surpassing knowledge in clarity or ignorance in opacity?

GLAUCON: No, it does neither.

SOCRATES: Then does belief seem to you to be more opaque than knowledge but clearer than ignorance?

GLAUCON: Very much so.   15

SOCRATES: It lies within the boundaries determined by them?   d

GLAUCON: Yes.

SOCRATES: So belief will lie in between the two?

GLAUCON: Absolutely.

SOCRATES: Now, didn't we say earlier that if something turned out both   5
to be and not to be at the same time, it would lie in between what purely is
and what in every way is not, and that neither knowledge nor ignorance
would deal with it; but whatever it was again that turned out to lie in
between ignorance and knowledge would?

GLAUCON: Correct.   10

SOCRATES: And now, what we are calling belief has turned out to lie in
between them?

GLAUCON: It has.

SOCRATES: Apparently, then, it remains for us to find what partakes in   e
both being and not being, and cannot correctly be called purely one or the
other, so that if we find it, we can justifiably call it the object of belief,
thereby assigning extremes to extremes and in-betweens to in-betweens.
Isn't that so?   5

GLAUCON: It is.

SOCRATES: Now that all that has been established, I want him to tell me
this—the excellent fellow who believes that there is no beautiful itself, no
form of beauty itself that remains always the same in all respects, but who   479a
does believe that there are many beautiful things—I mean, that lover of seeing who cannot bear to hear anyone say that the beautiful is one thing, or
the just, or any of the rest—I want him to answer this question: "My very
good fellow," we will say, "of all the many beautiful things, is there one that   5
won't also seem ugly? Or any just one that won't seem unjust? Or any pious
one that won't seem impious?"

GLAUCON: There is not. On the contrary, it is inevitable that they would
somehow seem both beautiful and ugly; and the same with the other things   b
you asked about.

SOCRATES: What about the many things that are doubles? Do they seem
to be any the less halves than doubles?

GLAUCON: No.   5

SOCRATES: And again, will things that we say are big, small, light, or
heavy be any more what we say they are than they will be the opposite?

173

GLAUCON: No, each of them is always both.

SOCRATES: Then is each of the many things any more what one says it is
than it is not what one says it is?

GLAUCON: No, they are like those puzzles one hears at parties, or the children's riddle about the eunuch who threw something at a bat—the one about what he threw at it and what it was in.[51] For these things, too, are ambiguous, and one cannot understand them as fixedly being or fixedly not being, or as both, or as neither.

SOCRATES: Do you know what to do with them, then, or anywhere better to put them than in between being and not being? Surely they cannot be more opaque than what is not, by not-being more than it; nor clearer than what is, by *being* more than it.

GLAUCON: That's absolutely true.

SOCRATES: So, we have now discovered, it seems, that the majority of people's many conventional views about beauty and the rest are somehow rolling around between what is not and what purely is.[52]

GLAUCON: We have.

SOCRATES: And we agreed earlier that if anything turned out to be of that sort, it would have to be called an object of belief, not an object of knowledge—a wandering, in-between object grasped by the in-between power.

GLAUCON: We did.

SOCRATES: As for those, then, who look at many beautiful things but do not see the beautiful itself, and are incapable of following another who would lead them to it; or many just things but not the just itself, and similarly with all the rest—these people, we will say, have beliefs about all these things, but have no knowledge of what their beliefs are about.

GLAUCON: That is what we would have to say.

SOCRATES: On the other hand, what about those who in each case look at the things themselves that are always the same in every respect? Won't we say that they have knowledge, not mere belief?

GLAUCON: Once again, we would have to.

---

[51] The riddle seems to have been this: a man who is not a man saw and did not see a bird that was not a bird in a tree (*xulon*) that was not a tree; he hit (*ballein*) and did not hit it with a stone that was not a stone. The answer is that a eunuch with bad eyesight saw a bat on a rafter, threw a pumice stone at it, and missed. For "he saw a bird" is ambiguous between "he saw what was actually a bird" and "he saw what he took to be a bird," *xulon* means both "tree" and "rafter" or "roof tree," and *ballein* means both "to throw" and "to hit." The rest is obvious.

[52] See 484c6–d3, 493a6–494a4.

SOCRATES: Shall we say, then, that these people are passionately devoted to and love the things with which knowledge deals, as the others are devoted to and love the things with which belief deals? We have not forgotten, have we, that the latter love and look at beautiful sounds, colors, and things of that sort, but cannot even bear the idea that the beautiful itself is a thing that is?

GLAUCON: No, we have not.

SOCRATES: Will we be striking a false note,[53] then, if we call such people "philodoxers" (lovers of belief) rather than "philosophers" (lovers of wisdom or knowledge)? Will they be very angry with us if we call them that?

GLAUCON: Not if they take my advice. It is not in accord with divine law to be angry with the truth.

SOCRATES: So, those who in each case are passionately devoted to the thing itself are the ones we must call, not "philodoxers," but "philosophers"?

GLAUCON: Absolutely.

---

[53] See 451b3.

Book 6

SOCRATES: Who the philosophers are, then, Glaucon, and who they aren't has, through a somewhat lengthy argument and with much effort, somehow been made clear.

GLAUCON: That's probably because it could not easily have been done through a shorter one.

SOCRATES: I suppose not. Yet I, at least, think that the matter would have been made even clearer if we had had only that topic to discuss, and not the many others that remain for us to explore if we are to discover the difference between the just life and the unjust one.

GLAUCON: What comes after this one, then?

SOCRATES: What else but the one that comes next? Since the philosophers are the ones who are able to grasp what is always the same in all respects, while those who cannot—those who wander among the many things that vary in every sort of way—are not philosophers, which of the two should be the leaders of a city?

GLAUCON: What would be a reasonable answer for us to give?

SOCRATES: Whichever of them seems capable of guarding a city's laws and practices should be established as guardians.

GLAUCON: That's right.

SOCRATES: So, is the answer to the following question clear: should a guardian who is going to keep watch over something be blind or keen-sighted?

GLAUCON: Of course it is.

SOCRATES: Well, do you think there is any difference, then, between the blind and those who are really deprived of the knowledge of each thing that is, and have no clear model of it in their souls—those who cannot look away, like painters, to what is most true, and cannot, by making constant reference to it and by studying it as exactly as possible, establish here on earth conventional views about beautiful, just, or good things[1] when

---

[1] See 479d3–5 for what happens to conventions not established in this way.

they need to be established, or guard and preserve those that have been established?

GLAUCON: No, by Zeus, there is not much difference between them.

SOCRATES: Shall we appoint these blind people as our guardians, then, or those who know each thing that is, have no less experience than the others,[2] and are not inferior to them in any other part of virtue?

GLAUCON: It would be absurd to choose anyone but philosophers, if indeed they are not inferior in these other things. For the very area in which they are superior is just about the most important one.

SOCRATES: Shouldn't we explain, then, how the same men can have both sets of qualities?

GLAUCON: Certainly.

SOCRATES: Then, as we were saying at the beginning of this discussion, it is first necessary to understand the nature of philosophers.[3] And I think that if we can agree sufficiently about that, we will also agree that the same people *can* have both qualities, and that they alone should be leaders in cities.

GLAUCON: How so?

SOCRATES: Let's agree that philosophic natures always love the sort of learning that makes clear to them some feature of the being[4] that always is and does not wander around between coming-to-be and decaying.

GLAUCON: Yes, let's.

SOCRATES: And further, let's agree that they love all of it and are not willing to give up any part, whether large or small, significant or insignificant, just like the honor-lovers and passionate men we described before.[5]

GLAUCON: That's right.

SOCRATES: Consider next whether there is a further feature they must have in their nature if they are going to be the way we described.

GLAUCON: What?

SOCRATES: Truthfulness; that is to say they must never willingly tolerate falsehood in any form. On the contrary, they must hate it and have a natural affection for the truth.

GLAUCON: They probably should have that feature.

---

[2] See 539e2–540c2, 581c10–583a11.

[3] See 474b3–c3.

[4] See Glossary of Terms s.v. being.

[5] See 474d3–475b2.

SOCRATES: But it is not only *probable,* my friend; it is entirely necessary for a naturally passionate man to love everything akin to or related to the boys he loves.

GLAUCON: That's right.

SOCRATES: Well, could you find anything that is more intimately related to wisdom than truth?

GLAUCON: Of course not.

SOCRATES: Then is it possible for the same nature to be a philosopher (lover of wisdom) and a lover of falsehood?

GLAUCON: Certainly not.

SOCRATES: So, right from childhood, a genuine lover of learning must strive above all for truth of every kind.

GLAUCON: Absolutely.

SOCRATES: But in addition, when someone's appetites are strongly inclined in one direction, we surely know that they become more weakly inclined in the others, just like a stream that has been partly diverted into another channel.

GLAUCON: Of course.

SOCRATES: Then when a person's desires flow toward learning and everything of that sort, they will be concerned, I imagine, with the pleasures that the soul experiences just by itself, and will be indifferent to those that come through the body—if indeed the person is not a counterfeit, but rather a true, philosopher.[6]

GLAUCON: That's entirely inevitable.

SOCRATES: A person like that will be temperate, then, and in no way a lover of money. After all, money and the big expenditures that go along with it are sought for the sake of things that other people may take seriously, but that he does not.

GLAUCON: That's right.

SOCRATES: And of course, there is also this to consider when you are going to judge whether a nature is philosophic or not.

GLAUCON: What?

SOCRATES: You should not overlook its sharing in illiberality; for surely petty-mindedness is altogether incompatible with that quality in a soul that is always reaching out to grasp all things as a whole, whether divine or human.

GLAUCON: That's absolutely true.

[6] See *Phaedo* 64c10–67c3.

SOCRATES: And do you imagine that a thinker who is high-minded enough to look at all time and all being will consider human life to be a very important thing? 10

GLAUCON: He couldn't possibly.

SOCRATES: Then he won't consider death to be a terrible thing either, will he? b

GLAUCON: Not in the least.

SOCRATES: Then a cowardly and illiberal nature could not partake, apparently, in true philosophy.

GLAUCON: Not in my opinion. 5

SOCRATES: Well, then, is there any way that an orderly person, who is not money-loving, illiberal, a lying imposter, or a coward, could come to drive a hard bargain or be unjust?

GLAUCON: There is not.

SOCRATES: Moreover, when you are considering whether someone has a philosophic soul or not, you will consider whether he is just and gentle, 10 right from the time he is young, or unsociable and savage.

GLAUCON: Of course.

SOCRATES: And you won't ignore this either, I imagine. c

GLAUCON: What?

SOCRATES: Whether he is a slow learner or a fast one. Or do you expect someone to love something sufficiently well when it pains him to do it and a lot of effort brings only a small return? 5

GLAUCON: No, it could not happen.

SOCRATES: What if he could retain nothing of what he learned, because he was completely forgetful? Could he fail to be empty of knowledge?

GLAUCON: Of course not.

SOCRATES: Then if he is laboring in vain, don't you think that in the end 10 he is bound to hate himself and what he is doing?

GLAUCON: Of course.

SOCRATES: So let's never include a person with a forgetful soul among those who are sufficiently philosophical; the one we look for should be d good at remembering.

GLAUCON: Absolutely.

SOCRATES: Moreover, we would deny that an unmusical and graceless nature is drawn to anything besides what is disproportionate. 5

GLAUCON: Of course.

SOCRATES: And do you think that truth is akin to what is disproportionate or to what is proportionate?

GLAUCON: To what is proportionate.

SOCRATES: Then, in addition to those other things, let's look for a mind that has a natural sense of proportion and grace, one whose innate disposi-
10   tion makes it easy to lead to the form of each thing which is.

GLAUCON: Indeed.

e   SOCRATES: Well, then, do you think the properties we have gone through aren't interconnected, or that any of them is in any way unnecessary to a soul that is going to have a sufficiently complete grasp of what is?

487a GLAUCON: No, they are all absolutely necessary.

SOCRATES: Is there any criticism you can find, then, of a pursuit that a person cannot practice adequately unless he is naturally good at remembering, quick to learn, high-minded, graceful, and a friend and relative of
5   truth, justice, courage, and temperance?

GLAUCON: Not even Momus could criticize a pursuit like that.

SOCRATES: Well, then, when people of this sort are in perfect condition because of their education and their stage of life, wouldn't you entrust the city to them alone?

And Adeimantus replied:

b   No one, Socrates, would be able to contradict these claims of yours. But all the same, here is pretty much the experience people have on any occasion on which they hear the sorts of things you are now saying: they think that because they are inexperienced in asking and answering questions, they are
5   led astray a little bit by the argument at every question, and that when these little bits are added together at the end of the discussion, a big false step appears that is the opposite of what they said at the outset. Like the unskilled, who are trapped by the clever checkers players in the end and
c   cannot make a move, they too are trapped in the end, and have nothing to say in this different kind of checkers, which is played not with pieces, but with words. Yet they are not a bit more inclined to think that what you claim is true. I say this in relation to the present case. You see, someone might well say now that he is unable to find the words to oppose you as you
5   ask each of your questions. Yet, when it comes to facts rather than words, he sees that of all those who take up philosophy—not those who merely dabble in it while still young in order to complete their upbringing, and
d   then drop it, but those who continue in it for a longer time—the majority become cranks, not to say completely bad, while the ones who seem best
5   are rendered useless to the city because of the pursuit you recommend.

When I had heard him out, I said:

Do you think that what these people say is false?

ADEIMANTUS: I do not know. But I would be glad to hear what you think.

SOCRATES: You would hear that they seem to me to be telling the truth.

ADEIMANTUS: How, then, can it be right to say that there will be no end to evils in our cities until philosophers—people we agree to be useless to cities—rule in them?

SOCRATES: The question you ask needs to be answered by means of an image.[7]

ADEIMANTUS: And you, of course, are not used to speaking in images!

SOCRATES: So! After landing me with a claim that is so difficult to establish, are you mocking me, too? Anyway, listen to my image, and you will appreciate all the more how I have to strain to make up images. What the best philosophers experience in relation to cities is so difficult to bear that there is no other single experience like it. On the contrary, one must construct one's image and one's defense of these philosophers from *many* sources, just as painters paint goat-stags by combining the features of different things.

Imagine, then, that the following sort of thing happens either on one ship or on many. The shipowner is taller and stronger than everyone else on board. But he is hard of hearing, he is a bit shortsighted, and his knowledge of seafaring is correspondingly deficient. The sailors are quarreling with one another about captaincy.[8] Each of them thinks that he should captain the ship, even though he has not yet learned the craft and cannot name his teacher or a time when he was learning it. Indeed, they go further and claim that it cannot be taught at all, and are even ready to cut to pieces anyone who says it can. They are always crowding around the shipowner himself, pleading with him, and doing everything possible to get him to turn the rudder over to them. And sometimes, if they fail to persuade him and others succeed, they execute those others or throw them overboard. Then, having disabled their noble shipowner with mandragora[9] or drink or in some other way, they rule the ship, use up its cargo drinking and feasting, and make the sort of voyage you would expect of such people. In addition, they praise anyone who is clever at persuading or forcing the shipowner to let them rule, calling him a "sailor," a "skilled captain," and "an expert about ships" while dismissing anyone else as a

---

[7] *Eikos:* also, likeness.

[8] See Glossary of Terms s.v. captain.

[9] An intoxicant.

5 good-for-nothing. They do not understand that a true captain must pay attention to the seasons of the year, the sky, the stars, the winds, and all that pertains to his craft if he is really going to be expert at ruling a ship. As for *how* he is going to become captain of the ship, whether people want him e to or not, they do not think it possible to acquire the craft or practice of doing this at the same time as the craft of captaincy. When that is what is happening onboard ships, don't you think that a true captain would be sure 489a to be called a "stargazer," a "useless babbler," and a "good-for-nothing" by those who sail in ships so governed?

ADEIMANTUS: I certainly do.

SOCRATES: I do not think you need to examine the image to see the
5 resemblance to cities and how they're disposed toward true philosophers, but you already understand what I mean.

ADEIMANTUS: Indeed, I do.

SOCRATES: First teach this image, then, to the person who is surprised
10 that philosophers are not honored in cities, and try to persuade him that it
b would be far more surprising if they were honored.

ADEIMANTUS: I will.

SOCRATES: Furthermore, try to persuade him that you are speaking the truth when you say that the best among the philosophers are useless to the masses. But tell him to blame their uselessness on those who do not make
5 use of them, not on those good philosophers. You see, it is not natural for the captain to beg the sailors to be ruled by him, nor for the wise to knock at the doors of the rich. The man who came up with that bit of sophistry was lying.[10] What is truly natural is for the sick person, rich or poor, to go to doctors' doors, and for anyone who needs to be ruled to go to the doors
c of the one who can rule him. It is not for the ruler—if he is truly any use—to beg the subjects to accept his rule. Tell him he will make no mistake if he likens our present political rulers to the sailors we mentioned a
5 moment ago, and those who are called useless stargazers by them to the true ship's captains.

ADEIMANTUS: That's absolutely right.

SOCRATES: For those reasons, then, and in these circumstances, it is not easy for the best pursuit to be highly honored by those whose pursuits are its
10 very opposites. But by far the greatest and most serious slander is brought
d on philosophy by those who claim to practice it—the ones about whom the prosecutor of philosophy declares, as you put it, that the majority of those

---

[10] Aristotle, *Rhetoric* 1391a7–12, says that when Simonides was asked whether it was better to be rich or wise, he replied: "Rich—because the wise spend their time at the doors of the rich."

who take it up are completely bad, while the best ones are useless. And I admitted that what you said was true, didn't I?[11]

ADEIMANTUS: Yes.

SOCRATES: Haven't we now explained why the good ones are useless?

ADEIMANTUS: We certainly have.

SOCRATES: Do you next want us to discuss why it is inevitable that the greater number are bad, and try to show, if we can, that philosophy is not responsible for this either?

ADEIMANTUS: Certainly.

SOCRATES: Then let's begin our dialogue by recalling the starting point of our description of the nature that someone must have if he is to become a fine and good person. First of all, if you remember, he was led by truth,[12] and he had to follow it wholeheartedly and unequivocally, on pain of being a lying imposter with no share at all in true philosophy.

ADEIMANTUS: That's what we said.

SOCRATES: Well, isn't that fact alone completely contrary to the belief currently held about him?

ADEIMANTUS: It certainly is.

SOCRATES: So, won't it be reasonable, then, for us to plead in his defense that a real lover of learning naturally strives for what is? He does not linger over each of the many things that are believed to be, but keeps on going, without losing or lessening his passion, until he grasps what the nature of each thing itself is[13] with the part of his soul that is fitted to grasp a thing of that sort because of its kinship with it.[14] Once he has drawn near to it, has intercourse with what really is, and has begotten understanding and truth, he knows, truly lives, is nourished, and—at that point, but not before—is relieved from his labor pains.

ADEIMANTUS: Nothing could be more reasonable.

SOCRATES: Well, then, will a person of that sort love falsehood or, in completely opposite fashion, will he hate it?

ADEIMANTUS: He will hate it.

SOCRATES: And if truth led the way, we would never say, I imagine, that a chorus of evils could follow it.

---

[11] 487d10.

[12] 485c3.

[13] *Autou ho estin hekastou tês phuseôs:* literally, "the what it is of the nature of each thing itself." See Glossary of Terms s.v. what it is.

[14] See 611e1–612a6.

ADEIMANTUS: Of course not.

SOCRATES: On the contrary, it is followed by a healthy and just character, and the temperance that accompanies it.

ADEIMANTUS: That's right.

SOCRATES: What need is there, then, to go back to the beginning and compel the rest of the philosophic nature's chorus to line up all over again? You surely remember that courage, high-mindedness, ease in learning, and a good memory all belong to philosophers. Then you objected that anyone would be compelled to agree with what we are saying, but that if he left the arguments aside and looked at the very people the argument is about, he would say that some of those he saw were useless, while the majority of them were thoroughly bad. Trying to discover the reason for this slander, we have arrived now at this question: why are the majority of them bad? And *that* is why we have again taken up the nature of the true philosophers and defined what it necessarily has to be.

ADEIMANTUS: That's right.

SOCRATES: What we now have to do is look at the ways this nature gets corrupted; how it gets completely destroyed in the majority of cases, while a small number escape—the very ones that are called useless, rather than bad. After that, we must next look at those who imitate this nature and adopt its pursuit. We must see what natures the souls have that enter into a pursuit that is too valuable and too high for them—souls that, by often striking false notes, give philosophy the reputation that you said it has with everyone everywhere.

ADEIMANTUS: What sorts of corruption do you mean?

SOCRATES: I will try to explain them to you if I can. I imagine that everyone would agree with us about this: the sort of nature that possesses all the qualities we prescribed just now for the person who is going to be a complete philosopher, is seldom found among human beings, and there will be few who possess it. Or don't you think so?

ADEIMANTUS: I most certainly do.

SOCRATES: Consider, then, how many great sources of destruction there are for these few.

ADEIMANTUS: What are they?

SOCRATES: The most surprising thing of all to hear is that each one of the things we praised in that nature tends to corrupt the soul that has it and drag it away from philosophy. I mean courage, temperance, and the other things we mentioned.

ADEIMANTUS: That does sound strange.

SOCRATES: Furthermore, in addition to those, all so-called good things   c
also corrupt it and drag it away—beauty, wealth, physical strength, powerful
family connections in the city, and all that goes along with these. You
understand the general pattern of thing I mean?

ADEIMANTUS: I do, and I would be glad to acquire a more precise understanding of it.   5

SOCRATES: Grasp the general principle correctly and the matter will
become clear to you, and what I said about it before won't seem so strange.

ADEIMANTUS: What are you telling me to grasp?   10

SOCRATES: In the case of every seed or growing thing, whether plant or   d
animal, we know that if it fails to get the food, climate, or location suitable
for it, then the more vigorous it is, the more it is deficient in the qualities
proper to it. For surely bad is more opposed to good than to not-good.   5

ADEIMANTUS: Of course.

SOCRATES: So, I suppose it is reasonable that the best nature comes off
worse than an inferior one from unsuitable nurture.

ADEIMANTUS: It is.

SOCRATES: Well, then, Adeimantus, won't we also say that if *souls* with the   e
best natures get a bad education, they become exceptionally bad? Or do
you think that great injustices and unalloyed evil originate in an inferior
nature, rather than in a vigorous one that has been corrupted by its
upbringing? Or that a weak nature is ever responsible for great good things   5
or great bad ones?

ADEIMANTUS: No, you are right.

SOCRATES: Well, then, if the nature we proposed for the philosopher hap-   492a
pens to receive the proper instruction, I imagine it will inevitably grow to
attain every virtue. But if it is not sown, planted, and grown in a suitable
environment, it will develop in entirely the opposite way, unless some god
comes to its aid. Or do you too believe, as the masses do, that some young   5
people are corrupted by sophists—that there are sophists, private individuals, who corrupt them to a significant extent? Isn't it, rather, the very people who say this who are the greatest sophists of all, who educate most
effectively and produce young and old men and women of just the sort   b
they want?

ADEIMANTUS: When do they do that?

SOCRATES: When many of them sit together in assemblies, courts, the-   5
aters, army camps, or any other gathering of a majority in public and, with
a loud uproar, object excessively to some of the things that are said or
done, then approve excessively of others, shouting and clapping; and

185

c   when, in addition to these people themselves, the rocks and the surrounding space itself echo and redouble the uproar of their praise or blame. In a situation like that, how do you think—as the saying goes—a young man's heart is affected?[15] How will whatever sort of private education he received

5   hold up for him, and not get swept away by such praise and blame, and go be carried off by the flood wherever it goes, so that he will call the same things beautiful or ugly as these people, practice what they practice, and become like them?

d   ADEIMANTUS: The compulsion to do so will be enormous, Socrates.

SOCRATES: And yet we have not mentioned the greatest compulsion of all.

ADEIMANTUS: What is that?

5   SOCRATES: It is what these educators and sophists impose by their actions if their words fail to persuade. Or don't you know that they punish anyone who is not persuaded, with disenfranchisement, fines, or death?

ADEIMANTUS: They most certainly do.

SOCRATES: What other sophist, then, or what sort of private conversations

10   do you think will oppose these and prove stronger?

e   ADEIMANTUS: None, I imagine.

SOCRATES: No, indeed, even to try would be very foolish. You see, there is not now, never has been, nor ever will be, a character whose view of virtue goes contrary to the education these provide. I mean a human charac-

5   ter, comrade—the divine, as the saying goes, is an exception to the rule. You may be sure that if anything is saved and turns out well in the political

493a   systems that exist now, you won't be mistaken in saying that divine providence saved it.

ADEIMANTUS: That is what I think, too.

SOCRATES: Well, then, you should also agree to this.

5   ADEIMANTUS: What?

SOCRATES: Each of those private wage-earners—the ones these people call sophists and consider to be their rivals in craft[16]—teaches anything other than the convictions the masses hold when they are assembled together, and this he calls wisdom. It is just as if someone were learning

10   the passions and appetites of a huge, strong beast that he is rearing—how

b   to approach and handle it, when it is most difficult to deal with or most docile and what makes it so, what sounds it utters in either condition, and what tones of voice soothe or anger it. Having learned all this through

---

[15] See Homer, *Iliad* 24.367.

[16] I.e., rivals in the craft of teaching virtue. See *Apology* 24c–25c, *Protagoras* 317e–328d, and Glossary of Terms s.v. sophist.

associating and spending time[17] with the beast, he calls this wisdom, gathers his information together as if it were a craft, and starts to teach it. Knowing nothing in reality about which of these convictions or appetites is fine or shameful, good or bad, just or unjust, he uses all these terms in conformity with the great beast's beliefs—calling the things it enjoys good and the things that anger it bad. He has no other account to give of them, but calls everything he is compelled to do just and fine, never having seen how much the natures of necessity and goodness really differ, and being unable to explain it to anyone. Don't you think, by Zeus, that someone like that would make a strange educator?

ADEIMANTUS: I do, indeed.

SOCRATES: Then does this person seem any different from the one who believes that wisdom is understanding the passions and pleasures of the masses—multifarious people—assembled together, whether in regard to painting, music, or politics for that matter? For if a person associates with the masses and exhibits his poetry or some other piece of craftsmanship to them or his service to the city, and gives them mastery over him to any degree beyond what is unavoidable, he will be under Diomedean compulsion,[18] as it is called, to produce the things of which they approve. But that such things are truly good and beautiful—have you ever heard anyone presenting an argument for that conclusion that was not absolutely ridiculous?

ADEIMANTUS: No, and I do not suppose I ever will.

SOCRATES: So then, bearing all that in mind, recall our earlier question: can the majority in any way tolerate or accept that the beautiful itself (as opposed to the many beautiful things), or each thing itself (as opposed to the corresponding many), exists?

ADEIMANTUS: Not in the least.

SOCRATES: It is impossible, then, for the majority to be philosophic.

ADEIMANTUS: It is impossible.

SOCRATES: And so, those who practice philosophy are inevitably disparaged by them?

ADEIMANTUS: Inevitably.

SOCRATES: And also by those private individuals who associate with the majority and want to please them.

ADEIMANTUS: Clearly.

---

[17] *Chronou tribê:* On the distinction between a craft (*technê*) and an experience-based knack (*tribê, empeiria*), see *Gorgias* 462b–465a.

[18] An inescapable compulsion. The origin of the phrase is uncertain.

SOCRATES: On the basis of these facts, then, do you see any way to pre-serve a philosophic nature and ensure that it will continue to practice phi-losophy and reach the end? Consider the question in light of what we said before. We agreed that ease in learning, a good memory, courage, and high-mindedness belong to the philosophic nature.

ADEIMANTUS: Yes.

SOCRATES: Right from the start, then, won't someone like that be first among the children in everything, especially if his body's nature matches that of his soul?

ADEIMANTUS: Of course he will.

SOCRATES: So as he gets older, I imagine his family and fellow citizens will want to make use of him in connection with their own affairs.

ADEIMANTUS: Certainly.

SOCRATES: They will get down on their knees, begging favors from him and honoring him, flattering ahead of time the power that is going to be his, so as to secure it for themselves.

ADEIMANTUS: That's usually what happens, at least.

SOCRATES: What do you think someone like that will do in such circum-stances—especially if he happens to be from a great city where he is rich and noble, and if he is good-looking and tall as well? Won't he be filled with an impractical expectation and think himself capable of managing the affairs, not only of the Greeks, but of the barbarians, too? And won't he exalt himself to great heights, as a result, and be brimming with pretension and empty, senseless pride?[19]

ADEIMANTUS: He certainly will.

SOCRATES: Now, suppose someone gently approaches a young man in that state of mind and tells him the truth: that he has no sense, although he needs it, and that it cannot be acquired unless he works like a slave to attain it. Do you think it will be easy for him to hear that message through the evils that surround him?

ADEIMANTUS: Far from it.

SOCRATES: And suppose that, because of his noble nature and his natural affinity for such arguments, he somehow sees the point and is turned around and drawn toward philosophy. What do we suppose those people will do if they believe that they are losing his services and companionship? Is there anything they won't do or say in his regard to prevent him from

---

[19] Plato seems to have had Alcibiades in mind here and in what follows. See *Alcibiades* 104a–c, 105b–c, *Symposium* 215d–216d. Alcibiades' extraordinary career is described in Thucydides, Books 6–8.

being persuaded? Or anything they won't do or say in regard to his per-
suader to prevent him from succeeding, whether it is in private plots or
public court cases?[20]

ADEIMANTUS: There certainly is not.

SOCRATES: Then is there any chance that such a person will practice philosophy?

ADEIMANTUS: None at all.

SOCRATES: Do you see, then, that we weren't wrong to say that when a
philosophic nature is badly brought up, its very components—together
with the other so-called goods, such as wealth and every provision of that
sort—are somehow the cause of its falling away from the pursuit?

ADEIMANTUS: No, we were not. What we said was right.

SOCRATES: There you are, then, you amazing fellow! That is the extent of
the sort of destruction and corruption that the nature best suited for the
noblest pursuit undergoes. And such a nature is a rare occurrence anyway,
we claim. Moreover, men who possess it are the ones that do the worst
things to cities and individuals, and also—if they happen to be swept that
way by the current[21]—the greatest good. For a petty nature never does anything great, either to a private individual or a city.

ADEIMANTUS: That's very true.

SOCRATES: So when these men, for whom philosophy is most appropriate, fall away from her, they leave her desolate and unwed, and themselves
lead a life that is inappropriate and untrue. Then others, who are unworthy
of her, come to her as to an orphan bereft of kinsmen, and shame her. They
are the ones responsible for the reproaches that you say are cast upon philosophy by her detractors—that some of her consorts are useless, while the
majority deserve many evils.

ADEIMANTUS: Yes, that is what they say.

SOCRATES: And it is a reasonable thing to say. For other worthless little
men see that this position has become vacant, even though it is brimming
with fine accolades and pretensions, and—like prisoners escaping from jail
who take refuge in a temple—leap gladly from their crafts to philosophy.
These are the ones who are most sophisticated at their own petty craft. You
see, at least in comparison to other crafts, and even in its present state, philosophy still has a grander reputation. And that is what many people are
aiming at, people with defective natures, whose souls are as cramped and
spoiled by their menial tasks as their bodies are warped by their crafts and
occupations. Isn't that inevitably what happens?

[20] The trial of Socrates in 399 BCE is the obvious case in point.
[21] See 485d.

ADEIMANTUS: It certainly is.

SOCRATES: Do you think that they look any different than a little, bald-
headed blacksmith who has come into some money and, newly released
from debtor's prison, has taken a bath, put on a new cloak, got himself up
as a bridegroom, and is about to marry the master's daughter because she is
poor and abandoned?

496a ADEIMANTUS: They are no different at all.

SOCRATES: What sort of offspring are they likely to beget, then? Won't
their children be wretched illegitimates?

ADEIMANTUS: Inevitably.

SOCRATES: What about when men who are unworthy of education
approach philosophy and associate with her in a way unworthy of her?
What kinds of thoughts and beliefs are we to say they beget? Won't they be
what are truly and appropriately called sophisms, since they have nothing
genuine or truly wise about them?

ADEIMANTUS: Absolutely.

SOCRATES: Then there remains, Adeimantus, only a very small group who
associate with philosophy in a way that is worthy of her: a noble and well
brought-up character, perhaps, kept down by exile, who stays true to his
nature and remains with philosophy because there is no one to corrupt
him; or a great soul living in a small city, who disdains the city's affairs and
looks beyond them. A very few might perhaps come to philosophy from
other crafts that they rightly despise because they have good natures. And
some might be held back by the bridle that restrains our friend Theages—
you see, he meets all the other conditions needed to make him fall away
from philosophy, but his physical illness keeps him out of politics and prevents it. Finally, my own case is hardly worth mentioning—my daimonic
sign[22]—since I don't suppose it has happened to anyone else or to only a
few before. Now, those who have become members of this little group
have tasted how sweet and blessed a possession philosophy is. At the same
time, they have also seen the insanity of the masses and realized that there is
nothing healthy, so to speak, in public affairs, and that there is no ally with
whose aid the champion of justice can survive; that instead he would perish
before he could profit either their city or his friends, and be useless both to
himself and to others—like a man who has fallen among wild animals and
is neither willing to join them in doing injustice nor sufficiently strong to
oppose the general savagery alone. Taking all this into his calculations, he
keeps quiet and does his own work, like someone who takes refuge under a

---

[22] See Plato, *Apology* 31c–32a, where Socrates explains that his *daimonion* has kept
him out of politics.

little wall from a storm of dust or hail driven by the wind. Seeing others filled with lawlessness, the philosopher is satisfied if he can somehow lead his present life pure of injustice and impious acts, and depart from it with good hope, blameless and content.

e

ADEIMANTUS: Well, that is no small thing for him to have accomplished before departing.

497a

SOCRATES: But no very great one either, since he did not chance upon a suitable constitution. In a suitable one, his own growth will be fuller and he will save the community, as well as himself. Anyway, it seems to me that we have now said enough about the slander brought against philosophy and why it is unjust—unless, of course, you have got something to add.

5

ADEIMANTUS: I have nothing further to add on that issue. But which of our present constitutions do you think is suitable for philosophy?

10

SOCRATES: None of them. But that is exactly my complaint. There is not one city today with a constitution worthy of the philosophic nature. That is precisely why it is perverted and altered. It is like foreign seed sown in alien ground: it tends to be overpowered and to fade away into the native species. Similarly, the philosophic species does not maintain its own power at present, but declines into a different character. But if it were to find the best constitution, as it is itself the best, it would be clear that it is really divine and that other natures and pursuits are merely human. Obviously, you are going to ask next what that constitution is.

b

5

c

ADEIMANTUS: You are wrong there. You see, I was not going to ask that, but whether it was the constitution we described when we were founding our city or a different one.

5

SOCRATES: In all other respects, it is that one. But we said even then[23] that there must always be some people in the city who have a rational account of the constitution, the same one that guided you, the lawgiver, when you made the laws.

d

ADEIMANTUS: Yes, we did say that.

SOCRATES: But we did not explain it clearly enough, for fear of what our own objections have made clear: namely, that the demonstration of it would be long and difficult. Indeed, even what remains is not the easiest of all things to discuss.

5

ADEIMANTUS: What is that?

SOCRATES: How a city can engage in philosophy without being destroyed. You see, all great things are prone to fall and, as the saying goes, beautiful things are really difficult.

10

[23] See 412a–b, which gives a hint of this need.

ADEIMANTUS: All the same, the demonstration won't be complete until this has been cleared up.

SOCRATES: If anything prevents that, it won't be lack of willingness, but lack of ability. At any rate, you will see how passionate *I* am. Look now, in fact, at how passionately and recklessly I am going to argue that a city should practice philosophy in the opposite way to the present one.

ADEIMANTUS: How?

SOCRATES: At present, those who take it up at all do so as young men, just out of childhood, who have yet to take up household management and moneymaking. Then, just when they reach the most difficult part they abandon it and are regarded as the most fully trained philosophers. By the most difficult part, I mean the one concerned with arguments.[24] In later life, if others are engaged in it and they are invited and deign to listen to them, they think they have done a lot, since they think this should only be a sideline. And, with a few exceptions, by the time they reach old age they are more thoroughly extinguished than the sun of Heraclitus, since they are never rekindled.[25]

ADEIMANTUS: What should they do instead?

SOCRATES: Entirely the opposite. As young men and children, they should occupy themselves with an education and philosophy suitable to the young. Their bodies are blooming and growing into manhood at this time, and they should take very good care of them, so as to acquire a helper for philosophy. But as they grow older and their soul begins to reach maturity, they should make its exercises more rigorous. Then, when their strength begins to fail and they have retired from politics and military service, they should graze freely in the pastures of philosophy and do nothing else, except as a sideline—I mean those who are going to live happily and, when the end comes, crown the life they have lived with a fitting providence in that other place.

ADEIMANTUS: You seem to be arguing with real passion, Socrates. But I am sure that most of your hearers will oppose you with even greater passion and won't be convinced in the least—beginning with Thrasymachus.

SOCRATES: Please do not try to raise a quarrel between me and Thrasymachus just as we have become friends—not that we were enemies before. You see, we won't relax our efforts until we convince him and the others— or at least do something that may benefit them in a later incarnation when, reborn, they happen upon these arguments again.[26]

---

[24] I.e., dialectic.

[25] Heraclitus' sun was extinguished at night but rekindled the next morning.

[26] See 614b ff.

ADEIMANTUS: You are talking about the short term, I see! 5

SOCRATES: It is certainly nothing compared to the whole of time! However, it is no wonder that the masses are not convinced by our arguments. I
mean, they have never seen a *man* that matched our *plan*—though they
have more often seen words purposely chosen to rhyme with one another e
than just happening to do so as in the present case.[27] But a man who, as far
as possible, matched and rhymed with virtue in word and deed, and
wielded dynastic power in a city of the same type—that is something they
have never seen even once. Or do you think they have? 499a

ADEIMANTUS: No, definitely not.

SOCRATES: Nor, bless you, have they spent enough time listening to fine
and free arguments that vigorously seek the truth in every way, so as to 5
acquire knowledge and keep their distance from all the sophistries and eristic quibbles that—whether in public trials or private gatherings—strive for
nothing except reputation and disputation.

ADEIMANTUS: No, they have not. 10

SOCRATES: It was for these reasons, and because we foresaw these difficulties, that we were afraid. All the same, we were compelled by the truth to b
say that no city, no constitution, and no individual man will ever become
perfect until some chance event compels those few philosophers who are
not vicious (the ones who are now called useless) to take care of a city,
whether they are willing to or not, and compels the city to obey them—or 5
until a true passion for true philosophy flows by some divine inspiration
into the sons of the men now wielding dynastic power or sovereignty, or
into the men themselves. Now, it cannot be reasonably maintained, in my c
view, that either or both of these things is impossible. But if they were, we
would be justly ridiculed for indulging in wishful thinking. Isn't that so? 5

ADEIMANTUS: It is.

SOCRATES: Then if, in the limitless past, some necessity forced those who
were foremost in philosophy to take charge of a city, or is doing so now in
some barbaric place far beyond our ken, or will do so in the future, this is d
something we are prepared to fight about—our argument that the constitution we have described has existed, does exist, and will exist, at any rate,
whenever it is that the muse of philosophy gains mastery of a city. It is not
impossible for this to happen, so we are not speaking of impossibilities—
that it is *difficult,* we agree ourselves. 5

ADEIMANTUS: *I* certainly think so.

---

[27] Plato is mocking the rhetoricians who were fond of forced rhyme. His own words
ou gar pôpote eidon genomenon to nun legomenon—"they've never seen anything come
into existence that matches our account"—exhibit the phenomenon he is mocking.

SOCRATES: But the masses do not—is that what you are going to say?

ADEIMANTUS: They probably don't.

SOCRATES: Bless you, you should not make such a wholesale charge against the masses! They will surely come to hold a different belief if, instead of wanting to win a victory at their expense, you soothe them and try to remove their slanderous prejudice against the love of learning. You must show them what you mean by philosophers and define their nature and pursuit the way we did just now. Then they will realize you do not mean the same people they do. And if they once see it that way, even you will say that they will have a different opinion from the one you just attributed to them and will answer differently. Or do you think that anyone who is gentle and without malice is harsh to one who is not harsh, or malicious to one who is not malicious? I will anticipate you and say that I think a few people may have such a harsh character, but not the majority.

ADEIMANTUS: And I agree, of course.

SOCRATES: Then don't you also agree that the harshness of the masses toward philosophy is caused by those outsiders who do not belong and who have burst in like a band of revelers, abusing one another, indulging their love of quarreling, and always arguing about human beings—something that is least appropriate in philosophy?

ADEIMANTUS: I do, indeed.

SOCRATES: For surely, Adeimantus, someone whose mind is truly directed toward the things that are has not the leisure to look down at human affairs and be filled with malice and hatred as a result of entering into their disputes. Instead, as he looks at and contemplates things that are orderly and always the same, that neither do injustice to one another nor suffer it, being all in a rational order, he imitates them and tries to become as like them as he can. Or do you think there is any way to prevent someone from associating with something he admires without imitating it?

ADEIMANTUS: He can't possibly.

SOCRATES: Then the philosopher, by associating with what is orderly and divine, becomes as divine and orderly as a human being can. Though, mind you, there are always plenty of slanders around.

ADEIMANTUS: Absolutely.

SOCRATES: And if he should come to be compelled to make a practice—in private and in public—of stamping what he sees there into the people's characters, instead of shaping only his own, do you think he will be a poor craftsman of temperance, justice, and the whole of popular virtue?

ADEIMANTUS: Not at all.

SOCRATES: And when the masses realize that what we are saying about him is true, will they be harsh with philosophers or mistrust us when we say that there is no way a city can ever find happiness unless its plan is drawn by painters who use the divine model? e10

ADEIMANTUS: They won't be harsh, if they do realize this. But what sort of drawing do you mean? 5
501a

SOCRATES: They would take the city and people's characters as their sketching slate, but first they would wipe it clean—which is not at all an easy thing to do. And you should be aware that this is an immediate differ-ence between them and others—that they refuse to take either a private individual or a city in hand, or to write laws, unless they receive a clean slate or are allowed to clean it themselves. 5

ADEIMANTUS: And rightly so.

SOCRATES: And after that, don't you think they would draw the plan of the constitution? 10

ADEIMANTUS: Of course.

SOCRATES: And I suppose that, as they work, they would look often in each direction: on the one hand, toward what is in its nature just, beautiful, b temperate, and all the rest; and, on the other, toward what they are trying to put into human beings, mixing and blending pursuits to produce a human likeness, based on the one that Homer too called divine and godly 5 when it appeared among human beings.[28]

ADEIMANTUS: Right.

SOCRATES: They would erase one thing, I suppose, and draw in another, until they had made people's characters as dear to the gods as possible. c

ADEIMANTUS: At any rate, the drawing would be most beautiful that way.

SOCRATES: Are we at all persuading the people you said were rushing to attack us, then, that the philosopher we were praising to them is really this 5 sort of painter of constitutions? They were angry because we were entrust-ing cities to him; are they any calmer at hearing it now?

ADEIMANTUS: They will be much calmer, if they have any sense.

SOCRATES: After all, how could they possibly dispute it? Will they deny d that philosophers are lovers both of what is and of the truth?

ADEIMANTUS: That would be silly.

SOCRATES: Or that their nature, as we have described it, is akin to the best? 5

ADEIMANTUS: They cannot deny that either.

[28] See, e.g., *Iliad* 1.131.

SOCRATES: Or that such a nature, when it happens to find appropriate pursuits, will not be as completely good and philosophic as any other? Or are they going to claim that the people we excluded are more so?

ADEIMANTUS: Certainly not.

SOCRATES: Will they still be angry, then, when we say that until the philosopher class gains mastery of a city, there will be no respite from evils for either city or citizens, and the constitution we have been describing in our discussion will never be completed in practice?

ADEIMANTUS: They will probably be less so.

SOCRATES: If it is all right with you, then, let's not say that they will simply be less angry, but that they will become altogether gentle and persuaded; so that out of shame, if nothing else, they will agree.

ADEIMANTUS: All right.

SOCRATES: So let's assume that they have been convinced of this. Will anyone contend, then, that there is no chance that the offspring of kings or men in power could be natural-born philosophers?

ADEIMANTUS: No one could.

SOCRATES: Could anyone claim that if such offspring are born, they must inevitably be corrupted? We agree ourselves that it is difficult for them to be saved. But that in the whole of time not one of them could be saved— could anyone contend that?

ADEIMANTUS: Of course not.

SOCRATES: But surely the occurrence of one such individual is enough, provided his city obeys him, to bring to completion all the things that now seem so incredible.

ADEIMANTUS: Yes, one is enough.

SOCRATES: For I suppose that if a ruler established the laws and practices we have described, it is hardly impossible that the citizens would be willing to carry them out.

ADEIMANTUS: Not at all.

SOCRATES: Would it be either surprising or impossible, then, that others should think as we do?

ADEIMANTUS: I don't suppose so.

SOCRATES: But I think our earlier discussion was sufficient to show that these arrangements are best, provided they are possible.

ADEIMANTUS: Indeed, it was.

SOCRATES: It seems, then, that the conclusion we have now reached about legislation is that the one we are describing is best, provided it is possible; and that while it is difficult for it to come about, it certainly is not impossible.

ADEIMANTUS: Yes, that is the conclusion we have reached.

SOCRATES: Now that this conclusion has, with much effort, been reached, we must next deal with the remaining issues—in what way, by means of what subjects and pursuits, the saviors of our constitution will come to exist, and at what ages they will take up each of them.

ADEIMANTUS: Yes, we must deal with that.

SOCRATES: I gained nothing by my cleverness, then, in omitting from our earlier discussion the troublesome topic of acquiring women, begetting children, and establishing rulers, because I knew the whole truth would provoke resentment and would be difficult to bring about. As it turned out, the need to discuss them arose anyway. Now, the subject of women and children has already been discussed. But that of the rulers has to be taken up again from the beginning. We said,[29] if you remember, that they must show themselves to be lovers of the city, when tested by pleasures and pains, by not abandoning this conviction through labors, fears, and all other adversities. Anyone who was incapable of doing so was to be rejected, while anyone who always came through pure—like gold tested in a fire— was to be made ruler and receive gifts and prizes, both while he lived and after his death. These were the sorts of things we were saying while our argument veiled its face and slipped by, for fear of stirring up the very problems that now confront us.

ADEIMANTUS: That's absolutely true. I do remember.

SOCRATES: I was reluctant, my friend, to say the things we have now dared to say anyway. But now, let's also dare to say that we must establish philosophers as guardians in the most exact sense.

ADEIMANTUS: Let's do so.

SOCRATES: Bear in mind, then, that there will probably be only a few of them. You see, they have to have the nature we described, and its parts rarely consent to grow together in one person; rather, its many parts grow split off from one another.

ADEIMANTUS: How do you mean?

SOCRATES: Ease of learning, good memory, astuteness, and smartness, as you know, and all the other things that go along with them, such as youthful passion and high-mindedness, are rarely willing to grow together simultaneously with a disposition to live an orderly, quiet, and completely stable

[29] At 412b–414a. The conviction referred to is identified at 412e6.

197

5　life. On the contrary, those who possess the former traits are carried by their quick wits wherever chance leads them, and have no stability at all.

ADEIMANTUS: That's true.

SOCRATES: Those with stable characters, on the other hand, who do not change easily, whom one would employ because of their greater reliability,

d　and who in battle are not easily moved by fears, act in the same way when it comes to their studies. They are hard to get moving and learn with difficulty, as if they are anesthetized, and are constantly falling asleep and yawn-

5　ing whenever they have to work hard at such things.

ADEIMANTUS: They are.

SOCRATES: Yet we say that someone must have a good and fine share of both characters, or he won't receive the truest education or honor, or be

10　allowed to rule.

ADEIMANTUS: That's right.

SOCRATES: Then don't you think this will rarely occur?

ADEIMANTUS: Of course.

e　SOCRATES: He must be tested, then, in the labors, fears, and pleasures we mentioned before. He must also be exercised in many other subjects, how-ever, which we did not mention but are adding now, to see whether his nature can endure the most important subjects or will shrink from them

504a　like the cowards who shrink from the other tests.

ADEIMANTUS: It is certainly important to find that out. But what do you mean by the most important subjects?

SOCRATES: Do you remember when we distinguished three kinds of

5　things in the soul in order to help bring out what justice, temperance, courage, and wisdom each is?[30]

ADEIMANTUS: If I didn't, I would not deserve to hear the rest.

SOCRATES: Do you also remember what preceded it?

10　ADEIMANTUS: No, what?

b　SOCRATES: We said, I believe, that in order to get the finest view of these matters, we would need to take a longer road, which would make them plain to anyone who took it, but that it was possible to give demonstrations that would be up to the standard of the previous discussion.[31] All of you said that was enough. The result was that our subsequent discussion, as it

5　seemed to me, was less than exact. But whether or not it satisfied all of you is for you to say.

[30] 434d–444e.
[31] 435d.

ADEIMANTUS: I, at any rate, thought you gave us good measure. And so, apparently, did the others.

SOCRATES: No, my friend, any measure of such things that falls short in any way of what is, is not good measure at all, since nothing incomplete is a measure of anything. Some people, however, are occasionally of the opinion that an incomplete treatment is already adequate and that there is no need for further inquiry.

ADEIMANTUS: Yes, a lot of people feel like that. Laziness is the cause.

SOCRATES: Well, that is a feeling that is least appropriate in a guardian of a city and its laws.

ADEIMANTUS: No doubt.

SOCRATES: He will have to take the longer road then, comrade, and put no less effort into learning than into physical training. For otherwise, as we were just saying, he will never pursue the most important and most appropriate subject to the end.

ADEIMANTUS: Why, aren't these virtues the most important things? Is there something yet more important than justice and the other virtues we discussed?

SOCRATES: Not only is it more important, but, even in the case of the virtues themselves, it is not enough to look at a mere sketch as we are doing now, while neglecting the most finished portrait. I mean, it is ridiculous, isn't it, to strain every nerve to attain the utmost exactness and clarity about other things of little value, while not treating the most important things as meriting the most exactness?

ADEIMANTUS: It certainly is. But do you think that anyone is going to let you off without asking you what you mean by this most important subject, and what it is concerned with?

SOCRATES: No, I do not. And you may ask it, too. You have certainly heard the answer often, but now either you are not thinking or you intend to make trouble for me again by interrupting. And I suspect it is more the latter. You see, you have often heard it said that the form of the good is the most important thing to learn about, and that it is by their relation to it that just things and the others become useful and beneficial. And now you must be pretty certain that that is what I am going to say, and, in addition, that we have no adequate knowledge of it. And if we do not know it, you know that even the fullest possible knowledge of other things is of no benefit to us, any more than if we acquire any possession without the good. Or do you think there is any benefit in possessing everything but the good? Or to know everything without knowing the good, thereby knowing nothing fine or good?

ADEIMANTUS: No, by Zeus, I do not.

SOCRATES: Furthermore, you also know that the masses believe pleasure to be the good, while the more refined believe it to be knowledge.

ADEIMANTUS: Of course.

SOCRATES: And, my friend, that those who believe this cannot show us what sort of knowledge it is, but in the end are forced to say that it is knowledge of the good.

ADEIMANTUS: Which is completely ridiculous.

SOCRATES: How could it not be, when they blame us for not knowing the good and then turn around and talk to us as if we did know it? I mean, they say it is knowledge of the good—as if we understood what they mean when they utter the word "good."

ADEIMANTUS: That's absolutely true.

SOCRATES: What about those who define the good as pleasure? Are they any less full of confusion than the others? Or aren't even they forced to admit that there are bad pleasures?

ADEIMANTUS: Most definitely.

SOCRATES: I suppose it follows, doesn't it, that they have to admit that the same things are both good and bad?

ADEIMANTUS: It certainly does.

SOCRATES: Isn't it clear, then, that there are lots of serious disagreements about the good?

ADEIMANTUS: Of course.

SOCRATES: Well, isn't it also clear that many people would choose things that are believed to be just or beautiful, even if they are not, and would act, acquire things, and form beliefs accordingly? Yet no one is satisfied to acquire things that are *believed* to be good. On the contrary, everyone seeks the things that *are* good. In this area, everyone disdains mere reputation.

ADEIMANTUS: Right.

SOCRATES: That, then, is what every soul pursues, and for its sake does everything. The soul has a hunch that the good is something, but it is puzzled and cannot adequately grasp just what it is or acquire the sort of stable belief about it that it has about other things, and so it misses the benefit, if any, that even those other things may give. Are we to accept that even the best people in the city, to whom we entrust everything, must remain thus in the dark about something of this kind and importance?

ADEIMANTUS: That's the last thing we would do.

SOCRATES: Anyway, I imagine that just and fine things won't have acquired much of a guardian in someone who does not even know why they are good. And I have a hunch that no one will have adequate knowledge of them until he knows this.

ADEIMANTUS: That's a good hunch.

SOCRATES: But won't our constitution be perfectly ordered if such a guardian, one who knows these things, oversees it?

ADEIMANTUS: It is bound to be. But you yourself, Socrates, do you say the good is knowledge or pleasure, or is it something else altogether?

SOCRATES: What a man! You made it good and clear long ago that other people's opinions about these matters would not satisfy you.

ADEIMANTUS: Well, Socrates, it does not seem right to me for you to be willing to state other people's convictions but not your own, when you have spent so much time occupied with these matters.

SOCRATES: What? Do you think it is right to speak about things you do not know as if you do know them?

ADEIMANTUS: Not as if you know them, but you ought to be willing to state what you believe as what you believe.

SOCRATES: What? Haven't you noticed that beliefs without knowledge are all shameful and ugly things, since the best of them are blind? Do you think that those who have a true belief without understanding are any different from blind people who happen to travel the right road?

ADEIMANTUS: They are no different.

SOCRATES: Do you want to look at shameful, blind, and crooked things, then, when you might hear fine, illuminating ones from other people?

And Glaucon said:

By Zeus, Socrates, do not stop now, with the end in sight, so to speak! We will be satisfied if you discuss the good the way you discussed justice, temperance, and the rest.

SOCRATES: That, comrade, would well satisfy me too, but I am afraid that I won't be up to it and that I will disgrace myself and look ridiculous by trying. No, bless you, let's set aside what the good itself is for the time being. You see, even to arrive at my current beliefs about it seems beyond the range of our present discussion.[32] But I am willing to tell you about what seems to be an offspring of the good and most like it, if that is agreeable to you; or otherwise to let the matter drop.

[32] See 532a–534d.

GLAUCON: Tell us, then. The story about the father remains a debt you will pay another time.

507a SOCRATES: I wish I could repay it, and you recover the debt, instead of just the interest. So here, then, is this child and offspring of the good itself. But take care I do not somehow deceive you unintentionally by giving you 5 an illegitimate account of the child.[33]

GLAUCON: We will take as much care as possible. So speak on.

SOCRATES: I will once I have come to an agreement with you and reminded you of things we have already said here as well as on many other occasions.

b GLAUCON: Which things?

SOCRATES: We say that there are many beautiful, many good, and many other such things, thereby distinguishing them in words.[34]

GLAUCON: We do.

SOCRATES: We also say there is a beautiful itself and a good itself. And so, 5 in the case of all the things that we then posited as many, we reverse ourselves and posit a single form belonging to each, since we suppose there is a single one, and call it what each is.[35]

GLAUCON: That's true.

SOCRATES: And we say that the one class of things is visible but not intel-
10 ligible, while the forms are intelligible but not visible.

GLAUCON: Absolutely.

c SOCRATES: With what of ours do we see visible things?

GLAUCON: With our sight.

SOCRATES: And don't we hear audible things with hearing and perceive all other perceptible things with our other senses?

5 GLAUCON: Of course.

SOCRATES: Have you ever thought about how lavish the craftsman of our senses was in making the power to see and be seen?

GLAUCON: No, not really.

10 SOCRATES: Well, think of it this way. Do hearing and sound need another kind of thing in order for the former to hear and the latter to be heard—a
d third thing in whose absence the one won't hear or the other be heard?

---

[33] Throughout, Socrates is punning on the word *tokos,* which means either a child or the interest on capital.
[34] See 596b5–10.
[35] See Glossary of Terms s.v. what it is.

GLAUCON: No.

SOCRATES: And I think there cannot be many—not to say any—others that need such a thing. Or can you think of one?

GLAUCON: No, I cannot.

SOCRATES: Aren't you aware that sight and the visible realm have such a need?

GLAUCON: In what way?

SOCRATES: Surely sight may be present in the eyes and its possessor may try to use it, and colors may be present in things; but unless a third kind of thing is present, which is naturally adapted for this specific purpose, you know that sight will see nothing and the colors will remain unseen.

GLAUCON: What kind of thing do you mean?

SOCRATES: The kind you call light.

GLAUCON: You are right.

SOCRATES: So it is no insignificant form of yoke, then, that yokes the sense of sight and the power to be seen. In fact, it is more honorable than any that yokes other yoked teams. Provided, of course, that light is not something without honor.

GLAUCON: And it is surely far from being without honor.

SOCRATES: Which of the gods in the heavens would you say is the controller of this—the one whose light makes our sight see best and visible things best seen?

GLAUCON: The very one you and others would name. I mean, it is clear that what you are asking about is the sun.[36]

SOCRATES: And isn't sight naturally related to that god in the following way?

GLAUCON: Which one?

SOCRATES: Neither sight itself nor that in which it comes to be—namely, the eye—is the sun.

GLAUCON: No, it is not.

SOCRATES: But it is, I think, the most sunlike of the sense organs.

GLAUCON: By far the most.

SOCRATES: And doesn't it receive the power it has from the sun, just like an influx from an overflowing treasury?

GLAUCON: Certainly.

[36] Helios—the sun—was considered a god.

SOCRATES: The sun is not sight either; yet as its cause, isn't it seen by sight itself?

GLAUCON: It is.

SOCRATES: Let's say, then, that this is what I called the offspring of the good, which the good begot as its analogue. What the latter is in the intelligible realm in relation to understanding and intelligible things, the former is in the visible realm in relation to sight and visible things.

GLAUCON: How? Tell me more.

SOCRATES: You know that when our eyes no longer turn to things whose colors are illuminated by the light of day, but by the lights of night, they are dimmed and seem nearly blind, as if clear sight were no longer in them.

GLAUCON: Of course.

SOCRATES: Yet I suppose that whenever they are turned to things illuminated by the sun, they see clearly and sight is manifest in those very same eyes?

GLAUCON: Indeed.

SOCRATES: Well, think about the soul in the same way. When it focuses on something that is illuminated both by truth and what is, it understands, knows, and manifestly possesses understanding. But when it focuses on what is mixed with obscurity, on what comes to be and passes away, it believes and is dimmed, changes its beliefs this way and that, and seems bereft of understanding.

GLAUCON: Yes, it does seem like that.

SOCRATES: You must say, then, that what gives truth to the things known and the power to know to the knower is the form of the good. And as the cause of knowledge and truth, you must think of it as an object of knowledge. Both knowledge and truth are beautiful things. But if you are to think correctly, you must think of the good as other and more beautiful than they. In the visible realm, light and sight are rightly thought to be sunlike, but wrongly thought to be the sun. So, here it is right to think of knowledge and truth as goodlike, but wrong to think that either of them is the good—for the state of the good is yet more honored.

GLAUCON: It is an incredibly beautiful thing you are talking about, if it provides both knowledge and truth but is itself superior to them in beauty. I mean, you surely do not think that *it* could be pleasure.

SOCRATES: No words of ill omen, please! Instead, examine our analogy in more detail.

GLAUCON: How?

SOCRATES: The sun, I think you would say, not only gives visible things the power to be seen but also provides for their coming-to-be, growth, and nourishment—although it is not itself coming to be.

GLAUCON: I would.

SOCRATES: Therefore, you should also say that not only do the objects of knowledge owe their being known to the good, but their existence and being are also due to it; although the good is not being, but something yet beyond being, superior to it in rank and power.

And Glaucon quite ridiculously replied:

By Apollo, what daimonic hyperbole![37]

SOCRATES: It is your own fault, you forced me to tell my beliefs about it.

GLAUCON: And don't you stop, either—at least, not until you have finished discussing the good's similarity to the sun, if you are omitting anything.

SOCRATES: I am certainly omitting a lot.

GLAUCON: Well don't, not even the smallest detail.

SOCRATES: I think I will have to omit a fair amount. All the same, as far as is now possible, I won't purposely omit anything.

GLAUCON: Please don't.

SOCRATES: Then you should think, as we said, that there are these two things, one sovereign of the intelligible kind and place, the other of the visible—I do not say "of heaven," so as not to seem to you to be playing the sophist with the name.[38] In any case, do you understand these two kinds, visible and intelligible?

GLAUCON: I do.

SOCRATES: Represent them, then, by a line divided into two unequal sections. Then divide each section—that of the visible kind and that of the intelligible—in the same proportion as the line.[39] In terms now of relative clarity and opacity, you will have as one subsection of the visible, images. By images I mean, first, shadows, then reflections in bodies of water and in

[37] Socrates' claim ends with the words *dunamei huperechontas* ("superior in . . . power"), Glaucon responds with the punning *daimonias huperbolês*. Hence the joke.

[38] The play seems to be on the similarity of sound between *orano* ("heaven") and *orato* ("visible").

[39]

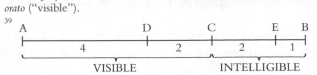

all close-packed, smooth, and shiny materials, and everything of that sort. Do you understand?

GLAUCON: I do understand.

SOCRATES: Then, in the other subsection of the visible, put the originals
5   of these images—that is, the animals around us, every plant, and the whole class of manufactured things.

GLAUCON: I will.

SOCRATES: Would you also be willing to say, then, that, as regards truth and untruth, the division is in this ratio: as what is believed is to what is
10   known, so the likeness is to the thing it is like?

b   GLAUCON: Certainly.

SOCRATES: Next, consider how the section of the intelligible is to be divided.

GLAUCON: How?

SOCRATES: As follows: in one subsection, the soul, using as images the things that were imitated before, is forced to base its inquiry on hypotheses, proceed-
5   ing not to a first principle, but to a conclusion. In the other subsection, by contrast, it makes its way to an unhypothetical first principle, proceeding from a hypothesis, but without the images used in the previous subsection, using forms themselves and making its investigation through them.

10   GLAUCON: I do not fully understand what you are saying.

SOCRATES: Let's try again. You see, you will understand it more easily after
c   this explanation. I think you know that students of geometry, calculation, and the like hypothesize the odd and the even, the various figures, the three kinds of angles, and other things akin to these in each of their investiga-
5   tions, regarding them as known. These they treat as hypotheses and do not think it necessary to give any argument for them, either to themselves or to others, as if they were evident to everyone. And going from these first prin-
d   ciples through the remaining steps, they arrive in full agreement at the point they set out to reach in their investigation.

GLAUCON: I certainly know that much.

5   SOCRATES: Then don't you also know that they use visible forms and make their arguments about them, although they are not thinking about them, but about those other things that they are like? They make their arguments with a view to the square itself and the diagonal itself, not the
e   diagonal they draw, and similarly with the others. The very things they make and draw, of which shadows and reflections in water are images, they now in turn use as images in seeking to see those other things themselves
511a   that one cannot see except by means of thought.

GLAUCON: That's true.

SOCRATES: This, then, is the kind of thing that I said was intelligible. The soul is forced to use hypotheses in the investigation of it, not traveling up to a first principle, since it cannot escape or get above its hypotheses, but using as images those very things of which images were made by the things below them, and which, by comparison to their images, were thought to be clear and to be honored as such.

GLAUCON: I understand that you mean what is dealt with in geometry and related crafts.

SOCRATES: Also understand, then, that by the other subsection of the intelligible I mean what reason itself[40] grasps by the power of dialectical discussion, treating its hypotheses, not as first principles, but as genuine hypotheses (that is, stepping stones and links in a chain), in order to arrive at what is unhypothetical and the first principle of everything. Having grasped this principle, it reverses itself and, keeping hold of what follows from it, comes down to a conclusion, making no use of anything visible at all, but only of forms themselves, moving on through forms to forms, and ending in forms.

GLAUCON: I understand, though not adequately—you see, in my opinion you are speaking of an enormous task. You want to distinguish the part of what is and is intelligible, the part looked at by the science of dialectical discussion, as clearer than the part looked at by the so-called sciences—those for which hypotheses are first principles. And although those who look at the latter part are forced to do so by means of thought rather than sense perception, still, because they do not go back to a genuine first principle in considering it, but proceed from hypotheses, you do not think that they have true understanding of them, even though—given such a first principle—they are intelligible. And you seem to me to call the state of mind of the geometers—and the others of that sort—thought but not understanding; thought being intermediate between belief and understanding.

SOCRATES: You have grasped my meaning most adequately. Join me, then, in taking these four conditions in the soul as corresponding to the four subsections of the line: understanding dealing with the highest, thought dealing with the second; assign belief to the third, and imagination to the last. Arrange them in a proportion and consider that each shares in clarity to the degree that the subsection it deals with shares in truth.

GLAUCON: I understand, agree, and arrange them as you say.

---

[40] *Autos ho logos.*

Book 7

SOCRATES: Next, then, compare the effect of education and that of the
lack of it on our nature to an experience like this. Imagine human beings
living in an underground, cavelike dwelling, with an entrance a long way
up that is open to the light and as wide as the cave itself. They have been
there since childhood, with their necks and legs fettered, so that they are
fixed in the same place, able to see only in front of them, because their fet-
ter prevents them from turning their heads around. Light is provided by a
fire burning far above and behind them. Between the prisoners and the fire,
there is an elevated road stretching. Imagine that along this road a low wall
has been built—like the screen in front of people that is provided by pup-
peteers, and above which they show their puppets.

GLAUCON: I am imagining it.

SOCRATES: Also imagine, then, that there are people alongside the wall
carrying multifarious artifacts that project above it—statues of people and
other animals, made of stone, wood, and every material. And as you would
expect, some of the carriers are talking and some are silent.

GLAUCON: It is a strange image you are describing, and strange prisoners.

SOCRATES: They are like us. I mean, in the first place, do you think these
prisoners have ever seen anything of themselves and one another besides
the shadows that the fire casts on the wall of the cave in front of them?

GLAUCON: How could they, if they have to keep their heads motionless
throughout life?

SOCRATES: What about the things carried along the wall? Isn't the same
true where they are concerned?

GLAUCON: Of course.

SOCRATES: And if they could engage in discussion with one another,
don't you think they would assume that the words they used applied to the
things they see passing in front of them?

GLAUCON: They would have to.

SOCRATES: What if their prison also had an echo from the wall facing
them? When one of the carriers passing along the wall spoke, do you think

they would believe that anything other than the shadow passing in front of them was speaking?

GLAUCON: I do not, by Zeus. 10

SOCRATES: All in all, then, what the prisoners would take for true reality is nothing other than the shadows of those artifacts. c

GLAUCON: That's entirely inevitable.

SOCRATES: Consider, then, what being released from their bonds and cured of their foolishness would naturally be like, if something like this 5 should happen to them. When one was freed and suddenly compelled to stand up, turn his neck around, walk, and look up toward the light, he would be pained by doing all these things and be unable to see the things whose shadows he had seen before, because of the flashing lights. What do you think he would say if we told him that what he had seen before was d silly nonsense, but that now—because he is a bit closer to what is, and is turned toward things that *are* more—he sees more correctly? And in partic-ular, if we pointed to each of the things passing by and compelled him to answer what each of them is, don't you think he would be puzzled and 5 believe that the things he saw earlier were more truly real than the ones he was being shown?

GLAUCON: Much more so.

SOCRATES: And if he were compelled to look at the light itself, wouldn't e his eyes be pained and wouldn't he turn around and flee toward the things he is able to see, and believe that they are really clearer than the ones he is being shown?

GLAUCON: He would. 5

SOCRATES: And if someone dragged him by force away from there, along the rough, steep, upward path, and did not let him go until he had dragged him into the light of the sun, wouldn't he be pained and angry at being treated that way? And when he came into the light, wouldn't he have his 516a eyes filled with sunlight and be unable to see a single one of the things now said to be truly real?

GLAUCON: No, he would not be able to—at least not right away.

SOCRATES: He would need time to get adjusted, I suppose, if he is going to see the things in the world above. At first, he would see shadows most 5 easily, then images of men and other things in water, then the things them-selves. From these, it would be easier for him to go on to look at the things in the sky and the sky itself at night, gazing at the light of the stars and the moon, than during the day, gazing at the sun and the light of the sun. b

GLAUCON: Of course.

SOCRATES: Finally, I suppose, he would be able to see the sun—not reflections of it in water or some alien place, but the sun just by itself in its own
place—and be able to look at it and see what it is like.

GLAUCON: He would have to.

SOCRATES: After that, he would already be able to conclude about it that
it provides the seasons and the years, governs everything in the visible
world, and is in some way the cause of all the things that he and his fellows
used to see.

GLAUCON: That would clearly be his next step.

SOCRATES: What about when he reminds himself of his first dwelling
place, what passed for wisdom there, and his fellow prisoners? Don't you
think he would count himself happy for the change and pity the others?

GLAUCON: Certainly.

SOCRATES: And if there had been honors, praises, or prizes among them
for the one who was sharpest at identifying the shadows as they passed by;
and was best able to remember which usually came earlier, which later, and
which simultaneously; and who was thus best able to prophesize the future,
do you think that our man would desire these rewards or envy those among
the prisoners who were honored and held power? Or do you think he
would feel with Homer that he would much prefer to "work the earth as a
serf for another man, a man without possessions of his own,"[1] and go
through any sufferings, rather than share their beliefs and live as they do?

GLAUCON: Yes, I think he would rather suffer anything than live like that.

SOCRATES: Consider this too, then. If this man went back down into the
cave and sat down in his same seat, wouldn't his eyes be filled with darkness, coming suddenly out of the sun like that?

GLAUCON: Certainly.

SOCRATES: Now, if he had to compete once again with the perpetual prisoners in recognizing the shadows, while his sight was still dim and before
his eyes had recovered, and if the time required for readjustment was not
short, wouldn't he provoke ridicule? Wouldn't it be said of him that he had
returned from his upward journey with his eyes ruined, and that it is not
worthwhile even to try to travel upward? And as for anyone who tried to
free the prisoners and lead them upward, if they could somehow get their
hands on him, wouldn't they kill him?

GLAUCON: They certainly would.

---

[1] *Odyssey* 11.489–90. The shade of Achilles speaks these words to Odysseus, who is
visiting Hades. Plato is likening the cave dwellers to the dead.

SOCRATES: This image, my dear Glaucon, must be fitted together as a whole with what we said before. The realm revealed through sight should be likened to the prison dwelling, and the light of the fire inside it to the sun's power. And if you think of the upward journey and the seeing of things above as the upward journey of the soul to the intelligible realm, you won't mistake my intention—since it is what you wanted to hear about. Only the god knows whether it is true. But this is how these phenomena seem to me: in the knowable realm, the last thing to be seen is the form of the good, and it is seen only with toil and trouble. Once one has seen it, however, one must infer that it is the cause of all that is correct and beautiful in anything, that in the visible realm it produces both light and its source, and that in the intelligible realm it controls and provides truth and understanding; and that anyone who is to act sensibly in private or public must see it.

GLAUCON: I agree, so far as I am able.

SOCRATES: Come on, then, and join me in this further thought: you should not be surprised that the ones who get to this point are not willing to occupy themselves with human affairs, but that, on the contrary, their souls are always eager to spend their time above. I mean, that is surely what we would expect, if indeed the image I described before is also accurate here.

GLAUCON: It is what we would expect.

SOCRATES: What about when someone, coming from looking at divine things, looks to the evils of human life? Do you think it is surprising that he behaves awkwardly and appears completely ridiculous, if—while his sight is still dim and he has not yet become accustomed to the darkness around him—he is compelled, either in the courts or elsewhere, to compete about the shadows of justice, or about the statues of which they are the shadows; and to dispute the way these things are understood by people who have never seen justice itself?

GLAUCON: It is not surprising at all.

SOCRATES: On the contrary, anyone with any sense, at any rate, would remember that eyes may be confused in two ways and from two causes: when they change from the light into the darkness, or from the darkness into the light. If he kept in mind that the same applies to the soul, then when he saw a soul disturbed and unable to see something, he would not laugh absurdly. Instead, he would see whether it had come from a brighter life and was dimmed through not having yet become accustomed to the dark, or from greater ignorance into greater light and was dazzled by the increased brilliance. Then he would consider the first soul happy in its experience and life, and pity the latter. But even if he wanted to ridicule it, at least his ridiculing it would make him less ridiculous than ridiculing a soul that had come from the light above.

5 GLAUCON: That's an entirely reasonable claim.

SOCRATES: Then here is how we must think about these matters, if that is true: education is not what some people boastfully declare it to be. They presumably say they can put knowledge into souls that lack it, as if they c could put sight into blind eyes.

GLAUCON: Yes, they do say that.

SOCRATES: But here is what our present account shows about this power to learn that is present in everyone's soul, and the instrument with which each of us learns: just as an eye cannot be turned around from darkness to light except by turning the whole body, so this instrument must be turned around from what-comes-to-be together with the whole soul, until it is able 10 to bear to look at what is and at the brightest thing that is—the one we call d the good. Isn't that right?

GLAUCON: Yes.

SOCRATES: Of this very thing, then, there would be a craft—namely, of this turning around—concerned with how this instrument can be most easily 5 and effectively turned around, not of putting sight into it. On the contrary, it takes for granted that sight is there, though not turned in the right way or looking where it should look, and contrives to redirect it appropriately.

GLAUCON: That's probably right.

SOCRATES: Then the other so-called virtues of the soul do seem to be 10 closely akin to those of the body: they really are not present in it initially, e but are added later by habit and practice. The virtue of wisdom, on the other hand, belongs above all, so it seems, to something more divine, which never loses its power, but is either useful and beneficial or useless and 519a harmful, depending on the way it is turned. Or haven't you ever noticed in people who are said to be bad, but clever, how keen the vision of their little soul is and how sharply it distinguishes the things it is turned toward? This shows that its sight is not inferior, but is forced to serve vice, so that the 5 sharper it sees, the more evils it accomplishes.

GLAUCON: I certainly have.

SOCRATES: However, if this element of this sort of nature had been hammered at right from childhood, and struck free of the leaden weights, as it were, of kinship with becoming, which have been fastened to it by eating b and other such pleasures and indulgences, which pull its soul's vision downward[2]—if, I say, it got rid of these and turned toward truly real things, then the same element of the same people would see them most sharply, just as it 5 now does the things it is now turned toward.

---

[2] See 611b9–612a6.

212

GLAUCON: That's probably right.

SOCRATES: Isn't it also probable, then—indeed, doesn't it follow necessarily from what was said before—that uneducated people who have no experience of true reality will never adequately govern a city, and neither will people who have been allowed to spend their whole lives in education. The former fail because they do not have a single goal in life at which all their actions, public and private, inevitably aim; the latter because they would refuse to act, thinking they had emigrated, while still alive, to the Isles of the Blessed.

GLAUCON: True.

SOCRATES: It is our task as founders, then, to compel the best natures to learn what was said before[3] to be the most important thing: namely, to see the good; to ascend that ascent. And when they have ascended and looked sufficiently, we must not allow them to do what they are allowed to do now.

GLAUCON: What's that, then?

SOCRATES: To stay there and refuse to go down again to the prisoners in the cave and share their labors and honors, whether the inferior ones or the more excellent ones.

GLAUCON: You mean we are to treat them unjustly, making them live a worse life when they could live a better one?

SOCRATES: You have forgotten again, my friend, that the law is not concerned with making any one class in the city do outstandingly well, but is contriving to produce this condition in the city as a whole, harmonizing the citizens together through persuasion or compulsion, and making them share with each other the benefit they can confer on the community.[4] It produces such men in the city, not in order to allow them to turn in whatever direction each one wants, but to make use of them to bind the city together.

GLAUCON: That's true. Yes, I had forgotten.

SOCRATES: Observe, then, Glaucon, that we won't be unjustly treating those who have become philosophers in our city, but that what we will say to them, when we compel them to take care of the others and guard them, will be just. We will say: "When people like you come to be in other cities, they are justified in not sharing in the others' labors. After all, they have grown there spontaneously, against the will of the constitution in each of them. And when something grows of its own accord and owes no debt for

[3] 505a–b.
[4] 420b–421c, 462a–466c.

its upbringing, it has justice on its side when it is not keen to pay anyone
for its upbringing. But both for your own sakes and for that of the rest of
the city, we have bred you to be leaders and kings in the hive, so to speak.
You are better and more completely educated than the others, and better
able to share in both types of life.[5] So each of you in turn must go down to
live in the common dwelling place of the other citizens and grow accustomed to seeing in the dark. For when you are used to it, you will see infi-
nitely better than the people there and know precisely what each image is,
and also what it is an image of, because you have seen the truth about fine,
just, and good things. So the city will be awake, governed by us and by you;
not dreaming like the majority of cities nowadays, governed by men who
fight against one another over shadows and form factions in order to rule—
as if that were a great good.[6] No, the truth of the matter is surely this: a city
in which those who are going to rule are least eager to rule is necessarily
best and freest from faction, whereas a city with the opposite kind of rulers
is governed in the opposite way."

GLAUCON: Yes, indeed.

SOCRATES: Then do you think the people we have nurtured will disobey
us when they hear these things, and be unwilling to share the labors of the
city, each in turn, and wish instead to live the greater part of their time
with one another in the pure realm?

GLAUCON: No, they couldn't possibly. After all, we will be giving just
orders to just people. However, each of them will certainly go to rule as to
something necessary, which is exactly the opposite of what is done by those
who now rule in each city.

SOCRATES: That's right, comrade. If you can find a way of life that is better than ruling for those who are going to rule, your well-governed city
will become a possibility. You see, in it alone the truly rich will rule—those
who are rich not in gold, but in the wealth the happy must have: namely, a
good and rational life. But if beggars—people hungry for private goods of
their own—go into public life, thinking that the good is there for the seizing, then such a city is impossible. For when ruling is something fought
over, such civil and domestic war destroys these men and the rest of the city
as well.

GLAUCON: That's absolutely true.

SOCRATES: Do you know of any other sort of life that looks down on
political offices besides that of true philosophy?

GLAUCON: No, by Zeus, I do not.

---

[5] I.e., the practical life of ruling and the theoretical life of doing philosophy.
[6] See 476c–d.

SOCRATES: But surely it is those who are not lovers of ruling who must go do it. Otherwise, the rivaling lovers will fight over it.

GLAUCON: Of course.

SOCRATES: Who else, then, will you compel to go be guardians of the city if not those who know best what results in good government, and have different honors and a better life than the political?

GLAUCON: No one else.

SOCRATES: Do you want us to consider now how such people will come to exist, and how we will lead them up to the light, like those who are said to have gone up from Hades to the gods?

GLAUCON: Yes, of course that's what I want.

SOCRATES: It seems, then, that this is not a matter of flipping a potsherd,[7] but of turning a soul from a day that is a kind of night in comparison to the true day—that ascent to what is, which we say is true philosophy.

GLAUCON: Yes, indeed.

SOCRATES: Then mustn't we try to discover what subjects have the power to bring this about?

GLAUCON: Of course.

SOCRATES: So what subject is it, Glaucon, that draws the soul from what is coming to be to what is? It occurs to me as I am speaking that we said, didn't we, that these people must be athletes of war when they are young?[8]

GLAUCON: Yes, we did say that.

SOCRATES: Then the subject we are looking for must also have this characteristic in addition to the former one.

GLAUCON: Which?

SOCRATES: It must not be useless to warlike men.

GLAUCON: If possible, it must not.

SOCRATES: Now, earlier they were educated by us in musical and physical training.

GLAUCON: They were.

SOCRATES: And surely physical training is concerned with what-comes-to-be and dies, since it oversees the growth and decay of the body.

---

[7] A proverbial expression, referring to a children's game. The players were divided into two groups. A shell or potsherd—white on one side, black on the other—was thrown into space between them to the cry of "night or day?" (Note the reference to night and day in what follows.) According as the white or black fell uppermost, one group ran away pursued by the other.

[8] 404a, 412b–417b.

GLAUCON: Obviously.

SOCRATES: So it could not be the subject we are looking for.

522a GLAUCON: No, it could not.

SOCRATES: Is it, then, the musical training we described before?

GLAUCON: But it is just the counterpart of physical training, if you remember. It educated the guardians through habits, conveying by harmony a certain harmoniousness of temper, not knowledge; and by rhythm a certain rhythmical quality. Its stories, whether fictional or nearer the truth, cultivated other habits akin to these. But as for a subject that leads to the destination you have in mind, of the sort you are looking for now, there was nothing of that in it.

SOCRATES: Your reminder is exactly to the point. It really does not have anything of that sort. You're a marvelous fellow, Glaucon, but what is there that does? The crafts all seemed to be somehow menial.[9]

GLAUCON: Of course. And yet, what subject is left that is separate from musical and physical training, and from the crafts?

SOCRATES: Well, if we have nothing left beyond these, let's consider one of those that touches all of them.

GLAUCON: Which?

SOCRATES: Why, for example, that common thing, the one that every type of craft, thought, and knowledge uses, and that is among the first things everyone has to learn.

GLAUCON: Which one is that?

SOCRATES: That inconsequential matter of distinguishing the numbers one, two, and three. In short, I mean number and calculation. Or isn't it true that every type of craft and knowledge must share in them?

GLAUCON: Indeed it is.

SOCRATES: Then warfare must too.

GLAUCON: It must.

SOCRATES: In tragedies, at any rate, Palamedes is always showing up Agamemnon as a totally ridiculous general. Haven't you noticed? He says that by inventing numbers he established how many troops there were in the army at Ilium and counted their ships and everything else. The implication is that they had not been counted before, and that Agamemnon apparently did not even know how many feet he had, since he did not know how to count. What kind of general do you think that made him?

[9] 495c–e.

216

GLAUCON: A very strange one, I'd say, if there is any truth in that.

SOCRATES: Won't we posit this subject, then, as one a warrior has to learn   e
so he can count and calculate?

GLAUCON: It is more essential than anything else—if, that is, he is going
to know anything at all about marshaling his troops—or if he is even going
to be human, for that matter.

SOCRATES: Then do you notice the same thing about this subject as I do?   5

GLAUCON: What?

SOCRATES: That in all likelihood it is one of the subjects we were looking
for that naturally stimulate the understanding. But no one uses it correctly,   523a
as something that really is fitted in every way to draw us toward being.

GLAUCON: How do you mean?

SOCRATES: I will try to make what I believe clear, at any rate. I will distin-   5
guish for myself the things that lead in the direction we mentioned from
those that do not. Then you must look at them along with me, and either
agree or disagree, so that we may see more clearly whether the distinction is
as I imagine.

GLAUCON: Show me the things you mean.

SOCRATES: All right, I will show you, if you can see that some sense-   10
perceptions do not summon the understanding to look into them, because   b
the judgment of sense-perception is itself adequate; whereas others encourage it in every way to look into them, because sense-perception does not
produce a sound result.

GLAUCON: You are obviously referring to things appearing in the distance   5
and illusionist paintings.

SOCRATES: No, you are not quite getting what I mean.

GLAUCON: Then what do you mean?

SOCRATES: The ones that do not summon the understanding are all those
that do not at the same time result in an opposite sense-perception. But the
ones that do I call *summoners*. That is when sense-perception does not make   c
one thing any more clear than its opposite, regardless of whether what
strikes the senses is close by or far away. What I mean will be clearer if you
look at it this way: these, we say, are three fingers—the smallest, the second,
and the middle finger.   5

GLAUCON: Of course.

SOCRATES: Assume that I am talking about them as being seen from close
by. Now consider this about them with me.

GLAUCON: What?   10

217

SOCRATES: It is obvious, surely, that each of them is equally a finger, and it
d makes no difference whether it is seen to be in the middle or at either end;
whether it is dark or pale, thick or thin, or anything else of that sort. You
see, in all these cases, the soul of most people is not compelled to ask the
understanding what a finger is, since sight does not at any point suggest to
5 it that a finger is at the same time the opposite of a finger.

GLAUCON: No, it does not.

SOCRATES: It is likely, then, that a perception of that sort would not sum-
e mon or awaken the understanding.

GLAUCON: It is likely.

SOCRATES: Now, what about their bigness and smallness? Does sight perceive them adequately? Does it make no difference to it whether one of
them is in the middle or at the end? And is it the same with the sense of
5 touch, as regards thickness and thinness, hardness and softness? What about
the other senses, then—do they make such things sufficiently clear? Or
doesn't each of them work as follows: in the first place, the sense that deals
524a with hardness must also deal with softness; and it reports to the soul that it
perceives the same thing to be both hard and soft?

5 GLAUCON: That's right.

SOCRATES: In cases of this sort then, isn't the soul inevitably puzzled as to
what this sense-perception means by hardness, if it says that the same thing
is also soft; and in the case of the sense-perception of lightness and heaviness, what it means lightness and heaviness are, if what is heavy is light or
10 what is light heavy?

b GLAUCON: Yes, indeed, those are strange messages for the soul to receive
and do need to be examined.

SOCRATES: It is likely, then, that it is in cases of this sort that the soul,
summoning calculation and understanding, first tries to determine whether
5 each of the things reported to it is one or two.

GLAUCON: Of course.

SOCRATES: If there are obviously two, won't each of them be obviously
one and distinct?

GLAUCON: Yes.

10 SOCRATES: If each of them is one, then, and both together are two, the
soul will understand that the two are separate. I mean, it would not under-
c stand inseparable things as two, but as one.

GLAUCON: That's right.

SOCRATES: But sight, we say, saw bigness and smallness, not as separate,
but as mixed up together. Right?

GLAUCON: Yes.   5

SOCRATES: And to get clear about this, understanding was compelled to see bigness and smallness, too, not mixed up together, but distinguished— the opposite way from sight.

GLAUCON: True.

SOCRATES: Isn't it in cases like this that it first occurs to us to ask what   10
bigness is, and smallness, too?

GLAUCON: Absolutely.

SOCRATES: Which is why we called one section the intelligible and the other the visible.

GLAUCON: Right.   d

SOCRATES: That, then, is what I was trying to express before when I said that some things summon thought, while others do not. I define summoners as those that strike the relevant sense at the same time as do their oppo- sites. Those that do not do this, I said, do not wake up the understanding.   5

GLAUCON: I understand now, and I think you are right.

SOCRATES: Well then, to which of them does number, including the number one, belong?

GLAUCON: I do not know.

SOCRATES: Use what has already been said as an analogy. If the number one is adequately *seen* just by itself, or grasped by any of the other senses,   10
then just as we were saying in the case of fingers, it would not draw the soul e
toward being. But if something opposite to it is always seen at the same time, so that it no more appears to be one than the opposite of one, then there would be a need at that point for someone to decide the matter. And he would compel the soul within him to be puzzled, to inquire, to stir up the understanding within itself, and to ask what the number one itself is.   5
So, learning about the number one will be among the subjects that lead the soul and turn it around to look at what is.   525a

GLAUCON: But surely the visual perception of it has just that feature, since we do see the same thing as one and as an unlimited number at the same time.   5

SOCRATES: Then if this is true of the number one, won't it also be true of all numbers?

GLAUCON: Of course.

SOCRATES: But now, calculation and arithmetic are wholly concerned with numbers.   10

GLAUCON: Right.

b SOCRATES: Then they obviously lead toward truth.

GLAUCON: To an unnatural degree.

SOCRATES: Then they would belong, it seems, among the subjects we are seeking. I mean, a soldier must learn them in order to marshal his troops; and a philosopher, because it is necessary to be rising up out of becoming
5 so as to grasp being, or he will never become able to calculate.

GLAUCON: That's right.

SOCRATES: And our guardian is, in fact, both a warrior and a philosopher.

10 GLAUCON: Of course.

SOCRATES: Then it would be appropriate, Glaucon, to prescribe this sub-
c ject in our legislation and to persuade those who are going to take part in what is most important in the city to go in for calculation and take it up, not as laymen do, but staying with it until they reach the point at which they see the nature of the numbers by means of understanding itself; not like tradesmen and retailers, caring about it for the sake of buying and sell-ing, but for the sake of war and for ease in turning the soul itself around
5 from becoming to truth and being.

GLAUCON: Very well put.

SOCRATES: Moreover, it occurs to me now that the subject of calculation has been mentioned, how refined it is and in how many ways it is useful for
d our purposes, provided you practice it for the sake of knowledge rather than trade.

GLAUCON: Which ways?

SOCRATES: Why, in the very one we were talking about just now. It gives
5 the soul a strong lead upward and compels it to discuss the numbers them-selves, never permitting anyone to propose for discussion numbers attached to visible or tangible bodies. I mean, you surely know what people who are clever in these matters are like. If, in the course of the argument, someone
e tries to divide the number one itself, they laugh and won't permit it. If *you* divide it, they multiply it, taking care that the number one never appears to be, not one, but many parts.

5 GLAUCON: That's very true.

SOCRATES: Then what do you think would happen, Glaucon, if someone
526a were to ask them: "What kind of numbers are you amazing fellows discuss-ing, where the number one is as you assume it to be, wholly equal in each and every case, without the least difference, and having no internal parts?"
5 What do you think they would answer?

GLAUCON: I think they would answer that they are talking about those that are accessible only to thought and can be grasped in no other way.

220

SOCRATES: Do you see then, my friend, that this subject really does seem to be necessary to us, since it apparently compels the soul to use understanding itself on the truth itself?

GLAUCON: It does so very strongly, in fact.

SOCRATES: Now, have you ever noticed that those who are naturally good at calculation are also naturally quick in all subjects, so to speak, and that those who are slow, if they are educated and exercised in it, even if they are benefited in no other way, nonetheless improve and become generally sharper than they were?

GLAUCON: That's right.

SOCRATES: Moreover, I do not think you will easily find many subjects that are harder to learn or practice than it.

GLAUCON: No indeed.

SOCRATES: For all these reasons, then, this subject is not to be neglected. On the contrary, the very best natures must be educated in it.

GLAUCON: I agree.

SOCRATES: Well, then, let's require that one. Second, let's consider whether the subject that follows after it is also appropriate for our purposes.

GLAUCON: Which one? Or do you mean geometry?

SOCRATES: That's it exactly.

GLAUCON: Insofar as it pertains to war, it is clearly appropriate. You see, when it comes to setting up camp, occupying a region, gathering and ordering troops, and all the other maneuvers armies make whether in battle itself or on the march, it makes all the difference whether someone is skilled in geometry or not.

SOCRATES: But still, for things like that, even a little bit of geometry—and of calculation—would suffice. What we need to consider is whether the greater and more advanced part of it tends to make it easier to see the form of the good. And that tendency, we say, is to be found in anything that compels the soul to turn itself around toward the region in which lies the happiest of the things that are; the one the soul must do everything possible to see.

GLAUCON: You are right.

SOCRATES: Therefore, if geometry compels one to look at being, it is appropriate; but if at becoming, it is inappropriate.

GLAUCON: Yes, that's what we are saying.

SOCRATES: Now, no one with even a little experience of geometry will dispute with us that this science is itself entirely the opposite of what is said about it in the accounts of its practitioners.

221

GLAUCON: How so?

SOCRATES: Well, they say completely ridiculous things about it because they are so hard up. I mean, they talk as if they were practical people who make all their arguments for the sake of action. They talk of squaring, applying, adding, and the like; whereas, in fact, the entire subject is practiced for the sake of acquiring knowledge.

GLAUCON: Absolutely.

SOCRATES: Mustn't we also agree on a further point?

GLAUCON: What?

SOCRATES: That it is knowledge of what always is, not of something that comes to be and passes away.

GLAUCON: That's easy to agree to, since geometry is knowledge of what always is.

SOCRATES: In that case, my noble fellow, it can draw the soul toward truth and produce philosophical thought by directing upward what we now wrongly direct downward.

GLAUCON: More than anything else.

SOCRATES: More than anything else, then, we must require the inhabitants of your beautiful city not to neglect geometry in any way, since even its byproducts are not insignificant.

GLAUCON: What are they?

SOCRATES: The ones you mentioned that are concerned with war. And in addition, when it comes to being better able to pick up any subject, we surely know there is a world of difference between someone with a grasp of geometry and someone without one.

GLAUCON: Yes, by Zeus, a world of difference.

SOCRATES: Shall we prescribe it, then, as a second subject for the young?

GLAUCON: Let's.

SOCRATES: What about astronomy? Shall we make it the third? What do you think?

GLAUCON: That's fine with me, at least. I mean, a better awareness of the seasons, months, and years is no less appropriate for a general than for a farmer or navigator.

SOCRATES: You are funny! You are like someone who is afraid that the masses will think he is prescribing useless subjects. It is no inconsequential task—indeed it is a very difficult one—to become persuaded that in everyone's soul there is an instrument that is purified and rekindled by such subjects when it has been blinded and destroyed by other pursuits—an

222

instrument that it is more important to preserve than 10,000 eyes, since only with it can the truth be seen. Those who share your belief that this is so will think you are speaking incredibly well, while those who are completely unaware of it will probably think you are talking nonsense, since they can see no other benefit worth mentioning in these subjects. So, decide right now which group you are engaging in discussion. Or is it neither of them, and are you making your arguments mostly for your own sake—though you do not begrudge anyone else whatever profit he can get from them?

GLAUCON: That's what I prefer—to speak, question, and answer mostly for my own sake.

SOCRATES: Let's backtrack a bit. You see, we were wrong just now about the subject that comes after geometry.

GLAUCON: How so?

SOCRATES: After a plain surface, we went immediately to a solid that was revolving, without taking one just by itself. But the right way is to take up the third dimension after the second. And it, I suppose, consists of cubes and of whatever shares in depth.

GLAUCON: Yes, you are right. But Socrates, that subject has not even been investigated yet.

SOCRATES: There are two reasons for that. Because no city values it, it is not vigorously investigated, due to its difficulty. And investigators need a director if they are to discover anything. Now, in the first place, such a director is difficult to find. Second, even if he could be found, as things stand now, those who investigate it are too arrogant to obey him. But if an entire city served as his co-director and took the lead in valuing this subject, then they would obey him, and consistent and vigorous investigation would reveal the facts about it. For even now, when it is not valued by the masses and is hampered by investigators who lack any account of its usefulness—all the same, in spite of all these handicaps, the force of its appeal has caused it to be developed. So it would not be at all surprising if the facts about it were revealed in any case.

GLAUCON: Yes, indeed, it *is* an outstandingly appealing subject. But explain more clearly to me what you were saying just now. You took geometry, presumably, as dealing with plane surface.

SOCRATES: Yes.

GLAUCON: Then at first you put astronomy after it, but later you went back on that.

SOCRATES: Yes, the more I hurried to get through them all, the slower I went! You see, the subject dealing with the dimension of depth was next.

But because of the ridiculous state the investigation of it is in, I passed it by and spoke of astronomy—which deals with the motion of things having depth—after geometry.

GLAUCON: That's right.

SOCRATES: Let's then prescribe astronomy as the fourth subject, on the assumption that solid geometry, which we are now omitting, will be available if a city takes it up.

GLAUCON: That seems reasonable. And since you reproached me just now, Socrates, for praising astronomy in a vulgar manner, I will now praise it your way. You see, I think it is clear to everyone that it compels the soul to look upward and leads it from things here to things there.

SOCRATES: It is clear to everyone except me, then, since that is not how I think of it.

GLAUCON: Then how do you think of it?

SOCRATES: As it is handled today by those who teach philosophy, it makes the soul look very much downward.

GLAUCON: How do you mean?

SOCRATES: In my opinion, your conception of "higher studies" is a good deal too generous! I mean, if someone were looking at something by leaning his head back and studying ornaments on a ceiling, it seems as though you would say that he is looking at them with his understanding, not with his eyes! Maybe you are right and I am foolish. You see, I just cannot conceive of any subject making the soul look upward except the one that is concerned with what is—and that is *invisible*. If anyone tries to learn something about perceptible things, whether by gaping upward or squinting downward, I would say that he never really learns—since there is no knowledge to be had of such things—and that his soul is not looking up but down, whether he does his learning lying on his back on land or on sea!

GLAUCON: A fair judgment! You are right to reproach me. But what did you mean, then, when you said that astronomy must be learned in a different way than people learn it at present, if it is going to be useful with regard to what we are talking about?

SOCRATES: It is like this: these ornaments in the heavens, since they are ornaments in something visible, may certainly be regarded as having the most beautiful and most exact motions that such things can have. But these fall far short of the true ones—those motions in which the things that are really fast or really slow, as measured in true numbers and as forming all the true geometrical figures, are moved relative to one another, and that move the things that are in them. And these, of course, must be grasped by reason and thought, not by sight. Don't you agree?

GLAUCON: Of course.

SOCRATES: Therefore, we should use the ornaments in the heavens as models to help us study these other things.[10] It is just as if someone chanced to find diagrams by Daedalus or some other craftsman or painter, which were very carefully drawn and worked out. I mean, anyone experienced in geometry who saw such things would consider them to be very beautifully executed, I suppose. But he would think it ridiculous to examine them seriously in order to find there the truth about equals, doubles, or any other ratio.

e

530a

GLAUCON: How could it be anything but ridiculous?

SOCRATES: Don't you think, then, that a real astronomer will feel the same way when he looks at the motions of the stars? He will believe that the craftsman of the heavens arranged them and all that is in them in the most beautiful way possible for such things. But as for the ratio of night to day, of these to a month, of a month to a year, or of the motions of the stars to them or to each other, don't you think he will consider it strange to believe that they are always the same and never deviate in the least, since they are connected to body and are visible things, or to seek by every means possible to grasp the truth about them?

5

b

GLAUCON: That's what I think—anyway, now that I hear it from you!

5

SOCRATES: Just as in geometry, then, it is by making use of problems that we will pursue astronomy too. We will leave the things in the heavens alone, if we are really going to participate in astronomy and make the naturally wise element in the soul useful instead of useless.

c

GLAUCON: The task you are prescribing is a lot bigger than anything now attempted in astronomy.

SOCRATES: And I suppose we will prescribe other subjects in the same way, if we are to be of any benefit as lawgivers. But can you in fact suggest any other appropriate subjects?

5

GLAUCON: Not at the moment, anyway.

SOCRATES: But motion, it seems to me, presents itself, not just in one form, but in several. A wise person could probably list them all, but there are two that are evident even to us.

d

GLAUCON: What are they?

SOCRATES: Besides the one we have discussed, there is also its counterpart.

GLAUCON: What's that?

5

SOCRATES: It is probable that as the eyes fasten on astronomical motions, so the ears fasten on harmonic ones, and that these two sciences are somehow akin, as the Pythagoreans say. And we agree, Glaucon. Don't we?

10

[10] See 510d–511a.

GLAUCON: We do.

e   SOCRATES: Then, since the task is so huge, shouldn't we ask them their opinion and whether they have anything to add, all the while guarding our own requirement?

GLAUCON: What's that?

SOCRATES: That those we will be rearing should never attempt to learn
5   anything incomplete,[11] anything that does not always come out at the place all things should reach—the one we mentioned just now in the case of astronomy.[12] Or don't you know that people do something similar with
531a   harmony, too? They measure audible concordances and sounds against one another, and so labor in vain, just like astronomers.

GLAUCON: Yes, by the gods, and pretty ridiculous they are, too. They talk about something they call a "dense interval" or quarter tone[13]—putting
5   their ears to their instruments, like someone trying to overhear what the neighbors are saying. And some say they hear a tone in between, and that *it* is the shortest interval by which they must measure, while others argue that this tone sounds the same as a quarter tone. Both groups put ears before the
b   understanding.

SOCRATES: You mean those excellent fellows who vex their strings, torturing them and stretching them on pegs. I won't draw out the analogy by
5   speaking of blows with the pick, or the charges laid against strings that are too responsive or too unresponsive. Instead, I will drop the analogy and say that I do not mean these people, but the ones we just said we were going to question about harmonics. You see, they do the same as the astronomers do.
c   I mean, it is in these audible concordances that they search for numbers, but they do not ascend to problems or investigate which numbers are in concord and which are not, or what the explanation is in each case.

5   GLAUCON: But that would be a daimonic task!

SOCRATES: Yet, it is useful in the search for the beautiful and the good! Pursued for any other purpose, though, it is useless.

GLAUCON: I suppose so.

SOCRATES: Moreover, I take it that if the investigation of all the subjects we have mentioned arrives at what they share in common with one
d   another and what their affinities are, and draws conclusions about their kinship, it does contribute something to our goal and is not labor in vain; but that otherwise it is in vain.

[11] 504c.

[12] 528b.

[13] A dense interval is evidently the smallest difference in pitch that was recognized in ancient music.

GLAUCON: I have the same hunch myself. But you are still talking about a very big task, Socrates.

SOCRATES: Do you mean the prelude, or what? Or don't you know that all these subjects are merely preludes to the theme[14] itself that must be learned? I mean, you surely do not think that people who are clever in these matters are dialecticians.

GLAUCON: No, by Zeus, I do not. Although, I have met a few exceptions.

SOCRATES: But did it ever seem to you that those who can neither give an account nor approve one know what any of the things are that we say they must know?

GLAUCON: Again, the answer is no.

SOCRATES: Then isn't this at last, Glaucon, the theme itself that dialectical discussion sings? It itself is intelligible. But the power of sight imitates it. We said that sight tries at last to look at the animals themselves, the stars themselves, and, in the end, at the sun itself.[15] In the same way, whenever someone tries, by means of dialectical discussion and without the aid of any sense-perceptions, to arrive through reason at the being of each thing itself, and does not give up until he grasps what good itself is[16] with understanding itself, he reaches the end of the intelligible realm, just as the other reached the end of the visible one.

GLAUCON: Absolutely.

SOCRATES: Well, then, don't you call this journey[17] dialectic?

GLAUCON: I do.

SOCRATES: Then the release from bonds and the turning around from shadows to statues and the light; and then the ascent out of the cave to the sun; and there the continuing inability to look directly at the animals, the plants, and the light of the sun, but instead at divine reflections in water and shadows of the things that are, and not, as before, merely at shadows of statues thrown by another source of light that, when judged in relation to the sun, is as shadowy as they—all this practice of the crafts we mentioned has the power to lead the best part of the soul upward until it sees the best among the things that are, just as before the clearest thing in the body was led to the brightest thing in the bodily and visible world.

GLAUCON: I accept that this is so. And yet, I think it is very difficult to accept; although—in another way—difficult not to accept! All the same,

---

[14] *Nomos:* also, law.

[15] See 516a–b.

[16] *Auto ho estin agathon:* See Glossary of Terms s.v. what it is.

[17] *Poreia:* An *aporia* (puzzle, problem—literally, a blockage on one's journey forward) is what dialectic attempts to solve.

since the present occasion is not our only opportunity to hear these things,
but we will get to return to them often in the future, let's assume that what
you said about them just now is true and turn to the theme itself, and discuss it in the same way as we did the prelude. So, tell us then, in what way
the power of dialectical discussion works, into what kinds it is divided, and
what roads it follows. I mean, it is these, it seems, that would lead us at last
to that place which is a rest from the road, so to speak, for the one who
reaches it, and an end of his journey.

SOCRATES: You won't be able to follow me any farther, my dear Glaucon—though not because of any lack of eagerness on my part. You would
no longer see an image of what we are describing, but the truth itself as it
seems to me, at least.[18] Whether it is really so or not—that's not something
on which it is any longer worth insisting. But that there is some such thing
to be seen, *that* is something on which we must insist. Isn't that so?

GLAUCON: Of course.

SOCRATES: And mustn't we also insist that the power of dialectical discussion could reveal it only to someone experienced in the subjects we
described, and cannot do so in any other way?

GLAUCON: Yes, that is worth insisting on, too.

SOCRATES: At the very least, no one will dispute our claim by arguing that
there is another road of inquiry that tries to acquire a systematic and wholly
general grasp of what each thing itself is. By contrast, all the other crafts are
concerned with human beliefs and appetites, with growing or construction,
or with the care of growing or constructed things. As for the rest, we
described them as to some extent grasping what is—I mean, geometry and
the subjects that follow it. For we saw that while they do dream about what
is, they cannot see it while wide awake as long as they make use of hypotheses that they leave undisturbed, and for which they cannot give any argument. After all, when the first principle is unknown, and the conclusion
and the steps in between are put together out of what is unknown, what
mechanism could possibly turn any agreement reached in such cases into
knowledge?[19]

GLAUCON: None.

SOCRATES: Therefore, dialectic is the only investigation that, doing away
with hypotheses, journeys to the first principle itself in order to be made
secure. And when the eye of the soul is really buried in a sort of barbaric
bog,[20] dialectic gently pulls it out and leads it upward, using the crafts we

[18] See 506d8–e5.
[19] See 510c1–511c2.
[20] See 519a7–519b5.

described to help it and cooperate with it in turning the soul around. From force of habit, we have often called these branches of knowledge. But they need another name, since they are clearer than belief and darker than knowledge. We distinguished them by the term "thought" somewhere before.[21] But I don't suppose we will dispute about names, with matters as important as those before us to investigate.

GLAUCON: Of course not, just as long as they express the state of clarity the soul possesses.

SOCRATES: It will be satisfactory, then, to do what we did before and call the first section knowledge, the second thought, the third opinion, and the fourth imagination. The last two together we call belief, the other two, understanding.[22] Belief is concerned with becoming; understanding with being. And as being is to becoming, so understanding is to belief; and as understanding is to belief, so knowledge is to belief and thought to imagination. But as for the ratios between the things these deal with, and the division of either the believable or the intelligible section into two, let's pass them by, Glaucon, in case they involve us in discussions many times longer than the ones we have already gone through.

GLAUCON: I agree with you about the rest of them, anyway, insofar as I am able to follow.

SOCRATES: So don't you, too, call someone a dialectician when he is able to grasp an account of the being of each thing? And when he cannot do so, won't you, too, say that to the extent that he cannot give an account of something either to himself or to another, to that extent he does not understand it?

GLAUCON: How could I not?

SOCRATES: Then the same applies to the good. Unless someone can give an account of the form of the good, distinguishing it from everything else, and can survive all examination as if in a battle, striving to examine[23] things not in accordance with belief, but in accordance with being; and can journey through all that with his account still intact, you will say that he does not know the good itself or any other good whatsoever. And if he does manage to grasp some image of it, you will say that it is through belief, not knowledge, that he grasps it; that he is dreaming and asleep throughout his

---

[21] 511d6–511e4.

[22] The reference is to 511d6–e5, where the first section is called understanding (*noêsis*), not knowledge (*epistêmê*). Since thought (*dianoia*) is not now a kind of knowledge, *noêsis* and *epistêmê* have in effect become one and the same. *Epistêmê* and *dianoia* are now jointly referred to as *noêsis*, because that whole section of the line on which they appear consists of intelligible objects (*noêton*).

[23] *Elengchein:* ("to examine," "to refute")—as in the Socratic elenchus.

d present life; and that, before he wakes up here, he will arrive in Hades and go to sleep forever.

GLAUCON: Yes, by Zeus, I will certainly say all that.

SOCRATES: Then as for those children of yours, the ones you are rearing and educating in your discussion, if you ever reared them in fact, I don't suppose that, while they are still as irrational as the proverbial lines,[24] you

5 would allow them to rule in your city or control the most important things.

GLAUCON: No, of course not.

SOCRATES: Won't you prescribe in your legislation, then, that they are to give the most attention to the education that will enable them to ask and

10 answer questions most knowledgeably?

e GLAUCON: I will prescribe it—together with you.

SOCRATES: Doesn't it seem to you, then, that dialectic is just like a capstone we have placed on top of the subjects, and that no other subject can rightly be placed above it, but that our account of the subjects has now

535a come to an end?

GLAUCON: It does.

SOCRATES: Then it remains for you to deal with the distribution of these subjects: to whom we will assign them and in what way.

5 GLAUCON: Clearly.

SOCRATES: Do you remember what sort of people we chose in our earlier selection of rulers?[25]

GLAUCON: How could I not?

SOCRATES: Well then, as regards the other requirements too, you must suppose that these same natures are to be chosen, since we have to select

10 the most secure, the most courageous, and—as far as possible—the best-looking.[26] In addition, we must look not only for people who have a noble

b and valiant character, but for those who also have natural qualities conducive to this education of ours.

GLAUCON: Which ones in particular?

5 SOCRATES: They must be keen on the subjects, bless you, and learn them without difficulty. For people's souls are much more likely to give up during strenuous studies than during physical training. The pain is more their own, you see, since it is peculiar to them and not shared with the body.

---

[24] A pun made possible by the fact that *alogon* can mean "irrational" (as applied to people) and "incommensurable" (as applied to lines in geometry).

[25] 412b8–417b9.

[26] See 402d1–4.

GLAUCON: That's true.

SOCRATES: We must also look for someone who has a good memory, is
persistent, and is wholeheartedly in love with hard work. How else do you   c
suppose he would be willing to carry out such hard physical labors and also
complete so much learning and training?

GLAUCON: He would not, not unless his nature were an entirely good one.

SOCRATES: In any case, the mistake made at present—which, as we said   5
before, explains why philosophy has fallen into dishonor—is that unworthy
people take it up. For illegitimate people should not have taken it up, but
genuine ones.

GLAUCON: How do you mean?

SOCRATES: In the first place, the one who takes it up must not be half-
hearted in his love of hard work, with one half of him loving hard work
and the other shirking it. That is what happens when someone is a lover of   d
physical training and a lover of hunting and a lover of all kinds of hard
bodily labor; yet is not a lover of learning, a lover of listening, or a keen
investigator, but hates the work involved in all such things. And someone   5
whose love of hard work tends in the opposite direction is also defective.

GLAUCON: That's absolutely true.

SOCRATES: Similarly with regard to truth, won't we say that a soul is
maimed if it hates a voluntary lie, cannot endure to have one in itself, and is
greatly angered when others lie; but is nonetheless content to accept an
involuntary lie, does not get irritated when it is caught being ignorant, and
bears its ignorance easily, wallowing in it like a pig?[27]   5

GLAUCON: Absolutely.   536a

SOCRATES: And with regard to temperance, courage, high-mindedness,
and all the other parts of virtue, too, we must be especially on our guard to
distinguish the illegitimate from the genuine. You see, when private individuals or cities do not know how to investigate all these things fully, they   5
unwittingly employ defectives and illegitimates as their friends or rulers for
whatever services they happen to need.

GLAUCON: Yes, that's just what happens.

SOCRATES: So we must take good care in all these matters, since, if we
bring people who are sound of limb and mind to so important a subject,   b
and train and educate them in it, justice itself will not find fault with us,
and we will save both the city and its constitution. But if we bring people

---

[27] The difference between voluntary and involuntary lies is explained at 382a1–
383a7.

of a different sort to it, we will achieve precisely the opposite and let loose

5 an even greater flood of ridicule upon philosophy as well.

GLAUCON: That would be a shame.

SOCRATES: It certainly would. But I seem to have made myself a little ridiculous just now.

GLAUCON: In what way?

c SOCRATES: I forgot we were playing and spoke too vehemently. You see, while I was speaking I looked upon philosophy, and when I saw it undeservedly showered with abuse, I suppose I got irritated and, as if I were angry with those responsible, I said what I had to say in too serious a

5 manner.

GLAUCON: Not too serious for me, by Zeus, as a member of the audience.

SOCRATES: But too serious for me as the speaker. In any case, let's not forget that in our earlier selection we chose older people, but here that is not

d permitted. You see, we must not believe Solon when he says that as someone grows older, he is able to learn a lot. On the contrary, he is even less able to learn than to run. It is to young people that all large and frequent labors properly belong.

GLAUCON: Necessarily so.

5 SOCRATES: Well, then, calculation, geometry, and all the preparatory education that serves as preparation for dialectic must be offered to them in childhood—and not in the shape of compulsory instruction, either.

GLAUCON: Why's that?

SOCRATES: Because a free person should learn nothing slavishly. For while compulsory physical labors do no harm to the body, no compulsory instruction remains in the soul.

5 GLAUCON: That's true.

SOCRATES: Well, then, do not use compulsion, my very good man, to train the children in these subjects; use play instead. That way you will also

537a be able to see better what each of them is naturally suited for.

GLAUCON: What you say makes sense.

SOCRATES: Don't you remember that we also said that the children were

5 to be led into war on horseback as observers, and that, wherever it is safe, they should be brought to the front and given a taste of blood, just like young dogs?

GLAUCON: I do remember.

SOCRATES: Those who always show the greatest facility in dealing with all

10 these labors, studies, and fears must be enrolled in a unit.

232

GLAUCON: At what age?   b

SOCRATES: After they are released from compulsory physical training. For
during that period, whether it is two or three years, they are incapable of
doing anything else, since weariness and sleep are enemies of learning. At
the same time, one of the important tests of each of them is how he fares in   5
physical training.

GLAUCON: It certainly is.

SOCRATES: Then, after that period, those selected from among the
twenty-year-olds will receive greater honors than the others. Moreover, the
subjects they learned in no particular order in their education as children,   c
they must now bring together into a unified vision of their kinship with
one another and with the nature of what is.

GLAUCON: That, at any rate, is the only instruction that remains secure in
those who receive it.   5

SOCRATES: It is also the greatest test of which nature is dialectical and
which is not. For the person who can achieve a unified vision is dialectical,
and the one who cannot isn't.

GLAUCON: I agree.

SOCRATES: Well, then, you will have to look out for those among them
who most possess that quality; who are resolute in their studies and also res- d
olute in war and the other things conventionally expected of them. And
when they have passed their thirtieth year, you will have to select them in
turn from among those selected earlier and assign them yet greater honors,
and test them by means of the power of dialectical discussion to see which
of them can relinquish his eyes and other senses, and travel on in the com-   5
pany of truth to what itself is. And here, comrade, you have a task that
needs a lot of safeguarding.

GLAUCON: How so?

SOCRATES: Don't you realize the harm caused by dialectical discussion as   e
it is currently practiced?

GLAUCON: What harm?

SOCRATES: Its practitioners are filled with lawlessness.

GLAUCON: They certainly are.   5

SOCRATES: Do you think it is at all surprising that this happens to them?
Aren't you sympathetic?

GLAUCON: Why should I be?

SOCRATES: It is like the case of a supposititious child brought up amid
great wealth, a large and powerful family, and many flatterers, who finds   538a
out, when he has become a man, that he is not the child of his professed

parents and that he cannot discover his real ones. Do you have any hunch as to what his attitude would be to the flatterers, and to his supposed parents, during the time when he did not know about the exchange, and, on the other hand, when he did know? Or would you rather hear my hunch?

GLAUCON: I would.

SOCRATES: Well, then, my hunch is that he would be more likely to honor his father, his mother, and the rest of his supposed family than the flatterers, less likely to overlook any of their needs, less likely to treat them lawlessly in word or deed, and less likely to disobey them than the flatterers in any matters of importance, in the time when he did not know the truth.

GLAUCON: Probably so.

SOCRATES: But when he became aware of the truth, on the other hand, my hunch is that he would withdraw his honor and devotion from his family and increase them for the flatterers, whom he would obey far more than before, and he would begin to live the way they did, spend time with them openly, and—unless he was thoroughly good by nature—care nothing for that father of his or any of the rest of his supposed family.

GLAUCON: All that would probably happen as you say. But how is it like the case of those who take up argument?

SOCRATES: As follows. I take it we hold from childhood convictions about what things are just and fine; we are brought up with them as with our parents; we obey and honor them.

GLAUCON: Yes, we do.

SOCRATES: And there are also other practices, opposite to those, which possess pleasures that flatter our soul and attract it to themselves, but which do not persuade people who are at all moderate—who continue to honor and obey the convictions of their fathers.

GLAUCON: That's right.

SOCRATES: What happens, then, when someone of that sort is met by the question, "What is the fine?" and, when he answers what he has heard from the traditional lawgiver, the argument refutes him; and by refuting him often and in many ways, reduces him to the belief that the fine is no more fine than shameful, and the same with the just, the good, and the things he honored most—what do you think he will do after that about honoring and obeying his earlier convictions?

GLAUCON: It is inevitable that he won't honor or obey them in the same way.

SOCRATES: Then when he no longer regards them as honorable or as his own kin the way he did before, and cannot discover the true ones, will he be likely to adopt any other sort of life than the one that flatters him?

[left margin, handwritten: What finding out about her does to someone even a philosopher.]

GLAUCON: No, he won't.

SOCRATES: And so he will be taken, I suppose, to have changed from being law-abiding to being lawless.

GLAUCON: Inevitably.

SOCRATES: Isn't it likely, then, that this is what will happen to people who take up argument in that way, and, as I said just now, don't they deserve a lot of sympathy?

GLAUCON: Yes, and pity too.

SOCRATES: Then if you do not want your thirty-year-olds to be objects of such pity, won't you have to employ every sort of precaution when they take up argument?

GLAUCON: Yes, indeed.

SOCRATES: And isn't one very effective precaution not to let them taste argument while they are young? I mean, I don't suppose it has escaped your notice that when young people get their first taste of argument, they misuse it as if it were playing a game, always using it for disputation.[28] They imitate those who have refuted them by refuting others themselves,[29] and, like puppies, enjoy dragging and tearing with argument anyone within reach.

GLAUCON: Excessively so.

SOCRATES: Then, when they have refuted many themselves and been refuted by many, they quickly fall into violently disbelieving everything they believed before. And as a result of this, they themselves and the whole of philosophy as well are discredited in the eyes of others.

GLAUCON: That's absolutely true.

SOCRATES: But an older person would not be willing to take part in such madness. He will imitate someone who is willing to engage in dialectical discussion and look for the truth, rather than someone who plays at disputation as a game. He will be more moderate himself and will bring honor, rather than discredit, to the practice.

GLAUCON: That's right.

SOCRATES: And wasn't everything we said before this also said as a precaution—that those with whom one takes part in arguments are to be orderly and steady by nature, and not, as now, those, however unsuitable, who chance to come along?

GLAUCON: Yes, it was.

---

[28] See Glossary of Terms s.v. disputation.
[29] See *Apology* 23c.

235

SOCRATES: Is it enough, then, if someone devotes himself continuously and strenuously to taking part in argument, doing nothing else, but training in it just as he did in the physical training that is its counterpart, but for twice as many years?

10

e   GLAUCON: Do you mean six years or four?

SOCRATES: It does not matter. Make it five. You see, after that, you must make them go down into the cave again, and compel them to take command in matters of war and the other offices suitable for young people, so that they won't be inferior to the others in experience. And in these offices, too, they must be tested to see whether they will remain steadfast when they are pulled in different directions, or give way.

5

540a

GLAUCON: How much time do you assign to that?

SOCRATES: Fifteen years. Then, at the age of fifty, those who have survived the tests and are entirely best in every practical task and every science must be led at last to the end and compelled to lift up the radiant light of their souls, and to look toward what itself provides light for everything. And once they have seen the good itself, they must use it as their model and put the city, its citizens, and themselves in order throughout the remainder of their lives, each in turn. They will spend most of their time doing philosophy, but, when his turn comes, each must labor in politics and rule for the city's sake, not as something fine, but rather as something that must be done.[30] In that way, always having educated others like themselves to take their place as guardians of the city, they will depart for the Isles of the Blessed and dwell there. And the city will publicly establish memorials and sacrifices to them as daimons,[31] if the Pythia agrees; but if not, as happy and divine people.

5

b

5

c

GLAUCON: Like a sculptor,[32] Socrates, you have produced thoroughly beautiful ruling men!

5   SOCRATES: And ruling women, too, Glaucon. You see, you must not think that what I have said applies any more to men than it does to those women of theirs who are born with the appropriate natures.

GLAUCON: That's right, if indeed they are to share everything equally with the men, as we said.

SOCRATES: Well, then, do you agree that the things we have said about the city and its constitution are not altogether wishful thinking; that it is difficult for them to come about, but possible in a way, and in no way except the one we described: namely, when one or more true philosophers

d

---

[30] See 346e3–347d8, 520e4–521a8.

[31] See Glossary of Terms s.v. daimon.

[32] See 361d4–6.

come to power in a city—people who think little of present honors, regarding them as illiberal and worthless, who prize what is right and the honors that come from it above everything, and who consider justice as the most important and most essential thing, serving it and fostering it as they set their city in order?

GLAUCON: How will they do that?

SOCRATES: Everyone in the city who is over ten years old they will send into the country. They will take over the children, and far removed from current habits, which their parents possess, they will bring them up in their own ways and laws, which are the ones we described before. And with the city and constitution we were discussing thus established in the quickest and easiest way, it will itself be happy and bring the greatest benefit to the people among whom it comes to be.

GLAUCON: That's by far the quickest and easiest way. And in my opinion, Socrates, you have well described how it would come into existence, if it ever did.

SOCRATES: Haven't we said enough, then, about this city and the man who is like it? For surely it is clear what sort of person we will say he has to be.

GLAUCON: Yes, it is clear. And as for your question, I think we have reached the end of this topic.

Book 8

543a SOCRATES: All right. We are agreed, then, Glaucon, that if a city is going to be eminently well governed, women must be shared; children and their entire education must be shared; in both peace and war, pursuits must be shared; and their kings must be those among them who have proved best
5 both in philosophy and where war is concerned.

GLAUCON: We are agreed.

b SOCRATES: Moreover, we also granted this: once the rulers are established, they will lead the soldiers and settle them in the kind of dwellings we described earlier, which are in no way private, but wholly shared. And surely we also came to an agreement, if you remember, about what sort of
5 possessions they should have.

GLAUCON: Yes, I do remember. We thought that none of them should acquire any of the things that others now do; but that, as athletes of war and
c guardians, they should receive their minimum yearly upkeep from the other citizens as a wage for their guardianship, and take care of themselves and the rest of the city.[1]

SOCRATES: That's right. But since we have completed that discussion, let's recall the point at which we began the digression that brought us here, so
5 that we can continue on the same path again.

GLAUCON: That is not difficult. You see, much the same as now, you were talking as if you had completed the description of the city.[2] You were saying that you would class both the city you described and the man who is like it
d as good, even though, as it seems, you had a still finer city and man to tell
544a us about. But in any case, you were saying that the others were defective, if it was correct. And you said, if I remember, that of the remaining kinds of constitution four were worth discussing, each with defects we should observe; and that we should do the same for the people like them in order
5 to observe them all, come to an agreement about which man is best and which worst, and then determine whether the best is happiest and the worst most wretched, or whether it is otherwise. I was asking you which

previous city defective

---

[1] 415d6–420a7.
[2] 445c1–450c5.

238

four constitutions you had in mind, when Polemarchus and Adeimantus b
interrupted.[3] And that is when you took up the discussion that led here.

SOCRATES: That's absolutely right.

GLAUCON: Like a wrestler, then, give me the same hold again, and when I 5
ask the same question, try to tell me what you were about to say before.

SOCRATES: If I can.

GLAUCON: In any case, I really want to hear for myself what four constitutions you meant.

SOCRATES: It won't be difficult for you to hear them. You see, the ones I
mean are the very ones that already have names: the one that is praised by c
"the many," your Cretan or Laconian[4] constitution. The second—and second in the praise it receives—is called oligarchy, a constitution filled with a
host of evils. Antagonistic to it, and next in order, is democracy. And 5
"noble" tyranny, surpassing all of them, is the fourth and most extreme disease of cities. Can you think of another form of constitution—I mean,
another distinct in form from these? For, no doubt, there are dynasties and
purchased kingships and other similar constitutions in between these, d
which one finds no less among barbarians than among Greeks.

GLAUCON: Many strange ones are certainly mentioned, at least. 5

SOCRATES: Are you aware, then, that there must be as many forms of
human character as there are of constitutions? Or do you think constitutions arise from oak or rock[5] and not from the characters of the people in
the cities, which tip the scales, so to speak, and drag the rest along with
them?

GLAUCON: No, they could not possibly arise from anything other than that.

SOCRATES: So, if there are five of cities, there must also be five ways of
arranging private individual souls.5

GLAUCON: Of course.

SOCRATES: Now, we have already described the one who is like aristocracy, the one we rightly describe as good and just.

GLAUCON: Yes, we have described him.545a

SOCRATES: Mustn't we next describe the inferior ones—the victory-loving and honor-loving, which correspond to the Laconian constitution, followed by the oligarchic, democratic, and tyrannical—so that, having
discovered the most unjust of all, we can oppose him to the most just and5

---

[3] 449b1–2.

[4] I.e., Spartan.

[5] Homer, *Odyssey* 19.163.

complete our investigation into how pure justice and pure injustice stand with regard to the happiness or wretchedness of the one who possesses them; and be persuaded either by Thrasymachus to practice injustice or by the argument that is now coming to light to practice justice.

GLAUCON: That's exactly what we must do.

SOCRATES: Then just as we began by looking for the virtues of character in constitutions before looking for them in private individuals, thinking they would be clearer in the former,[6] shouldn't we first examine the honor-loving constitution? I do not know another name that is commonly applied to it; it should be called either timocracy or timarchy. Then shouldn't we examine that sort of man by comparing him to it, and, after that, oligarchy and the oligarchic man, and democracy and the democratic man? Fourth, having come to a city that is under a tyrant and having examined it, shouldn't we look into a tyrannical soul, and so try to become adequate judges of the topic we proposed for ourselves?[7]

GLAUCON: That, at any rate, would be a reasonable way for us to go about observing and judging.

SOCRATES: Come on, then, let's try to describe how timocracy emerges from aristocracy. Or is it simply the case that, in all constitutions, change originates in the ruling element itself when faction breaks out within it; but that if this group remains of one mind, then—however small it is—change is impossible?

GLAUCON: Yes, that's right.

SOCRATES: How, then, Glaucon, will our city be changed? How will faction arise, either between the auxiliaries and the rulers or within either group? Or do you want us to be like Homer and pray to the Muses to tell us "how faction first broke out,"[8] and have them speak in tragic tones, playing and jesting with us, as if we were children and they were speaking in earnest?

GLAUCON: How do you mean?

SOCRATES: Something like this: "It is difficult for a city constituted in this way to change. However, since everything that comes-to-be must decay, not even one so constituted will last forever. On the contrary, it, too, must face dissolution. And this is how it will be dissolved: not only plants that grow in the earth, but also animals that grow upon it, have periods of fertility and infertility of both soul and bodies each time their cycles complete a revolution. These cycles are short for what is short-lived and the opposite for what

---

[6] See 368c7–369a3.

[7] Most recently at 544a2–8.

[8] Apparently an adaptation of *Iliad* 16.112–3.

is the opposite. However, even though they are wise, the people you have educated to be leaders in your city will, by using rational calculation combined with sense-perception, nonetheless fail to ascertain the periods of good fertility and of infertility for your species. Instead, these will escape them, and so they will sometimes beget children when they should not.

"Now, for the birth of a divine creature there is a cycle comprehended by a perfect number;[9] while for a human being, it is the first number in which are found increases involving both roots and powers, comprehending three intervals and four terms, of factors that cause likeness and unlikeness, cause increase and decrease, and make all things mutually agreeable and rational in their relations to one another. Of these factors, the base ones—four in relation to three, together with five—give two harmonies when thrice increased. One is a square, so many times a hundred. The other is of equal length one way, but oblong. One of its sides are 100 squares of the rational diameter of five each diminished by one, or alternatively 100 squares of the irrational diameter each diminished by two. The other side are 100 cubes of three. This whole geometrical number controls better and worse births.[10]

[9] The divine creature seems to be the world or universe. See *Timaeus* 30b–d, 32d, 34a–b. Plato does not specify what its number is.

[10] The human geometrical number is the product of 3, 4, and 5 "thrice increased": if $(3 \times 4 \times 5) \times (3 \times 4 \times 5) = (3 \times 4 \times 5)^2$ is one increase, $(3 \times 4 \times 5) \times (3 \times 4 \times 5) \times (3 \times 4 \times 5) \times (3 \times 4 \times 5) = (3 \times 4 \times 5)^4$ is three. This formula included "increases involving both roots and powers": $(3 \times 4 \times 5)$ is a root; its indices are powers. It "comprehends" three "intervals," symbolized by $\times$, and four "terms"—namely, the roots. The resulting number, 12,960,000, can be represented geometrically as: (1) a square whose sides are 3,600, or (2) an "oblong" or rectangle whose sides are 4,800 and 2,700. (1) is "so many times 100": 36 times. (2) is obtained as follows. The "rational diameter" of 5 is the nearest rational number to the real diameter of a square whose sides are 5. This diameter = $\sqrt{5^2 + 5^2} = \sqrt{50} = 7$. Since the square of 7 is 49, we get the longer side of the rectangle by diminishing 49 by 1 and multiplying the result by 100. This gives 4,800. The "irrational diameter" of 5 is $\sqrt{50}$. When squared (= 50), diminished by 2 (= 48), and multiplied by 100, this, too, is 4,800. The short side, "100 cubes of three," = 2,700. The significance of the number is more controversial. The factors "that cause likeness and unlikeness, cause increase and decrease, and make all things mutually agreeable and rational in their relations to one another" are probably the numbers, since odd numbers were thought to cause likeness and even ones unlikeness (Aristotle, *Physics* 203ª13–5). Of the numbers significant in human life, one is surely the 100 years of its maximum span (615a8–b1). Another might be the number of days in the year (roughly 360), and a third might be the divisions of those days into smaller units determined by the sun's place in the sky, since it is the sun that provides for "the coming-to-be, growth, and nourishment" of all visible things (509b2–4). Assuming that those units are the 360 degrees of the sun's path around the earth (a suggestion due to Robin Waterfield), the number of moments in a human life that have a potential effect on its coming-to-be, growth, and nourishment would be $100 \times 360 \times 360$, or 12,960,000—Plato's human geometrical number.

d "And when, through ignorance of these, your guardians join brides and grooms at the wrong time, the children will be neither good-natured nor fortunate. The older generation will choose the best of these children, even though they do not deserve them. And when they in turn acquire their fathers' powers, the first thing they will begin to neglect as guardians will

5 be us, by paying less attention to musical training than they should; and the second is physical training. Hence your young people will become more unmusical. And rulers chosen from among them won't be able to guard

e well the testing of Hesiod's and your own races—gold, silver, bronze, and

547a iron.[11] The intermixing of iron with silver and bronze with gold will engender lack of likeness and unharmonious inequality, and these always breed war and hostility wherever they arise. We must declare faction to be

5 'of this lineage,'[12] wherever and whenever it arises."

GLAUCON: And we will declare that they have answered correctly.

SOCRATES: They must. They are Muses, after all!

b GLAUCON: What do the Muses say next?

SOCRATES: When faction arose, each of these two races, the iron and the bronze, pulled the constitution toward moneymaking and the acquisition of land, houses, gold, and silver. The other two, by contrast, the gold and sil-

5 ver races—since they are not poor, but naturally rich in their souls[13]—led toward virtue and the old political system. Striving and struggling with one another, they compromised on a middle way: they distributed the land and houses among themselves as private property; enslaved and held as serfs and

c servants those whom they had previously guarded as free friends and providers of upkeep; and took responsibility themselves for making war and for guarding against the ones they had enslaved.

5 GLAUCON: I think that is how the transformation begins.

SOCRATES: Wouldn't this constitution, then, be somehow in the middle between aristocracy and oligarchy?

GLAUCON: Of course.

SOCRATES: Anyway, that is how the transformation occurs. But once transformed, how will it be managed? Or isn't it obvious that it will imi-

d tate the first constitution in some respects and oligarchy in others, since it is in the middle between them; and that it will also have some features unique to itself?

GLAUCON: That's right.

[11] 414d1–415c7; Hesiod, *Works and Days* 109–202.
[12] Homer, *Iliad* 6.211.
[13] See 416e4–417a1.

SOCRATES: In honoring the rulers, then, and in the fighting class's abstention from farming, handicrafts, and other ways of making money, in providing communal meals and being devoted to physical training and training for war—in all such ways, won't the constitution be like the previous one?

GLAUCON: Yes.

SOCRATES: But in its fear of appointing wise people as rulers, on the grounds that men of that sort are no longer simple and earnest but mixed; in its inclination toward spirited and simpler people, who are more naturally suited for war than peace; in its honoring the tricks and stratagems of war; and spending all its time making war—in these respects, by contrast, isn't it pretty much unique?

GLAUCON: Yes.

SOCRATES: Such men will have an appetite for money just like those in oligarchies, passionately adoring gold and silver in secret, owning storehouses and private treasuries where they can deposit them and keep them hidden; and they will have walls around their houses, real private nests, where they can spend lavishly on their women or on anyone else they please.

GLAUCON: That's absolutely true.

SOCRATES: They will be stingy with money, since they honor it and do not possess it openly, but they will love to spend other people's money because of their appetites. They will enjoy their pleasures in secret, running away from the law like boys from their father, since they have not been educated by persuasion but by force. This is because they have neglected the true Muse, the companion of discussion and philosophy,[14] and honored physical training more than musical training.

GLAUCON: The constitution you are describing is a thorough mixture of good and bad.

SOCRATES: Yes, it is mixed. But because of its mastery by the spirited element, only one thing really stands out in it—the love of victories and honors.

GLAUCON: And very noticeable it is.

SOCRATES: That, then, is how this constitution would come to exist, and that is what it would be like. It is just an outline sketch of the constitution in words, not an exact account of it, since even from a sketch we will be able to see the most just man and most unjust one. It would be an incredibly long task to discuss every constitution and every character without omitting any detail.

GLAUCON: Yes, that's right.

[14] See *Phaedo* 61a3–4.

SOCRATES: Who, then, is the man corresponding to this constitution? How does he come to exist and what sort of man is he?

ADEIMANTUS: I think he would be very like Glaucon here, at least as far as the love of victory is concerned.

SOCRATES: Maybe in that respect, but in the following ones I do not think his nature would be like that.

e   ADEIMANTUS: Which ones?

SOCRATES: He would have to be more stubborn and less well trained in
5   music; a lover of music and of listening, yet not at all skilled in speaking; the
549a   sort of person who is harsh to slaves instead of looking down on them, as
       an adequately educated person does; gentle to free people and very submissive to rulers; a lover of ruling and of honor, who does not base his claim to
5   rule on his ability to speak or anything like that, but on his exploits in war
       and anything having to do with war; a lover of physical training and of
       hunting.

ADEIMANTUS: Yes, that is indeed the character belonging to this constitution.

SOCRATES: As regards money, too, wouldn't someone like that look down
b   on it when he is young; but as he grows older, wouldn't he love it more
       and more because he shares in the money-lover's nature and is not pure in
       his attitude to virtue, since he lacks the best guardian?

5   ADEIMANTUS: What's that?

SOCRATES: Reason mixed with musical training. You see, only it dwells within the person who possesses it as the lifelong preserver of his virtue.

ADEIMANTUS: Well put.

SOCRATES: That, then, is what a timocratic youth is like; he is like the
10   corresponding city.

c   ADEIMANTUS: Yes, indeed.

SOCRATES: And he comes to exist in some such way as this: sometimes he is the young son of a good father, who lives in a city that is not politically well governed; avoids honors, political office, lawsuits, and all such meddling in other people's affairs; and who is even willing to be put at a disad-
5   vantage so as to avoid trouble.

ADEIMANTUS: Yes, but how does he become timocratic?

SOCRATES: It first happens when he listens to his mother complaining that her man is not one of the rulers and that she is at a disadvantage among the other women as a result. Next, she sees that he is not very serious about
d   money, either; does not fight or exchange insults in private lawsuits or in the public assembly, but takes easily everything of that sort; has a mind

always absorbed in its own thoughts; and does not overvalue her or under-value her either. As a result of all those things, she complains and tells her son that his father is unmanly and too easygoing, and makes a litany of the other sorts of things women love to recite on such occasions.

ADEIMANTUS: Yes, indeed, it is just like them to have lots of such complaints.

SOCRATES: You know, then, that the servants of such men—the ones thought to be loyal—also say similar things to the sons in private. If they see someone who owes the father money or has wronged him in some other way, whom he does not prosecute, they urge the son to punish all such people when he becomes a man, and be more of a man than his father. And when he goes out, the boy hears and sees other similar things: those who do their own work in the city are called fools and held to be of little account, while those who do not are honored and praised. When the young man hears and sees all this, then, and, on the other hand, also listens to what his father says, and sees his practices from close at hand and compares them with those of the others, he is pulled by both—his father nourishing the rational element in his soul and making it grow; the others nourishing the appetitive and spirited elements. And, because he is not a bad man by nature, but has kept bad company, he compromises on a middle way when he is pulled in these two directions, and surrenders the rule within him to the middle element—the victory-loving and spirited one—and becomes a proud and honor-loving man.

ADEIMANTUS: I think you have exactly described how such a man comes to exist.

SOCRATES: So, we now have the second constitution and the second man.

ADEIMANTUS: We have.

SOCRATES: Next then, shall we, like Aeschylus, talk of "another man ordered like another city,"[15] or follow our plan and talk about the city first?

ADEIMANTUS: The latter, of course.

SOCRATES: And I suppose oligarchy would come next after such a constitution.

ADEIMANTUS: And what kind of political system do you mean by oligarchy?

SOCRATES: The constitution based on a property assessment, the one in which the rich rule and the poor man does not participate in ruling.

ADEIMANTUS: I understand.

SOCRATES: So, mustn't we first describe how timarchy is transformed into oligarchy?

---

[15] The line does not occur in the extant plays, but it may be an adaptation of *Seven against Thebes* 451.

5 ADEIMANTUS: Yes.

SOCRATES: And surely the way it is transformed is clear even to the blind.

ADEIMANTUS: How?

10 SOCRATES: That storehouse filled with gold we mentioned,[16] which each possesses, destroys such a constitution. First, you see, the timocrats find ways of spending their money, then they alter the laws to allow them to do so, and then they and their women disobey the laws altogether.

ADEIMANTUS: Probably so.

e SOCRATES: Next, I suppose, through one person seeing another and envying him, they make the majority behave like themselves.

ADEIMANTUS: Probably so.

5 SOCRATES: After that then, they become further involved in moneymaking; and the more honorable they consider it, the less honorable they consider virtue. Or isn't virtue so opposed to wealth that if they were set on the scale of a balance, they would always incline in opposite directions?

ADEIMANTUS: It certainly is.

551a SOCRATES: So, when wealth and the wealthy are honored in a city, virtue and good people are honored less.

ADEIMANTUS: Clearly.

5 SOCRATES: And what is honored is always practiced, and what is not honored, neglected.

ADEIMANTUS: Yes.

SOCRATES: So, in the end, victory-loving and honor-loving men become lovers of making money and money-lovers, and they praise and admire the 10 wealthy man and appoint him as ruler, and dishonor the poor one.

ADEIMANTUS: Of course.

SOCRATES: Isn't it then that they pass a law, which is a defining characteristic of an oligarchic constitution, establishing a wealth qualification— b higher where it is more oligarchic, lower where it is less so—and proclaim that anyone whose property does not reach the stated assessment cannot participate in ruling? And they either put this through by force of arms, or else, without resorting to that, they use intimidation to establish this sort of 5 constitution. Isn't that so?

ADEIMANTUS: It is.

SOCRATES: That, then, is, generally speaking, how it is established.

[16] 548a7–8.

ADEIMANTUS: Yes, it is. But what is the constitution like? What are the defects we said it had?[17]

SOCRATES: First of all, consider its defining characteristic. I mean, what would happen if ship captains were appointed like that, on the basis of property assessments, and a poor person was turned away even if he were a better captain?

ADEIMANTUS: People would make a very bad voyage!

SOCRATES: And doesn't the same apply to any other sort of rule whatsoever?

ADEIMANTUS: I suppose so.

SOCRATES: Except of a city? Or does it apply to that of a city, too?

ADEIMANTUS: It applies to it most of all, since it is the most difficult and most important kind of rule there is.

SOCRATES: That, then, is one major defect in oligarchy.

ADEIMANTUS: So it seems.

SOCRATES: And what about this one? Is it any smaller than the other?

ADEIMANTUS: Which?

SOCRATES: That a city of this sort is not one, but inevitably two—a city of the poor and one of the rich, living in the same place and always plotting against one another.

ADEIMANTUS: By Zeus, that's no smaller a defect.

SOCRATES: And this is hardly a good quality either: the likelihood of being unable to fight a war because of having to arm and use the majority, and so having to fear them more than the enemy; or else, because of not using them, and so having to show up as true oligarchs[18] on the battlefield; and because, at the same time, the fact that they are money-lovers makes them unwilling to pay mercenaries.

ADEIMANTUS: That is not good.

SOCRATES: And what about what we condemned long ago[19]—the fact that in this constitution there is the meddling in other people's affairs that occurs when the same people are farmers, moneymakers, and soldiers simultaneously? Or do you think it is right for things to be that way?

ADEIMANTUS: Not at all.

SOCRATES: Now, let's see whether it is the first to admit the greatest of all evils.

---

[17] 544c4–5.

[18] I.e., as being few in number. *Oligos* means few.

[19] 374b6–c2.

ADEIMANTUS: Which is?

SOCRATES: Allowing someone to sell all his possessions and someone else to buy them, and then allowing the seller to continue living in the city while not being any one of its parts—neither moneymaker nor craftsman, nor cavalryman, nor hoplite, but a poor person without means.

b   ADEIMANTUS: It is the first.

SOCRATES: Anyway, this sort of thing certainly is not forbidden in oligarchies. I mean, if it were, some of their citizens would not be super rich and others totally impoverished.

5   ADEIMANTUS: That's right.

SOCRATES: Now, consider this: when a person like that was rich and spending his money, was he then of any greater use to the city in the ways we have just mentioned? Or did he merely seem to be one of the rulers, while in fact he was neither ruler nor subject of it, but only a squanderer of property?

ADEIMANTUS: That's right. He seemed to be a ruler but was nothing but a
c   squanderer.

SOCRATES: Do you want us to say of him, then, that as a drone existing in a cell is an affliction to the hive, so this person existing in a household is a drone and affliction to the city?

5   ADEIMANTUS: Yes, indeed, Socrates.

SOCRATES: And hasn't the god, Adeimantus, made all the winged drones stingless, as well as some of the footed ones, while other footed ones have terrible stings? And don't those who end up as beggars in old age come from
d   among the stingless ones, while all those with stings are called evildoers?

ADEIMANTUS: That's absolutely true.

SOCRATES: Clearly then, in any city where you see beggars, somewhere in the neighborhood there are thieves hidden, and pickpockets, temple rob-
5   bers, and craftsmen of all such sorts of evil.

ADEIMANTUS: Clearly.

SOCRATES: What about oligarchic cities? Don't you see beggars in them?

10   ADEIMANTUS: Nearly everyone is one, apart from the rulers.

e   SOCRATES: Mustn't we suppose, then, that there are also many evildoers there with stings, whom the rulers forcibly keep in check by their cautiousness?

ADEIMANTUS: We certainly must suppose it.

5   SOCRATES: And aren't we saying that the presence of such people is the result of lack of education, bad rearing, and a bad constitutional system?

ADEIMANTUS: We are.

SOCRATES: Well, then, that is roughly what the oligarchic city would be like. It would contain all these evils and probably others as well.

ADEIMANTUS: That's pretty much it.

SOCRATES: Let's take it, then, that we have disposed of the constitution they call oligarchy, which gets its rulers on the basis of a property assessment. Next, let's consider how the person who is like it comes to exist, and what sort of person he is when he does.

ADEIMANTUS: Yes, let's.

SOCRATES: Doesn't the transformation from timocrat to oligarch mostly occur in this way?

ADEIMANTUS: Which?

SOCRATES: It happens when a son of his is born who begins by emulating his father and following in his footsteps, and then sees him suddenly crashing against the city as against a reef, and sees him and all his possessions spilling overboard. He had held a generalship or some other high office, was brought to court by sycophants,[20] and was put to death or exiled, or was disenfranchised and had all his property confiscated.

ADEIMANTUS: Probably so.

SOCRATES: Anyway, my friend, after seeing and experiencing all that, and losing his property, the son is afraid, I imagine, and immediately throws the honor-loving and spirited element headlong from the throne in his own soul. And humbled by poverty, he turns greedily to moneymaking and, little by little, saving and working, he amasses property. Don't you think that someone like that will then establish the appetitive and moneymaking element on that throne, and make it a great king within himself, adorned with golden tiaras and collars and Persian swords?[21]

ADEIMANTUS: I do.

SOCRATES: And I suppose he makes the rational and spirited elements sit on the ground beneath it, one on either side, and be slaves. He won't allow the first to calculate or consider anything except how a little money can be made into more; or the second to admire or honor anything except wealth and wealthy people, or to love being honored for anything besides the possession of wealth and whatever contributes to it.

ADEIMANTUS: There is no other way to turn an honor-loving young man into a money-loving one that is as swift and sure as that!

---

[20] See Glossary of Terms s.v. sycophants.

[21] For the Greeks, the king of Persia was emblematic of absolute rule.

e   SOCRATES: Isn't this, then, the oligarchic person?

ADEIMANTUS: Well, he certainly developed from the sort of man who resembled the constitution from which oligarchy came.

SOCRATES: Then let's see whether he resembles it.

554a   ADEIMANTUS: Let's.

SOCRATES: Wouldn't he resemble it, primarily, by attaching the greatest importance to money?

ADEIMANTUS: Of course.

SOCRATES: And also by being a thrifty worker who satisfies only his nec-
5   essary appetites and spends nothing on other things but enslaves his other appetites as pointless.

ADEIMANTUS: Yes, indeed.

SOCRATES: A pretty squalid fellow, at any rate, who tries to make a profit
10   from everything: a treasury-builder—the sort the majority admire. Isn't that
b   the sort of man who resembles this sort of constitution?

ADEIMANTUS: *I* certainly think so. At any rate, money is honored more than anything else by both the city and the one who is like it.

SOCRATES: Because I don't suppose someone like that has paid any attention to education.

ADEIMANTUS: I don't think so. I mean, if he had, he would not have cho-
5   sen a blind leader for his chorus and honored him most.[22]

SOCRATES: Well put! But consider this. Wouldn't we say that though the dronish appetites exist in him because of his lack of education, some of them beggars and others evildoers, they are forcibly kept in check by his
c   general cautiousness?[23]

ADEIMANTUS: Certainly.

SOCRATES: Do you know, then, where you should look to see the evils
5   such people do?

ADEIMANTUS: Where?

SOCRATES: Where they are guardians of orphans, or any other situation like that, where they have ample opportunity to do injustice.

10   ADEIMANTUS: True.

SOCRATES: So, doesn't that make it clear that in other contractual matters, where someone like that has a good reputation and is thought to be just, something good of his is forcibly holding in check the other bad appetites

---

[22] I.e., Plutus, the god of wealth, who is often represented as being blind.
[23] See 552e1–2.

within; not persuading them that they had better not, nor taming them   d
with arguments, but using compulsion and fear, because he is terrified of
losing his other possessions?

ADEIMANTUS: Exactly.

SOCRATES: Yes, by Zeus, my friend, you will find that most of them,   5
when they have other people's money to spend, have appetites in them akin
to those of the drone.

ADEIMANTUS: Indeed, you certainly will!

SOCRATES: So, someone like that would not be entirely free from internal
faction, and would not be a single person but somehow a twofold one,[24]   10
although his better appetites would generally master his worse appetites.   e

ADEIMANTUS: That's right.

SOCRATES: Because of this, I suppose someone like that would be more
respectable than many other people; but the true virtue of a single-minded
and harmonious soul would somehow far escape him.   5

ADEIMANTUS: I suppose so.

SOCRATES: Furthermore, the thrifty man is a worthless individual contes-
tant in the city for any prize of victory or any of the other fine things the
love of honor craves. He is unwilling to spend money for the sake of fame   555a
or other such results of competition, and, fearing to arouse his appetites for
spending by allying them with love of victory, he fights in true oligarchic
fashion, with only a few of his resources,[25] and is mostly defeated, but
remains rich!   5

ADEIMANTUS: Exactly.

SOCRATES: Are we still in any doubt, then, that, as regards resemblance, a
thrifty moneymaker corresponds to an oligarchic city?   b

ADEIMANTUS: Not at all.

SOCRATES: Then democracy, it seems, must be considered next—both
the way it comes to exist and what it is like when it does—so that when
we know the character of this sort of man, we can present him for judg-   5
ment in turn.

ADEIMANTUS: At any rate, that would be consistent with what we have
been doing.

SOCRATES: Well, then, isn't the change from an oligarchy to a democracy
due in some way or other to the insatiable desire for the good set before
it—the need to become as rich as possible?   10

[24] See 443c9–444a2.
[25] See 551e2 note.

ADEIMANTUS: How so?

c   SOCRATES: Since the rulers rule in it because they own a lot, I suppose they are not willing to enact laws to prevent young people who have become intemperate from spending and wasting their wealth, so that by buying and making loans on the property of such people, the rulers them-
5   selves can become even richer and more honored.

ADEIMANTUS: That's their primary goal, at any rate.

SOCRATES: So, isn't it clear by now that you cannot honor wealth in a city and maintain temperance in the citizens at the same time, but must inevita-
d   bly neglect one or the other?

ADEIMANTUS: That is pretty clear.

SOCRATES: The negligent encouragement of intemperance in oligarchies,
5   then, sometimes reduces people who are not ill born to poverty.

ADEIMANTUS: Indeed, it does.

SOCRATES: And these people sit around in the city, I suppose, armed with stings or weapons—some of them in debt, some disenfranchised, some
10   both—hating and plotting against those who have acquired their property,
e   and all the others as well; passionately longing for revolution.

ADEIMANTUS: That's right.

SOCRATES: These moneymakers, with their heads down,[26] pretending not to see them, inject the poison of their money into any of the rest who do not
5   resist, and, carrying away a multitude of offspring in interest from their prin-
556a   cipal,[27] greatly increase the size of the drone and beggar class in the city.

ADEIMANTUS: They certainly do increase it greatly.

SOCRATES: In any case, they are not willing to quench evil of this sort as it flares up, either by preventing a person from doing whatever he likes with
5   his own property, or alternatively by passing this other law to do away with such abuses.

ADEIMANTUS: What law?

SOCRATES: The one that is next best and that compels the citizens to care
10   about virtue. You see, if someone prescribed that most voluntary contracts
b   be entered into at the lender's own risk, money would be less shamelessly pursued in the city and fewer of those evils we were mentioning just now would develop in it.

5   ADEIMANTUS: Far fewer.

---

[26] Their heads are down because their appetite for money forces their souls to look downward. See 518c4–519b5.

[27] See 507a5 and note.

SOCRATES: But as it is, and for all these reasons, the rulers in the city treat their subjects in the way we described. And as for themselves and those belonging to them, don't they bring up the young to be fond of luxury, incapable of effort either mental or physical, too soft to endure pleasures or pains, and lazy?

ADEIMANTUS: Of course.

SOCRATES: And haven't they themselves neglected everything except making money and been no more concerned about virtue than poor people are?

ADEIMANTUS: Yes, they have.

SOCRATES: And when rulers and subjects, socialized in this way, meet on journeys or some other shared undertakings, whether in an embassy or a military campaign; or as shipmates or fellow soldiers; or when they watch one another in dangerous situations—in these circumstances, don't you think the poor are in no way despised by the rich? On the contrary, don't you think it is often the case that a poor man, lean and suntanned, is stationed in battle next to a rich one, reared in the shade and carrying a lot of excess flesh, and sees him panting and completely at a loss? And don't you think he believes that it is because of the cowardice of the poor that such people are rich and that one poor man says to another when they meet in private: "These men are ours for the taking; they are good for nothing"?

ADEIMANTUS: I know very well they do.

SOCRATES: Well, just as a sick body needs only a slight shock from outside to become ill and sometimes, even without external influence, becomes divided into factions, itself against itself, doesn't a city in the same condition need only a small pretext—such as one side bringing in allies from an oligarchy or the other from a democracy—to become ill and fight with itself? And doesn't it sometimes become divided into factions even without any external influence?

ADEIMANTUS: Yes, violently so.

SOCRATES: Then democracy comes about, I suppose, when the poor are victorious, kill or expel the others, and give the rest an equal share in the constitution and the ruling offices, and the majority of offices in it are assigned by lot.

ADEIMANTUS: Yes, that is how a democratic political system gets established, whether it comes to exist by force of arms or because intimidation drives its opponents into exile.[28]

SOCRATES: In what way, then, do these people live? What sort of constitution do they have? For clearly the sort of man who is like it will turn out to be democratic.

[28] See 551a12–b5.

ADEIMANTUS: Clearly.

SOCRATES: Well, in the first place, aren't they free? And isn't the city full
5 of freedom and freedom of speech? And isn't there license in it to do whatever one wants?

ADEIMANTUS: That's what they say, anyway.

SOCRATES: And where there is license, clearly each person would arrange
10 his own life in whatever way pleases him.

ADEIMANTUS: Clearly.

c SOCRATES: I imagine it is in this constitution, then, that multifarious people come to exist.

ADEIMANTUS: Of course.

SOCRATES: It looks, then, as though it is the most beautiful of all the constitutions. For just like an embroidered cloak embroidered with every kind
5 of ornament, it is embroidered with every sort of character, and so would
appear to be the most beautiful. And presumably, many people would
behave like women and children looking at embroidered objects and actually judge it to be the most beautiful.

10 ADEIMANTUS: They certainly would.

SOCRATES: What is more, bless you, it is also a handy place in which to
d look for a constitution!

ADEIMANTUS: Why is that?

SOCRATES: Because it contains all kinds of constitutions, as a result of its
license. So whoever wants to organize a city, as we were doing just now,
probably has to go to a democracy and, as if he were in a supermarket of
constitutions, pick out whatever pleases him and establish it.

e ADEIMANTUS: He probably wouldn't be at a loss for examples, anyway!

SOCRATES: There is no compulsion to rule in this city, even if you are
qualified to rule, or to be ruled if you do not want to be; or to be at war
when the others are at war, or to keep the peace when the others are keep-
5 ing it, if you do not want peace; or, even if there happens to be a law preventing you from ruling or from serving on a jury, to be any the less free to
558a rule or serve on a jury—isn't that a heavenly and pleasant way to pass the
time, while it lasts?

ADEIMANTUS: It probably is—while it lasts.

SOCRATES: And what about the calm of some of their condemned crim-
inals? Isn't that a sophisticated quality? Or have you never seen people
5 who have been condemned to death or exile in a constitution of this sort
staying on all the same and living right in the middle of things, without

anyone giving them a thought or staring at them, while they stroll around like a hero?[29]

ADEIMANTUS: Yes, I have seen it a lot.

SOCRATES: And what about the city's tolerance, its complete lack of petty-mindedness, and its utter disregard for the things we took so seriously when we were founding the city—that unless someone had transcendent natural gifts, he would never become a good man if he did not play fine games right from early childhood and engage in practices that are all of that same sort? Isn't it magnificent how it tramples all that underfoot, gives no thought to what sort of practices someone went in for before he entered politics, and honors him if only he tells them he wishes the majority well?

b

5

c

ADEIMANTUS: That's true nobility!

SOCRATES: These, then, and others akin to them are the characteristics a democracy would possess. And it would, it seems, be a pleasant constitution—lacking rulers but not complexity, and assigning a sort of equality to equals and unequals alike.

5

ADEIMANTUS: Yes, that's well known!

SOCRATES: Look and see, then, what sort of private individual resembles it. Or should we first consider, as we did in the case of the constitution, how he comes to exist?

ADEIMANTUS: Yes.

10

SOCRATES: Well, doesn't it happen this way? Mightn't we suppose that our thrifty oligarchic man had a son brought up by his father with his father's traits of character?

d

ADEIMANTUS: Of course.

SOCRATES: Then he too would rule by force the pleasures that exist in him—the spendthrift ones that do not make money; the ones that are called unnecessary.

5

ADEIMANTUS: Clearly.

SOCRATES: In order not to have a discussion in the dark, would you like us first to define which appetites are necessary and which are not?

ADEIMANTUS: I would.

10

SOCRATES: Well, then, wouldn't those we cannot deny rightly be called necessary? And also those whose satisfaction benefits us? For we are by nature compelled to try to satisfy them both. Isn't that so?

e

ADEIMANTUS: Of course.

---

[29] Dead heroes were worshipped as minor deities in Greek religion, particularly in their birthplaces, where their spirits were thought to linger.

559a   SOCRATES: So, we would be right to apply the term "necessary" to them?

ADEIMANTUS: We would be right.

SOCRATES: What about those someone could get rid of if he started practicing from childhood, those whose presence does no good but may even
do the opposite? If we said that all of them were unnecessary, would we be
5   right?

ADEIMANTUS: We would be right.

SOCRATES: Let's pick an example of each, so that we have a pattern to follow.

10   ADEIMANTUS: Yes, let's.

SOCRATES: Wouldn't the desire to eat to the point of health and well-
b   being, and the desire for bread and relishes[30] be necessary ones?

ADEIMANTUS: I suppose so.

SOCRATES: The desire for bread is surely necessary on both counts, in that
it is beneficial and that unless it is satisfied, we die.[31]

5   ADEIMANTUS: Yes.

SOCRATES: And so is the one for relishes, insofar as it is beneficial and
conduces to well-being.

ADEIMANTUS: Indeed.

SOCRATES: What about an appetite that goes beyond these and seeks other
sorts of foods; that, if it is restrained from childhood and educated, most
10   people can get rid of; and that is harmful to the body and harmful to the
soul's capacity for wisdom and temperance? Wouldn't it be correct to call it
c   unnecessary?

ADEIMANTUS: Entirely correct.

SOCRATES: Wouldn't we also say that the latter desires are spendthrift,
then, whereas the former are moneymaking because they are useful where
work is concerned?

5   ADEIMANTUS: Certainly.

SOCRATES: And won't we say the same about sexual appetites and the rest?

ADEIMANTUS: Yes.

SOCRATES: And didn't we say that the person we just now called a drone is
full of such pleasures and appetites and is ruled by the unnecessary ones,
d   while the one who is ruled by his necessary appetites is a thrifty oligarch?

ADEIMANTUS: Of course we did.

---

[30] See 372c4 note.

[31] Bread is used here to mean "the staff of life." That is why one dies for want of it.

SOCRATES: Let's go back, then, and say how the democrat develops from the oligarch. It seems to me as if it mostly happens this way.

ADEIMANTUS: What way?

SOCRATES: When a young man who is reared in the uneducated and thrifty manner we described just now tastes the honey of the drones and associates with wild and terrible creatures who can provide multifarious pleasures of every degree of complexity and sort, that probably marks the beginning of his transformation from having an oligarchic constitution within him to having a democratic one.

ADEIMANTUS: It most certainly does.

SOCRATES: So, just as the city changed when one party received help from a like-minded alliance outside, doesn't the young man change in turn when external appetites of the same type and quality as it come to the aid of one of the parties within him?

ADEIMANTUS: Absolutely.

SOCRATES: And I suppose if a counter-alliance comes to the aid of the oligarchic party within him—whether from his father or from the rest of his family, who exhort and reproach him—then there is a faction and an opposing faction within him, and he battles against himself.

ADEIMANTUS: Of course.

SOCRATES: And sometimes, I suppose, the democratic party yields to the oligarchic, some of its appetites are overcome while others are expelled, and a kind of shame rises in the young man's soul and order is restored.

ADEIMANTUS: That does sometimes happen.

SOCRATES: Moreover, I suppose, as some appetites are expelled, others akin to them are being nurtured undetected because of the father's ignorance of upbringing, and become numerous and strong.

ADEIMANTUS: At any rate, that's what usually happens.

SOCRATES: Then these desires draw him back to his old associates[32] and, in secret intercourse, breed a multitude of others.

ADEIMANTUS: Of course.

SOCRATES: Finally, I suppose, they seize the citadel of the young man's soul, since they realize that it is empty of the fine studies and practices and the true arguments that are the best watchmen and guardians in the minds of men loved by the gods.

ADEIMANTUS: By far the best.

---

[32] Described at 559d7–e2.

SOCRATES: Then, I suppose, beliefs and arguments that are lying imposters rush up and occupy this same part of him in place of the others.

ADEIMANTUS: They do, indeed.

SOCRATES: Won't he then return to those Lotus-eaters and live with them openly? And if any help should come to the thrifty part of his soul from his relatives, don't those imposter arguments, having barred the gates of the royal wall within him, prevent the allied force itself from entering and even refusing to admit arguments of older, private individuals as ambassadors? Proving stronger in the battle, won't they call reverence foolishness and drive it out as a dishonored fugitive? And calling temperance cowardliness, won't they shower it with abuse and banish it? As for moderate and orderly expenditure, won't they persuade him that it is boorish and illiberal, and join with a multitude of useless appetites to drive it over the border?

ADEIMANTUS: They will indeed.

SOCRATES: And when they have somehow emptied and purged these from the soul of the one they are seizing hold of and initiating with solemn rites, they then immediately proceed to return arrogance, anarchy, extravagance, and shamelessness from exile in a blaze of torchlight, accompanied with a vast chorus of followers and crowned with garlands. They praise them and give them fine names, calling arrogance "good breeding," anarchy "freedom," extravagance "magnificence," and shamelessness "courage." Isn't it in some such way as this that a young person exchanges an upbringing among necessary appetites for the freeing and release of useless and unnecessary pleasures?

ADEIMANTUS: Yes, that's clearly the way it happens.

SOCRATES: Then in his subsequent life, I suppose, someone like that spends no less money, effort, and time on the necessary pleasures than on the unnecessary pleasures. But if he is lucky and does not go beyond the limits in his bacchic frenzy, and if, as a result of his growing somewhat older, the great tumult within him passes, he welcomes back some of the exiles and ceases to surrender himself completely to the newcomers. Then, putting all his pleasures on an equal footing, he lives, always surrendering rule over himself to whichever desire comes along, as if it were chosen by lot,[33] until it is satisfied; and after that to another, dishonoring none but satisfying all equally.

ADEIMANTUS: He does, indeed.

SOCRATES: And he does not accept or admit true argument into the guardhouse if someone tells him that some pleasures belong to fine and good appetites and others to bad ones, and that he must practice and honor the

---

[33] Many public officials in democratic Athens were elected by lot.

former and restrain and enslave the latter. On the contrary, he denies all this and declares that they are all alike and must be honored on an equal basis.

ADEIMANTUS: That's exactly what he feels and does.

SOCRATES: And so he lives from day to day, gratifying the appetite of the moment. Sometimes he drinks heavily while listening to the flute, while at others he drinks only water and is on a diet. Sometimes he goes in for physical training, while there are others when he is idle and neglects everything. Sometimes he spends his time engaged in what he takes to be philosophy. Often, though, he takes part in politics, leaping to his feet and saying and doing whatever happens to come into his mind. If he admires some military men, that is the direction in which he is carried; if some moneymakers, then in that different one. There is neither order nor necessity in his life, yet he calls it pleasant, free, and blessedly happy, and follows it throughout his entire life.

ADEIMANTUS: You have perfectly described the life of a man devoted to legal equality.[34]

SOCRATES: I certainly think he is a multifarious man and full of all sorts of characters, beautiful and complex, like the democratic city. Many men and women would envy his life because of the great number of examples of constitutions and characters it contains within it.

ADEIMANTUS: Yes, that's right.

SOCRATES: Well, then, will we set this man alongside democracy as the one who would rightly be called democratic?

ADEIMANTUS: We will.

SOCRATES: The finest constitution and the finest man remain for us to discuss: tyranny and the tyrant.

ADEIMANTUS: Absolutely.

SOCRATES: Come on, then; tell me, my dear comrade, how does tyranny come to exist? That it evolves from democracy, you see, is fairly clear.

ADEIMANTUS: It is clear.

SOCRATES: So, isn't the way democracy evolves from oligarchy much the same as that in which tyranny evolves from democracy?

ADEIMANTUS: How do you mean?

SOCRATES: The good they proposed for themselves, and because of which oligarchy was established, was wealth, wasn't it?

ADEIMANTUS: Yes.

[34] *Isonomia:* an important democratic value.

SOCRATES: And its insatiable desire for wealth and its neglect of other things for the sake of moneymaking was what destroyed it.

ADEIMANTUS: True.

SOCRATES: So, isn't democracy's insatiable desire for what it defines as the good also what destroys it?

ADEIMANTUS: What do you think it does define as the good?

SOCRATES: Freedom. For surely, in a democratic city, that is what you would hear described as its finest possession, and as what makes it the only place worth living in for someone who is naturally free.

ADEIMANTUS: Yes, you often hear that said.

SOCRATES: As I was about to say, then, isn't it the insatiable desire for this good and the neglect of other things that changes this constitution and prepares it to need a dictatorship?

ADEIMANTUS: How does it do that?

SOCRATES: I suppose it is when a democratic city, athirst for freedom, happens to get bad cupbearers for its leaders and gets drunk by drinking more than it should of unmixed wine.[35] Then, if the rulers are not very gentle and do not provide plenty of freedom, it punishes them and accuses them of being filthy oligarchs.

ADEIMANTUS: Yes, that is what it does.

SOCRATES: It showers with abuse those who obey the rulers as voluntary slaves and nonentities, but both in public and private it praises and honors rulers who are like subjects, and subjects who are like rulers. And isn't it inevitable in such a city that freedom should spread everywhere?

ADEIMANTUS: Of course.

SOCRATES: Yes, my friend, and so it is bound to make its way into private households until finally it breeds anarchy among the very animals.

ADEIMANTUS: What do you mean by that?

SOCRATES: For instance, a father gets into the habit of behaving like a child and fearing his son, and the son gets into the habit of behaving like a father, feeling neither shame nor fear in front of his parents—all in order to be *free*. A resident alien feels himself equal to a citizen and a citizen to him, and a foreigner likewise.

ADEIMANTUS: Yes, those sorts of things do happen.

SOCRATES: They do—and so do other little things of the same sort. A teacher in such circumstances is afraid of his students and flatters them, while the students belittle their teachers and do the same to their tutors,

---

[35] The Greeks drank their wine mixed with water.

too. In general, the young are the spitting images of their elders and compete with them in words and deeds, while the old stoop to the level of the
young and are full of wit and indulgence, imitating the young for fear of
being thought disagreeable and masterful.

ADEIMANTUS: Absolutely.

SOCRATES: The ultimate freedom for the majority, my friend, comes
about in such a city, when males and females bought as slaves are no less
free than those who bought them. Then there is the case of women in relation to men, and men to women, and the extent of their legal equality and
freedom—we almost forgot to mention that!

ADEIMANTUS: Are we not, with Aeschylus, going to "say whatever it was
came to our lips just now?"[36]

SOCRATES: Certainly. At any rate, *I am* going to say it. I mean, no one
who had not experienced it would believe how much freer domestic animals are here than in any other city. Bitches follow the proverb exactly and
become like their mistresses. Horses and donkeys are in the habit of proceeding with complete freedom and dignity, bumping into anyone they
meet on the road who does not get out of their way. And everything else is
full of freedom, too.

ADEIMANTUS: It is my own dream you are telling me.[37] That often happens to me when I go to the country.

SOCRATES: Summing up all these things together, then, do you notice
how sensitive they make the citizens' souls, so that if anyone tries to impose
the least degree of slavery, they get irritated and cannot bear it? In the end,
as I am sure you are aware, they take no notice of the laws—written or
unwritten—in order to avoid having any master at all.

ADEIMANTUS: I certainly am aware.

SOCRATES: This, my friend, is the fine and impetuous beginning from
which tyranny seems to me to grow.

ADEIMANTUS: It is certainly impetuous. But what comes next?

SOCRATES: The same disease that developed in oligarchy and destroyed it
also develops here—only more widespread and virulent because of the general permissiveness—and eventually enslaves democracy. In fact, excessive
action in one direction usually sets up a great reaction in the opposite
direction. This happens in seasons, in plants, in bodies, and particularly in
constitutions.

ADEIMANTUS: That's probably right.

---

[36] At 562e4–5. We no longer possess the play from which this fragment comes.

[37] I.e., you are telling me what I already know.

SOCRATES: For extreme freedom probably cannot lead to anything but a change to extreme slavery, whether in a private individual or a city.

5 ADEIMANTUS: No, it probably can't.

SOCRATES: Tyranny probably does not evolve from any constitution other than democracy, then—the most severe and cruel slavery evolving from what I suppose is the most eminent degree of freedom.

ADEIMANTUS: Yes, that's reasonable.

10 SOCRATES: But I think you were asking, not that, but rather what sort of
b disease develops both in oligarchy and democracy alike, and enslaves the latter.

ADEIMANTUS: That's true.

SOCRATES: Well, then, I meant that class of idle and extravagant men,
5 with the bravest as leaders and the more cowardly as followers. We compared them to drones: the leaders to drones with stings, the followers to stingless ones.[38]

ADEIMANTUS: Rightly so.

SOCRATES: These two cause problems in any constitution in which they
10 arise, like phlegm and bile in the body.[39] And it is against them that the
c good doctor and lawgiver of a city must take no less advance precaution than a wise beekeeper. He should preferably prevent them from arising at all. But if they should happen to arise, he must cut them out, cells and all, as quickly as possible.

5 ADEIMANTUS: Yes, by Zeus, and as thoroughly as possible.

SOCRATES: Then let's take up the question in this way, in order to see what we want more distinctly.

ADEIMANTUS: In what way?

SOCRATES: Let's in our discussion divide a democratic city into three parts—which is also how it is actually divided. One part is surely this class
d of drones, which, because of the general permissiveness, grows in it no less than in an oligarchy.

ADEIMANTUS: So it does.

SOCRATES: But it is much fiercer in it than in the other.

5 ADEIMANTUS: How so?

SOCRATES: There, because it is not honored but is excluded from the ranks of the rulers, it does not get any exercise and does not become vigor-

---

[38] 552c2–e3.

[39] Phlegm and bile were two of the so-called humors Greek medicine thought responsible for health and disease.

ous. However, in a democracy, with few exceptions, it is surely the dominant class. Its fiercest part does all the talking and acting, while the other one settles near the speaker's platform. It buzzes and does not tolerate any dissent. As a result, this class is in charge of everything in such a constitution—with a few exceptions.[40]

ADEIMANTUS: That's right.

SOCRATES: Then, there is a second distinct class that is constantly emerging from the majority.

ADEIMANTUS: Which one?

SOCRATES: Surely, when everyone is trying to make money, the ones who are by nature most orderly generally become the wealthiest.

ADEIMANTUS: Probably so.

SOCRATES: Then that is where the most plentiful honey for the drones exists, I take it, and the easiest for them to extract.

ADEIMANTUS: How could anyone extract it from those who have very little?

SOCRATES: I suppose, then, that these rich people, as they are called, are fodder for the drones.

ADEIMANTUS: Pretty much.

SOCRATES: The people—those who work their own land, take no part in politics, and own few possessions—would be the third class. This is the largest and most powerful class in a democracy when it meets in assembly.

ADEIMANTUS: Yes, it is. But it is not willing to meet often, if it does not get a share of the honey.

SOCRATES: So, it always does get a share—one that allows the leaders, in taking the wealth of the rich and distributing it to the people, to keep the greatest share for themselves.

ADEIMANTUS: Yes, that is the sort of share they get.

SOCRATES: Then I suppose that those whose wealth is taken away are compelled to defend themselves by speaking in the popular assembly and doing whatever else they can.

ADEIMANTUS: Of course.

SOCRATES: At which point—even if they have no appetite for revolution at all—they get accused by the others of plotting against the people and of being oligarchs.

[40] The exceptions in question are presumably the various offices—such as the chief military official—to which in the Athenian democracy were appointed on the basis of expertise.

ADEIMANTUS: They do.

SOCRATES: Finally, when they see the people—not intentionally, but
through misapprehension and being misled by the accusers—trying to do
injustice to them, then, whether they wish it or not, they really do become
oligarchs—not from choice, though, but because the drone, by stinging
them, engenders this evil.

ADEIMANTUS: Absolutely.

SOCRATES: Then there are impeachments, judgments, and trials on both
sides.

ADEIMANTUS: Right.

SOCRATES: And don't the people always tend to set up one man as their
special leader, nurturing him and making him great?

ADEIMANTUS: Yes.

SOCRATES: And it is clear that when a tyrant arises, the position of popular leader is the sole root from which he springs.

ADEIMANTUS: It is.

SOCRATES: What is the beginning, then, of the transformation from popular leader to tyrant? Isn't it clear that it happens when the popular leader
begins to behave like the character in the story told about the temple of the
Lycaean Zeus[41] in Arcadia?

ADEIMANTUS: What story?

SOCRATES: That whoever tastes the one piece of human innards cut up
with those of all the other sacrificial victims inevitably becomes a wolf.
Haven't you heard that story?

ADEIMANTUS: I have.

SOCRATES: Isn't it the same, then, with a popular leader? Once he really
takes over a docile mob, he does not restrain himself from shedding a fellow
citizen's blood. But by leveling the usual false charges and bringing people
into court, he commits murder. And by blotting out a man's life, his impious tongue and lips taste kindred blood. Then he banishes and kills and
drops hints about the cancellation of debts and the redistribution of land.
And after that, isn't such a man inevitably fated either to be killed by his
enemies or to be a tyrant, transformed from a man into a wolf?

ADEIMANTUS: Yes. That is the inevitable outcome.

SOCRATES: He is the one, then, who stirs up faction against the rich.

ADEIMANTUS: He is.

---

[41] Zeus the wolf-god.

SOCRATES: And if he happens to be exiled but, despite his enemies, manages to return, doesn't he come back as a full-fledged tyrant?[42]

ADEIMANTUS: Obviously.

SOCRATES: And if they are unable to expel him or put him to death by accusing him before the city, they plot a violent death for him by covert means.

ADEIMANTUS: That's what tends to happen, anyway.

SOCRATES: And everyone who has reached this stage soon discovers the famous tyrannical request—to ask the people to give him a bodyguard to keep their popular leader safe for them.

ADEIMANTUS: Right.

SOCRATES: And the people give it to him, I suppose, fearing for his safety but confident of their own.

ADEIMANTUS: Right.

SOCRATES: So, when a wealthy man sees this and is charged with being an enemy of the people because of his wealth, then, comrade, in the words of the oracle to Croesus, he "flees without delay to the banks of the many-pebbled Hermus, and is not ashamed at all of his cowardice."[43]

ADEIMANTUS: He would certainly never get a second chance to be ashamed!

SOCRATES: If he is caught, I would imagine he is put to death.

ADEIMANTUS: Inevitably.

SOCRATES: As for this popular leader of ours, he clearly does not lie on the ground "mighty in his might,"[44] but, having brought down all those others, he stands in the chariot of the city as a complete tyrant instead of a popular leader.

ADEIMANTUS: That's for sure.

SOCRATES: Shall we next describe the happiness of this man and of the city in which such a creature arises?

ADEIMANTUS: Yes, let's.

SOCRATES: To start with, in the early days of his reign, won't he greet everyone he meets with a smile, deny he is a tyrant, promise all sorts of

---

[42] Plato seems to be alluding to the tyrant Peisistratus. In 560 BCE, Peisistratus made himself tyrant with the help of a bodyguard granted to him by the Athenian people. After five years, he was expelled. Eventually he returned to Athens and used mercenaries to establish himself firmly as tyrant. He died in 527. See Herodotus 1.59–64.

[43] The story of the Delphic oracle to Croesus is found in Herodotus 1.55.

[44] See *Iliad* 16.776.

e things in private and in public, free the people from debt, redistribute the land to them and to his followers, and pretend to be gracious and gentle to all?

5 ADEIMANTUS: Inevitably.

SOCRATES: But once he has dealt with his exiled enemies by making peace with some and destroying others, and all is calm on that front, his primary concern, I imagine, is to be constantly stirring up some war or other, so that the people will need a leader.

10 ADEIMANTUS: Very likely.

567a SOCRATES: And also, wouldn't you say, so that impoverished by war taxes, they will be forced to concentrate on their daily needs and be less likely to plot against him?

ADEIMANTUS: Clearly.

SOCRATES: And in addition, I suppose, so that if there are some free-
5 thinking people he suspects of rejecting his rule, he can find pretexts for putting them at the mercy of the enemy and destroying them? For all these reasons, isn't a tyrant bound to be always stirring up war?

ADEIMANTUS: He is.

10 SOCRATES: Don't all these actions tend to make him more hateful to the
b citizens?

ADEIMANTUS: Of course.

SOCRATES: And don't some of those who helped establish his tyranny and hold positions of power within it, the ones who are bravest, speak freely to
5 him and to each other, criticizing what is happening?

ADEIMANTUS: Probably.

SOCRATES: Then the tyrant will have to do away with all of them if he intends to rule, until he is left with no friend or enemy who is worth any-
10 thing at all.

ADEIMANTUS: Obviously.

SOCRATES: He will have to keep a sharp lookout, then, for anyone who is brave, magnanimous, wise, or rich. He is so happy, you see, that he is
c forced, whether he wants to or not, to be their enemy and plot against all of them until he has purged the city.

ADEIMANTUS: A fine purge that is!

5 SOCRATES: Yes. The opposite of the one doctors perform on our bodies. They draw off the worst and leave the best, whereas he does just the opposite!

ADEIMANTUS: Yet that's what he has to do, it seems, if he is to rule.

SOCRATES: It is a blessedly happy necessity he is bound by, then, which requires him to live with inferior masses even though hated by them, or not live at all! d

ADEIMANTUS: It is.

SOCRATES: And the more he makes the citizens hate him by doing those things, the larger and more trustworthy a bodyguard he will need, won't he? 5

ADEIMANTUS: Of course.

SOCRATES: And who will these trustworthy people be? And from where will he get them?

ADEIMANTUS: Lots of them will come swarming of their own accord, if he pays them. 10

SOCRATES: Drones again, by the dog![45] That is what I think you are talking about. Foreign, multifarious ones! e

ADEIMANTUS: Yes, you are right.

SOCRATES: What about the domestic ones? Wouldn't he be willing to deprive citizens of their slaves somehow, set them free, and enlist them in his bodyguard? 5

ADEIMANTUS: He certainly would, since they are the ones he can trust the most.

SOCRATES: What a blessedly happy thing this tyrant business is on your view, if these are the sorts of friends and trusted men he must employ after destroying his former ones! 568a

ADEIMANTUS: Nonetheless, they are the sorts he does employ.

SOCRATES: And these friends and new citizens admire and associate with him, whereas the good ones hate and avoid him? 5

ADEIMANTUS: Of course.

SOCRATES: It is no wonder, then, that tragedy seems to be something wholly wise, or that Euripides is outstanding in it.

ADEIMANTUS: Why is that? 10

SOCRATES: Because, among other things, he expressed the following shrewd thought: "tyrants are wise by associating with the wise." He meant evidently that these associates of the tyrant are the wise ones.[46] b

---

[45] See 399e5 note.

[46] The fragment is from an unknown play. Euripides meant that tyrants gain wisdom from the wise people who, as Simonides said, "knock at the doors of the rich" (489b7–8). Plato twists his words to mean that the drones and slaves, who are the tyrant's last resort, are wise, since they associate with him.

ADEIMANTUS: Yes. And he also praises tyranny as godlike, and lots of other things besides—and the other poets do, too.

5 SOCRATES: Then surely, since the tragic poets are so wise, they will forgive us and those with constitutions like ours if we do not admit them into our city, since they hymn the praises of tyranny.

ADEIMANTUS: For my part, I think they will forgive us—the more refined
c of them, anyway.

SOCRATES: They can go around to all the other cities instead, I suppose, drawing large crowds and hiring actors with fine, loud, persuasive voices,
5 and lead their constitutions to become tyrannies and democracies.

ADEIMANTUS: Yes, indeed.

SOCRATES: What's more, they are paid and honored for it, primarily—as one might expect—by tyrants and secondly by democracy. But the higher they go on the ascending scale of constitutions, the more their honor
d diminishes, as if unable to proceed for lack of breath.

ADEIMANTUS: Absolutely.

SOCRATES: But all that is a digression. Let's return to our tyrant's camp—
5 the one that is beautiful, populous, complex, and never the same—and ask how he is going to maintain it.

ADEIMANTUS: If there are sacred treasuries in the city, he will obviously use them for as long as they last, as well as the property of those he has destroyed, so the taxes he will require from the people will be smaller.

e SOCRATES: What about when these resources give out?

ADEIMANTUS: Clearly, his father's estate will have to support him, his drinking companions, and his boyfriends and girlfriends, too.

SOCRATES: I understand. You mean the people who fathered the tyrant
5 will have to support him and his friends.

ADEIMANTUS: They will have no choice.

SOCRATES: What if the people get irritated and say it is not just for a grown-up son to be supported by his father? On the contrary, the father should be supported by his son. They did not father him and establish
569a him in power, they say, so that, when he had become strong, they would be enslaved to their own slave and have to support him, his slaves, and other assorted rabble as well; but so that, with him as their popular leader, they would get free from the rule of the rich and the so-called
5 fine and good people in the city. At that point, they order him and his friends to leave the city, as a father might drive a son and his troublesome drinking companions from his house. What do you think would happen then?

ADEIMANTUS: Then, by Zeus, the people will soon learn what kind of creature they have fathered, welcomed, and made strong, and that it is a case of the weaker trying to drive out the stronger.

b

SOCRATES: What do you mean? Will the tyrant dare to use force against his father or hit him if he does not obey?

ADEIMANTUS: Yes—once he has taken away his weapons.

5

SOCRATES: A tyrant is a parricide as you describe him, then, and a harsh nurse of old age; and we do now seem to have an acknowledged tyranny. And so the people, by trying to avoid the proverbial frying pan of enslavement to free men, have fallen into the fire of having slaves as their masters; and, in exchange for the excessive and inappropriate freedom they had before, have put upon themselves the harshest and most bitter slavery to slaves.

c

ADEIMANTUS: That's exactly what happens.

5

SOCRATES: Well, then, wouldn't we be justified in saying that we have adequately described how tyranny evolves from democracy, and what it is like once it has come to exist?

ADEIMANTUS: We would. Our description was entirely adequate.

Book 9

571a SOCRATES: The tyrannical man himself remains to be investigated: how he evolves from a democratic one, what he is like once he has come to exist, and whether the way he lives is wretched or blessedly happy.

ADEIMANTUS: Yes, he still remains.

5 SOCRATES: Do you know what else I still miss?

ADEIMANTUS: What?

SOCRATES: I do not think we have adequately distinguished the nature and number of our appetites.[1] And if that subject is not adequately dealt
b with, our investigation will lack clarity.

ADEIMANTUS: Well, isn't now as fine a time as any?

SOCRATES: It certainly is. So, consider what I want to look at in them. It is this: among unnecessary pleasures and appetites, there are some that seem
5 to me to be lawless. These are probably present in all of us, but they are held in check by the laws and by our better appetites allied with reason. In a few people they have been eliminated entirely or only a few weak ones remain,
c while in others they are stronger and more numerous.

ADEIMANTUS: Which ones do you mean?

SOCRATES: The ones that wake up when we are asleep, whenever the rest of the soul—the rational, gentle, and ruling element—slumbers. Then the
5 bestial and savage part, full of food or drink, comes alive, casts off sleep, and seeks to go and gratify its own characteristic instincts. You know it will dare to do anything in such a state, released and freed from all shame and wisdom. In fantasy, it does not shrink from trying to have sex with a mother or
d with anyone else—man, god, or beast. It will commit any foul murder, and there is no food it refuses to eat. In a word, it does not refrain from anything, no matter how foolish or shameful.

5 ADEIMANTUS: That's absolutely true.

SOCRATES: On the other hand, I suppose someone who keeps himself healthy and temperate will awaken his rational element before going to

---

[1] A topic briefly discussed at 558d4–559d2.

270

sleep and feast it on fine arguments and investigations, which he has brought to an agreed conclusion within himself. As for the appetitive element, he neither starves nor overfeeds it, so it will slumber and not disturb the best element with its pleasure or pain but will leave it alone, just by itself and pure, to investigate and reach out for the perception of something—whether past, present, or future—that it does not know. He soothes the spirited element in a similar way and does not get angry and fall asleep with his spirit still aroused. And when he has calmed these two elements and stimulated the third, in which wisdom resides, he takes his rest. You know this is the state in which he most readily grasps the truth and in which the visions appearing in his dreams are least lawless.

ADEIMANTUS: I completely agree.

SOCRATES: Well, we have been led a bit astray and said a bit too much. What we want to pay attention to is this: there are appetites of a terrible, savage, and lawless kind in everyone—even in those of us who seem to be entirely moderate. This surely becomes clear in sleep. Do you think I am talking sense? Do you agree with me?

ADEIMANTUS: Yes, I do agree.

SOCRATES: Now, recall what we said the democratic man is like.[2] He was the result, we presumed, of a childhood upbringing by a thrifty father who honored only appetites that made money and despised the unnecessary ones whose objects are amusement and showing off. Isn't that right?

ADEIMANTUS: Yes.

SOCRATES: And by associating with more sophisticated men who are full of the appetites we just described, he starts to indulge in every kind of arrogance and adopt their kind of behavior, because of his hatred of his father's thrift. But, since he has a better nature than his corrupters, he is pulled in both directions and settles in the middle between their two ways of life. And enjoying each in what he takes to be moderation, he lives a life that is neither illiberal nor lawless, transformed now from an oligarch to a democrat.

ADEIMANTUS: Yes, that was—and still is—our belief about someone like that.

SOCRATES: Suppose, then, that this man has now in turn become older and has a son who is also brought up in his father's way of life.

ADEIMANTUS: I will.

SOCRATES: Suppose, too, that the same things happen to him as happened to his father: he is led into all the kinds of lawlessness that those leading him call total freedom. His father and the rest of his family come to the aid of

---

[2] 558c–562a2.

the appetites that are in the middle, while the others help the opposite ones. And when these terrible enchanters and tyrant-makers have no hope of keeping hold of the young man in any other way, they contrive to implant a powerful passion in him as the popular leader of those idle and profligate appetites—a sort-of great, winged drone. Or do you think passion is ever anything else in such people?

ADEIMANTUS: I certainly do not think it is.

SOCRATES: And when the other appetites come buzzing around—filled with incense, perfumes, wreaths, wine, and all the other pleasures found in such company, they feed the drone, make it grow as large as possible, and plant the sting of longing in it. Then this popular leader of the soul adopts madness as its bodyguard and is stung to frenzy. If it finds any beliefs or appetites in the man that are regarded as good or are still moved by shame, it destroys them and throws them out, until it has purged him of temperance and filled him with imported madness.

ADEIMANTUS: You have perfectly described how a tyrannical man comes to exist.

SOCRATES: Is that, then, why Passion has long been called a tyrant?

ADEIMANTUS: Probably so.

SOCRATES: And hasn't a drunken man, my friend, something of a tyrannical cast of mind, too?

ADEIMANTUS: He has.

SOCRATES: And of course someone who is mad and deranged attempts to rule not only human beings, but gods as well, and expects to be able to rule them.

ADEIMANTUS: Of course.

SOCRATES: A man becomes tyrannical in the precise sense, then, you marvelous fellow, when his nature or his practices or both together lead him to drunkenness, passion, and melancholia.

ADEIMANTUS: Absolutely.

SOCRATES: So, that, it seems, is how a tyrannical man comes to exist. Now, what is his life like?

ADEIMANTUS: Why don't *you* tell *me,* as askers of riddles usually do?

SOCRATES: I will tell you. You see, I think someone in whom the tyrant of Passion dwells, and in whom it serves as captain of everything in the soul, next goes in for festivals, revelries, luxuries, girlfriends, and all that sort of thing.

ADEIMANTUS: Inevitably.

SOCRATES: And don't lots of terrible appetites sprout up each day and night beside it, creating needs for all sorts of things?

ADEIMANTUS: Indeed, they do.

SOCRATES: So, any income someone like that has is soon spent.

ADEIMANTUS: Of course.

SOCRATES: And the next thing, surely, is borrowing and expenditure of capital.

ADEIMANTUS: What else?

SOCRATES: And when everything is gone, won't the violent crowd of appetites that have nested within him inevitably shout in protest? And when people of this sort are driven by the stings of these other appetites, but particularly of Passion itself, which leads all the others as if they were its bodyguard, stung to frenzy, don't they look to see who possesses anything that can be taken from him by deceit or force?

ADEIMANTUS: Certainly.

SOCRATES: He must take it from every source, then, or live in great suffering and pain.

ADEIMANTUS: He must.

SOCRATES: And just as the late-coming pleasures within him do better than the older ones and steal away their satisfactions, won't he himself, young as he is, think he deserves to do better[3] than his father and mother? And if he has spent his own share, won't he try to take some of his father's wealth by converting it to his own use?

ADEIMANTUS: Of course.

SOCRATES: And if his parents resist him, won't he first try to steal it and deceive them?

ADEIMANTUS: Certainly.

SOCRATES: And if he cannot, won't he next try to seize it by force?

ADEIMANTUS: I suppose so.

SOCRATES: And if, you amazing man, the old man and woman stand their ground and put up a fight, would he take care and be reluctant to act like a tyrant?

ADEIMANTUS: I am not very optimistic about the parents of someone like that!

SOCRATES: But in the name of Zeus, Adeimantus, do you really think that for the sake of his latest love, an unnecessary girlfriend, he would strike his

___

[3] See Glossary of Terms s.v. do better.

c

5

mother, who is his oldest and necessary friend? Or that for the sake of his latest and unnecessary boyfriend, who is in the bloom of youth, he would strike his aged and necessary father, the oldest of his friends, who is no longer in the bloom of youth? Or that he would enslave his parents to them, if he brought them into the same house?

ADEIMANTUS: Yes, by Zeus, he would.

SOCRATES: It seems to be a great blessing to produce a tyrannical son!

ADEIMANTUS: It certainly does!

d

5

e

575a

SOCRATES: What happens to someone like that when the possessions of his father and mother give out and the swarm of pleasures now inside him has grown dense? Won't he first try to break into someone's house or snatch the cloak of someone walking late at night? Next, won't he try to clean out some temple? And in the course of all that, his old childhood beliefs about fine or shameful things—beliefs that are accounted just—are mastered by the new ones that have been released from slavery and, as the bodyguard of Passion, hold sway along with it. These are the ones that used to be freed in sleep as a dream, when he himself, since he was still subject to the laws and his father, had a democratic constitution within him. But under the tyranny of Passion, what he used to become occasionally in his dreams he has now become permanently while awake, and so there is no terrible murder, no food, and no act from which he will refrain. On the contrary, Passion lives like a tyrant within him in complete anarchy and lawlessness, as his sole ruler, and drives him, as if he were a city, to dare anything that will provide sustenance for itself and the unruly mob around it—some of which have come in from the outside as a result of his bad associates, while others have come from within, freed and let loose by his own bad habits. Isn't this the life such a man leads?

ADEIMANTUS: It is.

b

5

SOCRATES: And if there are only a few men like that in a city, and the majority of the others are temperate, they emigrate in order to become the bodyguard of some other tyrant or serve as paid auxiliaries if there happens to be a war somewhere. But if they chance to live in a time of peace and calm, they stay right there in the city and cause lots of little evils.

ADEIMANTUS: What sort of evils do you mean?

SOCRATES: They steal, break into houses, snatch purses, steal clothes, rob temples, and kidnap people. Sometimes, if they are capable speakers, they become sycophants and bear false witness and accept bribes.[4]

c

ADEIMANTUS: You mean they are small evils—provided there are only a few such people.

[4] See Glossary of Terms s.v. sycophants.

SOCRATES: Yes. After all, small evils are small by comparison to big ones. And when it comes to producing corruption and misery in a city, all these evils together do not—as the saying goes—come within a mile of a tyrant. But when you get a large number of these people and their followers in a city, and they become aware of their numbers, they are the ones who— together with the foolishness of the people—create the tyrant out of the one among them who has in his soul the greatest and strongest tyrant of all.

ADEIMANTUS: Naturally, since he would be the most tyrannical.

SOCRATES: That's if they submit willingly. But if the city doesn't put itself in his hands, then just as he once chastised his mother and father, he will now punish his fatherland in the same way, if he can, bringing in new friends and making and keeping his once beloved motherland—as the Cretans call it—or fatherland their slaves. And that is surely the end at which the appetites of a man like that aim.

ADEIMANTUS: It most certainly is.

SOCRATES: So, isn't this what such men are like in private life, before they start to rule? In the first place, don't they associate with flatterers who are ready to do anything to serve them? Or, if they need something from someone themselves, won't they grovel and willingly engage in any sort of posturing, the way slaves do? But once they get what they need, isn't it a different story altogether?

ADEIMANTUS: Yes, completely different.

SOCRATES: So, those with a tyrannical nature live their entire lives without ever being friends with anyone, always masters to one man or slaves to another, but never getting a taste of freedom or true friendship.

ADEIMANTUS: Exactly.

SOCRATES: Wouldn't we be right to call people like that untrustworthy?

ADEIMANTUS: Of course.

SOCRATES: And as unjust as anyone can be—assuming we were right in our earlier conclusions about what justice is like.

ADEIMANTUS: And we certainly were right.

SOCRATES: Let's sum up the worst type of man, then. He is surely the one who, when awake, is like the dreaming person we described earlier.[5]

ADEIMANTUS: Exactly.

SOCRATES: And he evolves from someone who, since he is by nature most tyrannical, achieves sole rule. And the longer he lives as tyrant, the more like that he becomes.

[5] See 571c–d.

10   "Inevitably," *said Glaucon, taking over the argument.*

SOCRATES: Well, then, won't the one who is plainly worst also be plainly

c   most wretched? And the one who for the longest time is most a tyrant, won't he also be most wretched for the longest time, if truth be told? Though the views of the masses[6] on the subject are naturally also many.

5   GLAUCON: All that, at any rate, must be true.

SOCRATES: Doesn't a tyrannical man correspond to and most resemble a city ruled by a tyrant, a democratic man a democratically ruled city, and similarly with the others?

GLAUCON: Of course.

SOCRATES: And the comparison between city and city, as regards their vir-

10   tue and happiness, isn't it the same as the comparison between man and man?

d   GLAUCON: Certainly.

SOCRATES: As regards virtue, then, how does a city ruled by a tyrant compare to a city of the sort we described first that is ruled by a king?

GLAUCON: They are absolute opposites: one is the best, and the other is

5   the worst.

SOCRATES: I won't ask you which is which, since it is obvious. But as regards happiness and wretchedness, is your judgment the same or different? And let's not become dazzled by looking at the tyrant—since he is just one man—or at the few who surround him. Instead, as is necessary, let's go in and study the city as a whole and, when we have gone down and looked

e   into every corner, only then present what we believe.

GLAUCON: That's a good suggestion. And it is clear to everyone that there is no city more wretched than a tyrannical one and none happier than one

5   ruled by a king.

SOCRATES: Would it also be right, then, to suggest the same thing about

577a   the men—that the only fit judge of them is someone who can, in thought, go down into a man's character and discern it—not someone who sees it from the outside, the way a child does, and is dazzled by the façade that tyrants adopt for the outside world, but someone who discerns it ade-

5   quately? And what if I were to assume that the person we must all listen to is the one who has this capacity to judge; who has lived in the same house as a tyrant and witnessed his behavior at home; who has seen how he deals with each member of his household, when he can best be observed

b   stripped of his tragic costume;[7] and who has also seen how he deals with

---

[6] Literally, the many.

[7] I.e., the façade referred to earlier. Greek tragedies often had tyrants as characters.

public dangers? Shouldn't we ask the one who has seen all that to tell us how the tyrant compares to the others with respect to happiness and wretchedness?

GLAUCON: That's also a very good suggestion.

SOCRATES: Then, in order to have someone to answer our questions, do you want us to pretend that we are among the ones who can make such a judgment, and that we have met tyrannical people already?[8]

GLAUCON: I certainly do.

SOCRATES: Come on, then, and examine the matter like this for me. Bearing in mind the resemblance between the city and the man, examine each in turn and describe its condition.

GLAUCON: What kinds of things do you want me to describe?

SOCRATES: Describe the city first. Would you say that a tyrannical city is free or enslaved?

GLAUCON: As enslaved as it is possible to be.

SOCRATES: Yet you can surely see masters and free people in it.

GLAUCON: I can certainly see a small group of people like that. But pretty much the whole population, and the best part of it, is shamefully and wretchedly enslaved.

SOCRATES: If a man and his city are similar, then, mustn't the same structure exist in him, too? Mustn't his soul be full of slavery and illiberality, with those same parts of it enslaved, while a small part, the most wicked and most insane, is master?

GLAUCON: It must.

SOCRATES: Will you describe such a soul as enslaved, then, or as free?

GLAUCON: Enslaved, of course.

SOCRATES: And, to go back, isn't the enslaved, tyrannical city least able to do what it wishes?

GLAUCON: By far the least.

SOCRATES: So, a tyrannical soul will also least do what it wishes—I am talking about the soul as a whole—and will be full of disorder and regret, since it is always forcibly driven by a gadfly.

GLAUCON: Of course.

SOCRATES: Rich or poor? Which must a tyrannical city be?

GLAUCON: Poor.

---

[8] Plato spent time with Dionysius I, tyrant of Sicily.

578a SOCRATES: So, a tyrannical soul, too, must always be poor and insatiable.

GLAUCON: It must.

SOCRATES: What about fear? Mustn't a city of this sort and a man of this
5 sort be filled with it?

GLAUCON: They certainly must.

SOCRATES: And do you think you will find more wailing, groaning,
lamenting, or painful suffering in any other city?

GLAUCON: No.

SOCRATES: What about in a man? Do you think such things are more
10 common in anyone than in this tyrannical man, maddened by his appetites
and passions?

GLAUCON: How could I?

SOCRATES: I imagine it is in view of all these things, then, as well as others
b like them, that you judged this city to be the most wretched of cities.

GLAUCON: And wasn't I right?

SOCRATES: Yes, of course. But how, again, do you describe the tyrannical
5 man in view of these same things?

GLAUCON: He is by far the most wretched of them all.

SOCRATES: There your description is no longer right.

GLAUCON: How so?

SOCRATES: This man, I think, is not yet the most wretched.

10 GLAUCON: Then who is?

SOCRATES: Presumably, you will regard this next one as even more
wretched.

GLAUCON: What one?

SOCRATES: The tyrannical man who does not live out his life as a private
c individual, but is unlucky, in that some misfortune gives him the opportunity of becoming an actual tyrant.

GLAUCON: On the basis of what we have already said, I infer that what
you are saying is true.

5 SOCRATES: Yes. But it is not good enough to believe these claims; one
must carefully examine someone like that by means of argument. After
all, the investigation concerns the most important thing—a good life and
a bad one.[9]

GLAUCON: That's absolutely right.

---

[9] See 344e1–3.

SOCRATES: So, consider, then, whether there is anything in what I say. You
see, I think we should investigate him on the basis of the following.   d

GLAUCON: What?

SOCRATES: On the basis of each and every one of the wealthy private citizens in our cities who own many slaves. For they resemble a tyrant in ruling
over many, although the number ruled by the tyrant is different.   5

GLAUCON: It is different.

SOCRATES: You know, then, that these people feel secure and do not fear
their slaves.

GLAUCON: Of what have they to be afraid, after all?

SOCRATES: Nothing. But do you know why?

GLAUCON: Yes. Because the whole city is ready to defend each of its private citizens.

SOCRATES: That's right. But now, suppose some god were to lift one of
these men, who has fifty or more slaves, out of the city, and put him   e
down—with his wife, his children, his slaves, and his other property—in a
deserted place, where no free men could come to his assistance? Can you
imagine the sort and amount of fear he would feel that he and his wife and   5
children would be killed by his slaves?

GLAUCON: It would be huge, if you ask me.

SOCRATES: Wouldn't he at that point be compelled to start fawning on
some of his slaves, promising them all sorts of things and setting them   579a
free—even though there was nothing he wanted to do less—and wouldn't
he turn out to be a flatterer of slaves?

GLAUCON: He would have to be. Otherwise, he would be killed.

SOCRATES: Now, suppose the god were to settle many other neighbors
around him who would not tolerate anyone claiming to be master of
another, but if they caught such a person, would inflict the most extreme   5
punishments on him?

GLAUCON: I suppose he would be in even worse trouble, since he would
be surrounded by nothing but enemies.   b

SOCRATES: So, isn't this, then, the kind of prison in which the tyrant is
held—the one whose nature we have described, filled with multifarious
fears and passions? Though his soul is really greedy, he is the only one in the   5
city who cannot go abroad or look at the sights at which other free people
yearn to look. Instead, he is mostly stuck in house, living like a woman,[10]
envying any other citizen who goes abroad and sees some good thing.   c

[10] See 451d7 note.

GLAUCON: Absolutely.

SOCRATES: Isn't such a harvest of evils, then, a measure of the difference between a tyrannical man who is badly governed politically on the inside—whom you judged just now to be most wretched—and one who does not live out his life as a private individual, but is compelled by some chance to become an actual tyrant and try to rule others, when he cannot even master himself? It is as if someone with a body that is sick and cannot master itself were compelled, not to spend his life in private pursuits, but to compete and fight with other bodies.

GLAUCON: That's exactly what he is like. Your description is absolutely true, Socrates.

SOCRATES: And so, my dear Glaucon, isn't his condition completely wretched, and isn't the life of a tyrant even harsher than the one you judged to be harshest?

GLAUCON: It certainly is.

SOCRATES: So, in truth, then, and whatever some people may think, a real tyrant is really a slave to the worst sorts of fawning and slavery, and a flatterer of the worst kind of people. He is so far from satisfying his appetites in any way that he is in the greatest need of most things and truly poor—as is apparent if one knows how to look at a whole soul. He is full of fear throughout his life and overflowing with convulsions and pains, if in fact his condition is like that of the city he rules. And it is like it, isn't it?

GLAUCON: Yes, of course.

SOCRATES: And, in addition, shouldn't we also attribute to the man the qualities we mentioned earlier? We said that he is inevitably envious, untrustworthy, unjust, friendless, impious, and a host and nurse to every kind of vice; that ruling makes him even more so than before; and that, as a consequence, he is extremely unfortunate and goes on to make those near him so.

GLAUCON: No one with any sense could possibly contradict that.

SOCRATES: Come on, then, and tell me now at last, like the judge who makes the final decision,[11] who you believe is first in happiness and who second, and judge the others similarly, making five altogether—kingly, timocratic, oligarchic, democratic, tyrannical.

GLAUCON: That's an easy judgment. You see, I rank them in the order of their appearance, just as if they were choruses, both in virtue and vice and in happiness and its opposite.

[11] The reference is to the way plays were judged at dramatic festivals in Athens. A herald announced the results.

SOCRATES: Shall we, then, hire a herald, or shall I myself announce that the son of Ariston[12] has given as his verdict that the best and most just is the most happy, and that he is the one who is most kingly and rules like a king over himself; whereas the worst and most unjust is the most wretched, and he, again, is the one who, because he is most tyrannical, is the greatest tyrant over himself and his city?

GLAUCON: You have announced it!

SOCRATES: And shall I add that it holds whether or not their characters remain hidden from all human beings and gods?[13]

GLAUCON: Do add it.

SOCRATES: Well, then, that is one of our demonstrations. But look at this second one and see if you think there is anything in it.

GLAUCON: What is it?

SOCRATES: In just the way a city is divided into three classes, the soul of each person is also divided in three. That is the reason I think there is another demonstration.

GLAUCON: What is it?

SOCRATES: The following. It seems to me that the three also have three kinds of pleasure, one peculiar to each. The same holds of appetites and kinds of rule.

GLAUCON: How do you mean?

SOCRATES: One element, we say, is that with which a person learns; another, that with which he feels anger. As for the third, because it is multiform, we had no one special name for it but named it after the biggest and strongest thing it has in it. I mean we called it the appetitive element because of the intensity of its appetites for food, drink, sex, and all the things that go along with them. We also called it the money-loving element,[14] because such appetites are most easily satisfied by means of money.

GLAUCON: And we were right.

SOCRATES: So, if we said its pleasure and love are for profit, wouldn't that best bring it together under one heading for the purposes of our argument and make clear to us what we mean when we speak of this part of the soul? And would we be right in calling it money-loving and profit-loving?

GLAUCON: I think so, anyway.

[12] Glaucon, but also, perhaps, his brother Plato.
[13] See 367e1–5, 612a8–b5.
[14] At 553c5.

SOCRATES: What about the spirited element? Don't we say that its whole aim is always mastery, victory, and high repute?

GLAUCON: Certainly.

SOCRATES: Then wouldn't it strike the right note for us to call it victory-loving and honor-loving?

GLAUCON: The absolutely right one.

SOCRATES: But surely it is clear to everyone that the element we learn with is always wholly straining to know where the truth lies, and that of the three it cares least for money and reputation.

GLAUCON: By far the least.

SOCRATES: Wouldn't it be appropriate, then, for us to call it learning-loving and philosophic?

GLAUCON: Of course.

SOCRATES: And doesn't it rule in some people's souls, while one of the others—whichever it happens to be—rules in other people's?

GLAUCON: Yes.

SOCRATES: And isn't that why we say there are three primary types of people, philosophic, victory-loving, and profit-loving?

GLAUCON: Absolutely.

SOCRATES: And also three kinds of pleasure, one assigned to each of them?

GLAUCON: Exactly.

SOCRATES: You realize, then, that if you chose to ask each of these three types of people in turn to tell you which of their lives is most pleasant, each would give the highest praise to his own? Won't the moneymaker say that, compared to that of making a profit, the pleasures of being honored or of learning are worthless unless there is something in them that makes money?

GLAUCON: True.

SOCRATES: What about the honor-lover? Doesn't he think the pleasure of making money is vulgar, while the pleasure of learning—except to the extent that learning brings honor—is smoke and nonsense?

GLAUCON: He does.

SOCRATES: As for the philosopher, what do you suppose he thinks of the other pleasures in comparison to that of knowing where the truth lies and always enjoying some variety of it while he is learning? Won't he think they are far behind? And won't he call them really necessary,[15] since he would have no need for them if they were not necessary for life?

[15] See 559a1–b7.

GLAUCON: He will. We can be sure of that.   5

SOCRATES: Since the pleasures of each kind and the lives themselves dispute with one another—not about which life is finer or more shameful or better or worse—but about which is more pleasant and less painful, how are we to know which of them is speaking the absolute truth?   582a

GLAUCON: I have no idea how to answer that.

SOCRATES: Consider the matter this way: how should we judge things if we want to judge them well? Isn't it by experience, knowledge, and argu-   5 ment? Or could someone have better criteria than these?

GLAUCON: No, of course not.

SOCRATES: Consider, then. Of the three types of men, which has most experience of the pleasures we mentioned? Do you think the profit-lover learns what the truth itself is like, or has more experience of the pleasure of   10 knowing, than the philosopher does of making a profit?   b

GLAUCON: There is a big difference between them. You see, the latter has to have tasted the other kinds of pleasure beginning from childhood. But it is not necessary for the profit-lover to taste or experience how sweet is the pleasure of learning the nature of the things that are—and even if he were   5 eager to, he could not easily do so.

SOCRATES: So, the philosopher is far superior to the profit-lover in his experience of both kinds of pleasures.

GLAUCON: Very far superior.   c

SOCRATES: What about compared to the honor-lover? Is he more inexperienced in the pleasure of being honored than the latter is in the pleasure of knowing?

GLAUCON: No. Honor comes to all of them, provided they accomplish their several aims. For the rich man, too, is honored by many people, as   5 well as are the courageous and the wise ones. So, all have experienced what the pleasure of being honored is like. But the pleasure pertaining to the sight of what is cannot be tasted by anyone except the philosopher.

SOCRATES: So, as far as experience goes, then, he is the finest judge among the three types of men.   d

GLAUCON: By far.

SOCRATES: And he alone will have gained his experience with the help of knowledge.   5

GLAUCON: Of course.

SOCRATES: Moreover, the tool that should be used to judge is not the tool of the profit-lover or the honor-lover, but of the philosopher.

10   GLAUCON: What one is that?

SOCRATES: Surely we said that judgment should be made by means of arguments. Didn't we?

GLAUCON: Yes.

SOCRATES: And arguments are, above all, his tool.

GLAUCON: Absolutely.

15
e

SOCRATES: If the things being judged were best judged by means of wealth and profit, the praise and criticism of the profit-lover would necessarily be closest to the truth.

GLAUCON: It would indeed.

5

SOCRATES: And if by means of honor, victory, and courage, wouldn't it be those of the honor-lover and victory-lover?

GLAUCON: Clearly.

SOCRATES: But since it is by means of experience, knowledge, and argument?

GLAUCON: The praise of the philosopher and argument-lover must be closest to the truth.

583a

SOCRATES: So, of the three pleasures, then, the most pleasant would be that of the part of the soul with which we learn, and the one of us in whom it rules has the most pleasant life.

5

GLAUCON: How could it be otherwise? The knowledgeable person at least praises with authority when he praises his own life.

SOCRATES: What life and pleasure does the judge say are in second place?

GLAUCON: Clearly, those of the warrior and honor-lover, since they are closer to his own than those of the moneymaker.

SOCRATES: Then those of the profit-lover come last, apparently.

GLAUCON: Of course.

b

5

SOCRATES: Well, then, that makes two in a row. And twice the just person has defeated the unjust one. Now comes the third, which is dedicated in Olympic fashion to our savior, Olympian Zeus.[16] Observe, then, that the other pleasures—apart from that of the knowledgeable person—are neither entirely true nor pure. On the contrary, they are like some sort of illusionist painting, as I think I have heard some wise person say. Yet, if that were true, it would be the greatest and most decisive of the overthrows.

---

[16] The first toast at a banquet was to the Olympian Zeus, the third to our savior, Zeus. By combining both in a single form of address, Plato seems to be emphasizing the importance of this final proof.

284

GLAUCON: By far the greatest. But what exactly do you mean?

SOCRATES: I will find out, if you answer the questions while I ask them.   c

GLAUCON: Start asking, then.

SOCRATES: Tell me, then, don't we say that pain is the opposite of pleasure?

GLAUCON: Yes.

SOCRATES: Isn't there also a state of feeling neither enjoyment nor pain?   5

GLAUCON: There is.

SOCRATES: Isn't it in the middle between these two, a sort of quiet state of the soul where they are concerned? Or wouldn't you describe it that way?

GLAUCON: I would.

SOCRATES: So then do you recall the sorts of things ill people say when   10
they are ill?

GLAUCON: Which ones?

SOCRATES: That nothing is more pleasant than being healthy, but they had not realized it was most pleasant until they fell ill.   d

GLAUCON: I do remember that.

SOCRATES: Don't you also hear people who are in great pain saying that nothing is more pleasant than the cessation of one's suffering?

GLAUCON: I do.   5

SOCRATES: And there are many similar circumstances, I presume, in which you see people in pain praising not enjoyment, but freedom from pain, and respite from that sort of thing, as most pleasant.

GLAUCON: Yes. For at such times, the respite presumably becomes pleasant enough to content them.   10

SOCRATES: And when someone ceases to enjoy something, this respite from pleasure will be painful.   e

GLAUCON: Presumably.

SOCRATES: So, the quiet state we just now described as being in between the two will sometimes be both pain and pleasure.   5

GLAUCON: Apparently.

SOCRATES: And is it possible for what is neither to become both?

GLAUCON: Not in my view.

SOCRATES: Furthermore, when what is pleasant and what is painful arise in the soul, they are both a sort of motion, aren't they?   10

GLAUCON: Yes.

285

SOCRATES: And didn't we see just now that what is neither painful nor pleasant is a respite and in the middle between the two?

GLAUCON: Yes, we did.

SOCRATES: How can it be right, then, to think that the absence of pain is pleasant or the absence of enjoyment painful?

GLAUCON: There's no way it can be.

SOCRATES: So, it is not right. But when the quiet state is next to what is painful, it appears pleasant; and when it is next to what is pleasant, it appears painful. And there is nothing sound in these illusions as far as the truth about pleasure is concerned. On the contrary, they are a sort of sorcery.

GLAUCON: That's what the argument suggests, at any rate.

SOCRATES: Well, then, take a look at pleasures that do not derive from pains, so that you won't be likely to think that, *in their case,* it is the nature of pleasure to be just the cessation of pain or of pain to be just the cessation of pleasure.

GLAUCON: Where am I to look? What pleasures do you mean?

SOCRATES: There are lots of others, but you might especially want to think about the pleasures of smell. You see, without being preceded by pain, they suddenly become incredibly intense. And when they cease, they leave no pain behind.

GLAUCON: That's absolutely true.

SOCRATES: So, let's not be persuaded that pure pleasure is relief from pain, or pure pain relief from pleasure.

GLAUCON: No, let's not.

SOCRATES: However, of the so-called pleasures that reach the soul through the body, pretty much the greatest number—and the most intense ones, too—are of that kind: they are some sort of relief from pains.

GLAUCON: Yes, they are.

SOCRATES: And aren't those pleasures and pains of anticipation, which arise from the expectation of future pleasures or pains, of the same kind?

GLAUCON: They are.

SOCRATES: Do you know what they are like and what they most resemble?

GLAUCON: What?

SOCRATES: Do you think there is such a thing in the natural world as an up, a down, and a middle?

GLAUCON: I do.

SOCRATES: Don't you imagine, then, that if someone were brought from down below to the middle, he would think anything other than that he was moving upward? And if he stood at the middle and saw where he had come from, could he possibly think he was anywhere other than the upper region, since he hadn't seen the one that is truly up above?

GLAUCON: By Zeus, I do not see how he could think anything else.

SOCRATES: But if he were brought back again, wouldn't he think he was being brought down? And wouldn't he be thinking the truth?   e

GLAUCON: Of course.

SOCRATES: And wouldn't all this happen to him because he is inexperienced in what is truly and really up, middle, and down?   5

GLAUCON: Clearly.

SOCRATES: Would it surprise you, then, if those who are inexperienced in the truth have unsound beliefs about lots of other things as well—that they are so disposed toward pleasure, pain, and the middle state that, whenever they descend to the painful, they think the truth and really are in pain; but   585a
that, when they ascend from the painful to the middle state, they firmly think they have reached fulfillment and pleasure? Like people who compare black to gray without having experienced white, don't they compare pain to painlessness while being inexperienced in pleasure, and so get deceived?   5

GLAUCON: No, by Zeus, it would not surprise me! In fact, I would be very surprised if it were not like that.

SOCRATES: Think of it this way, then: Aren't hunger, thirst, and the like some sort of emptiness related to the state of the body?   b

GLAUCON: They are.

SOCRATES: And isn't foolishness and lack of knowledge, in turn, some sort of emptiness related to the state of the soul?

GLAUCON: It certainly is.   5

SOCRATES: Aren't people filled when they take in nourishment or gain understanding?

GLAUCON: Of course.

SOCRATES: Does the truer filling belong to what *is* less or to what *is* more?   10

GLAUCON: Clearly, it belongs to what is more.

SOCRATES: Which of the two types, then, partakes more of pure being? The sorts belonging to bread, drink, relishes, and nourishment in general? Or the kind belonging to true belief, knowledge, understanding, and, in sum, to all of virtue? Judge it this way: what belongs to what is always the   c
same, immortal, and true, is itself of that sort, and comes to be in something

287

of that sort—it *is* more, don't you think, than what belongs to what is never the same and mortal, is itself of that kind, and comes to be in something of that kind?

5

GLAUCON: Far more. What belongs to what is always the same is far superior.

SOCRATES: And does the being of what is always the same partake any more of being than of knowledge?[17]

GLAUCON: Not at all.

10 SOCRATES: What about of truth?

GLAUCON: Not of it, either.

SOCRATES: And if less of truth, less of being, too?

GLAUCON: Necessarily.

SOCRATES: Isn't it generally true that the types concerned with the care of the body partake less in truth and being than do those concerned with the care of the soul?

d

GLAUCON: Yes, much less.

SOCRATES: Don't you think the same holds of the body in comparison to the soul?

5

GLAUCON: I do.

SOCRATES: Then isn't what is filled with things that are more, and is itself more, more really filled than what is filled with things that are less, and is itself less?

10 GLAUCON: Of course.

SOCRATES: So, then, if being filled with what is appropriate to our nature is pleasant, what is more filled with things that *are* more is more really and truly caused to enjoy a more true pleasure; whereas what partakes of things that *are* less is less truly and surely filled and partakes of a less trustworthy and less true pleasure.

e

5 GLAUCON: That's absolutely inevitable.

586a SOCRATES: So, those who lack experience of knowledge or virtue, but are always occupied with feasts and the like, are brought down, apparently, and then back up to the middle state; and wander in this way throughout their lives, never reaching beyond this to what is truly higher up, never looking up at it or brought up to it, never filled with what really is, and never tasting any stable or pure pleasure. On the contrary, they are always looking downward like cattle and, with their heads bent over the earth or the dinner table, they feed, fatten, and fornicate. And, in order to do better than

5

---

[17] See 477a2–4.

others in these things, they kick and butt with iron horns and hooves, kill-[b
ing each other, because their desires are insatiable.[18] For they aren't using
things that *are* to fill the part of themselves that *is* a thing that is, and a leak-
proof vessel.[19]

GLAUCON: You have described the life of "the many," Socrates, just like an   5
oracle!

SOCRATES: So, isn't it necessary, then, for these people to live with pleasures that are mixed with pains, mere phantoms and illusionist paintings of
true pleasures? And aren't they so colored by their juxtaposition with one
another that they appear intense, beget mad passions for themselves in the   c
foolish, and are fought over—as Stesichorus tells us the phantom of Helen
was fought over at Troy—through ignorance of the truth?[20]   5

GLAUCON: Something like that must be what happens.

SOCRATES: Mustn't similar things happen to someone who succeeds in
satisfying the spirited element? Mustn't his love of honor be so colored by
envy, his love of victory by violence, and his spiritedness by peevishness,[21]
that he pursues the satisfactions of honor, victory, and spiritedness without   d
rational calculation or understanding?

GLAUCON: The same sorts of things must happen with regard to that element, too.

SOCRATES: Can't we confidently assert, then, that, even where the desires /
of the profit-loving and honor-loving parts are concerned, those that fol-   5
low knowledge and argument, and pursue with their help the pleasures that /
wisdom prescribes, will attain—to the degree that they can attain true pleasure at all—the truest pleasures, because they follow truth, and those that
are most their own; if, indeed, what is the best for each thing is also what is \ e
most its own?

GLAUCON: But that, of course, is what is most its own.

SOCRATES: So, when the entire soul follows the philosophic element and
does not engage in faction, the result is that each element does its own
work and is just; and, in particular, each enjoys its own pleasures, the best
pleasures and—to the degree possible—the truest.   587a

---

[18] See 372e2–373e7.

[19] *Stegnon:* contrasted in the *Gorgias* (493a1–b3) with the "leaking jar" in which the
appetites are located.

[20] According to the story, Stesichorus wrote a poem defaming Helen and was punished by being struck with blindness. His sight was restored when he added a verse to
the poem in which he claimed that it was a phantom of Helen and not Helen herself
who was at Troy. See *Phaedrus* 243a.

[21] Envy, violence, and peevishness are all painful conditions that enhance the honor-
lover's pleasures through contrast.

GLAUCON: Absolutely.

SOCRATES: So, when one of the other parts gains mastery, the result is that it cannot discover its own pleasure and compels the other parts to pursue an alien, and not a true pleasure.

GLAUCON: Yes.

SOCRATES: And wouldn't what is most distant from philosophy and reason be most likely to produce that result?

GLAUCON: By far.

SOCRATES: And isn't what is most distant from reason the very thing that is most distant from law and order?

GLAUCON: Clearly.

SOCRATES: And wasn't it made evident that the passionate and tyrannical appetites are most distant?

GLAUCON: By far the most.

SOCRATES: And the kingly and orderly ones least distant?

GLAUCON: Yes.

SOCRATES: Then the tyrant, I suppose, will be most distant from a true pleasure that is his own, while the king will be least distant.

GLAUCON: It is inevitable.

SOCRATES: And so, the tyrant will live most unpleasantly and the king most pleasantly.

GLAUCON: It is absolutely inevitable.

SOCRATES: Do you know, then, how much more unpleasant the tyrant's life is than the king's?

GLAUCON: Not unless you tell me.

SOCRATES: There are, it seems, three pleasures: one genuine and two illegitimate. The tyrant is at the extreme end of the illegitimate ones, since he flees both law and reason and lives with a bodyguard of slavish pleasures. But it is not at all easy to say just how inferior he is—except perhaps as follows.

GLAUCON: How?

SOCRATES: The tyrant is somehow at a third remove from the oligarch, since the democrat was in the middle between them.[22]

GLAUCON: Yes.

---

[22] Third because the Greeks always counted the first as well as the last member of a series. The day after tomorrow was the third day.

SOCRATES: Won't he also live with a phantom of pleasure, then, that, as regards truth, is at a third remove from that other—if what we said before is true?

GLAUCON: He will.

SOCRATES: But the oligarch, in turn, is at a third remove from the king,[23] if we assume king and aristocrat to be the same.

GLAUCON: Yes, third.

SOCRATES: So a tyrant is removed from true pleasure by a numerical value of three times three.

GLAUCON: Apparently.

SOCRATES: So, on the basis of the size of this numerical value, it seems the phantom of the tyrant's pleasure is a plane figure.

GLAUCON: Exactly.

SOCRATES: On the basis of its square and cube, in that case, it becomes clear how far removed it is.

GLAUCON: Clear to someone skilled in calculation, anyway!

SOCRATES: Turning it the other way around, then, if someone wants to say how far the king is removed from the tyrant in terms of true pleasure, he will find, if he completes the calculation, that he lives 729 times more pleasantly, while the tyrant lives the same number of times more painfully.[24]

GLAUCON: That's an extraordinary calculation of the difference between the two men—the just one and the unjust one—in terms of their pleasure and pain!

[23] Because the timocrat is between them.

[24] Socrates' mathematics is difficult to follow. He seems to have something like this in mind: the tyrant's pleasure is a two-dimensional image (a plane figure) of the true, three-dimensional pleasure of the philosopher. Hence, if a one-unit square represents the degree of closeness to true pleasure of an image nine times removed from it, true pleasure should be represented by a nine-unit cube. It follows that the king lives 729 times more pleasantly than the tyrant. However, in order to reach the significant number 729—there are 729 days and nights in a year of 364 twenty-four–hour days and 729 months in the "great year" recognized by the Pythagorean philosopher Philolaus—Socrates has had to make two rather fast moves. First, he illegitimately capitalizes on the Greek manner of counting series in order to count the oligarch twice, once as the last term in his first series (tyrant, democrat, oligarch) and again as the first term in his second series (oligarch, timocrat, king). Second, he multiplies the number of times the tyrant is removed from the oligarch by the number of times the oligarch is removed from the king, when he should have added them. In fact, the tyrant is only five times removed from the king, and so lives only 125 times less pleasantly!

SOCRATES: And yet it is a number that is both true and appropriate to human lives—if indeed days, nights, months, and years are appropriate to them.

GLAUCON: And of course they are appropriate.

SOCRATES: If the victory of the good and just person over the bad and unjust one in terms of pleasure is as great as that, won't his victory in terms of its grace, beauty, and virtue be extraordinarily greater?

GLAUCON: Extraordinarily greater, indeed, by Zeus!

SOCRATES: All right, then. Since we have reached this point in the argument, let's return to the first things we mentioned that led us here. I think someone said that doing injustice profits a completely unjust person who is believed to be just. Wasn't that the claim?[25]

GLAUCON: Yes, it was.

SOCRATES: Let's discuss it with its proponent, then, since we have now agreed on the respective effects of doing unjust and doing just things.[26]

GLAUCON: How?

SOCRATES: By fashioning an image of the soul in words, so that the one who said that will know what he was saying.

GLAUCON: What sort of image?

SOCRATES: One of those creatures that ancient legends say used to exist. The Chimera, Scylla, Cerberus, and the numerous other cases where many different kinds are said to have grown together into one.

GLAUCON: Yes, they do describe such things.

SOCRATES: Well, then, fashion a single species of complex, many-headed beast, with a ring of tame and savage animal heads that it can grow and change at will.

GLAUCON: That's a task for a clever fashioner of images![27] Still, since language is easier to fashion than wax and the like, consider the fashioning done.

SOCRATES: Now, fashion another single species—of lion—and a single one of human being. But make the first much the largest and the second, second in size.

GLAUCON: That's easier—the fashioning is done.

SOCRATES: Now, join the three in one, so that that they somehow grow together naturally.

---

[25] See 348b9–10, 360c8–361d3, 392c2–4.

[26] See 358b4–7, 367e1–5.

[27] See 596b12–e4.

292

GLAUCON: They are joined.

SOCRATES: Then fashion around the outside the image of one of them, that of the human being, so that to anyone who cannot see what is inside, but sees only the outer shell, it will look like a single creature, a human being.

GLAUCON: The surrounding shell has been fashioned.

SOCRATES: When someone claims, then, that it profits this human being to do injustice, but that doing what is just brings no advantage, let's tell him that he is saying nothing other than that it profits him to feed well and strengthen the multifarious beast, as well as the lion and everything that pertains to the lion; to starve and weaken the human being, so that he is dragged along wherever either of the other two leads; and not to accustom the two to one another or make them friends, but leave them to bite and fight and devour one another.

GLAUCON: Yes, that's exactly what someone who praises doing injustice is saying.

SOCRATES: On the other hand, wouldn't someone who claims that what is just be profitable be saying we should do and say what will give the inner human being the greatest mastery over the human being, to get him to take care of the many-headed beast like a farmer, feeding and domesticating the gentle heads and preventing the savage ones from growing; to make the lion's nature his ally; and to care for all in common, bringing them up in such a way that they will be friends with each other and with himself?

GLAUCON: Yes, that's exactly what someone who praises justice is saying.

SOCRATES: From every point of view, then, the one who praises what is just speaks truly while the one who praises what is unjust speaks falsely. For whether we consider pleasure or good reputation or advantage, the one who praises the just tells the truth while the one who condemns it has nothing sound to say and condemns with no knowledge of what he is condemning.

GLAUCON: None at all, in my opinion.

SOCRATES: Then let's persuade him gently—after all, he is not getting it wrong intentionally—by questioning him as follows: "Bless you, but shouldn't we claim that this is also the basis of the conventional views about what is fine and what is shameful: what is fine is what subordinates the beastlike elements in our nature to the human one—or better, perhaps, to the divine, whereas what is shameful is what enslaves the tame element to the savage"? Will he agree, or what?

GLAUCON: He will if he takes my advice.

SOCRATES: Is there anyone, then, in light of this argument, who profits by acquiring gold unjustly, if the result is something like this: in taking the

293

e

gold, he simultaneously enslaves the best element in himself to the most wicked? If he got the gold by enslaving his son or daughter to savage and evil men, it would not profit him, no matter how much he got for doing it. So, if he ruthlessly enslaves the most divine element in himself to the most godless and polluted, how could he fail to be wretched, when he accepts

5

590a

golden gifts in return for a far more terrible destruction than that of Eriphyle, who took the necklace in return for her husband's soul?[28]

GLAUCON: A much more terrible one. I will answer for him.

SOCRATES: And don't you think intemperance has long been condemned

5

for reasons of this sort; that it is because of vices like it that that terrible creature, the large and multiform beast, is given more freedom than it should be?

GLAUCON: Clearly.

SOCRATES: And aren't stubbornness and peevishness condemned because they inharmoniously increase and stretch the lionlike and snakelike[29]

b

element?

GLAUCON: Certainly.

SOCRATES: And aren't luxury and softness condemned for slackening and loosening this same part, because that produces cowardice in it?

5

GLAUCON: Of course.

SOCRATES: And aren't flattery and illiberality condemned because they subject this same spirited element to the moblike beast, allow it to be showered with abuse for the sake of money and the latter's insatiability, and habituate it from youth to be an ape instead of a lion?

c

GLAUCON: Yes, indeed.

SOCRATES: Why do you think someone is reproached for menial work or handicraft? Or shall we say that it is for no other reason than because the best element is naturally weak in him, so that it cannot rule the beasts

5

within him, but can only serve them and learn what flatters them?

GLAUCON: Apparently.

---

[28] Eriphyle was bribed by Polynices to persuade her husband, Amphiaraus, to take part in an attack on Thebes. He was killed, and she was murdered by her son in revenge. See *Odyssey* 11.326–7.

[29] The snakelike element hasn't been previously mentioned, although it may be included in "all that pertains to" the lion (588e6). It symbolizes some of the meaner components of the spirited part, such as peevishness, which it would be unnatural to attribute to the noble lion. Snakes were thought to guard shrines and other sacred places. Including a snakelike element in the part of the soul dominant in guardians is, therefore, somewhat natural.

SOCRATES: In order to ensure, then, that someone like that is also ruled by something similar to what rules the best person, we say that he should be the slave of that best person who has the divine ruler within himself. It is not to harm the slave that we say he should be ruled, as Thrasymachus supposed was true of all subjects, but because it is better for everyone to be ruled by a divine and wise ruler—preferably one that is his own and that he has inside himself; otherwise one imposed on him from outside, so that we may all be as alike and as friendly as possible, because we are all captained by the same thing.

GLAUCON: Yes, that's right.

SOCRATES: This is clearly the aim of the law as well, which is the ally of everyone in the city. It is also our aim in ruling our children. We do not allow them to be free until we establish a constitution in them as in a city. That is to say, we take care of their best part with the similar one in ourselves and equip them with a guardian and ruler similar to our own to take our place. Only then do we set them free.

GLAUCON: Yes, that's clearly so.

SOCRATES: How, then, will we claim, Glaucon, and on the basis of what argument, that it profits someone to do injustice, or what is intemperate, or some shameful thing that will make him worse, even if it brings more money or power of some other sort?

GLAUCON: There's no way we can.

SOCRATES: Or how can we claim that it profits him to be undetected in his injustice and not pay the penalty? I mean, doesn't the one who remains undetected become even worse, while in the one who is discovered and punished, the bestial element is calmed and tamed and the gentle one freed? Doesn't his entire soul, when it returns to its best nature and acquires temperance and justice along with wisdom, achieve a condition that is as more honorable than that of a body when it acquires strength and beauty along with health, as a soul is more honorable than a body?

GLAUCON: Absolutely.

SOCRATES: Won't anyone with any sense, then, give everything he has to achieve it as long as he lives? First, won't he honor the studies that produce it and not honor the others?

GLAUCON: Clearly.

SOCRATES: Second, as regards the condition and nurture of his body, not only will he not give himself over to bestial and irrational pleasure, and live turned in that direction; but he won't make health his aim nor give precedence to the ways of becoming strong or healthy or beautiful, unless he is also going to become temperate as a result of them. On the contrary, it is

295

d clear that he will always be tuning the harmony of his body for the sake of the concord of his soul.

5 GLAUCON: He certainly will, if indeed he is going to be truly musical.

SOCRATES: Won't he also keep order and concord in his acquisition of money? He won't be dazzled, will he, by what the masses regard as blessed happiness, and—by increasing the size of his wealth without limit—acquire an unlimited number of evils?

GLAUCON: Not in my view.

SOCRATES: On the contrary, he will keep his eye fixed on the constitution
e within him and guard against disturbing anything there either with too much money or with too little. Captaining himself in that way, he will increase and spend his wealth, as far as possible by reference to it.

5 GLAUCON: That's exactly what he will do.

SOCRATES: Where honors are concerned, too, he will keep his eye on the
592a same thing. He will willingly share in and taste those he believes will make him better. But those that might overthrow the established condition of his soul, he will avoid, both in private and in public.

5 GLAUCON: So, he won't be willing to take part in politics, then, if that is what he cares about.

SOCRATES: Yes, by the dog,[30] in his own city, he certainly will. But he may not be willing to do so in his fatherland, unless some divine good luck chances to be his.

GLAUCON: I understand. You mean in the city we have just been founding
10 and describing; the one that exists in words, since I do not think it exists
b anywhere on earth.

SOCRATES: But there may perhaps be a model of it in the heavens for any-one who wishes to look at it and to found himself on the basis of what he sees. It makes no difference at all whether it exists anywhere or ever will.
5 You see, he would take part in the politics of it alone, and of no other.

GLAUCON: That's probably right.

---

[30] See 399e5 note.

Book 10

SOCRATES: You know that there are many other things about our city that   595a
make me think we were entirely right in founding it as we did, but I am
particularly thinking of poetry when I say that.

GLAUCON: What about it?

SOCRATES: Our refusal to admit any of it that is imitative. Indeed, the   5
need not to admit it seems even more evident, in my view, now that we
have distinguished the elements in the soul from one another.   b

GLAUCON: How do you mean?

SOCRATES: Between ourselves—for *you* won't denounce me to the tragic
poets or any of the other imitative ones—I think all such poetry is likely to   5
corrupt the mind of those of its hearers who do not have the knowledge of
what it is really like as a drug to counteract it.

GLAUCON: What do you have in mind in saying that?

SOCRATES: I will have to tell you, even though a sort of reverential love I
have had for Homer since childhood makes me hesitate to speak. You see,
he seems to have been the first teacher and leader of all these fine tragedi-   c
ans. All the same, a man should not be honored more than the truth. So, as
I say, I will have to tell you.

GLAUCON: Of course.

SOCRATES: Listen, then—or rather, answer my questions.   5

GLAUCON: Ask away.

SOCRATES: Could you tell me what imitation in general is? You see, I do
not entirely understand what it is supposed to be.

GLAUCON: So is it likely that *I* will?

SOCRATES: There would be nothing strange in that, since there are many   ouch 10
things the shortsighted see before the sharp-eyed!   596a

GLAUCON: That's right. But with you present, I could not possibly be very
eager to speak out even if there were something I saw. So, you will have to
do the looking yourself.

5 SOCRATES: Do you want us to begin our investigation with the following point, then, in accordance with our usual procedure? I mean, as you know, we usually posit some one particular form in connection with each set of many things to which we apply the same name.[1] Or don't you understand?

GLAUCON: I do.

10 SOCRATES: Then in the present case, too, let's take any set of many things
b you like. For example, there are, if you like, many couches and tables.

GLAUCON: Of course.

SOCRATES: But the forms connected to these manufactured items are surely just two, one of a couch and one of a table.

5 GLAUCON: Yes.

SOCRATES: Don't we usually say, too, that the craftsman who makes each manufactured item looks toward the form when he makes the couches or the tables we use, and similarly with other things? For surely no craftsman
10 makes the form itself—

GLAUCON: How could he?

SOCRATES: Well, now, see what you would call *this* craftsman?

c GLAUCON: Which?

SOCRATES: The one who makes everything each individual handicrafts-man makes.

GLAUCON: That's an amazingly clever man you are talking about!

SOCRATES: Wait a minute and you will have even more reason to say that! You see, this same handicraftsman is able to make not only every manufac-
5 tured item, but he also makes all the plants that grow from the earth, and produces all the animals, including himself; and, in addition, he produces earth and sky and gods and everything in the sky, and everything in Hades beneath the earth.

d GLAUCON: You are talking about a wholly amazing sophist!

SOCRATES: You do not believe me? Tell me, do you think such a crafts-man is completely impossible? Or do you think there is a way in which a maker of all these things could exist, and a way in which he could not? Don't you see there is a certain way in which even you yourself could
5 make all of them?

GLAUCON: What way is that?

SOCRATES: It is not difficult. On the contrary, it is a sort of craftsmanship that is widely available and quick—and quickest of all, I suppose, if you are

[1] See 478e7–480a13, 507b2–7.

willing to take a mirror and turn it around in all directions. That way you will quickly make the sun and the things in the sky; you will quickly make the earth, yourself and the other animals, manufactured items, plants, and everything else that was mentioned just now.

GLAUCON: Yes, their appearances, but certainly not the things themselves as they truly are.

SOCRATES: Right! You attack the argument at just the right place. For I think the painter is also one of these craftsmen, isn't he?

GLAUCON: Of course.

SOCRATES: But you will say, I think, that he does not make the things he makes as they truly are—even though there is a certain way in which the painter also makes a couch. Isn't that right?

GLAUCON: Yes, he also makes the appearance of one.

SOCRATES: What about the couch-maker? Didn't you just say that he does not make the form—which we say is what a couch is[2]—but only a particular couch?

GLAUCON: Yes, I did say that.

SOCRATES: Now, if he does not make what it is, he is not making what is, but something that is like what is, but is not. So, if someone were to say that the product of a couch-maker or any other handicraftsman completely is, he probably would not be speaking the truth?

GLAUCON: That, at any rate, is what those who occupy themselves with such arguments would think.

SOCRATES: So we should not be surprised if it also turns out to be somewhat dim in comparison to the truth.

GLAUCON: No, we should not.

SOCRATES: Would you like us, then, to use these same examples to search for that imitator of ours and what he really is?

GLAUCON: I would, if you would.

SOCRATES: Well, then, we have these three sorts of couches. One, that is in nature,[3] which I think we would say a god makes. Or is it someone else?

GLAUCON: No one, I suppose.

SOCRATES: One the carpenter makes.

GLAUCON: Yes.

---

[2] See Glossary of Terms s.v. what it is.

[3] I.e., that is in its nature a couch. See 597c2 and 490b3.

SOCRATES: And one the painter makes. Isn't that so?

GLAUCON: It is.

SOCRATES: So painter, carpenter, and god—these three oversee three kinds of couches?

15 GLAUCON: Yes, three.

SOCRATES: Now, the god, either because he did not want to, or because it

c was somehow necessary for him not to make more than one that is in its nature a couch, made only the one that is what a couch itself is.[4] Two or more of these have not been naturally developed by the god and never will

5 be naturally developed.

GLAUCON: Why is that?

SOCRATES: Because, if he were to make only two, one would again come to light whose form they in turn would both possess, and *it* would be what a couch itself is, not the two.

10 GLAUCON: That's right.

SOCRATES: The god knew this, I suppose, and, wishing to be the real

d maker of the real couch and not just some particular maker of some particular couch, naturally developed the one that is in its nature unique.

GLAUCON: Probably so.

5 SOCRATES: Would you like us to call him its natural maker, then, or something like that?

GLAUCON: It would be right to do so, at any rate, since it is by nature that he has made it and all the others.

SOCRATES: What about the carpenter? Shouldn't we call him the craftsman who makes a couch?

10 GLAUCON: Yes.

SOCRATES: And should we call a painter, too, a craftsman and maker of such a thing?

GLAUCON: Certainly not.

SOCRATES: In that case, what is it you say he is, of a couch?

e GLAUCON: In my view, the most reasonable thing to call him is this: he is an imitator of what the others are craftsmen of.

SOCRATES: All right. So the one whose product is three removed from the natural one, you call an imitator?

5 GLAUCON: Certainly.

---

[4] See 490b3, 532b1.

SOCRATES: So the tragedian too, if indeed he is an imitator, will be some-one who is by his nature third from king and truth,[5] and so will all the other imitators.

GLAUCON: It looks that way.

SOCRATES: We are agreed about the imitator, then. Now, tell me this about the painter: in each case, do you think it is what each thing itself is in its nature that he is trying to imitate, or the products of the craftsmen?

GLAUCON: Those of the craftsmen.

SOCRATES: As they are, or as they appear to be? You have still to make that distinction.

GLAUCON: How do you mean?

SOCRATES: This: if you look at a couch from the side or the front or from anywhere else, does it differ in any way from itself? Or, while not differing at all, does it appear different? And similarly with the others?

GLAUCON: The latter. It appears different, but is not different at all.

SOCRATES: Then consider this very point: at what does painting aim in each case? To imitate what is as it is? Or what appears as it appears? Is it an imitation of an illusion, or of truth?

GLAUCON: Of an illusion.

SOCRATES: So, imitation is surely far removed from the truth. And the reason that it produces everything, it seems, is that it grasps only a small part of each thing—and that is an illusion. For example, the painter, we say, can paint us a cobbler, a carpenter, or any other craftsman, even though he knows nothing about these crafts. All the same, if he is a good painter, by painting a carpenter and displaying him at a distance, he might deceive children and foolish adults into thinking it truly is a carpenter.

GLAUCON: Of course.

SOCRATES: In fact, my friend, I imagine that what we must bear in mind in all these cases is this: when someone tells us he has met a human being who knows every craft as well as everything else anyone knows, and that there is nothing of which he does not have a more exact knowledge than anyone else, we should assume we are talking to a naïve fellow. He has been deceived, it seems, by an encounter with some sort of sorcerer or imitator, whom he therefore considers to be all-wise. But that is because of his own inability to distinguish between knowledge, lack of knowledge, and imitation.

GLAUCON: That's absolutely true.

[5] God is called king at *Laws* 10.904a6.

301

SOCRATES: Well, then, we must next consider tragedy and its leader, Homer, since we hear from some that these men know every craft, every-

e thing relevant to human virtue and vice, and even all about divine matters. They claim, you see, that if a good poet is to write beautiful poetry about the things he writes about, he must have knowledge of them when he

5 writes, or else he would be unable to. We should consider, then, whether those who tell us this have been deceived by their encounters with these imitators and do not realize, when they see their works, that they are three

599a removes from what is, and are easy to produce without knowledge of the truth. For they produce illusions, not things that are. Or whether there is something in what they say, and good poets really do have knowledge of the things about which the masses think they speak so well.

5 GLAUCON: We certainly must consider that.

SOCRATES: Do you think, then, that if someone could make both what is imitated and its image, he would allow himself to take making images seri-

b ously, and put it at the forefront of his life as the best ability he had?

GLAUCON: No, I do not.

SOCRATES: But if he truly had knowledge of what he imitates, I suppose he would take deeds much more seriously than their imitations, would try

5 to leave behind many beautiful deeds as his own memorials, and would be much more eager to be the subject of a eulogy than the author of one.

GLAUCON: I suppose so. I mean, these things certainly are not equal either in honor or in benefit.

SOCRATES: Let's not demand an account, then, of the other things from

c Homer or any other poet. Let's not ask if any of them is a doctor or only an imitator of what doctors say; or which people any of the poets, old or new, has reportedly made healthy, as Asclepius did; or which students of medi-

5 cine he left behind, as Asclepius did his sons. And let's not ask them about the other crafts either, but leave them aside. When it comes, however, to the most important and most beautiful things of which Homer undertakes to speak—warfare, generalship, city government, and a person's educa- tion—surely, it *is* fair to question him as follows: "My dear Homer, if you

d are not third removed from the truth about virtue, and are not the sort of craftsman of an image, which is what we defined an imitator to be, but if you are even in second place and capable of knowing what practices make

5 people better or worse in private or in public life, tell us which cities are better governed because of you, as the Lacedaemonians are because of Lycurgus, and as many others—big and small—are because of many other

e men. What city gives you credit for having proved to be a good lawgiver who benefited it? Italy and Sicily give it to Charondas, and we give it to Solon. Who gives it to you?" Will he be able to name one?

GLAUCON: I suppose not. At any rate, none is mentioned even by the Homeridae themselves.[6]

SOCRATES: Then is any war in Homer's time remembered that was well fought because of his leadership or advice?

GLAUCON: None at all.

SOCRATES: Then as you would expect in the case of a man wise in deeds, are we told of his many ingenious inventions in the crafts or other activities, as we are about Thales of Miletus and Anacharsis the Scythian?

GLAUCON: There's nothing of that sort.

SOCRATES: Then if there is nothing of a public nature, is Homer said to have been a leader, during his own lifetime, in the education of people who loved associating with him and passed on a Homeric way of life to those who came later? Is he like Pythagoras, who was himself particularly loved for this reason, and whose followers even today still seem to be conspicuous for a way of life they call Pythagorean?

GLAUCON: Again, we are told nothing of this kind. Indeed, Socrates, Creophylus, the companion of Homer, would presumably seem even more ridiculous than his name[7] suggests as an example of such education, if the story told about Homer is true. You see, we are told that while he was alive, Creophylus completely neglected him.

SOCRATES: Yes, we are told that. But, Glaucon, if Homer had really been able to educate people and make them better, if he had been able, not to imitate such matters but to know about them, wouldn't he have had many companions who honored and loved him? Protagoras of Abdera, Prodicus of Ceos, and a great many others are able to convince anyone who associates with them in private that he wouldn't be able to manage his household or city unless they themselves supervised his education, and they are so intensely loved because of this wisdom of theirs that their disciples do everything except carry them around on their shoulders. Are we to believe, then, that if Homer had been able to help people become virtuous, his companions would have allowed either him or Hesiod to wander around as rhapsodes, and wouldn't have clung far tighter to them than to gold and compelled them to come home and live with them? And if persuasion failed, wouldn't they have followed them wherever they went until they had received sufficient education?

GLAUCON: I think what you say is entirely true, Socrates.

[6] The rhapsodes and poets who recited and expounded Homer throughout the Greek world.

[7] It derives from two words, *kreas* (meat) and *phylon* (race or kind). A modern equivalent might be "meathead."

303

SOCRATES: Are we to conclude, then, that all poets, beginning with Homer, imitate images of virtue and of all the other things they write about, and have no grasp of the truth? Although, as we were saying just now, a painter will make what seems to be a shoemaker to those who know as little about shoemaking as he does himself, but who look at things in terms of their colors and shapes.[8]

601a

GLAUCON: That's right.

SOCRATES: Similarly, I suppose, we will say that the poet uses words and phrases to paint colored pictures of each of the crafts, even though he knows only how to imitate them; so that others like himself, who look at things in terms of words, will think he speaks extremely well about shoe-making or generalship or anything else, provided he speaks with meter, rhythm, and harmony. That is how great a natural spell these things cast. For if a poet's works are stripped of their musical colorings and spoken just by themselves, I think you know what they look like. You have surely seen them.

5

b

5

GLAUCON: I certainly have.

SOCRATES: Don't they resemble the faces of those who are young but not really beautiful, after the bloom of youth has left them?

GLAUCON: Absolutely.

SOCRATES: Come on, then, consider this: the maker of an image—the imitator—knows nothing, we say, about what is, but only about what appears. Isn't that so?

10

c

GLAUCON: Yes.

SOCRATES: Then let's not leave the story half-told. Let's look at the whole thing.

GLAUCON: Go on.

5

SOCRATES: A painter, we say, will paint reins and a bit?

GLAUCON: Yes.

SOCRATES: But it is the saddler and the blacksmith who make them?

GLAUCON: Of course.

SOCRATES: Does the painter know what the reins and bit should be like, then? Or do not even their makers—the saddler and the blacksmith—know this, but only the one who knows how to use them, the horseman?

10

GLAUCON: That's absolutely true.

SOCRATES: So, won't we say that the same holds for everything?

[8] See 476b4–8.

GLAUCON: What?

SOCRATES: That for each thing there are these three crafts: one that will use, one that will make, one that will imitate?

GLAUCON: Yes.

SOCRATES: Then aren't the virtue, goodness, and correctness of each manufactured item, living creature, and activity related to nothing but the use for which each is made or naturally developed?

GLAUCON: They are.

SOCRATES: So it is entirely necessary, then, that the user of each thing has the most experience of it, and that he inform the maker about what the good and bad points are in the actual use of the thing he uses. For example, it is the flute player, I take it, who informs the flute-maker about which flutes respond well in actual playing, and prescribes how they should be made, while the maker obeys him.

GLAUCON: Of course.

SOCRATES: Doesn't the one who knows give information, then, about good and bad flutes, whereas the other, by relying on him, makes them?

GLAUCON: Yes.

SOCRATES: So, as regards the same manufactured item, its maker— through associating with the one who knows and having to listen to the one who knows—has correct belief about its good and bad qualities, while its user has knowledge.

GLAUCON: Exactly.

SOCRATES: What about the imitator? Will he, on the basis of using the things he paints, have knowledge of whether they are good and correct or not? Or will he have correct belief through having to associate with the one who knows and being told how he should paint them?

GLAUCON: Neither.

SOCRATES: So an imitator has neither knowledge nor correct belief about whether the things he makes are good or bad.

GLAUCON: Apparently not.

SOCRATES: How well situated the poetic imitator is, then, in relation to wisdom about the subjects of his poems!

GLAUCON: He isn't really.

SOCRATES: And yet he will go on imitating all the same, even though he does not know in what way each thing is good or bad. On the contrary, whatever appears good to the masses who know nothing—that, it seems, is what he will imitate.

305

5   GLAUCON: What else?

SOCRATES: Apparently, then, we are fairly well agreed on the following: that the imitator knows nothing worth mentioning about the things he imitates, but that imitation is a kind of game, not something to be taken seriously; and that tragic poets, whether in iambic or epic verse, are as imi-
10   tative as they could possibly be.

GLAUCON: Absolutely.

SOCRATES: In the name of Zeus, then, this business of imitation is con-
c   cerned with what is third removed from the truth. Isn't that right?

GLAUCON: Yes.

SOCRATES: Now, then, on which of the elements in a human being does
5   it have its effect?

GLAUCON: What sort of element do you mean?

SOCRATES: This sort: the same object, viewed from nearby, does not appear the same size, I presume, as when viewed from a distance.

GLAUCON: No, it does not.

SOCRATES: And the same things appear bent and straight when seen in
10   water or out of it, or concave and convex because sight is misled by colors;
d   and every other similar sort of confusion is clearly present in our soul. It is because it exploits this weakness in our nature that illusionist painting is nothing short of sorcery, and neither are jugglery or many other similar sorts of trickery.

5   GLAUCON: True.

SOCRATES: And haven't measuring, counting, and weighing proved to be most welcome assistants in these cases, ensuring that what appears bigger or smaller or more numerous or heavier does not rule within us, but rather what has calculated or measured or even weighed?

10   GLAUCON: Of course.

e   SOCRATES: And that is the task of the soul's rational element?

GLAUCON: Yes, of it.

SOCRATES: But quite often, when it has measured and indicates that some things are larger or smaller than others, or the same size, the opposite
5   simultaneously appears to hold of these same things.

GLAUCON: Yes.

SOCRATES: And didn't we say that it is impossible for the same thing to believe opposites about the same thing at the same time?[9]

> [9] 436b8–c1.

306

GLAUCON: Yes, and we were right to say it. 10

SOCRATES: So, the element in the soul that believes contrary to the measurements and the one that believes in accord with the measurements could not be the same. 603a

GLAUCON: No, they could not.

SOCRATES: But the one that puts its trust in measurement and calculation would be the best element in the soul. 5

GLAUCON: Of course.

SOCRATES: So the one that opposes it would be one of the inferior parts in us.

GLAUCON: Necessarily.

SOCRATES: That, then, was what I wanted to get agreement about when I said that painting—and imitation as a whole—are far from the truth when 10 they produce their work; and moreover that imitation really consorts with an element in us that is far from wisdom, and that nothing healthy or true can come from their relationship or friendship. b

GLAUCON: That's absolutely right.

SOCRATES: So, imitation is an inferior thing that consorts with another inferior thing to produce inferior offspring.

GLAUCON: So it seems. 5

SOCRATES: Does this apply only to the imitation that is visible, or also to the one that is audible—the one we call poetry?

GLAUCON: It probably applies to that as well.

SOCRATES: Well, let's not rely solely on a probable analogy with painting. 10 Instead, let's also go directly again to the very element in our mind with which poetic imitation consorts and see whether it is inferior or excellent. c

GLAUCON: Yes, we should.

SOCRATES: Then let's put it as follows. Imitative poetry, we say, imitates human beings acting under compulsion or voluntarily, who, as a result of these actions, believe they are doing either well or badly, and so experience 5 either pain or enjoyment in all these situations. Does it imitate anything apart from these?

GLAUCON: Not a thing. *Really? Not a thing?*

SOCRATES: So, is a human being of one mind in all these circumstances then? Or, just as in the case of visible representation, where he was split into factions and had opposite beliefs in him about the same things at the d same time, is he also split into factions and at war with himself in matters of action? But I am reminded that there is really no need now for us to reach

307

agreement on this question. You see, in our earlier arguments, we were suf-
5 ficiently agreed about all that when we said that our soul is filled with myriad opposites of that sort at the same time.¹⁰

GLAUCON: And rightly so.

SOCRATES: Yes, it *was* right. But we omitted something then that I now
e think we must discuss.

GLAUCON: What's that?

SOCRATES: When a good man suffers some stroke of bad luck, such as the
loss of a son or something else he values very highly, we also said in our ear-
5 lier arguments, as you know, that he will bear it more easily than others.¹¹

GLAUCON: We certainly did.

SOCRATES: Now, let's consider this: will he not grieve at all? Or, since that
is impossible, will he be somehow measured in the face of pain?

GLAUCON: The latter is probably closer to the truth.

SOCRATES: Now, tell me this about him: do you think he will be more
604a likely to fight and resist pain when he is seen by his equals, or when he is
just by himself in a solitary place?

5 GLAUCON: He's sure to fight it far more when he is being seen.

SOCRATES: But when he is alone, I imagine, he will venture to say many
things he would be ashamed if someone else heard, and to do many things
he would not want anyone else to see him doing.

GLAUCON: That's right.

SOCRATES: And isn't it reason and law that tell him to resist, while what
b urges him to give in to the pains is the feeling itself?

GLAUCON: True.

SOCRATES: And when there are opposite impulses in a human being in
relation to the same thing at the same time, we say that there must be two
elements in him.

5 GLAUCON: Of course.

SOCRATES: Isn't one part ready to be persuaded to follow the law, wherever the law leads?

GLAUCON: Can you explain how?

SOCRATES: The law says, as you know, that it is best to keep as quiet as
possible in misfortunes and not get irritated, since what is really good or
10 bad in such things is not clear. There is nothing to be gained by taking

---

¹⁰ 439c2–441c7.

¹¹ 387d4–e4.

them hard, nor is any aspect of human affairs worth getting very serious about. And the very thing whose aid we need as quickly as possible in such circumstances is the one our grieving hinders.

GLAUCON: Which do you mean?

SOCRATES: The capacity to deliberate about what has happened and, as with the fall of the dice, to arrange our affairs, given what has befallen us, in whatever way reason determines would be best. Instead of acting like children who have fallen over, and who hold on to the hurt part and spend their time wailing, we should always accustom our souls to turn as quickly as possible to curing and raising up the part that has suffered a fall and is sick, so as to banish lamentation by means of medicine.

GLAUCON: That would be the most correct way to deal with bad luck, anyway.

SOCRATES: So it is the best element, we say, that is willing to follow this rational calculation.

GLAUCON: Clearly.

SOCRATES: As for the part that leads us to recollections of our suffering and to lamentations, and is insatiable for these things, won't we say that it is the element that lacks reason, is idle, and is a friend of cowardice?

GLAUCON: We certainly will.

SOCRATES: Now, this element—the one that gets irritated—admits of much complex imitation; whereas the wise and quiet character, which always remains pretty much selfsame, is neither easy to imitate nor easy to understand when imitated—especially not at a festival where multifarious people are gathered together in theaters. For the experience being imitated is alien to them.

GLAUCON: Absolutely.

SOCRATES: The imitative poet, then, clearly does not naturally relate to this best element in the soul, and his wisdom is not directed to pleasing it—not if he is going to attain a good reputation with the masses—but to the irritable and complex character, because it is easy to imitate.

GLAUCON: Clearly.

SOCRATES: So, it would at last be right to take him and place him beside the painter as his counterpart. For he is like the latter in producing things that are inferior as regards truth, and is also similar to him in associating with the other element in souls, not with the best one. So, we would also at last be justified in not admitting him into a city that is to be well governed. You see, he arouses and nourishes this element in the soul and, by making it strong, destroys the rational one—just as someone in a city who makes

wicked people strong, by handing the city over to them, ruins the better
ones. Similarly, we will say an imitative poet produces a bad constitution in
the soul of each individual by making images that are very far removed
from the truth and by gratifying the element in it that lacks understanding
and cannot distinguish bigger from smaller, but believes the same things to
be now large, now small.[12]

GLAUCON: He does, indeed.

SOCRATES: But we haven't yet brought our chief charge against imitation.
For its power to corrupt all but a very few *good* people is surely an altogether terrible one.

GLAUCON: It certainly is, if it really can do that.

SOCRATES: Listen and consider. When even the best of us hear Homer, or
some other tragic poet, imitating one of the heroes in a state of grief and
making a long speech of lamentation, or even chanting and beating his
breast, you know we enjoy it and give ourselves over to it. We suffer along
with the hero and take his sufferings seriously. And we praise the one who
affects us most in this way as a good poet.

GLAUCON: Of course I know.

SOCRATES: But when one of us suffers a personal loss, you also realize we
do the opposite: we pride ourselves if we are able to keep quiet and endure
it, in the belief that that is what a *man* does, whereas what we praised before
is what a woman does.

GLAUCON: I do realize that.

SOCRATES: Is praise of that sort rightly bestowed, then? Is it right to look
at the sort of man we would be, not honored, but rather ashamed to resemble, and instead of being disgusted by what we see to enjoy and praise it?

GLAUCON: No, by Zeus, that does not seem reasonable.

SOCRATES: Yes, it does. At least, it does if you look at it in the following
way.

GLAUCON: How?

SOCRATES: If you reflect as follows: what is forcibly kept in check in our
personal misfortunes and has an insatiable hunger for weeping and lamenting—since that is what it has a natural appetite for—is the very factor that
gets satisfaction and enjoyment from the poets. Second, our naturally best
element, since it has not been adequately educated by reason or habit,
relaxes its guard over the lamenting one, since it is watching the sufferings
of somebody else and thinks there is no shame involved for it in praising
and pitying another purportedly good man who grieves excessively. On the

---

[12] See 523b9–524a5.

contrary, it thinks that to be a clear profit—I mean the pleasure it gets. And it would not want to be deprived of it by despising the whole poem. You see, I think only a few people are able to calculate that the enjoyment of other people's sufferings is inevitably transferred to one's own, since, when pity is nourished and strengthened by the former, it is not easily suppressed in the case of one's own sufferings.

GLAUCON: That's absolutely true.

SOCRATES: Doesn't the same argument also apply to humor? You see, if there are jokes you would be ashamed to tell yourself, but that you very much enjoy when you hear them imitated in a comedy or even in private, and that you don't hate as something bad, aren't you doing the same as with the things you pity? For the element in you that wanted to tell the jokes, but which you held back by means of reason because you were afraid of being reputed a buffoon, you now release; and having made it strong in that way, you have been led unawares into becoming a comedian in your own life.

GLAUCON: Exactly.

SOCRATES: And in the case of sexual desires, anger, and all the appetites, pains, and pleasures in the soul, which we say accompany every action of ours, the effect of poetic imitation on us is the same. I mean, it nurtures and waters them when they should be dried up, and establishes them as rulers in us when—if we are to be become better and happier rather than worse and more wretched—they should be ruled.

GLAUCON: I cannot disagree with you.

SOCRATES: In that case, Glaucon, when you meet admirers of Homer—who tell us that this is the poet who educated Greece, and that for the management of human affairs and education in them, one should take up his works and learn them and live guided by this poet in the arrangement of one's whole life—you should befriend and welcome them, since they are the best they are capable of being. And you should agree that Homer is the most poetic of the tragedians and the first among them. Nonetheless, be aware that hymns to the gods and eulogies of good people are the only poetry we can admit into our city. For if you admit the honeyed Muse, whether in lyric or epic poetry, pleasure and pain will be kings in your city instead of law and the thing that has always been generally believed to be best—reason.

GLAUCON: That's absolutely true.

SOCRATES: Let that, then, be our defense for our return to the topic of poetry, which shows that, given her nature, we were right to banish her from the city earlier, since our argument compelled us. But let's also tell her—in case we are charged with some harshness and boorishness—that there is an ancient quarrel between poetry and philosophy. For such expressions as "the

bitch yelping at its master" and "howling," and "great in the empty elo-
c   quence of fools," and "control by a mob of the omni-wise," and "the subtle
thinkers who are beggars all," and countless others are signs of this old oppo-
sition.[13] All the same, let it be said that, if the imitative poetry that aims at
pleasure has any argument to show it should have a place in a well-governed
5   city, we would gladly welcome it back, since we are well aware of being
charmed by it ourselves. Still, it is not pious to betray what one believes to be
the truth. What about you, my friend; aren't you also charmed by it, espe-
d   cially when it is through Homer that you look at it?

GLAUCON: Very.

SOCRATES: Isn't it just, then, for her to reenter in that way, when she has
defended herself in lyric or some other meter?

5   GLAUCON: Yes, indeed.

SOCRATES: Then we will surely allow her defenders—the ones who are
not poets themselves, but lovers of poetry—to argue without meter on her
behalf, showing that she gives not only pleasure but also benefit both to
constitutions and to human life. Indeed, we will listen to them graciously,
since we would certainly profit if poetry were shown to be not only pleas-
e   ant but also beneficial.

GLAUCON: How could we fail to profit?

SOCRATES: But if it is not, my dear comrade, we will behave like men
5   who have fallen in love. If they do not believe their passion is beneficial,
hard though it is, they nonetheless stay away. And we too, because of the
passion for this sort of poetry implanted in us by our upbringing in those
608a   fine constitutions, are well disposed to have her appear in the best and truest light. But as long as she is not able to produce such a defense, then
whenever we listen to her, we will chant to ourselves the argument we just
now put forward as a counter-charm to prevent us from slipping back into
5   the childish passion that the masses have. For we have come to see that such
poetry is not to be taken seriously, as a serious undertaking that grasps
truth; but that anyone who listens to it should be careful, if he is concerned
b   about the constitution within him, and should believe what we have said
about poetry.

GLAUCON: I completely agree.

SOCRATES: It is a great struggle, my dear Glaucon, greater than people
5   think, to become good rather than bad. So, we must not be tempted by

---

[13] Philosophers, such as Xenophanes and Heraclitus, attacked Homer and Hesiod for
their immoral tales about the gods. Poets, such as Aristophanes in his *Clouds,* attacked
philosophers for subverting traditional ethical and religious values. The sources of
these particular quotations, however, are unknown.

honor, money, or any sort of office whatever—not even by poetry!—into thinking that it is worthwhile to neglect justice and the rest of virtue.

GLAUCON: I agree with you on the basis of what we have said. And so, I think, would anyone else.

SOCRATES: And yet the greatest rewards of virtue, and the prizes proposed for it, have not been discussed.

GLAUCON: You must have something incredibly great in mind, if it is greater than those already mentioned!

SOCRATES: In a short period of time, could anything really great come to pass? I mean, the entire period from childhood to old age is surely short when compared to the whole of time.

GLAUCON: It's a mere nothing.

SOCRATES: Well, then, do you think an immortal thing should be seriously concerned with that period rather than the whole of time?

GLAUCON: I suppose not, but what exactly do you have in mind by that?

SOCRATES: Haven't you realized that our souls are immortal and never destroyed?

He looked at me and said in amazement:

No, by Zeus, I have not. But are you really in a position to assert that?

SOCRATES: I certainly ought to be, and I think you are, too. There is nothing difficult about it.

GLAUCON: There is for me. So I would be glad to hear from you about this non-difficult topic!

SOCRATES: Listen then.

GLAUCON: All you have to do is speak!

SOCRATES: Do you think there is a good and a bad?

GLAUCON: I do.

SOCRATES: And do you think about them the same way I do?

GLAUCON: What way?

SOCRATES: What destroys and corrupts coincides entirely with the bad, while what preserves and benefits coincides entirely with the good.

GLAUCON: I do.

SOCRATES: And do you think there is a good and a bad for each thing, such as ophthalmia for the eyes, sickness for the whole body, blight for grain, rot for wood, rust for iron and bronze, and, as I say, a natural badness and sickness for nearly everything?

5 GLAUCON: I certainly do.

SOCRATES: And when one of them attaches itself to something, doesn't it make the thing to which it attaches itself deficient? And in the end, doesn't it break it down completely and destroy it?

GLAUCON: Of course.

SOCRATES: So the badness natural to each thing—the deficiency peculiar to each—destroys it, but if that does not destroy it, there is nothing else left

b to destroy it. For obviously the good will never destroy anything, and again what is neither good nor bad won't either.

GLAUCON: How could it?

SOCRATES: So if we discover something, the badness of which causes it to

5 deteriorate but cannot break it down and destroy it, won't we immediately know that something with such a nature cannot be destroyed after all?

GLAUCON: That seems reasonable.

SOCRATES: Well, then, what about the soul? Isn't there something that

10 makes it bad?

GLAUCON: Certainly. All the things we were discussing earlier: injustice,

c intemperance, cowardice, and ignorance.

SOCRATES: Do any of these break it down and destroy it? Think about it, so we are not deceived into believing that when an unjust and foolish person is caught, he is destroyed by injustice, which is a deficiency in a soul.

5 Instead, let's proceed this way: just as the body's deficiency, which is disease, wastes and destroys a body, and brings it to the point of not being a body at all, so all the things we mentioned just now reach the point of not being

d when their own peculiar badness attaches itself to them, is present in them, and destroys them. Isn't that so?

GLAUCON: Yes.

SOCRATES: Come on, then, and look at the soul in the same way. When

5 injustice and the rest of vices are present in it, does their presence in it and attachment to it corrupt and wither it until they bring it to the point of death and separate it from the body?

GLAUCON: No, they never do that.

SOCRATES: But surely it is unreasonable to suppose that a thing is

10 destroyed by something else's deficiency and not by its own?

GLAUCON: It is unreasonable.

SOCRATES: Think about it, Glaucon. We do not even believe that a body

e would be destroyed by the deficiency belonging to foods, whether it is staleness, rottenness, or anything else. But if the foods' own deficiency

314

induces bodily deterioration, we will say the body was destroyed *through* them *by* its own badness, which is disease. But we will never admit that the body is destroyed *by* the deficiency belonging to foods—since they and the body are different things—except when external badness induces the natural badness.

GLAUCON: That's absolutely right.

SOCRATES: By the same argument, then, if the body's deficiency does not induce a soul's own deficiency in a soul, we will never admit that a soul is destroyed by external badness in the absence of its own peculiar deficiency—one thing by another's badness.

GLAUCON: Yes, that's reasonable.

SOCRATES: Well, then, let's refute these arguments and show that what we said was not right. Or, so long as they remain unrefuted, let's never say that the soul even comes close to being destroyed by a fever or any other disease, or by killing for that matter—not even if one were to cut the entire body up into the very smallest pieces—until someone demonstrates to us that these conditions of the body make the soul itself more unjust and more impious. But when an external badness is present, while its own particular badness is absent, let's not allow anyone to say that a soul or anything else whatever is destroyed.

GLAUCON: But you may be sure no one will ever prove that the souls of the dying are made more unjust by death!

SOCRATES: But suppose someone dares to come to grips with our argument and—simply in order to avoid having to agree that our souls are immortal—dares to say that a dying man does become worse and more unjust. We are sure to reply that if what he says is true, injustice must be as deadly as a disease to those who have it, and that those who catch it must die because of its own deadly nature—with the worst cases dying quickly and the less serious ones more slowly—and not as now in fact happens, where the unjust are put to death because of their injustice by others who inflict the penalty.

GLAUCON: By Zeus, injustice won't seem so altogether terrible if it will be deadly to the person who contracts it, since then it would be an *escape* from evils! But I am more inclined to think that it will be shown to be entirely the opposite—something that kills others if it can, but makes its possessor very lively indeed—and not just lively, but positively sleepless! That's how far it is, in my view, from being deadly.

SOCRATES: You are right. After all, if its own deficiency—its own badness—is not enough to kill and destroy the soul, an evil designed for the destruction of something else will hardly destroy the soul, or anything else except what it is designed to destroy.

GLAUCON: "Hardly" is right, it seems.

SOCRATES: Then when something is not destroyed by a single bad thing—whether its own or an external one—clearly it must always exist. And if it always exists, it is immortal.

GLAUCON: It must be.

SOCRATES: Well, then, let's assume it to be so. And if it is so, you realize that the same ones will always exist. I mean, they surely could not become fewer in number if none is destroyed, or more numerous either. For if anything immortal is increased, you know that the increase would have to come from the mortal, and then everything would end up being immortal.

GLAUCON: True.

SOCRATES: Then we must not think such a thing—for our argument does not allow it. And we must not think, either, that the soul in its truest nature is full of multicolored variety and dissimilarity and conflict with itself.

GLAUCON: How do you mean?

SOCRATES: It is not easy for something to be immortal when it is composed of many elements and is not composed in the most beautiful way—which is how the soul now seemed to us.

GLAUCON: It probably isn't.

SOCRATES: Yet both our recent argument and others as well require us to accept that the soul *is* immortal. But what it is like in truth, seen as it should be, not maimed by its partnership with the body and other bad things, which is how we see it now, what it is like when it has become pure—*that* we can adequately see only by means of rational calculation. And you will find it to be a much more beautiful thing than we thought and get a much clearer view of all the cases of justice and injustice and of all the other things that we have so far discussed. So far, what we have said about the soul is true of it as it appears at present. But the condition we have seen it in is like that of all the sea god Glaucus,[14] whose original nature cannot easily be made out by those who catch glimpses of him, because some of the original parts of his body have been broken off, others have been worn away and altogether mutilated by the waves, and other things—shells, seaweeds, and rocks—have grown into him, so that he looks more like any wild beast than what he naturally was. Such, too, is the condition of the soul when we see it beset by myriad bad things. But, Glaucon, we should be looking in another direction.

GLAUCON: Where?

[14] Ancient paintings may have represented Glaucus in the way Plato describes him here. His name appears in the accusative (*Glaukon*), suggesting a play on Glaucon (*Glaukôn*).

SOCRATES: To its love of wisdom.[15] We must keep in mind what it grasps and the kinds of things with which it longs to associate, because it is akin to what is divine and immortal and what always exists, and what it would become if it followed this longing with its whole being and if that impulse lifted it out of the sea in which it now is, and struck off the rocks and shells that, because it now feasts on earth, have grown around it in a wild, earthy, and stony profusion as a result of those so-called happy feastings.[16] And then you would see its true nature, whether multiform or uniform,[17] or somehow some other way. But we have given a pretty good account now, I think, of what its condition is and what form it takes in human life.

GLAUCON: We certainly have.

SOCRATES: In the course of our discussion, then, did we respond to the other points, without having to invoke the rewards and reputations of justice, as you all said Homer and Hesiod did?[18] Instead, haven't we found that justice itself is the best thing for the soul itself, and that the soul should do what is just, whether it has Gyges' ring or not, or even the cap of Hades as well.[19]

GLAUCON: That's absolutely true. We have.

SOCRATES: So, Glaucon, isn't it now at last unobjectionable, in addition, also to give back to justice and the rest of virtue both the kind and quantity of wages they bring to the soul, both from human beings and from gods, both during life and after death?

GLAUCON: Certainly.

SOCRATES: Then will you give *me* back what you borrowed from me in the course of the discussion?

GLAUCON: What in particular?

SOCRATES: I granted you that the just man should seem unjust and the unjust one just. For you thought that even if it would be impossible for these things to remain hidden from both gods and human beings, all the same, it had to be granted for the sake of argument, so that justice itself could be judged in relation to injustice itself.[20] Don't you remember?

---

[15] *Philosophia.*

[16] See 519a8–b5.

[17] *Eite polueidês eite monoeidês:* having many elements or only one.

[18] The reference is to the challenge posed by Glaucon and Adeimantus at 357a1–367e5. But they, of course, are renewing the challenge posed by Thrasymachus in Book 1 (see 358b1–c1).

[19] The ring of Gyges is discussed at 359c6–360c5. The cap of Hades also made its wearer invisible.

[20] See 360e1–361d3, 367b2–e5.

GLAUCON: *I* would be unjust if I didn't!

SOCRATES: Well, then, since they have now been judged, I ask on behalf of justice for a return of the reputation it in fact has among gods and human beings; and that we agree that it does indeed have such a reputation, and so may carry off the prizes it gains for someone by making him seem just; since we have already seen that it does give the good things that come from being just, and does not deceive those who really possess it.

GLAUCON: That's a just request.

SOCRATES: Then won't you first give this back, that it certainly does not remain hidden from the gods what each of the two is like?

GLAUCON: We will.

SOCRATES: But if it does not remain hidden, one would be loved by the gods and one hated, as we agreed at the beginning.[21]

GLAUCON: That's right.

SOCRATES: And won't we also agree that everything that comes to the one who is loved by gods—insofar as it comes from the gods themselves—is the best possible, unless it is some unavoidable bad thing due to him for an earlier mistake?[22]

GLAUCON: Certainly.

SOCRATES: Similarly, we must suppose that if a just man falls into poverty or disease or some of the other things that seem bad, it will end well for him during his lifetime or even in death. For surely the gods at least will never neglect anyone who eagerly wishes to become just and, by practicing virtue, to make himself as much like a god as a human being can.

GLAUCON: It is certainly reasonable to think that a man of that sort won't be neglected by one who is like him.

SOCRATES: And mustn't we think the opposite of the unjust one?

GLAUCON: Definitely.

SOCRATES: Those, then, are the sorts of prizes that come from the gods to the just man.

GLAUCON: That's certainly what I believe.

SOCRATES: What about from human beings? What does a just man get from them? If we are to assert what is really the case, isn't it this? Aren't clever but unjust men precisely like runners who run well on the first leg but not on the return one?[23] They leap away sharply at first, but in the end

---

[21] 352a10–b2, 363a5–e4.

[22] A foreshadowing of the doctrine of reincarnation introduced below.

[23] The race is a sprint from one end of the stadium to the other and back.

they become ridiculous and, heads drooping, run off the field uncrowned. True runners, on the other hand, make it to the end, collect the prizes, and are crowned as victors. And isn't it also generally what happens to just people? Toward the end of each course of action and association and of life as a whole, don't they enjoy a good reputation and collect the prizes that come from human beings?

GLAUCON: Of course.

SOCRATES: Will you then allow me to say about them what *you* said about the unjust?[24] For I will claim that it is the just who, when they are old enough, hold the ruling offices in their city if they choose, marry from whatever family they choose, and give their children in marriage to whomever they please. Indeed, all the things that you said about the others, I now say about these. As for the unjust, the majority of them, even if they remain hidden when they are young, are caught by the end of the race and ridiculed, and, by the time they get old, have become wretched and are showered with abuse by foreigners and citizens, beaten with whips, and made to suffer those punishments you rightly described as crude, such as racking and burning. Imagine I have claimed that they suffer all such things. Well, as I say, see if you will stand for it.

GLAUCON: Of course I will. What you say is right.

SOCRATES: Well, then, while the just man is alive, these are the sorts of prizes, wages, and gifts he receives from gods and human beings, in addition to those good things that justice itself provides.

GLAUCON: Fine and secure ones they are, too!

SOCRATES: Well, they are nothing in number or size compared to those that await each man after death. We must hear about them, too, so that, by hearing them, each of these men may get back in full what he is owed by the argument.

GLAUCON: Please describe them, then, since there are not many things it would be more pleasant to hear.

SOCRATES: Well, it is not an Alcinous-story I am going to tell you, but that of a brave man called Er, the son of Armenias, by race a Pamphylian.[25]

---

[24] 361d7–362c8.

[25] Books 9–11 of the *Odyssey* were traditionally referred to as *Alkinou apologoi,* the tales of Alcinous. Included among them is the story in Book 11 of Odysseus' descent into Hades. Since the word translated by "brave" is *alkimou,* which is very similar to *Alkinou,* some sort of pun seems to be involved. The following is one attractive way to interpret it. *Alkinou* might be taken as a compound of *alkê* (strength) + *nous* (understanding) and *alkimou* as a compound of *alkê* + *Mousa* (a Muse). Socrates would then be saying something like: it isn't a tale that shows strength of understanding that I'm going to tell but one that shows the strength of the Muse of storytelling.

Once upon a time, he was killed in battle. On the tenth day, when the rest of the dead were picked up, they were already putrefying, but he was picked up still quite sound. When he had been taken home and was lying on the pyre before his funeral on the twelfth day, he revived and, after reviving, told what he had seen in the other world.

He said that when his soul had departed, it traveled together with many others and came to a daimonic[26] place, where there were two adjacent openings in the earth and two in the heavens above and opposite them. Judges were seated between these. And, when they had made their judgments, they told the just to go to the right up through the heavens, with signs of the judgments attached to their fronts. But the unjust they told to travel to the left and down. And they too had on their backs signs of all their deeds. When he himself came forward, they said that he was to be a messenger to human beings to tell them about the things happening there, and they told him to listen to and look at everything in the place.

Through one of the openings in the heavens and one in the earth, he saw souls departing after judgment had been passed on them. Through the other two, they were arriving. From the one in the earth they came up parched and dusty, while from the one in the heavens they came down pure. And the ones that had just arrived seemed to have come from a long journey, and went off gladly to the meadow, like a crowd going to a festival, and set up camp there. Those that knew one another exchanged greetings and those coming up from the earth asked the others about the things up there, while those from the heavens asked about the others' experiences. They told their stories to one another, the former weeping and lamenting as they recollected all they had suffered and seen on their journey below the earth—which lasted a thousand years—and the ones from heaven telling, in turn, about their happy experiences and the inconceivably beautiful sights they had seen.

To tell it all, Glaucon, would take a long time. But the gist, he said, was this: for all the unjust things they had done and for all the people they had wronged, they had paid the penalty for every one in turn, ten times over for each. That is to say, they paid for each injustice once in every hundred years of their journey, so that, on the assumption that a hundred years is roughly the length of a human life, they paid a tenfold penalty for each injustice. For example, if some of them had caused many deaths or had betrayed cities or armies and reduced them to slavery, or had taken part in other evildoing, they would receive ten times the pain for each of them. On the other hand, if they had done good deeds and become just and pious, they received commensurate awards.

He said some other things about the stillborn and those who lived for only a short time, but they are not worth recounting. And he told of even

---

[26] See Glossary of Terms s.v. daimon.

greater wages for impiety or piety toward gods or parents, and for murder. He said he was there, you see, when someone asked where the great Ardiaius was. This Ardiaius had been a tyrant in a city in Pamphylia just a thousand years before that, and was said to have killed his aged father and older brother and committed many other impious deeds as well. He said the one who was asked responded: "He has not come here and never will. For in fact this, too, was one of the terrible sights we saw. When we were near the mouth, about to come up after all our sufferings were over, we suddenly saw Ardiaius together with some others, almost all of whom were tyrants— although there were also some private individuals among them who had committed great crimes. They thought that they were about to go up, but the mouth would not let them through. Instead, it roared whenever one of these incurably bad people, or anyone else who had not paid a sufficient penalty, tried to go up. At that location, there were savage men, all fiery to look at, standing by, paying attention to the sound, who grabbed some of these people and led them away. But in the case of Ardiaius and others, they bound their feet, hands, and neck and threw them down and flayed them. They dragged them along the road outside, lacerating them on thorn bushes. They explained to those who were passing by at the time why they were being dragged away, and said that they were to be thrown into Tartarus. He said that of the many and multifarious fears they experienced there, the greatest each of them had was that the sound would be heard as he came up, and that each was very pleased when it was silent as he went up. Such then were the penalties and punishments, and the rewards that were their counterparts.

When each group had spent seven days in the meadow, on the eighth they had to move on from there and continue their journey. In four days, they came to a place where they could see stretching from above, through the whole heaven and earth, a straight beam of light, like a column, very closely resembling a rainbow, but brighter and more pure. They reached the beam after traveling another day's journey. And there, in the middle of the light, they saw stretching from the heavens the ends of its bonds—for this light is what binds the heavens, like the cables underneath a trireme, thus holding the entire revolving thing together. From those ends hangs the spindle of Necessity, by means of which all the revolving things are turned. Its shaft and hook were adamant, while its whorl[27] was adamant mixed with materials of other kinds. The nature of the whorl was as follows. Its shape was like the ones here on Earth, but from Er's description, we must think of it as being like this: in one large whorl, hollow and scooped out, lay another just like it, only smaller, that fitted into it exactly, the way nested bowls fit together; and similarly a third and a fourth, and four others. For

---

[27] *Sphondulon:* the circular weight that twirls a spindle in weaving.

there were eight whorls altogether, lying inside one another, with their rims appearing as circles from above, while from the back they formed one continuous whorl around the shaft, which is driven right through the center of the eighth.

Now, the first or outermost whorl had the broadest circular rim, that of the sixth was second, third was that of the fourth, fourth that of the eighth, fifth that of the seventh, sixth that of the fifth, seventh that of the third, and eighth that of the second. That of the largest was spangled; that of the seventh was brightest; that of the eighth took its color from the seventh's shining on it; that of the second and fifth were very similar to one another, being yellower than the rest; the third was the whitest in color; the fourth was reddish; and the sixth was second in whiteness.

The spindle as a whole revolved at the same speed, but within the revolving whole the seven inner circles gently revolved in the opposite direction to the whole. Of these, the eighth moved fastest; second, and at the same speed as one another, were the seventh, sixth, and fifth; third, it seemed to them, in the speed of its counter-revolution, was the fourth; fourth was the third; and fifth the second.[28]

The spindle revolved on the lap of Necessity. On top of each of its circles stood a Siren, who was carried around by its rotation, emitting a single sound, one single note. And from all eight in concord, a single harmony was produced. And there were three other women seated around it equidistant from one another, each on a throne. They were the daughters of Necessity, the Fates, dressed in white with garlands on their heads—Lachesis, Clotho, and Atropos—and they sang to the accompaniment of the Sirens' harmony, Lachesis singing of the past, Clotho of the present, and Atropos of the future. Clotho, using her right hand, touched the outer

[28] Plato's description of the beam of light and the spindle is difficult. He compares the light to *hypozomata,* or the ropes that bind a trireme together. These ropes seem to have girded the trireme from stem to stern and to have entered it at both places. Within the trireme, they were connected to some sort of twisting device that allowed them to be tightened when the water caused them to stretch and become slack. The spindle of Necessity seems to be just such a twisting device. Hence, the extremities of the light's bonds must enter into the universe just as the *hypozomata* enter the trireme, and the spindle must be attached to these extremities, so that its spinning tightens the light and holds the universe together. The light is thus like two rainbows around the universe (or the whorl of the spindle), whose ends enter the universe and are attached to the spindle. The upper half of the whorl of the spindle consists of concentric hemispheres that fit into one another, with their lips or rims fitting together in a single plane. The outer hemisphere is that of the fixed stars; the second is the orbit of Saturn; the third of Jupiter; the fourth of Mars; the fifth of Mercury; the sixth of Venus; the seventh of the sun; and the eighth of the moon. The earth is in the center. The hemispheres are transparent and the width of their rims is the distance of the heavenly bodies from one another. A convincing discussion is J. S. Morrison, "Parmenides and Er." *The Journal of Hellenic Studies* (1955) 75: 59–68.

circumference of the spindle and helped it turn, pausing from time to time; Atropos, with her left, did the same to the inner ones; and Lachesis used each hand in turn to touch both.

When the souls arrived, they had to go straight to Lachesis. A sort of spokesman[29] first arranged them in ranks; then, taking lots and models of lives from the lap of Lachesis, he mounted a high platform, and said:

"The word of Lachesis, maiden daughter of Necessity! Ephemeral souls. The beginning of another death-bringing cycle for mortal-kind! Your daimon will not be assigned to you by lot; you will choose him. The one who has the first lot will be the first to choose a life to which he will be bound by necessity. Virtue has no master: as he honors or dishonors it, so shall each of you have more or less of it. Responsibility lies with the chooser; the god is blameless."

After saying that, the spokesman threw the lots out among them all, and each picked up the one that fell next to him—except for Er, who was not allowed. And to the one who picked it up, it was clear what number he had drawn. After that again the spokesman placed the models of lives on the ground before them—many more of them than those who were present. They were multifarious: all animal lives were there, as well as all human lives. There were tyrannies among them, some life-long, others ending halfway through in poverty, exile, and beggary. There were lives of famous men—some famous for the beauty of their appearance or for their other strengths or athletic prowess, others for their nobility and the virtues of their ancestors, and also some infamous in these respects—and similarly for women. But the structure of the soul was not included, because with the choice of a different life it would inevitably become different. But all the other qualities were mixed with each other and with wealth or poverty, sickness or health, or the states in between.

Here, it seems, my dear Glaucon, a human being faces the greatest danger of all, and because of that each must, to the neglect of all other subjects, take care above all else to be a seeker and student of that subject which will enable him to learn and discover who will give him the ability and the knowledge to distinguish a good life from a bad, so that he will always and in any circumstances choose the better one from among those that are possible. He must calculate the effect of all the things we have mentioned just now, both jointly and severally, on the virtue of a life, so as to know what the good and bad effects of beauty are when it is mixed with wealth or poverty and this or that state of the soul; what the effects are of high and low birth, private lives and ruling offices, physical strength and weaknesses, ease and difficulties in learning, and all the things that are either naturally part of the soul or can be acquired by it, when they are mixed with one another. On the basis of all that he will be able, by considering the nature

d

5

e

5

618a

5

b

5

c

5

d

5

---

[29] *Prophêtês:* a prophet. Here in the sense of someone who speaks on behalf of a god.

of the soul, to reason out which life is better and which worse and choose
e   accordingly, calling worse the one that will lead the soul to become more
unjust, and better the one that leads it to become more just. Everything else
he will ignore. For we have seen that this is the best way to choose,
whether in life or death.

Holding this belief with adamantine determination, he must go down to
619a   Hades, so that even there he won't be dazzled[30] by wealth and other such
evils, and won't rush into tyrannies or other similar practices and so commit
irreparable evils, and suffer even greater ones; but instead will know to
5   choose the middle life in such circumstances, and avoid either of the
extremes, both in this life, so far as is possible, and in the whole of the life
b   to come. For this is how a human being becomes happiest.

At that point our messenger from the other world also reported that the
spokesman said this: "Even for the one who comes last, if he chooses wisely
and lives earnestly, there is a satisfactory life available, not a bad one. Let not
5   the first to choose be careless, nor the last discouraged."

When the spokesman had told them that, Er said, the one who drew the
first lot came up and immediately chose the greatest tyranny. In his foolishness and greed, you see, he chose it without adequately examining everything, and did not notice that it involved being fated to eat his own
c   children, among other evils. When he examined the life at leisure, however,
he beat his breast and bemoaned his choice, ignoring the warning of the
spokesman. For he did not blame himself for these evils, but chance, dai-
5   mons, and everything except himself. He was one of those who had come
down from heaven, having lived his previous life in an orderly constitution,[31] sharing in virtue through habit but without philosophy.

d   Generally speaking, not the least number of the people caught out in
this way were souls who came from heaven, and so were untrained in sufferings. The majority of those from the earth, on the other hand, because
they had suffered themselves and had seen others doing so, were in no rush
5   to make their choices. Because of that, and also because of the chance of
the lottery, there was an exchange of evils and goods for most of the souls.
Yet, if a person, whenever he came to the life that is here, always practiced
philosophy in a sound manner, and if the fall of the lot did not put his
e   choice of life among the last, it is likely, from what was reported by Er
about the next world, that not only will he be happy here, but also that his
journey from here to there and back again will not be underground and
5   rough,[32] but smooth and through the heavens.

---

[30] See 364d3, 576d8.

[31] *Tetagmenê politeia:* see 500c2 where the forms the philosopher looks to in designing the constitution of Kallipolis are also said to be orderly.

[32] See 364d3, 516e7.

He said it was a sight worth seeing how the various souls chose their lives, since seeing it caused pity, ridicule, and surprise. For the most part, their choice reflected the character of their former life. He saw the soul that had once belonged to Orpheus, he said, choosing a swan's life: he hated the female sex because of his death at their hands, and so was unwilling to be conceived in a woman and born.[33] He saw the soul of Thamyris choosing a nightingale's life, a swan changing to the choice of a human life, and other musical animals doing the same. The twentieth soul chose the life of a lion. It was that of Ajax, son of Telamon, who avoided human life because he remembered the judgment about the armor.[34] The next was that of Agamemnon, which also hated the human race on account of what it suffered, and so changed to the life of an eagle. Allotted a place in the middle, the soul of Atalanta, when it saw the great honors of a male athlete, unable to pass them by, chose his life. After her, he saw the soul of Epeius, son of Panopeus, taking on the nature of a craftswoman. Further on, among the last, he saw the soul of the ridiculous Thersites clothing itself as an ape.

Now it chanced that Odysseus' soul drew the last lot of all, and came to make its choice. Remembering its former sufferings, it rejected love of honor, and went around for a long time looking for the life of a private individual who did his own work, and with difficulty it found one lying off somewhere neglected by the others. When it saw it, it said that it would have done the same even if it had drawn the first-place lot, and chose it gladly. Similarly, souls went from the other animals into human beings, or into one another; the unjust changing into savage animals, the just into tame ones; and every sort of mixture occurred.

When all the souls had chosen lives, in the same allotted order they went forward to Lachesis. She assigned to each the daimon it had chosen, as guardian of its life and fulfiller of its choices. This daimon first led the soul under the hand of Clotho as it turned the revolving spindle, thus ratifying the allotted fate it had chosen. After receiving her touch, he led the soul to the spinning of Atropos, to make the spun fate irreversible. Then, without turning around, it went under the throne of Necessity. When it had passed through that, and when the others had also passed through, they all traveled to the plain of Lethe, through burning and choking and terrible heat, for it was empty of trees and earthly vegetation. They camped, since evening was coming on, beside the river of forgetfulness, whose water no vessel can hold. All of them had to drink a certain measure of this water. But those not saved by wisdom drank more than the measure. And as each of them

[33] According to one myth, Orpheus was killed and dismembered by Thracian women, or Maenads.

[34] Ajax thought that he deserved to be awarded the armor of the dead Achilles, but instead it was awarded to Odysseus. Ajax was maddened by this injustice and later killed himself because of the terrible things he had done while mad.

620a

5

b

5

c

5

d

5

e

5

5

621a

5

b

5

drank, he forgot everything. When they were asleep and midnight came, there was a clap of thunder and an earthquake, and they were suddenly carried away from there, this way and that, up to their births, like shooting stars. But Er himself was prevented from drinking the water. Yet how or where he had come back to his body, he did not know, but suddenly recovering his sight he now saw himself lying on the pyre at dawn.

c

5

And so, Glaucon, his story was saved and not lost; and it would save us, too, if we were persuaded by it, since we would safely cross the river Lethe with our souls undefiled. But if we are persuaded by me, we will believe that the soul is immortal and able to endure every evil and also every good, and always hold to the upward path, practicing justice with wisdom every way we can, so that we will be friends to ourselves and to the gods, both while we remain here on Earth and when we receive the rewards of justice, and go around like victors in the games collecting prizes; and so both in this life and on the thousand-year journey we have described, we will fare well.

Glossary of Terms

being (*ousia*) Abstract noun derived from *einai* (to be). The being of (e.g.,) justice is what justice really is.

captain (*kubernêtês*) A combination of our ship's captain, helmsman, and navigator.

city (*polis*) A canonical Greek *polis* is a unique political organization. Unlike a modern city, it enjoyed the political sovereignty characteristic of a modern state: it could possess its own army and navy, enter into alliances, make war and peace, and so on. Unlike a typical modern state, however, it was culturally and religiously homogenous and quite small in scale. The territory of a typical *polis* included a single (usually) walled town (*astu*), with a citadel (*akropolis*) and a marketplace (*agora*), which, as the political and administrative center, is itself often referred to as a *polis*. But a *polis* also included the surrounding agricultural land, and the citizens lived both there and in the town proper.

cloak (*himation*) The draped mantle worn by Greek men—and eventually by women as well—throughout the eastern Mediterranean. It was a rectangle of cloth (approximately 9 × 6 feet), which was draped so as to be supported by the left arm, leaving the right one free. Originally worn without a tunic (a sleeveless garment made of two pieces of cloth joined at the sides and shoulders), it was usually worn with one by the fourth century. Men usually wore a triangular loincloth underneath it.

craft (*technê*) "*Technê*" has the sort of connotation for Socrates and Plato that "science" has for us. Thus fifth-century doctors tried to show that medicine is a *technê*.

daimon, daimonic (*to daimonion*) Daimons are either gods or children of gods and mortals (*Apology* 27d–e). They serve as intermediaries between gods and human beings (*Symposium* 202e). Socrates' famous *daimonion* is the voice or sign of a daimon, and so of either a god (Apollo, in this case) or his offspring (*Apology* 26b–28a, 31c–d).

disputation (*antilogikê*) Literally, antilogic. Also called **eristic.**

dithyramb Choral song to the god Dionysus.

do better (*pleonektein*) An important notion in the *Republic*. Connected to *pleonexia*—wanting to get and have more and more. *Pleonexia* is the chief cause of injustice (359c), since it leads one to try to get what belongs to other people, what isn't *one's own*. Contrasted with *doing or having one's own,* which is, or is the cause of, justice (434a, 441e).

eristic Argument that aims at scoring points against an opponent, rather than at discovering the truth (see 537e1–539c3). Contrasted with dialectic, which does aim at the truth (537c9–d8, 539d3–540c2). Also called **disputation**.

excellence See **virtue**.

flute (*aulos*) Unlike the flute, the *aulos* is a reed instrument, like an oboe. The *aulos* was thought to be especially good at conveying emotion.

illusionistic painting (*skiagraphos*) Literally, shadow-painting. Painting in black and white in which shading creates an illusion of volume, as in the cave analogy.

irony (*eirôneia*) Unlike irony as we understand it, *eirôneia* is correctly attributed only to someone who intends to deceive.

judge (*dikastês*) Literally, a member of a jury. However, Athenian juries combined the functions of deciding guilt or innocence and imposing a penalty that we divide between judge and jury.

justice (*dikaiosunê*) The topic of the *Republic*. Often broader in scope than our notion of justice and more nearly equivalent to ethical rightness in general. Its opposite, *adikia,* then has the sense of general wrongdoing.

masses, the (*hoi polloi*) Literally, the many. Ordinary, relatively poor people, who typically made up the majority of a city's inhabitants. Often contrasted in Greek political thought with "the few," who were typically rich and often aristocratic.

musical training (*mousikê*) Includes poetry and stories, as well as music proper. Effects characterized at 401d5–402d9, 410b10–412b1, 522a3–b1.

pancration A mixture of boxing and wrestling, combined with kicking and strangling. Biting and gouging were forbidden, but nearly everything else, including breaking and dislocating limbs, was permitted.

physical training (*gymnastikê*) Includes dance and training in warfare, as well as what we call physical training. Effects characterized at 401d5–402d9, 410b10–412b1, 522a3–b1.

relish (*opson*) Anything eaten with the staples, such as the barley and wheat breads.

rhapsode Someone who memorized epic poems and gave dramatic recitations of them.

sophists Itinerant teachers who charged sometimes substantial fees for popular lectures and specialized instruction in a wide variety of fields, including natural science, rhetoric, grammar, ethics, and politics. They did not constitute a single school or movement and were neither doctrinally nor organizationally united.

sycophants Athens had nothing corresponding to our public prosecutors. Private citizens prosecuted cases themselves. By the middle of the fifth century, some Athenians began to make a profession of bringing nuisance suits against others, which they dropped in exchange for a bribe. These people were called sycophants. A vivid sense of their power and importance is conveyed in L. B. Carter, *The Quiet Athenian* (Oxford: Clarendon Press, 1986).

temperance (*sôphrosunê*) Also self-mastery, self-discipline, good sense, reasonableness, moderation, and (in some contexts) chastity. Someone who keeps his head under pressure or temptation possesses *sôphrosunê*.

thing that is (*to on*) Because of the ambiguity of the verb *einai* ("to be"), a thing that is could be: (1) a thing that exists (existential "is"); (2) a thing that is, for example, beautiful (predicative "is"); (3) a thing that is true or something that is (veridical "is").

virtue *(arête)* If something is a knife or a man, its virtue, as knife or man, is that state or property of it that makes it good (*Charmides* 161a8–9; *Euthyphro* 6d9–e1; *Gorgias* 506d2–4; *Protagoras* 332b4–6; *Republic* 353d9–354a2). The *aretê* of a knife might include having a sharp blade; the *aretê* of a man might include being intelligent, well born, just, or courageous. *Aretê* is thus broader than our notion of moral virtue, which tends to be applied only to human beings, and restricted to good sexual behavior or helpfulness to others. *Aretê,* by contrast, applies to things (such as knives) that are not moral agents, and to aspects of moral agents (such as intelligence or family status) that have nothing to do with sex or with behavior toward others.

what it is *(ho estin)* If we ask what justice is, the correct answer will specify (the) what it is. What we might mean in speaking of the essence of justice.

Glossary and Index of Names

All dates are BCE.

Abdera Greek city on the coast of Thrace. 600c7

Achaeans Greek forces in the Trojan War. 389e8, 390e6, 393a1, 4, d5, 394a6

Achilles Hero of Homer's *Iliad*. Champion of the Greeks in the Trojan War. 388a6, 390e4, 7, 391a4, c1

Adeimantus Plato's older brother. With Glaucon, Socrates' chief interlocutor after Book 1.

Adrasteia Personification of fate or necessity and punisher of pride and proud words. The "bow to Adrasteia" is an apology for an act or statement that might otherwise spur her to take action. 451a4

Aeschylus of Eleusis (c. 525/4–456/5) Author of the *Oresteia, Seven against Thebes,* and other plays. 361b7, 362a3, 380a1, 383a9, 550c4, 563c1

Agamemnon King of Mycenae. Husband of Clytemnestra (who killed him) and father of Orestes (who killed Clytemnestra), Iphigenia (whom he killed), and Electra. He led the Greek forces in the Trojan War. 383a8, 390e9, 392e3, 393e4, 522d1, 6, 620b4

Aglaeon Father of Leontius. 439e7

Ajax One of the Greek heroes who fought at Troy. 468d, 620b2

Alcinous King of the Phaeacians in Homer's *Odyssey.* 614b2

Anacharsis of Scythia (6th cent.) A legendary sage. 600a6

Aphrodite Goddess of (sexual) love. 390c6

Apollo God of music, medicine, prophecy, and so on. 383a9, 391a5, 394a3, 399e2, 408b8, 427b2, 509c1

Arcadia Area in the central Peloponnese. 565d6

Archilochus of Paros (c. 756–716) Iambic and elegiac poet who composed the famous fable about the fox and the hedgehog. 365c5

Ardiaeus Probably fictional tyrant of Pamphylia (now coastal Turkey) in the myth of Er. 615c6, e6

Ares God of war. 390c6

Argos City of Agamemnon. 381d8, 393e7

Ariston Father of Adeimantus, Glaucon, and Plato. 327a1, 368a4, 427d1, 580b9

Aristonymus Father of Clitophon. 328b7

Armenius Father of Er. 614b3

Asclepius A mythical figure regarded as the first doctor. 405d4, 7, 406a6, c1, 407c7, e3, 408b6, 8, 599c4

Atalanta Mythical huntress who would marry only a man who could beat her at running. In most versions of the myth, losers were killed. Melanion received three golden apples from Aphrodite, which he dropped during his race with Atalanta. She stopped to pick them up, and he won the race. 620b6

Athena Virgin goddess of the arts and technical expertise of every kind. Patron goddess of Athens. 379e4

Athenian 330a3

Atreus Father of Agamemnon and Menelaus. 393a5

Atropos One of the Fates. 617c3, 5, 8, 620e5

Attic Pertaining to Attica, the area in which Athens is situated. 404d8

Autolycus Maternal grandfather of Odysseus. 334b1

Bendis A Thracian goddess about whose cult, which may have been orgiastic, little is known. Greek artists represent her as a booted huntress rather like Artemis. An Athenian decree of c. 413/2 assigned her a priestess and founded the festival in Piraeus mentioned at the beginning of Book 1. 354a11

Bias of Priene (6th cent.) One of the legendary seven sages of Greece. Priene is in Ionia. 335e8

Ceos Island in the northwest Cyclades. Home of the sophist Prodicus. 600c7

Cephalus A wealthy resident alien in Athens. Father of Polemarchus, Euthydemus, and Lysias.

Cerberus Three-headed dog with a snake's tail that guarded the gates to Hades. 588c3

Chalcedon On the Black Sea. Home of the sophist Thrasymachus. 328b6

Charmantides of Paeania (c. 500–420) Remains silent throughout the *Republic*. 328b7

Charondas of Catana (6th cent.) Created laws for his native Catane and other cities in Italy and Sicily. 599e3

Cheiron A centaur (half man, half horse), famous as tutor of Achilles. 391c3

Chimera Mythical beast, "lion in the front, serpent in the back, and she-goat in the middle" (*Iliad* 6.181). 588c3

Chryses Priest of Apollo in the *Iliad*. 392e3, 393a8, d4, 6

Clitophon Young Athenian who gives his name to a (pseudo-) Platonic dialogue. Supporter of Thrasymachus.

Clotho One of the three Fates. 617c3, 5, 6, 620e2

Cocytus River of Hades. 387b9

Corinthian Pertaining to the city of Corinth near the isthmus joining central Greece to the Peloponnese. 404d5

Creophylus Epic poet. Follower of Homer. 600b6

Cretans People of Crete, an island in the southern Aegean. 452c9

Croesus King of Lydia (560–546). 566c4

Cronus Greek god. Father of Zeus. 377e8, 378a1

Daedalus A legendary sculptor of great skill. His statues were so lifelike that they moved around by themselves just like living things. 529e1

Damon of Athens (5th cent.) Pioneering musicologist who had views on the psychological and political significance of music. The few surviving fragments of his writings are translated in Kathleen Freeman, *Ancilla to the Pre-Socratic Philosophers* (Cambridge, Mass.: Harvard University Press, 1977). 400b1, c4, 424c6

Delphi On the slopes of Mount Parnassus above the Gulf of Corinth. Site of the Delphic Oracle. 427b3

Diomedes, Diomedean Greek hero of the Trojan War. A type of necessity named after him. 389e5, 493d5

Dionysiac Pertaining to Dionysus, the god of wine, intoxication, madness, drama, and so on. 475d6

Dorian With the Ionians, one of the two Greek "tribes." Also the musical mode associated with them. 399a3

Egyptians 436a2

Epeius Mentioned at *Odyssey* 8.493 as the man who helped Athena make the Trojan Horse. 620c1

Er The son of Armenius. May be a Platonic creation. 614b3

Eriphyle Wife of Amphiaraus. Bribed with a gold necklace, she sent her husband to his death in Aeschylus' *Seven against Thebes*. 590a1

Erôs God of love. 573b7, d4, e6, 574d8, e2, 575a1

Euripides of Athens (c. 480–406) Author of the *Bacchae, Medea,* and many other tragedies. 568a9

Eurypylus Greek warrior at Troy whose wounds are treated by Patroclus in Homer's *Iliad*. 405e1, 408a7

Euthydemus Son of Cephalus and brother of Polemarchus. His role in the *Republic* is non-speaking. Not to be confused with Euthydemus, son of Diocles, after whom Plato named a dialogue. 328b5

Fates 617c2

Glaucon Plato's older brother. With Adeimantus, Socrates' chief interlocutor after Book 1.

Glaucus A human being transformed into a minor sea god by eating a magic herb. 611d1

Greece 606e2

Greeks 423a9, 452c7, 469b8, c4, 5, e8, 470a1, c5, 7, 8, 9, e9, 471a1, 9, b8, 494c8, 544d4

Gyges (c. 685–657) King of Lydia. The story of how he became king is described in Herodotus 1.8–13. 359d1, 612b4

Hades God of the underworld, ruler of the dead. Also the underworld itself. 330d8, 363c4, d7, 366a5, 386b4, 10, d9, 392a6, 521c3, 534c7, 596c8, (cap of Hades) 612b5, 619a1

Helen of Troy Wife of Menelaus, lover of Paris, and cause of the Trojan War. 586c4

Hellespont Narrow strait dividing Europe from Asia. 404c1

Hephaestus God of fire, blacksmiths, and craftsmen more generally. 378d3, 389a6, 390c7

Hera Wife of Zeus. Queen of the gods. 378d3, 381d6, 390c2

Heraclitus of Ephesus (c. 500) One of the greatest of the Presocratic philosophers. He believed that everything is in flux, and that apparent opposites (day and night, alive and dead, up and down) are in some sense unities. As a result, he seems to have denied the law of non-contradiction. 498b1

Hermus River on the west coast of Asia Minor. 566c5

Herodicus of Selymbria Physical trainer and medical theorist from Thrace, credited with the invention of dietetics. 406a7

Hesiod (c. 700) Early epic poet from Boeotia. Author of *Theogony* and *Works and Days*. 363a8, 377d4, e8, 466c2, 468e8, 546e1, 600d6, 612b2

Homer (c. 8th cent.) Greatest of the Greek epic poets. Author of the *Iliad* and *Odyssey*. 334a11, b4, 363a8, 364d4, 377d4, 378d5, 379c9, 383a7, 387b1, 388a5, 389a3, e5, 391a3, 393b1, d3, 6, 396e5, 404b10, c6, 441b4, c1, 468c10, d1, 7, 501b6, 516d4, 545d8, 595b10, 598d8, 599b9, c7, 600a1, 10, b7, 9, c4, d5, e4, 605c11, 606e1, 607a2, d1, 612b2

Homeridae Followers of Homer. 599e6

Hydra Mythical monster with many heads; when one was cut off, two grew in its place. 426e8

Ida Mountain in Crete. 391e8

Iliad 392e2

Ilium Troy. 393b4, 522d4

Inachus River god whose daughter, Io, was turned into a cow by Hera because of Zeus' lust for her. 381d8

Ionian With Dorians, one of the two Greek "tribes." Also the musical mode associated with them. 398e10

Isles of the Blessed A place where good people are said to live in eternal happiness, normally after death. 519c5, 540b6

Ismenias of Thebes (active 404–382) A democratic leader who aided the exiled Athenian democrats in 404. He is also mentioned at *Meno* 90a4–5. 336a6

Italy 599c3

Ithaca Island home of Odysseus. 393b4

Lacedaemonians Spartans. 452c9, 599d7

Lachesis One of the three Fates. 617c3, 4, 8, d2, 4, 6, 620d7

Laconian Spartan. 544c3, 545a3

Leontius Son of Aglaeon. 439e7

Lethe River in Hades. 621a2, c1

Lotus-eaters Mythical people visited by Odysseus on his ten-year voyage back to Ithaca after the Trojan War. 560c5

Lycaean (Zeus). 565d6

Lycurgus Tradition lawgiver to the Spartans. 599d7

Lydian Lydia was a territory in the west of Asia Minor. 359d1, 2, 398e10

Lysanias Father of Cephalus. 330b5

Lysias of Thurii and Athens (459–c. 380) Well-known writer of legal speeches and brother of Polemarchus. Socrates discusses a speech attributed to him in the *Phaedrus*.

Marsyas One of the mythical satyrs, part human, part animal. He was flayed alive by Apollo for challenging him to a musical contest and losing. 399e2

Megara City between Athens and Corinth. The battle of Megara took place in 409 BCE. 368a3

Menelaus Brother of Agamemnon. Husband of Helen. 408a3

Midas Legendary king of Phrygia (now central Turkey). As the result of a foolish wish, everything he touched turn to gold. 408b4

Milesian Pertaining to Miletus, an Ionian city in Asia Minor. 600a6

Momus The god of criticism, blame, and censure. 487a6

Musaeus A legendary poet closely associated with the mystery religion of Orphism. 363c3, 364e3

Muse(s) Patron goddesses of the various arts, including Calliope (epic), Erato (lyric), Euterpe (flute-playing), Melpomene (tragedy), Terpsichore (dancing), Thalia (comedy). 364e4, 411c9, 499d3, 545d8, 547a7, b1, 548b8, 607a5

Necessity 616c4, 617b4, c2, d6, 621a1

Niceratus of Cydantidae Son of Nicias. Like Polemarchus, a victim of the oligarchic coup of the Thirty Tyrants in 404 BCE. He remains silent throughout the *Republic.* 327c2

Nicias Athenian general during the Peloponnesian War with Sparta. 327c2

Niobe In mythology, daughter of Tantalus. She boasted that she was superior to Leto, mother of Apollo and Artemis, who, in revenge, killed her children. 380a6

Odysseus Greek hero of the Trojan War. Hero of Homer's *Odyssey.* 334b1, 620c4

Olympian (Zeus). 583b3

Olympic Olympia in Elis was a panhellenic sanctuary of Zeus. Site of the ancient Olympic games. 465d3, 466a9

Orpheus It is not clear whether Orpheus was a real person or a mythical figure. His fame in Greek myth rests on the poems in which the doctrines of Orphic religion are set forth. These are discussed in W. Burkert, *Greek Religion* (Cambridge, Mass.: Harvard University Press, 1985). 364e3, 620a4

Paeania A rural deme (parish) of Athens. 328b7

Palamedes Greek hero of the Trojan War credited with the invention of numbers, writing, and law. Odysseus hid gold in his tent, forged a letter that compromised him, accused him of treason, and had him stoned to death. Aeschylus, Sophocles, and Euripides wrote tragedies about his fate. 522d2

Pamphylian Pertaining to Pamphylia, a region in the southern coastal plain of what is now Turkey. 614b4, 615c7

Pandarus Trojan warrior, son of Lycaon. 379e3, 408a3

Panopeus Father of Epeius. 620c1

Patroclus Closest friend of Achilles in the *Iliad*. 388d1, 391b5

Peleus Father of Achilles. 391c2

Pelops Father of Atreus. Grandfather of Agamemnon and Menelaus. 380a6

Perdiccas Probably Perdiccas II, King of Macedon (c. 450–413). Also mentioned in the *Gorgias* 471a–e. 336a5

Periander (650–570) Tyrannical ruler of the city of Corinth. 336a5

Perithous Son of Zeus. 391c9

Phocylides of Miletus (6th cent.) Elegiac and hexameter poet best known for his epigrams. 407a7, b3

Phoebus Apollo. 383b5

Phoenician(s) Pertaining to Phoenicia, a region of the eastern Mediterranean. 414c4, 436a2

Phoenix Guardian of Achilles in the *Iliad*. 390e4

Phrygian A musical mode. Phrygia was a large region in Asia Minor. 399a4

Pindar of Cynoscephalae (518–438) Lyric poet from Boeotia, most famous for his poems celebrating the victors in the Olympian, Pythian, and other games. 331a3, 365b2, 408b8

Piraeus Harbor town of Athens. 327a1, 328c7, 439e7

Pittacus of Mytilene (6th cent.) One of the legendary seven sages of Greece. 335e8

Polemarchus Son of Cephalus. Brother of Lysias and Euthydemus. Executed by the Thirty Tyrants in 404. Mentioned at *Phaedrus* 257b.

Polydamas Famous athlete from Thessaly in northern Greece. 338c7

Pramneian Type of wine. 405e2

Priam King of Troy during the Trojan War. 388b4

Prodicus of Ceos (5th cent.) Teacher of rhetoric, with an interest in fine distinctions of meaning (*Protagoras* 337a1–c4, *Laches* 197d3–5) and the correctness of names (*Euthydemus* 277e4, *Cratylus* 384a8–c2). Socrates is described as attending some of his lectures (*Cratylus* 384b2–c1, *Charmides* 163d3–4) and as being educated by him (*Meno* 96d7). 600c7

Protagoras of Abdera (c. 490–420) Famous sophist who held that "man is the measure of all things." His views are criticized in the dialogue named for him and in the *Theaetetus*. 600c6

Proteus Minor sea god, able to change his shape at will. 381d5

Pythagoras of Samos (6th cent.) Developed a way of life in which natural science became a religion. He is credited with discovering the mathematical ratios determining the principal intervals of the musical scale. He seems to have been led by this to believe that all natural phenomena are explicable in terms of numbers. He may also have discovered some version of the famous theorem about right triangles that bears his name. 600b2

Pythagoreans 530d8

Pythia Priestess of Apollo at Delphi. 461e3, 540c1

Sarpedon Son of Zeus in the *Iliad*. 388c7

Scylla Mythical monster shaped like a woman with six heads and twelve feet (see *Odyssey* 12.85ff., 245ff.). 588c3

Scythia Lands to the north of Greece. 435e6, 600a7

Seriphian 330a2

Seriphus Small island in the Cyclades. 329e8

Selene The Moon. 364e4

Sicilian 404d1

Sicily Island off the toe of Italy. 599e3

Simonides of Ceos (c. 548–468) Lyric and elegiac poet. 331d5, e2, 5, 332a7, b3, 9, c6, 334b4, e4, 335e8

Siren One of eight Sirens responsible for "the harmony of the celestial spheres." 617b5, c4

Socrates of Athens (469–399) Son of Sophroniscus and Phaenarete of the deme (parish) of Alopece. Chief protagonist of most of Plato's dialogues and of those of other writers. See Introduction, pages xi–xii.

Solon of Athens (c. 640–560) Athenian statesman and poet and founder of the Athenian constitution. 536d1, 599e3

Sophocles of Colonus (c. 496–408) Athenian playwright, author of *Antigone, Oedipus Tyrannus,* and other tragedies. 329b7, c1, 8

Sparta Major city of the Peloponnese. Athens' rival in the 5th and 4th centuries. Sparta was a militaristic and somewhat closed society, always prepared for war. Its citizens, male and female, lived in military camps and ate communally. Plato's thinking about his guardians reflects Spartan influence.

Spercheius River (river god) in the *Iliad*. 391b2

Stesichorus of Himera (6th cent.) Lyric poet. 586c4

Styx River in Hades. 387b9

Syracusan Pertaining to Syracuse, a city on the east coast of Sicily. 404d1

Tartarus The deepest part of Hades. 616a4

Telamon Brother of Peleus. Father of Ajax. 620b2

Thales of Miletus (6th cent.) First philosopher we know of in ancient Greece. He seems to have regarded water as the fundamental principle of all things and is said to have predicted the solar eclipse of 585. 600a6

Thamyris A legendary poet and singer who boasted that he could defeat the Muses in a song contest. For this they blinded him and took away his voice. He is mentioned at *Iliad* 2.596–600. 620a6

Theages of Anagyrus Member of Socrates' circle. A pseudo-Platonic dialogue dealing with the relationship between politics and philosophy is named after him. 496b7, c1

Thebes City on the south edge of the eastern plain of Boeotia. 336a6

Themis Daughter of Gaia and Uranus, associated with divine law and justice. 380a1

Themistocles of Phrearrhi (c. 524–459) Athenian statesman and chief architect of the Greek victory in the war against the Persians. By building up the navy, he secured Athens' future as a naval power and paved the way for the increased political power of the poorer classes from which sailors were largely drawn. 329e7

Thersites Ordinary soldier who criticizes Agamemnon at *Iliad* 2.211–277. Odysseus beats him for his presumption and is widely approved for doing so. 620c3

Theseus Legendary king of Athens. 391c9

Thetis Sea nymph, wife of Peleus, and mother of Achilles. 381d5, 383a9

Thrace Area roughly corresponding to present-day northwestern Greece, Bulgaria, and northeastern Turkey. 327a5

Thracians 435e6

Thrasymachus of Chalcedon (5th cent.) Sophist and rhetorician of note. Some fragments of his writings are translated in Michael Gargarin and Paul Woodruff, *Early Greek Political Thought from Homer to the Sophists* (Cambridge: Cambridge University Press, 1995): 254–6.

Troy City in northwest Asia Minor. Site of Trojan War. 380a6, 393e2, 405e1, 408a1, 586c4

Uranus Divine personification of the sky, father of Cronus. 377e7

Xerxes (c. 486–465) King of Persia who invaded Greece in the second Persian war (begun in 480). 336a5

Zeus Chief among the Greek gods. 329a1, 332a9, c5, 334b7, 340a1, 345b7, e4, 350e8, 370a7, 374e10, 375b11, 376d6, 378b6, 379d3, 5, e1, 4, 380a1, 383a8, 386b3, 390b6, c8, 391c2, 9, e8, 9, 399e4, 400a4, c6, 403b3, 407b4, 423b3, 426b7, 440b8, 441b2, 443b6, 444a7, 445b8, 452b4, 453d4, 459a4, 462a1, 469e6, 472d8, 484d4, 493c7, 505b4, 506d2, 515b10, 521b3, 527c9, 531e2, 534d2, 536c6, 554d5, 564c5, 565d6, 568a8, 574b12, c6, 583b3, 585a6, 588a11, 602c1

General Index

account argument, discussion, word (*logos*) 328d4, 330a4, 331d7, e1, 334a9, d6, 8, 335a3, 336b2, 4, d8, 336e3, 337e3, 338d4, 339d1, 340d1, e2, 341a7, b2, 6 (sense), 8 (sense), c5 (sense), 342b7 (meaning), 343a1, 2, 344d3, 5, 6 (speech), 345b6, 348a8 (speech), d9, 349a4, 10, 351a1, b6, 352b3, d6, 353d1, e12, 354b7, 357a1, 358c1, 8, 359b5, 360d2, 361b6, d8, 362d3, e2, 363c5, e6, 364b2, c5, 365d2, 366b3, 7, d6, e2, 8, 367b3, e2, 368b2, c5, 369a6, c9, 376d2, 10, e9 (story), 11 (story), 377e1 (story), 378a7 (story), e4 (story), 380a8, 381a7, 382a1, b9, c6, e9, 10, 383a5, 388e2, 9, 389a7, d6, 390a1, 392a3, c1, 6, 394d8, 395a1, b8, 396a1, 3, e7, 398b7, d1, 5, 9, 11, 400a1, 2, c5, d4, 5, 401d2, 402a2, 3, 408d8, 411d3, 8, 414d1, 421a3, 425b8, 431a4, 435d2, 436b3, 437d11, 439a6, 440a5, b3, 5, 442a1, c2, 445c5, e1, 449c3, 7, 450a8, b1, 4, 7, d2, e2, 451b3, c8, 452d5, 453a8, c8, d10, 457c1, e2, 6, 461e8, 462d4, e5, 465e5, 472a2, 6, e1, 473a5, e2, 7, 475a3, 4, c1, d4, e2, 476a5, b1, 484a2, 485a4, 487b4, 6, c3, 5, e7, 490d1, 2, 491d7, 492a8, d5, 7, e6, 493c4, d8, 494e1, 497c8, 498a3, d4, e4, 499a4, c3, d1, 500b5, c4, 501e4, 503b1, 507b3, 509d7, 510c5, d6, 8, 511b4, e2, 518c4, 522a6, 7, 525e1, 527a3, 7, e6, 528a2, c5, 529d4, 531e5, 532a7, 533c2, 534a8, b3, 4, 9, c3, d3, 537a3, 538c5, d8, 539a5, 9, b3, 6, d5, 8, 541b2, 543c8, 544a4, b2, 545b1, c6, 548c10, 549b6, 550a3, 6, 554d2, 560c2, 8, d1, 561b7, 563a7, 564a9, c9, 565e1, 571b7, d3, 576b10, 578c6, 581a5, 582a5, d13, e7, 583c11, 584a11, 586d6, 587a7, 10, c2, 588b1, 10, 589d5, d2 (language), 591a5, 592a11, 596e5, 597a9, 599b9, 601a7, 602b7, 603d5, 604a10, c7, 606a8, c2, 5, 607a8, b3, c4, d7, 608a3, 610a5, 7, c6, 611a10, b9, 612a8, c5, 10, 614a8, 617d6

alien (*metoikos*) 562e9, 563a1

anger See **spirit**

ape (*pithêkon*) 590b9, 620c3

appetite (*epithumia*) 328d4, 329c7, 351a7 (want), 358b4 (want), 359c3, 367b1 (want), 390c1, 4, 420e5 (have a desire), 429d1, 430b1, e7, 431b9, c10, d1, 5, 432e8 (want), 436a10, 437b7, c2, 3, 8, d2, 9, e1, 5, 7, 438a2, 3, 4, 5, 439d7, e9 (appetitive desire), 440a1, 6, b1, 4, 458a4, b2 (want), 475b2, 4, 5, 8, c3, 485d6, 493b1, 8, 494a9 (want), 517b6 (want), 533b4, 544b9 (want), 548a5, b5, 554a6, 8, b7, d1, 7, 10, 555a3, 557e5 (want), 558d9, 559b9, c9, e6, 560a5, 9, d6, 561a3, c1, 7, 565b5, 571a7, b4, 7, 572b5, c2, 7, e2, 573a1, 4, b2, d7, e4, 6, 575d8, 578a11, 579b7 (yearn), e1, 580d8, e3, 581a1, 585d5, 587b1, 606a5

appetitive element (in the soul) (*epithumêtikon*) 439d8, e5, 440e3, 10, 441a6, 442a5, 516d2, 550b2, 553c5, 571e1, 580e2, 606d2

argument (*logos*) See **account**

338

472d5, 474a6, d7, 475e9, 476b5, 7 (b itself), 10 (b itself), c2 (b itself), 9 (b itself), 477e8, 479a1 (b itself), 2 (form of b itself), 3 (many b things), 4 (the b), 6 (many b things), b1, c7, d4, e1 (many b things, the b itself), 480a2, 4 (the b itself), 484d2, 489e4, 491c2, 492c7, 493b8, c5, d7, e3 (the b itself, many b things), 495c9, 496e2, 497d10, 499a4, 501b2, c3, 503d7, 504b1, 505b3, d5, 506a4, 8, b5, d1, 507b2 (many b things), 5 (a b), 508a5, e4, 6, 509a6, 7, 517c2, 520c5, 527c6, 529b3, c8, e4, 530a5, 531c6 (the b), 538c7, d7 (the b), e1 (the b), 540b4, 543d1, 549b8, 551d7, e5, 555a1, 557c4, 6, 8, 558b5, 559a5, 7, 560b9, 561c1, e4, 562a4, c1, 563e3, 568c3, d5, 569a4, 571b2, d8, 574d6, 578e1, 581e7, 582a4, d1, 587c4, 588a9, 589c7, 8, 591b6, c8, 595c1, 596e5, 598e4, 599b6, c7, 601b7, d4, e8, 602a4, 9, b3, 604b9, 605e4, 607e7, 610a10, e5, 611b6, c4, 614a4, 615a4, 618a8, c8

becoming (*genesis*) 519a9, 525b5, c5, 526e7, 534a3, 4

beginning See **first principle**

being (*ousia*) 359a5, 479c7, 485b2, 486a9, 509b8, 9, 523a3, 524e1, 525b5, c6, 526e6, 534a3, b4, c2, 585b12, c7, 12, d3

belief reputation (*doxa*) 346a3, 350e5, 358a5, 361a7, c5, 362a6, 363a3, 5, e1, 364a4, 365b7, 366e4, 367b5, d2, 4, 377b8, 378d8, 412e8, 10, 413a10, 429c1, 7, 430a3, b3, 7, 431c6, d9, 433c7, 435d1, 444a2, 451c5, 456d3, 466b8, 467d9, 470a8, 473e4, 476d6, 477b3, 7, e1, 3, 5, 8, 478a8, 13, b7, c8, 13, d3, 11, 480a1, 490a5, 491a4, 493c2, 496a7 (b), 499a7, e1, 505d8, 506c6, 508d8, 511d4, 533b4, d5, 9, 534a2, 4, c2, 6, 560c2, 572d4, 573b2,

574d5, 576e2, 580b2, 581b7, 584e8, 585b14, 602a4, 603d2, 606c7, 612b1, d4, 613b8, 619a1

(*pistis*) 505e2, 511e1, 534a1, 5, 601e7

body (*sôma*) 328d3, 332c9, 338c8, 341e2, 3, 5, 342c2, d6, 366c2, 369d9, 371c7, e3, 375b4, 376e4, 377c4, 380e4, 389c3, 395d3, 401a4, 402d11, 403d2, 4, 8, 404c8, d6, e5, 406e3, 407b6, c5, 8, d5, 408d12, e2, 4, 409a5, 410a1, 2, c2, 411c6, e7, 425b4, 442a8, b7, 443e3, 444c6, d3, 445a6, 455b9, 459c3, 461a1, 462c11, 464b2, d9, e6, 469d8, 476a6, 485d12, 491c3, 494b6, 495d8, 496c2, 498b4, 518c7, d10, 521e4, 525d8, 530b3, 532c7, 535b9, c2, d4, 536e2, 3, 539d10, 546a5, 556b9, e3, 559b10, 564a1, b10, 566b7, 567c5, 579c9, d1, 581b1, d5, 584c4, 585d1, 591b6, 7, c5, d2, 609a1, c6, 7, d7, e3, 5, 610a1, 5, b3, 5, 611c1, d2, 621b5

boxing (*puktikê*) 333e4, 422c5

brother (*adelphos*) 327c2, 328b6, 387e3, 362d2, 6, 376d4, 401a7, 8, 402c4, 404b4, 415a3, 421c8, 427d2, 436b1, 461e1, 2, 463c5, 6, 465b2, 471d3, 510c5, 511b2 (related), 522a7, 530d8, 558c3, 615d1

build builder, building (*oikodomein*) 333b5, 346d4, 369d7, 370d2, e1, 372a7, 374b7, 381a7 (manufactured), 394a5, 401a3, b6, 419a5, 424d2, 438d3

calculate calculation (rational) (*logizesthai*, *logismos*) 339a3, 340d3, 4, 366a6, 431c6, 439d1, 5, 440b1, 441a9, 496d6, 510c3, 522c7, e2, 524b4, 525d1, 526d8, 536d5, 546b1, 553d3, 586d2, 587c11, e5, 602d9, 603a4, 604d5, 606b5, 611c3

calculating element (in the soul)
(*logistikon*) 439d5, 440e6, 8, 9, 441a3,
5, e4, 442c11, 525a9, b6, c1, 526b5,
550b1, 553d1, 571c4, d7, 587d11,
602e1, 605b5, 606b5

captain captaincy (*kubernêtês*) 331a9,
332e2, 9, 333c3, 341c9, d2, 342d9,
e2, 3, 346a7, b2, 4, 360e7, 389c4,
397e5, 488b4, d1, 4, 8, e2, 4, 489b6,
c7, 551c3, 4, 590d6, 591e3 (direct)

carpenter (*tektôn*) 370d5, 389d3,
406d1, 407b1, 428b12, c1, 434a3, 4,
443c6, 454d5, 597b9, d9, 598b9,
c3, 4

cave (*spêlaion*) 514a3, 5, 515a8,
539e3

chance luck (*tuchê*) 383b3, 399b3,
460a9, 499b5, 579c7, 592a9, 603e3,
604d3, 619c5, d7, 620c3

charge (*katêgoria*) 420a7, 453e5,
499d10, 531b5, 605c6

charm (*kêlein*) 358b3, 411b1, 413c2,
601b1, 607c7, 8

child children, boy, son (*pais*) 327b3,
4, 330c4, e7, 363d3, 366a6, b1,
368a1, 4, 372c1, 374c7, 377b6, c3,
381d8, e5, 383b9, 386a2, 387b4,
388a6, 391c1, d2, 5, 395c4, 397d7,
401d1, 403c11, 407e4, 408b6,
408d10, 413c8, e6, 424e5, 7, 425a3,
427c6, 431c1, 432d2, 435d2, 449c5,
d4, 450c1, 451c5, 453d2, 457d2, 3, 8,
460b4, 461a5, b6, c2, d6, e6, 463d7,
464a9, b6, d2, e1, 465d9, 466c8, e5,
467a3, b3, c2, 5, 468b4, 471a12,
474e2, 479c1, 494b5, 498a1, b3,
502e1, 514a5, 519a9, 534d3, 536d7,
e5, 537a5, c1, 538c6, 541a2, 543a3,
545e2, 546b3, d3, 548b6, 553a9,
557c8, 558b4, 562e7, 574d6, 577a3,
578e3, 7, 582b3, 590e3, 595b10,
598c2, 604c8, 608c6, 619c1

citizen (*politês*) 344b5, c1, 370c7,
375b10, 378c7, 389b8, 409e5, 414e5,

416b2, d1, e1, 417b1, c8, 423d3,
426c1, 462b5, 463a4, 6, 10, 471b7,
494b10, 501e3, 502b9, 519e4, 555c8,
556a10, 563d5, 567b1, d5, e5, 564a4,
568a5, 579c1

city (*polis*) 330a1, 338d7, 10, 339a1,
c1, 343b4, d7, 345e2, 347d2, 348d5,
351b1, 7, 8, c8, e10, 362b2, 364e5,
366b1, 368e3, 5, 369a1, 5, b5, 7, c4,
9, d6, 11, 370e4, 5, 9, 371a8, b4, c7,
d5, 7, e7, 9, 372d4, e2, 3, 6, 8, 373b2,
4, c5, e7, 9, 374a5, e8, 376c5, d2,
378b2, c2, d6, 379a1, 380b8, 381d4,
389b7, 9, d1, 4, 394d6, 395c1, 397d1,
e4, 398a3, 5, 7, 399d3, 8, e6, 403b4,
405a1, 6, 406c4, 407b7, e2, 408c6,
409e5, 410a6, 412a9, c10, 13, e1, 8,
413c6, e5, 414a2, c2, d4, 415a2, c5,
d4, 9, 417a2, 6, 419a4, 420a1, b6, 8,
e7, 421a2, 4, 5, 6, b1, 2, 3, c3, 6, e8,
422a5, d1, 8, e4, 8, 423a6, 9, b5, c4,
d6, 424b4, 425a6, 426b8, 10, c1, d1,
427a4, b9, e7, d1, 428b3, 10, 13, c3,
d1, 2, 8, 11, e9, 429a6, 9, b2, 8,
430d1, 431b4, c9, d4, 9, 432a1, 9, b2,
4, 433a2, 5, b7, c4, d7, e1, 4, 434a7,
b7, c1, 4, 9, 10, e1, 4, 5, 435b1, 4, c2,
e3, 5, 440d5, 6, e10, 441c5, 9, d1, 6,
442d3, 8, e5, 443a4, b5, 8, 444a4,
445e2, 449a1, 3, 453b4, 455a2, b2,
d6, 456a11, d8, e6, 457a3, 8, 458b5,
e1, 460a5, c3, e5, 7, 461a5, 8, b7, e6,
462a3, 9, c1, 4, 7, d7, e1, 5, 463a1,
b11, e3, 464b1, 2, 5, c7, 465b9, d8,
e1, 466a4, c1, 8, 467b4, 469b9,
470d4, e4, 471a10, c8, 472e1, 4,
473a8, b5, 7, d1, 6, 475d7, 484b6, 10,
c2, 485a7, 487a8, d5, e2, 488a3,
489a5, 9, 491c3, 493d4, 494c5,
495b4, 6, 496b4, c8, d4, 497b2, c6, 8,
d8, e7, 499a1, b2, 6, c7, d4, 500e2,
501a2, 5, c7, e2, 3, 502b4, 504c7,
506a2, 519c1, e2, 3, 520a3, 4, b1, 5,
c6, d2, 7, e3, 521a2, 8, b8, 9, 528b6,
c2, e4, 534d6, 536a6, b3, 540a9, b4,

refined sophisticated (*kompsos*) 376a11, 405d4, 404a9, 408b6, 436d5, 460a8, 489b8, 495d4, 499a6, 505b6, 525d1, 558a4, 568c1, 572c6

ridicule ridiculous, laughter, humor (*geloios*) 331e1, 382d8, 388d3, e6, 389a1, 5, 392d8, 403e7, 406c6, 429e6, 430e11, 432d8, 435e3, 445a5, b5, 451a1, 452a7, 10, b4, c7, d5, 6, 7, 8, 454c6, 7, 455c8, 456d11, 463e1, 467a9, 473c7, 493d9, 499c4, 504d8, 505b11, 506d8, 509c1, 517a2, d6, 518b2, 3, 527a6, 528d9, 529e4, 530a2, 531a4, 536b5, 8, 600b8, 606c2, c3, 6 (jokes), 613c1, d7, 620a2, c3

rule See **first principle**

serious (*spoudaios*) See **excellent**

sex, sexual desire (*aphrodision*) 329a6, c1, 389e2, 390c1, 403a5, 426a8, 559c6, 580e4, 606d1

shame shameful, ashamed (*aischron*) 344b7, 347c3, 348e7, 364a4, 378c2, 381b11, 395c7, 396c8, d6, 402a1, 405a6, b1, 5, 6, c7, d4, 414e7, 416a3, 444e5, 452c7, 457b5, 475e9, 479a6, b1, 492c7, 493b8, 495c3, 502a2, 506c7, 11, 536b7, 538d, e1, 562e8, 571c9, 574d6, 581e8, 589c7, d2, 591a6, 604a7, 605e5, 606b2

share partnership, (*koinônia*) 333a13, 14, b7, 335e10, 343d4, 5, 362b4, 369e5, 370a3, 371b5, 402e4, 403b1, 411c9, 440b4, 449c8, d4, 450c1, 453a2, 457a7, 461e5, 462b4, c11, 464a4, 5, 6, 9, b6, 466c6, d2, 4, 8, 470e10, 476a7, 531d1, 540c8, 556c10, 611c1

sheep shepherd, shepherding, flock (*poimên*) 343a8, b1, 6, 345c2, 4, d1, 2, 5, 359d2, e2, 3, 370d10, 397a7, 415e3, 416a3, 4, 6, 422d6, 440d6, 451d9, 459e1

shepherd See **sheep**

slave slavery, enslave (*doulos*) 344b6, 351b2, 3, d10, 386b6, 387b5, 395e5, 433d3, 444b5, 463b5, 469c2, 4, 471a6, 494d6, 536e1, 547c2, 549a1, 2, 554a7, 561c3, 562d7, 563d6, 564a4, 8, b2, 567e5, 569a2, 3, c1, 3, 574d7, 575d6, 576a5, 577c6, 7, 10, d2, 4, 7, 9, 10, 579a2, d10, 587c2, 589d3, e2, 5, 590c9, d2, 615b4

slavishness unfreedom, lack of freedom (*aneleutheria*) 391c5, 395c6, 400b2, 401b5, 422a2, 469d6, 486a4, b3, 6, 540d6, 560d5, 572d2, 577d3, 590b6

sleep (*hupnos*) 330e7, 404a4, 476c5, 503d4, 537b4, 571c3, 6, d7, 572b6, 574e1

snakelike element (in the soul) 590b1

sophist 509d3, 596d1

sorcery (*goêteia*) 380d1, 381e10, 383a3, 412e7, 413b1, c1, c4, d7, 584a10, 598d3, 602d2

soul (*psuchê*) 330e2, 345b5, 353d3, 6, 9, 11, e1, 4, 7, 10, 358b6, 365a6, 366c2, e6, 9, 375b1, 7, 376e4, 377b7, c3, 381a3, 382b2, 8, 10, 386d5, 387a2, 400d7, 401c3, d7, e5, 402a, d1, 10, 403d3, 404e4, 408e3, 409a1, 2, b6, c4, 410a1, 3, c3, 5, 411a1, 6, b3, d1, e7, 412a5, 415b6, 416e5, 431a4, 435c1, 5, 436b1, 437c2, d9, 439a9, c6, d6, e3, 440e5, 9, 441a2, c6, e5, 442a6, b6, c, e1, 443d3, 444b3, c6, d3, 8, e1, 445b, c10, d1, 449a4, 454d2, 458a7, 462c12, 484c8, 485d11, 486a5, b10, d1, e3, 490b4, e, 491a2, b8, e1, 494b6, 495d, e1, 496b4, 498b7, 504a4, 505d11, 508d4, 510b5, 511a4, d7, 517b5, c9, 518a4, c1, 5, 8, 518c2, d9, 519a3, b3, 521c6, d3, 523d4, 524a3, 7, b1, 4, e5, 525c5, d6, 526b2, e2, 527b9, d8, 529a2, b4,